Taking Sides: Clashing Views
on Economic Issues, 16/e

http://create.mcgraw-hill.com

ISBN-10: 1259170993   ISBN-13: 9781259170997

Contents

Contents

Preface

Where there is much desire to learn, there of necessity will be much arguing.

—John Milton (1608–1674),
English poet and essayist

Presented here are debates on important economic issues, which are designed to stimulate critical thinking skills and initiate lively and informed discussion. These debates take economic theory and show how it is applied to current real-world public policy decisions, the outcomes of which will have an immediate and personal impact. How these debates are resolved will affect our taxes, our jobs, wages, the health care system, and so on; in short, they will shape the society in which we live.

The goal of *Taking Sides: Clashing Views on Economic Issues* has been to select issues that reveal something about the nature of economics itself and something about how economics relates to current everyday newspaper headlines and television news stories on public policy concerns. To assist the reader, we begin each issue with *Learning Outcomes* and an issue *Introduction*, which sets the stage for the debate as it is argued in the YES and NO selections. Each issue concludes with an *Exploring the Issue* section, which offers *Critical Thinking* questions, *Is There Common Ground*, *Additional Resources*, and *Internet References* for further exploration of the issue. The *Introduction* and *Exploring the Issue* section do not preempt what is the reader's own task: to achieve a critical and informed view of the economic issue at stake. Certainly, the reader should not feel confined to adopt one or the other of the positions presented. The views presented should be used as starting points.

As with all of the previous editions, the issues in this edition can be used in any sequence. Although the organization of the book loosely parallels the sequence of topics found in a standard introductory economics text-book, you can pick and choose which issues to read first, since they are designed to stand alone.

A word to the instructor An *Instructor's Resource Guide with Test Questions* (multiple choice and essay) is available through the publisher for the instructor using *Taking Sides* in the classroom. For more information on other McGraw-Hill Create™ titles and collections, visit www.mcgrawhillcreate.com.

Academic Advisory Board Members

Members of the Academic Advisory Board are instrumental in the final selection of articles for the *Taking Sides* series. Their review of the articles for content, level, and appropriateness provides critical direction to the editor(s) and staff. We think that you will find their careful consideration reflected in this book.

Tahereh Alavi Hojja
Desales University

Brian Bartel
Mid-State Technical College

Mary Ellen Benedict
Bowling Green State University

Charles A. Bennett
Gannon University

Arthur I. Cyr
Carthage College

Dennis Debrecht
Carroll University

Alexander Deshkovski
North Carolina Central University

Hardial Dulay
Butte College

Eric Eller
Upper Iowa University

Mary Ann Hendryson
Western Washington University

Ryan Herzog
Gonzaga University

Miren Ivankovic
Anderson University

Mary Lesser
Lenoir-Rhyne University

David Levenstam
Lord Fairfax Community College

Carlos Liard-Muriente
Central Connecticut State University

Tiong Kiong Lim
Carnegie Mellon University

Tim Muth
Florida Institute of Technology

Anthony Negbenebor
Gardner-Webb University

Samuel Onipede
Strayer University—North Charlotte

Reza Ramazani
Saint Michael's College

Malcolm Robinson
Thomas More College

Amy Scott
DeSales University

Pearl Steinbuch
Mount Ida College

Eric Strahorn
Florida Gulf Coast University

Michael Stroup
Stephen F. Austin State University

Kelly Whealan George
Embry Riddle Aeronautical University

Tetsuji Yamada
Rutgers University

Correlation Guide

The *Taking Sides* series presents current issues in a debate-style format designed to stimulate student interest and develop critical thinking skills. Each issue is thoughtfully framed with an issue summary, an issue introduction, and a postscript. The pro and con essays—selected for their liveliness and substance—represent the arguments of leading scholars and commentators in their fields.

Taking Sides: Clashing Views on Economic Issues, 16/e is an easy-to-use reader that presents issues on important topics in economics. For more information on *Taking Sides* and other *McGraw-Hill* Create™ titles and collections, visit www.mcgrawhillcreate.com.

This convenient guide matches the issues in **Taking Sides: Economics Issues, 16/e** with the corresponding chapters in one of our best-selling McGraw-Hill economics textbooks by Guell.

Taking Sides: Economics, 16/e	Issues in Economics Today, 7/e by Guell
Are Profits the Only Business of Business?	**Chapter 5:** Perfect Competition, Monopoly, and Economic versus Normal Profit
Should the Compensation of Executives Be Subject to Government Regulation?	**Chapter 4:** Firm Production, Cost, and Revenue **Chapter 42:** Wal-Mart: Always Low Prices (and Low Wages)—Always
Has the Supreme Court Made It Possible for Corporations to Buy Elections?	**Chapter 26:** So You Want to Be a Lawyer: Economics and the Law
Should the United States Stop All New Offshore Drilling for Oil?	**Chapter 38:** Energy Prices
Are Health Savings Accounts Working Effectively?	**Chapter 23:** Health Care **Chapter 24:** Government-Provided Health Insurance: Medicaid, Medicare, and the Child Health Insurance Program
Should NBC and Comcast Be Allowed to Merge?	**Chapter 2:** Supply and Demand **Chapter 5:** Perfect Competition, Monopoly, and Economic versus Normal Profit
Is Obamacare a Disaster for the Economy?	**Chapter 23:** Health Care **Chapter 24:** Government-Provided Health Insurance: Medicaid, Medicare, and the Child Health Insurance Program
Will Health Reform's Pilot Programs Lead to the Control of Health Care Costs?	**Chapter 23:** Health Care **Chapter 24:** Government-Provided Health Insurance: Medicaid, Medicare, and the Child Health Insurance Program
Did the American Recovery and Reinvestment Act of 2009 Create Jobs?	**Chapter 20:** Economic Growth and Development
Do American Consumers Need a Financial Protection Agency?	**Chapter 32:** Ticket Brokers and Ticket Scalping
Should Minimum Wage and Living Wage Laws Be Eliminated?	**Chapter 31:** Minimum Wage
Does Immigration Benefit the Economy?	**Chapter 28:** The Economics of Race and Sex Discrimination
Is a Fair Trade Policy Superior to a Free Trade Policy?	**Chapter 17:** International Trade: Does It Jeopardize American Jobs?
Is Loan Mitigation the Answer to the Housing Foreclosure Problem?	**Chapter 13:** The Housing Bubble
Are Biofuels Like Ethanol the Answer to U.S. Energy Problems?	**Chapter 38:** Energy Prices
Is Climate Change a Threat That Requires Urgent Action?	**Chapter 22:** Natural Resources, the Environment, and Climate Change
Can U.S. Deficit and Debt Problems Be Solved Without Increases in Taxes?	**Chapter 9:** Fiscal Policy **Chapter 37:** Personal Income Taxes
Is China's Currency Undervalued, and Should the United States Take Action to Correct This Undervaluation?	**Chapter 18:** International Finance and Exchange Rates
Do the Testing and Accountability Elements of the No Child Left Behind Act Prevent a Proper Cost-Benefit Evaluation?	**Chapter 33:** Economics of K-12 Education
Is the Inequality in U.S. Income Distribution Surging?	**Chapter 31:** Minimum Wage **Chapter 32:** Ticket Brokers and Ticket Scalping

Topic Guide

This topic guide suggests how the selections in this book relate to the subjects covered in your course.
All the articles that relate to each topic are listed below the bold-faced term.

Business

Did the American Recovery and Reinvestment Act of 2009 Create Jobs?
Do American Consumers Need a Financial Protection Agency?
Do the Testing and Accountability Elements of the No Child Left Behind Act Prevent a Proper Cost-Benefit Evaluation?
Does Immigration Benefit the Economy?
Is a Fair Trade Policy Superior to a Free Trade Policy?
Is China's Currency Undervalued, and Should the United States Take Action to Correct This Undervaluation?
Is Loan Mitigation the Answer to the Housing Foreclosure Problem?
Is the Inequality in U.S. Income Distribution Surging?
Should Minimum Wage and Living Wage Laws Be Eliminated?

Economy

Did the American Recovery and Reinvestment Act of 2009 Create Jobs?
Do the Testing and Accountability Elements of the No Child Left Behind Act Prevent a Proper Cost-Benefit Evaluation?
Does Immigration Benefit the Economy?
Has the Supreme Court Made It Possible for Corporations to Buy Elections?
Is Loan Mitigation the Answer to the Housing Foreclosure Problem?
Is the Inequality in U.S. Income Distribution Surging?

Employment

Did the American Recovery and Reinvestment Act of 2009 Create Jobs?

Energy

Are Biofuels Like Ethanol the Answer to U.S. Energy Problems?

Environment

Are Biofuels Like Ethanol the Answer to U.S. Energy Problems?
Is Climate Change a Threat That Requires Urgent Action?
Should the United States Stop All New Offshore Drilling for Oil?

Ethics

Has the Supreme Court Made It Possible for Corporations to Buy Elections?

Finance

Do American Consumers Need a Financial Protection Agency?
Is Loan Mitigation the Answer to the Housing Foreclosure Problem?

Global Warming

Is Climate Change a Threat That Requires Urgent Action?

Global Issues

Is Climate Change a Threat That Requires Urgent Action?

Government

Can U.S. Deficit and Debt Problems Be Solved Without Increases in Taxes?
Do American Consumers Need a Financial Protection Agency?
Does Immigration Benefit the Economy?
Should the Compensation of Executives Be Subject to Government Regulation?

Government Regulation

Do American Consumers Need a Financial Protection Agency?
Has the Supreme Court Made It Possible for Corporations to Buy Elections?
Should the Compensation of Executives Be Subject to Government Regulation?

Health Care

Is Obamacare a Disaster for the Economy?
Will Health Reform's Pilot Programs Lead to the Control of Health Care Costs?

Health Insurance

Are Health Savings Accounts Working Effectively?

Immigration

Does Immigration Benefit the Economy?

Mass Media

Should NBC and Comcast Be Allowed to Merge?

Natural Resources

Should the United States Stop All New Offshore Drilling for Oil?

Poverty

Should Minimum Wage and Living Wage Laws Be Eliminated?

Supreme Court

Has the Supreme Court Made It Possible for Corporations to Buy Elections?

Sustainability

Are Profits the Only Business of Business?

Taxes

Can U.S. Deficit and Debt Problems Be Solved Without Increases in Taxes?

Television

Should NBC and Comcast Be Allowed to Merge?

Trade

Is a Fair Trade Policy Superior to a Free Trade Policy?
Is China's Currency Undervalued, and Should the United States Take Action to Correct This Undervaluation?

Unemployment

Should Minimum Wage and Living Wage Laws Be Eliminated?

Introduction

Economics and Economists: The Basis for Controversy

> "I think that Capitalism, wisely managed, can probably be more efficient for attaining economic ends than any alternative system yet in sight, but that in itself it is in many ways extremely objectionable."
>
> —Lord John Maynard Keynes,
> *The End of Laissez-Faire* (1926)

Although more than 80 years have passed since Lord Keynes penned these lines, many economists still struggle with the basic dilemma he outlined. The paradox rests in the fact that a free-market system is extremely efficient. It is purported to produce more at a lower cost than any other economic system. But in producing this wide array of low-cost goods and services, problems arise. These problems—most notably a lack of economic equity and economic stability—concern some economists.

If the problems raised and analyzed in this book were merely the product of intellectual gymnastics undertaken by "egg-headed" economists, then we could sit back and enjoy these confrontations as theoretical exercises. Unfortunately, we are not afforded that luxury. The essays contained in this book touch each and every one of us in tangible ways. They are real-world issues. One set of issues deals with "microeconomic" topics. (We refer to these issues as "micro" problems not because they are small problems, but because they deal with small economic units, such as households, firms, or individual industries.) Another set focuses on "macroeconomic" topics that impact the whole economy or many industries. A third set of issues deals with matters that do not fall neatly into the macroeconomic or microeconomic classifications, including issues relating to the international aspects of economic activity.

The range of issues and disagreements raises a fundamental question. Why do economists disagree? One explanation is suggested by Lord Keynes's 1926 remark. How various economists will react to the strengths and weaknesses found in an economic system will depend on how they view the relative importance of efficiency, equity, and stability. These are central terms, and they will be defined in detail in the following pages. For now the important point is that some economists may view efficiency as overriding. In other cases, the same economists may be willing to sacrifice the efficiency generated by the market in order to ensure increased economic equity and/or increased economic stability.

Given this discussion of conflict, controversy, and diversity, it might appear that economists rarely, if ever, agree on any economic issue. It would be most misleading

to leave the reader with this impression. Economists rarely challenge the internal logic of the theoretical models that have been developed and articulated by their colleagues. Rather, they will challenge either the validity of the assumptions used in these models or the value of the ends these models seek to achieve. For example, it is most difficult to discredit the internal logic of the microeconomic models employed by the "free-market economist." These models are elegant, and their logical development is most persuasive. However, these models are challenged. The challenges typically focus on such issues as the assumption of functioning, competitive markets, and the desirability of perpetuating the existing distribution of income. In this case, those who support and those who challenge the operation of the market agree on a large number of issues. But they disagree most assuredly on a few issues that have dramatic implications.

This same phenomenon of agreeing more often than disagreeing is also true in the area of economic policy. In this area, where the public is most acutely aware of differences among economists, these differences are not generally over the kinds of changes that will be brought about by a particular policy. Again, the differences more typically concern the timing of the change, the specific characteristics of the policy, and the size of the resulting effect or effects. For example, a recent survey found that 85 percent of economists agree that the United States should eliminate tariffs and other trade restrictions (see "Do Economists Agree on Anything? Yes!" by Robert Whaples, *Economists Voice*, www.bwepress.com/ev, November 2006).

Economists: What Do They Represent?

Newspapers, magazines, TV commentators, and bloggers all use handy labels to describe certain members of the economics profession. What do the headlines mean when they refer to the "Chicago School," the "Keynesians," the "Institutional Economists," or the "Radical Economists"? What do these individuals stand for? Since these labels are used throughout this book, the principal groups or camps will be identified. This can be a misleading venture. Some economists, perhaps most economists, defy classification. They drift from one camp to another, selecting a gem of wisdom here and another there. These are practical men and women who believe that no one camp has all the answers to all the economic problems confronting society.

Recognizing this limitation, four major groups of economists can be identified. These groups are differentiated on the basis of two criteria: how they view efficiency relative to equity and stability, and what significance they attach to imperfectly competitive market structures. Before describing the views of the four groups on these criteria, it is essential to understand the meaning of certain terms to be used in this description.

Efficiency, equity, and stability represent goals for an economic system. An economy is efficient when it produces those goods and services that people want and does so without wasting scarce resources. Equity in an economic sense has several dimensions. It means that income and wealth are distributed according to accepted principles of fairness, that those who are unable to care for themselves receive adequate care, and that mainstream economic activity is open to all persons. Stability is viewed as the absence of sharp ups and downs in business activity, in prices, and in employment. In other words, stability is marked by steady increases in output, little inflation, and low unemployment while the recent Great Recession was a clear manifestation of undesirable economic instability.

When the term market structures is used, it refers to the number of buyers and sellers in the market and the amount of control they exercise over price. At one extreme is a perfectly competitive market where there are so many buyers and sellers that no one has any ability to influence market price. One seller or buyer obviously could have great control over price. This extreme market structure, called pure monopoly, and other market structures that result in some control over price are grouped under the broad label of imperfectly competitive markets. That is, imperfect competition is a situation where the number of market participants is limited and, as a consequence, the participants have the ability to influence price. With these terms in mind, the various schools of economic thought can be examined.

Free-Market Economists

One of the most visible groups of economists and perhaps the easiest group to identify and classify is the "free-market economists." In general, this is also the group of economists that persons have in mind when they speak of conservative economists. These economists believe that the market operating freely without interference from government or labor unions will generate the greatest amount of well-being for the greatest number of people.

Economic efficiency is one of the priorities for free-market economists. In their well-developed models, consumer sovereignty—consumer demand for goods and services—guides the system by directly influencing market prices. The distribution of economic resources caused by these market prices not only results in the production of an array of goods and services that are demanded by consumers, but also this production is undertaken in the most cost-effective fashion. The free-market economists claim that at any point, some individuals must earn incomes that are substantially greater than other individuals. They contend that these higher incomes are a reward for greater efficiency or productivity and that this reward-induced efficiency will result in rapid economic growth that will benefit all persons in the society. They might also admit that a system driven by these freely operating markets will be subject to occasional bouts of instability (slow growth, inflation, and unemployment). However, they maintain that government action to eliminate or reduce this periodic instability will be of little value and may only make matters worse. Consequently, government, according to the free-market or conservative economist, should play a minor role in the economic affairs of society.

Although the models of free-market economists are dependent upon functioning, competitive markets, the lack of these competitive markets in the real world does not seriously jeopardize their position. First, they assert that large firms are necessary to achieve low per-unit costs; that is, a single large firm may be able to produce a given level of output with fewer scarce resources than a large number of small firms. Second, they suggest that the benefits associated with the free operation of markets are so great compared to government intervention that even a "second best solution" of imperfectly competitive markets still yields benefits far in excess of government intervention.

These advocates of the free market have been given various labels over time. The oldest and most persistent label is "classical economists." This is because the classical economists of the eighteenth century, particularly Adam Smith, were the first to point out the virtues of the market. Smith captured the essence of the system with the following words:

> Every individual endeavors to employ his capital so that its produce may be of greatest value. He generally neither intends to promote the public interest nor knows how much he is promoting it. He intends only his own security, only his own gain. And he is in this led by an invisible hand to promote an end that was no part of his intention. By pursuing his own interest he frequently promotes that of society more effectively than when he really intends to promote it.
>
> —Adam Smith, *The Wealth of Nations* (1776)

Liberal Economists

Another significant group of economists in the United States can be classified as liberal economists. "Liberal" in this instance refers to the willingness to intervene in the free operation of the market. These economists share with the free-market economists a great respect for the market. However, the liberal economist does not believe that the explicit and implicit costs of a freely operating market should or can be ignored. Rather, the liberal economist maintains that the costs of an uncontrolled marketplace are often borne by those in society who are least capable of bearing them: the poor, the elderly, and the infirm. Additionally, liberal economists maintain that the freely operating market sometimes results in economic instability (that is, in bouts of inflation, unemployment, and slow or negative growth).

Consider for a moment the differences between free-market economists and liberal economists at the microeconomic level. Liberal economists take exception to the free market on two grounds. First, these economists find a basic problem with fairness in the marketplace. Since the forces of consumer spending drive the market, there are those who through no fault of their own (they may be aged, young, infirm, physically or mentally handicapped) may not have the wherewithal to participate in the economic system. Second, the unfettered marketplace does not and cannot handle spillover effects or what are known as "externalities." These are the third-party effects that may occur as a result of some action. Will a firm willingly compensate its neighbors for the pollutants it pours into the nearby lake? Will a truck driver willingly drive at an appropriately safe speed and in the process reduce the highway accident rate? Liberal economists think not. These economists are therefore willing to have the government intervene in these and other similar cases.

The liberal economists' role in macroeconomics is more readily apparent. Ever since the failure of free-market economics during the Great Depression of the 1930s, Keynesianism (still another label for liberal economics) has become widely known. In his 1935 book, *The General Theory of Employment, Interest, and Money,* Lord John Maynard Keynes laid the basic groundwork for this school of thought. Keynes argued that the history of freely operating market economies was marked by periods of recurring recessions, sometimes very deep recessions, called depressions. He maintained that government intervention through its fiscal policy—government tax and spending power—could eliminate, or at least soften these sharp reductions in economic activity and as a result move the economy along a more stable growth path. Thus for the Keynesians, or liberal economists, one of the "extremely objectionable" aspects of a free-market economy is its inherent instability.

The difference between liberal and conservative economists played itself out in terms of the policy response to the recent Great Recession. The Democrats took the liberal position, passing a stimulus package that combined spending increases with tax cuts. Republicans, on the other hand, took the conservative stance. If government was to do anything to impact the economy, it should do so in a way that reduces government involvement, that is, by reducing taxes.

Liberal economists are also far more concerned about the existence of imperfections in the marketplace than their free-market counterparts. They reject the notion that imperfect competition is an acceptable substitute for competitive markets. These economists may agree that the imperfectly competitive firms can achieve some savings because of their large size and efficiency, but they assert that since there is little or no competition the firms are not forced to pass these cost savings on to consumers. Thus liberal economists, who in some circles are labeled "anti-trusters," are willing to intervene in the market in two ways. In some cases, they are prepared to allow some monopolies, such as public utilities, to exist, but they contend that government must regulate these monopolies. In other cases, they maintain that there is no justification for monopolies, and they are prepared to invoke the powers of antitrust legislation to break up existing monopolies and/or prevent the formation of new monopolies.

The Mainstream Critics and Radical Reform Economists

There are two other groups of economists that must be identified. One group can be called mainstream critics. Included in this group are individuals like Thorstein Veblen (1857–1929) and his critique of conspicuous consumption and John Kenneth Galbraith (1908–2006) and his views on industrial structure. One reasonably cohesive group of mainstream critics are the post-Keynesians. They are post-Keynesians because they believe that as the principal economic institutions have changed over time, they have remained closer to the spirit of Keynes than the liberal economists. As some have suggested, the key aspect of Keynes as far as the post-Keynesians are concerned is his assertion that "expectations of the future are not necessarily certain." On a more practical level post-Keynesians assert, among other things, that the productivity of the economic system is not significantly affected by changes in income distribution, that the system can still be efficient without competitive markets, that conventional fiscal policies cannot control inflation, and that "incomes policies" are the means to an effective and equitable answer to the inflationary dilemma. (This characterization of post-Keynesianism is drawn from Alfred S. Eichner's "Introduction" in *A Guide to Post-Keynesian Economics,* White Plains: M. E. Sharpe, Inc., 1978.)

The fourth and last group can be called radical reformist economists. Many in this group trace their ideas to the nineteenth-century philosopher–economist Karl Marx and his most impressive work, the three volumes of *Das Kapital.* As with the other three groups of economists, there are subgroups of radical reform economists. One subgroup, which may be labeled contemporary Marxists, is best represented by those who have published their research over the years in the *Review of Radical Political Economy.* These economists examine issues that have been largely ignored by mainstream economists, issues such as war, sexism, racism, imperialism, and civil rights. In their analyses of these issues, they borrow from and refine the work of Marx. In the process, they emphasize the role of class in shaping society and the role of the economy in determining class structures. Moreover, they see a need to encourage explicitly the development of some form of democratic socialism, for only then will the greatest good for the greatest number be ensured.

Use these labels with extreme care. The categories are not hard and fast. There is much grayness around the edges and little that is black and white in these classifications. This does not mean, however, that they have no value. It is important to understand the philosophical background of the individual authors. This background does indeed color and shade their work.

Before the conclusion of this section, it deserves to be noted again that economists are pragmatic, they are responsive to evidence and events. Perhaps the best current example is that of Alan Greenspan, who served as chairman of the Federal Reserve System from 1987 to 2006. Greenspan is best described as a conservative economist and a strong supporter of free markets. He has been quoted as saying, "I do have an ideology. My judgment is that free competitive markets are by far the unrivaled way to organize economies. We have tried regulation, none meaningfully worked." But the events that unfolded with the bursting of the housing bubble and the credit crisis had a strong impact on Greenspan's thinking and his views on deregulation: In congressional testimony in late October 2008 (*Hearings on the Financial Crisis and the Role of Federal Regulators*, House of Representatives, Committee on Oversight and Government Reform [October 23, 2008]), Greenspan said, "The crisis has turned out to be much broader than anything I could have imagined. I made a mistake in presuming that the self interest of organizations, specifically banks and others, was such that they were best capable of protecting their own shareholders." To rectify the problems Greenspan, in this same testimony, called for regulatory action in the "areas of fraud, settlement and securitization."

Summary

It is clear that there is no shortage of economic problems. These problems demand solutions. At the same time there is no shortage of proposed solutions. In fact, the problem is often one of oversupply. The issues included in this volume will acquaint you or, more accurately, reacquaint you with some of these problems. And, of course, there are at least two proposed solutions for each of the problems. The hope is to provide new insights regarding the alternatives available and the differences and similarities of these alternative remedies.

If this introduction has served its purpose, you will be able to identify common elements in the proposed solutions to the different problems. For example, you will be able to identify the reliance on the forces of the market advocated by free-market economists as the remedy for several economic ills. This introduction should also help you understand why there are at least two proposed solutions for every economic problem; each group of economists tends to interpret a problem from its own philosophical position and to advance a solution that is grounded in that same philosophical framework.

The intention, of course, is not to connect persons to one philosophic position or another, but to generate discussion and promote understanding. To do this, each of us must see not only a proposed solution; we must also be aware of the foundation that supports that solution. With greater understanding, meaningful progress in addressing economic problems can be achieved.

Unit 1

UNIT

Microeconomic Issues

*E*conomic decisions made at the microeconomic level affect our lives in a variety of important ways. Public and private actions determine what goods and services are produced as well as the prices we pay for them. The actions also affect our incomes and even our health. In this unit, we examine the profit decisions of business, the pay of business leaders, election financing, offshore oil drilling, health savings accounts, and a corporate merger.

Selected, Edited, and with Issue Framing Material by:
Miren Ivankovic, *Anderson University*

ISSUE

Are Profits the Only Business of Business?

YES: Milton Friedman, from "The Social Responsibility of Business Is to Increase Its Profits," *The New York Times Magazine* (September 13, 1970)

NO: Mindy S. Lubber, from "Corporate Responsibility: Without Outside Pressure, Corporations Will Not Take Meaningful Action on Sustainability," *The Economist* (September 8, 2013)

Learning Outcomes

After reading this issue, you will be able to:

- Explain business's role in our society as a profit maximizer.
- Explain business's role in our society beyond profit maximization.
- Develop arguments and reasons for profit maximization as a firm's sole responsibility.
- Develop arguments and reasons for a firm to go beyond profit maximization.
- Explain about corporate social responsibility.
- Explain about moral and ethical explanation of firms' responsibility.

ISSUE SUMMARY

YES: Free-market economist and Nobel Laureate Milton Friedman contends that the sole responsibility of business is to increase its profits.

NO: Mindy S. Lubber, president of Ceres, argues that activist involvement is necessary for business to take sustainability seriously, but also believes that businesses should be socially responsible and help develop creative solutions.

As Dr. Milton Friedman states in his work from the above publication, a firm's main and pretty much only concern should be to focus on its profits. Most past and current corporate finance textbooks teach students that the most important task of a corporate manager is to maximize shareholder wealth. This differs a bit from profit maximization because profit maximizing behavior is focused on short-term goals, while wealth maximization is focused on a firm's long-term profitability and thus its wealth. This means that firms may even bypass some short-term profits in order to achieve long-term wealth creation. And the opposite is true as well. If a firm focuses its activity on short-term profitability (profit maximization), it might lose focus on the long-run opportunities and become obsolete in the future. We can find examples in the industry where a firm's managers are looking for opportunities to enhance the firm's wealth and shareholder's value; these firms engage in research and development that is costly but promises a degree of success over the long run. On the other hand, some firms focus on the present; these firms might be very successful in the short run

but forget to pay attention to the changes in demand and market dynamics. Eventually, they lose their market share, or even worse; they go bankrupt.

But what if the goal of a corporate manager was to maximize the firm's social responsibility, rather than to maximize shareholder wealth, which supports Friedman's thinking? Many CEOs and other top-level managers have made corporate social responsibility (CSR) a priority. According to knowledge@wharton, more than 8,000 businesses around the world have signed the UN Global Compact pledging to show good global citizenship in the areas of human rights, labor standards, and environmental protection. Milton Friedman was, to put it mildly, very skeptical about this goal. He called it a "hypocritical window dressing," where firms try to maximize profits and also to minimize their costs; the act of pursuing the CSR is costly. Higher wages, better labor conditions, and less pollution are all expensive propositions. Minimizing the cost means minimizing CSR as well.

The pros and cons will agree that for firms to be as efficient as they can be, they must try to maximize profits. However, in their journey to accomplish that task, should they also pay attention to CSR, thus acknowledging their stakeholders as well as their shareholders? Firms such as Coca Cola, Visa, and many other do follow these principles, and there are a number of private firms that do not have to meet shareholders' demands, thus focusing their operations toward maximization of CSR.

In summary, it is clear that in the capitalist society, firms can exist only if they make profits. So, the question is whether or not business firms have an obligation beyond making profits. This question will be addressed in the following YES and NO selections on the topic of "Are Profits the Only Business of Business?"

Milton Friedman

The Social Responsibility of Business
Is to Increase Its Profits

When I hear businessmen speak eloquently about the "social responsibilities of business in a free-enterprise system," I am reminded of the wonderful line about the Frenchman who discovered at the age of 70 that he had been speaking prose all his life. The businessmen believe that they are defending free enterprise when they declaim that business is not concerned "merely" with profit but also with promoting desirable "social ends; that business has a social conscience" and takes seriously its responsibilities for providing employment, eliminating discrimination, avoiding pollution and whatever else may be the catchwords of the contemporary crop of reformers. In fact they are—or would be if they or anyone else took them seriously—preaching pure and unadulterated socialism. Businessmen who talk this way are unwitting puppets of the intellectual forces that have been undermining the basis of a free society these past decades.

The discussions of the "social responsibilities of business" are notable for their analytical looseness and lack of rigor. What does it mean to say that "business" has responsibilities? Only people can have responsibilities. A corporation is an artificial person and in this sense may have artificial responsibilities, but "business" as a whole cannot be said to have responsibilities, even in this vague sense. The first step toward clarity in examining the doctrine of the social responsibility of business is to ask precisely what it implies for whom.

Presumably, the individuals who are to be responsible are businessmen, which means individual proprietors or corporate executives. Most of the discussion of social responsibility is directed at corporations, so in what follows I shall mostly neglect the individual proprietor and speak of corporate executives.

In a free-enterprise, private-property system, a corporate executive is an employee of the owners of the business. He has direct responsibility to his employers. That responsibility is to conduct the business in accordance with their desires, which generally will be to make as much money as possible while conforming to the basic rules of the society, both those embodied in law and those embodied in ethical custom. Of course, in some cases his employers may have a different objective. A group of persons might establish a corporation for an eleemosynary purpose—for example, a hospital or a school. The manager of such a corporation will not have money profit as his objective but the rendering of certain services.

In either case, the key point is that, in his capacity as a corporate executive, the manager is the agent of the individuals who own the corporation or establish the eleemosynary institution, and his primary responsibility is to them.

Needless to say, this does not mean that it is easy to judge how well he is performing his task. But at least the criterion of performance is straightforward, and the persons among whom a voluntary contractual arrangement exists are clearly defined.

Of course, the corporate executive is also a person in his own right. As a person, he may have many other responsibilities that he recognizes or assumes voluntarily—to his family, his conscience, his feelings of charity, his church, his clubs, his city, his country. He may feel impelled by these responsibilities to devote part of his income to causes he regards as worthy, to refuse to work for particular corporations, even to leave his job, for example, to join his country's armed forces. If we wish, we may refer to some of these responsibilities as "social responsibilities." But in these respects he is acting as a principal, not an agent; he is spending his own money or time or energy, not the money of his employers or the time or energy he has contracted to devote to their purposes. If these are "social responsibilities," they are the social responsibilities of individuals, not of business.

What does it mean to say that the corporate executive has a "social responsibility" in his capacity as businessman? If this statement is not pure rhetoric, it must mean that he is to act in some way that is not in the interest of his employers. For example, that he is to refrain from increasing the price of the product in order to contribute to the social objective of preventing inflation, even though a price increase would be in the best interests of the corporation. Or that he is to make expenditures on reducing pollution beyond the amount that is in the best interests of the corporation or that is required by law in order to contribute to the social objective of improving the environment. Or that, at the expense of corporate profits, he is to hire "hard-core" unemployed instead of better-qualified available workmen to contribute to the social objective of reducing poverty.

In each of these cases, the corporate executive would be spending someone else's money for a general social interest. Insofar as his actions in accord with his "social responsibility" reduce returns to stockholders, he is spending their money. Insofar as his actions raise the price to customers, he is spending the customers' money. Insofar as his actions lower the wages of some employees, he is spending their money.

The stockholders or the customers or the employees could separately spend their own money on the particular action if they wished to do so. The executive is exercising a distinct "social responsibility," rather than serving as an agent of the stockholders or the customers or the employees, only if he spends the money in a different way than they would have spent it.

But if he does this, he is in effect imposing taxes, on the one hand, and deciding how the tax proceeds shall be spent, on the other.

This process raises political questions on two levels: principle and consequences. On the level of political principle, the imposition of taxes and the expenditure of tax proceeds are governmental functions. We have established elaborate constitutional, parliamentary and judicial provisions to control these functions, to assure that taxes are imposed so far as possible in accordance with the preferences and desires of the public—after all, "taxation without representation" was one of the battle cries of the American Revolution. We have a system of checks and balances to separate the legislative function of imposing taxes and enacting expenditures from the executive function of collecting taxes and administering expenditure programs and from the judicial function of mediating disputes and interpreting the law.

Here the businessman—self-selected or appointed directly or indirectly by stockholders—is to be simultaneously legislator, executive and jurist. He is to decide whom to tax by how much and for what purpose, and he is to spend the proceeds—all this guided only by general exhortations from on high to restrain inflation, improve the environment, fight poverty and so on and on.

The whole justification for permitting the corporate executive to be selected by the stockholders is that the executive is an agent serving the interests of his principal. This justification disappears when the corporate executive imposes taxes and spends the proceeds for "social" purposes. He becomes in effect a public employee, a civil servant, even though he remains in name an employee of a private enterprise. On grounds of political principle, it is intolerable that such civil servants—insofar as their actions in the name of social responsibility are real and not just window-dressing—should be selected as they are now. If they are to be civil servants, then they must be selected through a political process. If they are to impose taxes and make expenditures to foster "social" objectives, then political machinery must be set up to guide the assessment of taxes and to determine through a political process the objectives to be served.

This is the basic reason why the doctrine of "social responsibility" involves the acceptance of the socialist view that political mechanisms, not market mechanisms, are the appropriate way to determine the allocation of scarce resources to alternative uses.

On the grounds of consequences, can the corporate executive in fact discharge his alleged "social responsibilities"? On the one hand, suppose he could get away with spending the stockholders' or customers' or employees' money. How is he to know how to spend it? He is told that he must contribute to fighting inflation. How is he to know what action of his will contribute to that end? He is presumably an expert in running his company—in producing a product or selling it or financing it. But nothing about his selection makes him an expert on inflation. Will his holding down the price of his product reduce inflationary pressure? Or, by leaving more spending power in the hands of his customers, simply divert it elsewhere? Or, by forcing him to produce less because of the lower price, will it simply contribute to shortages? Even if he could answer these questions, how much cost is he justified in imposing on his stockholders, customers and employees for this social purpose? What is the appropriate share and what is the appropriate share of others?

And, whether he wants to or not, can he get away with spending his stockholders', customers' or employees' money? Will not the stockholders fire him? (Either the present ones or those who take over when his actions in the name of social responsibility have reduced the corporation's profits and the price of its stock.) His customers and his employees can desert him for other producers and employers less scrupulous in exercising their social responsibilities.

This facet of "social responsibility" doctrine is brought into sharp relief when the doctrine is used to justify wage restraint by trade unions. The conflict of interest is naked and clear when union officials are asked to subordinate the interest of their members to some more general social purpose. If the union officials try to enforce wage restraint, the consequence is likely to be wildcat strikes, rank-and-file revolts and the emergence of strong competitors for their jobs. We thus have the ironic phenomenon that union leaders—at least in the U.S.—have objected to Government interference with the market far more consistently and courageously than have business leaders.

The difficulty of exercising "social responsibility" illustrates, of course, the great virtue of private competitive enterprise—it forces people to be responsible for their own actions and makes it difficult for them to "exploit" other people for either selfish or unselfish purposes. They can do good—but only at their own expense.

Many a reader who has followed the argument this far may be tempted to remonstrate that it is all well and good to speak of government's having the responsibility to impose taxes and determine expenditures for such "social" purposes as controlling pollution or training the hard-core unemployed, but that the problems are too urgent to wait on the slow course of political processes, that the exercise of social responsibility by businessmen is a quicker and surer way to solve pressing current problems.

Aside from the question of fact—I share Adam Smith's skepticism about the benefits that can be expected from "those who affected to trade for the public good"—this argument must be rejected on grounds of principle. What it amounts to is an assertion that those who favor the taxes and expenditures in question have failed to persuade a majority of their fellow citizens to be of like mind and that they are seeking to attain by undemocratic procedures what they cannot attain by democratic procedures. In a free society, it is hard for "good" people to do "good," but that is a small price to pay for making it hard for "evil" people to do "evil," especially since one man's good is another's evil.

I have, for simplicity, concentrated on the special case of the corporate executive, except only for the brief digression on trade unions. But precisely the same argument applies to the newer phenomenon of calling upon stockholders to require corporations to exercise social responsibility (the recent G.M. crusade, for example). In most of these cases, what is in effect involved is some stockholders trying to get other stockholders (or customers or employees) to contribute against their will to "social" causes favored by the activists. Insofar as they succeed, they are again imposing taxes and spending the proceeds.

The situation of the individual proprietor is somewhat different. If he acts to reduce the returns of his enterprise in order to exercise his "social responsibility," he is spending his own money, not someone else's. If he wishes to spend his money on such purposes, that is his right, and I cannot see that there is any objection to his doing so. In the process, he, too, may impose costs on employees and customers. However, because he is far less likely than a large corporation or union to have monopolistic power, any such side effects will tend to be minor.

Of course, in practice the doctrine of social responsibility is frequently a cloak for actions that are justified on other grounds rather than a reason for those actions.

To illustrate, it may well be in the long-run interest of a corporation that is a major employer in a small community to devote resources to providing amenities to that community or to improving its government. That may make it easier to attract desirable employees, it may reduce the wage bill or lessen losses from pilferage and sabotage or have other worthwhile effects. Or it may be that, given the laws about the deductibility of corporate charitable contributions, the stockholders can contribute more to charities they favor by having the corporation make the gift than by doing it themselves, since they can in that way contribute an amount that would otherwise have been paid as corporate taxes.

In each of these—and many similar—cases, there is a strong temptation to rationalize these actions as an exercise of "social responsibility." In the present climate of opinion, with its widespread aversion to "capitalism," "profits," the "soulless corporation" and so on, this is one way for a corporation to generate goodwill as a by-product of expenditures that are entirely justified in its own self-interest.

It would be inconsistent of me to call on corporate executives to refrain from this hypocritical window-dressing because it harms the foundations of a free society. That would be to call on them to exercise a "social responsibility"! If our institutions, and the attitudes of the public, make it in their self-interest to cloak their actions in this way, I cannot summon much indignation to denounce them. At the same time, I can express admiration for those individual proprietors or owners of closely held corporations or stockholders of more broadly held corporations who disdain such tactics as approaching fraud.

Whether blameworthy or not, the use of the cloak of social responsibility, and the nonsense spoken in its name by influential and prestigious businessmen, does clearly harm the foundations of a free society. I have been impressed time and again by the schizophrenic character of many businessmen. They are capable of being extremely far-sighted and clear-headed in matters that are internal to their businesses. They are incredibly short-sighted and muddleheaded in matters that are outside their businesses but affect the possible survival of business in general. This short-sightedness is strikingly exemplified in the calls from many businessmen for wage and price guidelines or controls or income policies. There is nothing that could do more in a brief period to destroy a market system and replace it by a centrally controlled system than effective governmental control of prices and wages.

The short-sightedness is also exemplified in speeches by businessmen on social responsibility. This may gain them kudos in the short run. But it helps to strengthen the already too prevalent view that the pursuit of profits is wicked and immoral and must be curbed and controlled by external forces. Once this view is adopted, the external forces that curb the market will not be the social consciences, however highly developed, of the pontificating executives; it will be the iron fist of Government bureaucrats. Here, as with price and wage controls, businessmen seem to me to reveal a suicidal impulse.

The political principle that underlies the market mechanism is unanimity. In an ideal free market resting on private property, no individual can coerce any other, all cooperation is voluntary, all parties to such cooperation benefit or they need not participate. There are no "social" values, no "social" responsibilities in any sense other than the shared values and responsibilities of individuals. Society is a collection of individuals and of the various groups they voluntarily form.

The political principle that underlies the political mechanism is conformity. The individual must serve a more general social interest—whether that be determined by a church or a dictator or a majority. The individual may have a vote and a say in what is to be done, but if he is overruled, he must conform. It is appropriate for some to require others to contribute to a general social purpose whether they wish to or not.

Unfortunately, unanimity is not always feasible. There are some respects in which conformity appears unavoidable, so I do not see how one can avoid the use of the political mechanism altogether.

But the doctrine of "social responsibility" taken seriously would extend the scope of the political mechanism to every human activity. It does not differ in philosophy from the most explicitly collectivist doctrine. It differs only by professing to believe that collectivist ends can be attained without collectivist means. That is why, in my book "Capitalism and Freedom," I have called it a "fundamentally subversive doctrine" in a free society, and have said that in such a society, "there is one and only one social responsibility of business—to use its resources and engage in activities designed to increase its profits so long as it stays within the rules of the game, which is to say,

engages in open and free competition without deception or fraud."

MILTON FRIEDMAN (1912–2006) is a graduate of University of Chicago and Columbia University. In 1948, Friedman joined the faculty at Chicago and stayed there until his retirement in 1977. After his academic work at the University of Chicago, he served as a senior fellow at the Hoover Institution at Stanford University. He was also president of the American Economic Association in 1967 and won the Nobel Prize in economics in 1976. He served as a columnist for *Newsweek*, wrote popular books, participated in educational television series, and delivered addresses to numerous groups.

Mindy S. Lubber

Corporate Responsibility: Without Outside Pressure, Corporations Will Not Take Meaningful Action on Sustainability

A question I am often asked is how, as an outsider to industry, Ceres can claim to be able to bring value to companies that focus on their bottom line every day.

The recent subprime mortgage meltdown is a painful example of how companies and whole industries can delude themselves into ignoring even the most fundamental issues. If anyone outside the financial markets had been scrutinizing the risks from easy mortgages, they could have helped avert millions of foreclosures and an economic recession, and saved themselves a fistful of dollars.

It is the same with global climate change, which presents far-reaching risks and opportunities that many companies—their heads stuck in the sands of the quarterly business cycle—are not grasping on their own. Outsiders warned Ford and General Motors for years that their gas-guzzling high-polluting cars were too big, but the carmakers did not listen. Now their large sports utility vehicles sit unsold in car lots and the company's very survival is at stake.

Outsiders—investors, environmentalists, public interest groups, other industry experts—have an essential role in pressuring companies on their handling of environmental and social threats. They should be asking tough questions; they should be offering creative, out-of-the-box ideas; they should be demanding real action; and they should be holding companies accountable.

Last year's buyout of TXU is a good example of how outside pressure can yield positive benefits. For years, the Texas utility battled with environmentalists over carbon emissions and other pollutants. When it proposed in 2006 to build 11 new coal-fired power plants, the battle became a full-blown war. When TXU's stock price sagged and two private equity firms began their bid to buy the company, we saw a significant shift in business strategy: making environmental factors a part of due diligence. After extensive discussions with Environmental Defense and the Natural Resources Defense Council on the judiciousness of the planned coal binge and possible green alternatives, the buyers scrapped most of the coal-fired power plants and agreed to cut global warming pollution and boost energy efficiency efforts. The result? A better place for their bottom line.

There are many other examples of positive results from outside pressure: companies like Nike, which responded to public-interest pressure on workplace issues by providing first-in-the-industry disclosure about the names and locations of its 700-plus contract factories; Bank of America, which heeded the advice of investors in setting a greenhouse gas reduction target in its lending; McDonalds, which teamed up with environmental groups in sourcing sustainable fishery stocks; and Dell, which listened to advocacy groups and investors by supporting electronics recycling legislation and improving the energy efficiency of its products. These efforts are all the result of listening and responding to outside parties in making smart business decisions that lower costs, reduce regulatory, reputation and litigation risks, and build long-term shareholder value.

But some forms of outside pressure work better than others. I prefer relationships between outsiders and companies that are steady and long-lasting, not one-night stands focused on one problem and one project only. That is one reason why the jury is still out on the TXU buyout. Yes, it is great that eight coal plants were not built, but let us hope that advocates keep the pressure on so that the company's owner's green commitments stand the test of time. The fact that the company is now privately held makes the task especially challenging since there is no public transparency.

For years, Ceres has used stakeholder teams consisting of investors, environmentalists and other outside experts to engage with companies on environmental and social challenges they face. Through conference calls and face-to-face meetings, these teams advise companies on sustainability reporting, emerging issues and specific performance improvements. Companies value this level of candour from outside experts who may have been adversaries in the past. These relationships often begin with one issue, but the dialogue broadens and expands over time to include much, much more. This kind of constructive long-term engagement with executives and board members is the best way to drill sustainability deep into the core of corporate decision-making. It creates a platform for measuring year-to-year progress on environmental performance and exposing potential "greenwashing."

An example of what I am talking about is our relationship with the apparel company, Timberland. Ceres has a long track record of working with apparel companies (including Nike) on workplace conditions at their overseas factories. Timberland is among the companies that have been responsive to our concerns on the issue. In just the past few years, this New Hampshire company has disclosed the name and locations of its 300 contract facilities and boosted its assessments at those sites, which has led to improvements in workplace conditions. But, with help from our stakeholder team, Timberland is now taking sustainability in exciting new directions. The company recently launched first-of-its-kind packaging with nutritional labels, detailing how and where each Timberland product was made and its impact on the environment. The company is also participating in our new Facility Reporting Project, a valuable way for companies to evaluate and address how individual facilities are affecting their local communities.

Still, outside engagement is hard, hard work with numerous challenges. The three keys for success are goal setting, continual performance improvement and accountability.

In the case of climate change, stakeholders will never be satisfied with companies making simple pledges toward carbon neutrality. It is relatively easy to buy carbon credits and renewable energy certificates (RECs) and then claim you are 100% powered by wind energy. But, as we all know, there is a vast gap between theoretical credits and RECs that are purchased and wind farms that are actually built.

Businesses that are really serious about tackling climate change need to go much further. Energy efficiency and other measures that directly reduce greenhouse gas emissions in their operations and supply chains should be a priority at all companies. Businesses should also work with outside experts to develop smart creative solutions that distinguish them from their peers. Several leading banks, for example, worked closely with environmental groups to develop and adopt the Carbon Principles, a tougher set of standards for scrutinizing loans for coal-fired power plants. Dell is working with outside groups and other companies, including TXU, to make it easier to site renewable energy projects and infrastructure in states such as Texas.

These collaborations are all works in progress. Stakeholders are ever mindful of pushing companies harder and making sure there is no backtracking.

Outside pressure may be resisted by corporations blinded by the age-old way of doing things. But they should listen: it just might save their company.

Mindy S. Lubber is president of Ceres, the leading coalition of investors, environmental organizations, and other public interest groups working with companies and investors to build sustainability into the capital markets and address sustainability challenges such as global climate change. She also directs the Investor Network on Climate Risk (INCR), a network of more than 95 investors representing nearly $10 trillion in assets that coordinates U.S. investor responses to the financial risks and opportunities of climate change. She was recently voted one of "The 100 Most Influential People in Corporate Governance for 2009" by *Directorship Magazine*, who noted Ceres's substantial influence in its field. Before coming to Ceres, Ms. Lubber was the Regional Administrator of the U.S. Environmental Protection Agency and Founder/CEO of Green Century Capital Management, an investment firm managing environmentally screened mutual funds.

EXPLORING THE ISSUE

Are Profits the Only Business of Business?

Critical Thinking and Reflection

1. As a shareholder of the XYZ Corporation, would you be willing to receive a smaller dividend so that a portion of the firm's profits could be allocated for saving endangered species? Explain.
2. According to Dr. M. Friedman, a firm's main goal is to maximize shareholders' wealth; if so, why do you think so many firms contribute large amounts of funds toward other causes and not the shareholders?
3. Explain the concept of a socially responsible firm and the concept of goodwill.
4. Should firms correct any negative externalities they might be creating on their own, such as pollution, or do you think we need to have government regulations, which will reinforce social responsibility?
5. We live in a global economy; thus how will the firms in poor nations be able to act socially responsible (think pollution) compared to their partners in wealthy nations? Remember—we all share the same air.

Is There Common Ground?

There are different types of firms. Some are private, some are public, some are for profit, and some are non-for-profit. Some are very large and have offices and plants on multiple continents, and some are small and operate in one location only. All of these firms, no matter where they are located will be subject to their government's regulations and probably at multiple levels from local, state, and federal governments. All of them will purchase inputs for production such as land, labor, capital, and managers. They will, in most of cases, purchase water, electricity, and a number of other items that will benefit that community.

Are firms responsible for going above and beyond the aforementioned responsibilities? If a firm is only focusing on shareholder wealth maximization, generating profits is crucial and thus cost minimization is an important part of the equation. Will they, therefore, divert their interests away from the socially responsible causes?

It is in the firm's interest to present itself to the stakeholders and shareholders as a responsible, law abiding, moral, and ethical enterprise because these are also profit-maximizing attributes. Firms are very careful about their image in the markets, and it is quantified on the balance sheet as a non-tangible asset: goodwill. McDonald's wraps its food in recyclable and biodegradable paper products because it is good business. It might be costly in the short run, but shareholder wealth is based on the firm's profits over the long run using the "time value of money" concept. Shareholder wealth maximization and social responsibility might have more in common than we think.

Create Central

www.mhhe.com/createcentral

Additional Resources

Primeaux, Patrick and Stieber, John A., *Profit Maximization* (Jan. 1, 1995)

SAGE Brief Guide to Corporate Social Responsibility (SAGE Publications, 2011)

Crowther, David, *International Dimensions of Corporate Social Responsibility, vol. 1* (2005)

Shiller, Robert J., *Finance and the Good Society* (2012)

Internet References . . .

Corporate Social Responsibility and Wealth Maximization—Scribd

www.scribd.com/doc/...Social-Responsibility-and -Wealth-Maximization

Profit Maximization Vs. Corporate Social Responsibility

www.tkf.org.in/blog/profit-maximization-vs -corporate-social

'Leveraging Corporate Responsibility': The Stakeholder Approach to Knowledge

wharton.upenn.edu/article/leveraging-corporate

TheRacetotheBottom: Social Responsibility—Profit Maximization

www.theracetothebottom.org/social-responsibility /profit

ISSUE

Should the Compensation of Executives Be Subject to Government Regulation?

YES: Joseph E. Stiglitz, from "Testimony before the U.S. House of Representatives Committee on Financial Services" (January 22, 2010)

NO: Kevin J. Murphy, from "Testimony before the U.S. House of Representatives Committee on Financial Services" (June 11, 2009)

Learning Outcomes

After reading this issue, you will be able to:

- Discuss the relationship between incentives and executive compensation.
- Appreciate the differences in consequence between risk taking and excessive risk taking.
- Identify the federal measure known as the Troubled Asset Relief Program (TARP).
- Assess the concept of "too big to fail."

ISSUE SUMMARY

YES: Joseph Stiglitz, the winner of the Nobel Prize in economics, argues that flawed incentive compensation systems played an important role in the financial crisis. He believes that better regulation including regulations that affect incentive structures are likely to produce a better alignment of private rewards and social returns and better innovation.

NO: University of Southern California professor Kevin J. Murphy argues that "there is nothing inherent in the current structure of compensation in financial service firms that leads to obvious incentives to take excessive risk." He believes that government-imposed regulations are "highly unlikely" to improve compensation policies of these firms.

As the most famous and best baseball player of his era, George Herman (Babe) Ruth earned a salary of $80,000 in 1930. While this figure, especially because it is unadjusted for inflation, seems incredibly low, it was the highest in professional baseball. What shocked most people was that it was higher than the $75,000 salary of then President Calvin Coolidge. Today, of course, almost every major league baseball player earns more than the president (the 2010 major league minimum player salary is exactly the same as President Obama's salary of $400,000). But back then when a reporter wondered whether Ruth deserved to be paid more than the president, the Babe supposedly replied: "Why not? I had a better year than he did."

As strange as it might seem, Ruth's reply has grounding in economic theory, which holds that someone's income should be related to his or her performance. More specifically, a worker's compensation should reflect that worker's marginal revenue product with it defined as the additional revenues or reduced costs generated by the employment of an additional worker. That is, if a worker adds $80,000 per year to a profit-maximizing firm's revenues, then the firm should be willing to pay the worker up to $80,000. The greater the worker's productivity and/or the greater the price at which the worker's output can be sold, the greater should be his or her earnings.

But reflections on incomes, like those of the reporter, are not typically based on economic theory. Instead of being based on estimates of marginal revenue product, they are more likely to be based on other, more abstract notions of worth and value. For example, people complain that truly valuable members of society, like nurses and teachers, are paid too little compared to marginal contributors to societal well-being, like a third-rate punk rock band member or a pro football team's third-string quarterback.

Recently, the controversy about pay has spilled over to the compensation of business executives, especially the earnings of persons who are the heads of financial services firms. This began well before the financial crisis erupted in 2007. Probably one of the most visible manifestations of this controversy involved Eliot Spitzer and Richard Grasso. In 2004, as attorney general of the state of New York, Spitzer sued Grasso, who had headed the New York Stock Exchange (NYSE). Spitzer charged that Grasso's compensation, reported at about $187 million, was excessive and a portion should be returned to the NYSE. The suit was eventually dismissed.

Today, in the background of the financial crisis, mortgage foreclosures, bank failures, and government bailouts, the controversy of executive compensation is on the front burner. According to a recent *Wall Street Journal* article ("Wall Street Pay: A Record $144 Billion," October 12, 2010), compensation at 35 banks, hedge funds, asset managers, and stock and commodities exchanges was $117 billion in 2007, $135 billion in 2008, $122 billion in 2009, and projected at $144 billion in 2010. To many American taxpayers, pay of this kind—especially the executive compensation of firms that received government funds from the Troubled Assets Relief Program (TARP)—is simply unjustified. Indeed, in passing TARP as part of the Emergency Economic Stabilization Act in 2008, Congress did seek to put some limits on executive compensation: for example, restricting the tax deductibility for executive compensation above a specific level.

As Congress began to consider additional regulation of the financial sector in the form of the Wall Street Reform and Investor Protection Act (generally referred to as Dodd-Frank), it reconsidered the issue of executive compensation. Both Joseph Stiglitz and Kevin Murphy appeared before the House Committee on Financial Services to argue the case for and against additional government regulation of executive compensation. Stiglitz believes that regulation can help to better align the private rewards and social returns. Murphy argues that there is nothing inherent in private compensation systems that encourage financial executives to take excessive risk.

YES

Joseph E. Stiglitz

Testimony before the U.S. House of Representatives Committee on Financial Services

In this brief testimony, I can only touch on a few key points. Many of these points I elaborate in my book *Freefall*,[1] which was published just a few days ago.

Our financial system failed to perform the key roles that it is supposed to perform for our society: managing risk and allocating capital. A good financial system performs these functions at low transaction costs. Our financial system created risk and mismanaged capital, all the while generating huge transaction costs, as the sector garnered some 40% of all of corporate profits in the years before the crisis.

The sector is also responsible for running the payments mechanism, without which our economy cannot function. But so badly did it manage risk and misallocate capital that our payments mechanism was in danger of collapse. So deceptive were the systems of creative accounting that the banks had employed that, as the crisis evolved, they didn't even know their own balance sheets, and so they knew that they couldn't know that of any other bank. No wonder then that no bank could trust another, and no one could trust our banks. No wonder then that our system of credit—the lifeblood on which the economy depends—froze. We may congratulate ourselves that we have managed to pull back from the brink, but we should not forget that it was the financial sector that brought us to the brink of disaster. . . .

While the failures of the financial system that led the economy to the brink of ruin are, by now, obvious, the failings of our financial system are more pervasive. Small- and medium-sized enterprises found it difficult to get credit, even as the financial system was pushing credit on poor people beyond their ability to repay. Modern technology allows for the creation of an efficient, low-cost electronic payment mechanism; but businesses pay 1 to 2 per cent or more in fees for a transaction that should cost pennies or less.

Our financial markets not only mismanaged risk—and created products that increased the risk faced by others—but they also failed to create financial products that would help ordinary Americans face the important risks that they confronted, such as the risks of home ownership or the risks of inflation. Indeed, I am in total

agreement with Paul Volcker—it is hard to find evidence of any real growth associated with the so-called innovations of our financial system, though it is easy to see the link between those innovations and the disaster that confronted our economy.

Underlying all of these failures is a simple point, which seems to have been forgotten: *financial markets are a means to an end, not an end in themselves.* If they allocate capital and manage risk well, then the economy prospers, and it is appropriate that they should garner for themselves some fraction of the resulting increases in productivity. But it is clear that pay was not connected with *social* returns—or even long-run profitability of the sector. For many financial institutions, losses after the crisis were greater than the cumulative profits in the four years preceding the crisis; from a longer-term perspective, profits were negative. Yet the executives walked off with ample rewards, sometimes in the millions. Most galling for many Americans was the fact that even when profits were negative, many financial institutions proposed paying large bonuses.

We should remember this is not the first time that our banks have been bailed out, saved from bearing the consequences of their bad lending. While this is only the second major bailout in twenty years in the US, past responses to financial crises abroad—in Mexico, Brazil, Russia, Indonesia, Thailand, Argentina, and many others— were really bailouts of American and European banks, at the expense of taxpayers in these countries, engineered through the bankers' allies at the IMF and the US Treasury. In each of these instances, the banks had made bad lending decisions, lending beyond the ability or willingness of borrowers to repay.

Market economies work to produce growth and efficiency, but only when private rewards and social returns are aligned. Unfortunately, in the financial sector, both individual and institutional incentives were misaligned. The consequences of the failures of the financial system were not borne just by those in the sector but by homeowners, retirees, workers, and taxpayers, and not just in this country but also around the world. The "externalities," as economists refer to these impacts

Stiglitz, Joseph E. United States Congress, January 22, 2010.

on others, were massive. . . . But in America's casino capitalism, when the banks gambled and lost, the entire nation paid the price. We need regulation because of these externalities.

So far, I have made four key points:

1. Banks have consistently failed to fulfill their basic societal mission.
2. Banks have repeatedly been bailed out from bearing the consequences of their flawed lending.
3. Incentives within the financial system are distorted at both the individual and institutional level—at both levels private rewards and social returns are misaligned.
4. The financial sector has imposed large costs on the rest of society—the presence of externalities is one of the reasons why the sector needs to be regulated. . . .

Incentives and Executive Compensation

. . . The one thing that economists agree upon is that incentives matter, and even a casual look at the conventional incentive structures—with payment focused on short-run performance and managers not bearing the full downside consequences of their mistakes—suggested that they would lead to short-sighted behavior and excessive risk taking. And so they did. Leverage ratios in excess of 30 to 1 meant that even a 4% decline in asset prices would wipe out an institution's net worth, and with even smaller declines a bank would fail to meet basic standards of capital adequacy. To put this in perspective: average housing prices have fallen from their peak by nearly 30%.

In some ways, the "apparent" incentive structures were worse than this, because compensation typically increased with stock prices, which provided incentives for management to provide distorted information that would result in higher stock prices. The banks excelled at this, moving risks off balance sheet, with consequences that I have already described. Markets can only work well when there is good information, and the banks' incentive structures encouraged the provision of distorted and misleading information.

Moreover, management was rewarded for higher returns, whether those returns were produced merely by increasing risk (higher beta, in the parlance of finance) or by truly outperforming the market (higher alpha). Anyone can do the former; the latter is almost impossible. Again, no wonder that all the financial wizards took the easier route—and it was this excessive risk taking that helped bring capitalism to the brink.

These problems in incentive pay have long been recognized. Unless appropriate care is paid to the quality of what is produced, those who are paid on the basis of the quantity produced will put more effort into quantity than quality. And that is what happened in finance;

with fees based, for instance, on the amount of mortgages written, there was little attention paid to the quality of the mortgages—and not surprisingly, quality deteriorated markedly, especially with securitization.

Opportunities for "product deterioration" are especially large in the financial sector, since the risks associated with, say, poorer mortgages (mortgages with a higher probability of default) won't be evident until years after the fees are earned. The financial sector has been particularly creative in finding accounting frameworks that increase apparent profits in the short run—with losses revealed only later. While some of the accounting practices may have gone outside the law, there are still ample opportunities within the law.

There is an ongoing dispute: was it poor models (which predicted that events such as those that occurred in 2007–2008 would occur less often than once in the lifetime of the universe), poor risk management, or the off-balance-sheet shenanigans that nearly brought down our banking system and with it the global economy? None of these possibilities puts a positive light on our bankers. But incentives played a key role in each of these interpretations. They had an incentive to engage in excessive risk taking, they had an incentive to engage in deceptive accounting, and they had an incentive to use—and seemingly believe—models that allowed them to undertake excessive risk. They had an incentive not to enquire too deeply into the assumptions used in those models. And they had an incentive not to think too deeply about how their incentive structures distorted, and continue to distort, behavior. And while they continue to emphasize the importance of incentive pay, they have been slow to acknowledge the failings in the incentive structures and to look for alternatives.[2]

Things might have been worse were it not for the fact that much of the so-called incentive (performance) pay was a mere charade: pay was high when performance was good, but as the country saw in 2008 and 2009, pay was also high when performance was poor. Only the name of the pay changed, e.g. from "incentive" bonus to "retention" bonus. Studies in other downturns have shown the same pattern.[3]

Indeed, had our bankers been serious about designing an efficient *performance-incentive* system, it would have been markedly different, with pay related to relative performance, not to the vagaries of the overall economy and the stock market.

While the financial sector's failure to perform its essential functions, all the while garnering high profits, casts a poor light on the sector, their predatory lending and deceptive credit card practices cast an even darker shadow. They have used all their political muscle resisting curbing these practices. The irony is that the bankers were hoisted on their own petard—it was the subprime mortgages, irresponsible loans made to uninformed individuals beyond their ability to pay, designed to generate bankers fees as they robbed the poor of the life savings, that began the unraveling of our financial system. Our bankers discovered that there was money at the bottom of the pyramid, and they did everything they could to make sure that it moved to the top.

Having done little to change either the incentives or the constraints facing the financial sector, we cannot expect a marked change in behavior. Of course, in the immediate aftermath of the crisis, they and their supervisors may be chastened, though at least for some seemingly far less than one might have thought, given the enormity of the recent calamity.

In some quarters, for instance, there is a concern that programs to restructure mortgages have given rise to new fees, added on to what is already owed. Rather than a reduction in what is owed, in some cases it may be increasing. Recorded profits—and bonuses—may increase, with little regard to the risks of non-payment in the future.

Critics of regulation worry that such regulation will stifle innovation. As I argued earlier, it is hard to identify significant social benefits—and easy to identify large social costs—associated with some of the recent financial innovations. Bankers were more innovative in figuring out ways of exploiting American consumers and extracting fees than they were at designing products that would help consumers manage the risks that they face. Their failure in this respect has had not only an economic cost, but also a large social cost: foreclosures this year, estimated between 2.5 and 3.5 million, are expected to be even larger than in the last two years.

At the same time, as I have noted, the financial sector not only has not innovated in ways that would have lowered transaction costs, increased the efficiency of capital allocation, or led to less societal risk, but in some cases they have even resisted such innovations. The new mortgages led to higher, not lower, default rates: they clearly made it more difficult for individuals to manage the risk of home ownership. In my book *Freefall*, I document other examples.

None of this should be a surprise: flawed incentives affect incentives to innovate. A better alignment of private rewards and social returns and better regulation—including regulations that affect incentive structures—holds out the prospect of better innovation.

I can summarize our discussion of incentives as follows:

1. Flawed incentives played an important role in this and other failures of the financial system to perform its central roles. They encouraged excessive risk taking and shortsighted behavior. They encouraged predatory behavior.
2. Flawed incentives also explain the failure of the financial sector to innovate in ways that would have served society better, e.g. better mortgages and an efficient electronic payment mechanism.
3. Poorly designed incentive systems can lead to a deterioration of product quality, and this happened in the financial sector. This is not surprising, given the ample opportunities provided by creative accounting.

4. Many of the compensation schemes actually provided incentives for deceptive accounting. Markets only allocate resources well when information is good; but the incentive structures encouraged distortions in the provision of information.
5. The design of the incentive system demonstrates a failure to understand risk and incentives and/or a deliberate attempt to deceive investors, exploiting deficiencies in our system of corporate governance.
6. There were alternative compensation schemes that would have provided better incentives, but few firms chose to implement such schemes.
7. Matters might have been worse but for the fact that some of the discussion of incentive pay was simply a charade: pay was high when performance was good, but pay was also high when performance was poor. Only the name of the compensation changed. There was less "pay for performance" than claimed.

Concluding Comments

Market economies yield growth and efficiency when private rewards and social returns are aligned. Unfortunately, in the financial sector, both individual and institutional incentives were misaligned. The result of the flawed incentives, perhaps even worse in the aftermath of the crisis, can be called ersatz capitalism, with losses socialized and profits privatized; it is an economic system that is neither fair nor efficient.

But in some critical ways, incentives are actually worse now than they were before the crisis. The way the bank bailout was managed—with money flowing to the big banks while the smaller banks were allowed to fail (140 failed in 2009 alone)—has led to a more concentrated banking system. Incentives have been worsened too by the exacerbation of the problem of moral hazard. A new concept—with little basis in economic theory or historical experience—was introduced: the largest financial institutions were judged to be too big to be resolved. We saved not just the banks, but also the bankers, the shareholders, and the bondholders.

I want to end with two broader notes on the societal impacts of compensation in the financial sector. The first has to do with the exploitive behavior of those in the financial sector, to which I have briefly referred earlier. The bankers have been criticized for their excessive greed. First-time homebuyers were deliberately exploited. Similar criticisms can be made about the exploitive behavior of credit card companies. I don't think that those who went into finance are greedier or more deficient in moral scruples than others. But the incentive structures led them to behave in the way that they did. Economists have an expression: "everyone has their price," and in finance, for too many, the rewards were simply too great to resist. The system even affected how they thought. In most professional jobs, one takes pride in one's work; one gives one's all. We don't pay heart surgeons on the basis of success, arguing higher pay will provide an incentive to exert more effort to save his patient. What kind of person says to his employer, "If you only pay me $5 million, I'll give you only half my effort? If you want me to really exert my energies, you have to pay me more if I succeed in increasing profits." But for those in finance, this kind of reasoning became not only acceptable but also became the conventional wisdom—with little thought, as we have seen, to the relationship between these "measured" profits and either long-term firm performance or, more importantly, societal returns.

Finally, I have emphasized how our financial sector failed in its essential societal roles, especially with respect to the allocation of capital, and how the sector's incentive structures may have contributed to that failure. But there is another misallocation of resources that resulted from the sector's compensation policies, one whose effects are graver and longer lasting, and one which, as a teacher, I have felt intensely. There was a misallocation of scarce human capital, as some of America's most talented young succumbed to the lure of easy money—brilliant minds that, in another era, might have made real discoveries that enhanced our knowledge or real innovations—that would have enhanced societal well-being. In earlier decades, our best students went into a variety of areas—some into medicine, many into research, still others into public service, and some into business. Each found fulfillment of their potential at the same time they served their communities in one way or another. At Amherst College, where I serve as a trustee, we talk of helping our youth live lives of consequence. In this modern era of a finance-dominated

economy, unfortunately, a disproportionate share of our most talented youth went into finance, lured by the outsized compensation. The costs to our society of this misallocation are incalculable.

Notes

1. Published by W. W. Norton, 2010.
2. There have been some efforts to make more of the compensation based on long-term performance, but little effort to separate out performance which is related to "better alpha" rather than "beta" or to outcomes that are the consequences of general market factors and outcomes that are the consequences of managers' contributions. (Systems based on *relative* performance can be shown to be far better than those currently in fashion. See, e.g. B. Nalebuff and J. E. Stiglitz, 1983, "Prizes and Incentives: Towards a General Theory of Compensation and Competition." *Bell Journal of Economics,* 14(1): 21–43.)
3. See, for instance, J. E. Stiglitz, *Roaring Nineties*, New York: W. W. Norton, 2003.

JOSEPH E. STIGLITZ is a university professor at Columbia University. He served as the chief economist of the World Bank from 1997 to 2000. He is the author of *Making Globalization Work* (W. W. Norton, 2006) and most recently, with Linda J. Bilmes of Harvard's Kennedy School, he coauthored *The Three Trillion Dollar War: The True Cost of the Iraq Conflict* (W. W. Norton, 2008). Along with two others, he received the Nobel Prize in Economic Science in 2001.

Kevin J. Murphy

→ **NO**

Testimony before the U.S. House of Representatives Committee on Financial Services

Introduction and Summary[1]

Compensation in the financial services industry became highly controversial in early 2009 amid revelations that Merrill Lynch paid substantial year-end bonuses to its executives and employees after receiving Federal bailout funds and just prior to completion of its acquisition by Bank of America. The outrage heightened following the revelation that AIG (which had received over $170 billion of federal bailout funds) was in the process of paying $168 million in "retention bonuses" to its executives. The anger over these bonuses—coupled with suspicions that the Wall Street bonus culture is a root cause of excessive risk taking that helped create the ongoing global financial crisis—has led to an effective prohibition on cash bonuses for participants in the government's Troubled Asset Relief Program (TARP), and is leading us today towards more-sweeping regulation of compensation in financial services firms.

Political pressures to reform pay have escalated in spite of limited evidence that compensation structures have, in fact, been responsible for excessive risk taking in the financial services industry. Indeed, the pressures have emerged even without a definition of "excessive risk taking" or how we might distinguish excessive risk from the normal risks inherent in all successful business ventures. While inappropriately designed compensation structures can certainly encourage risk taking, the risk-taking incentives caused by compensation in financial services are small relative to those created by "Too Big to Fail" guarantees, loose monetary policies, social policies on home ownership, and poorly implemented financial innovations such as exotic mortgages, securitization, and collateralized debt obligations. Moreover, the compensation constraints currently on TARP recipients will likely destroy these organizations unless they can quickly repay the government and avoid the constraints. Furthermore, regulating compensation in financial services will cripple one of our nations most important, and historically most productive, industries.

Risk Taking and the Wall Street Bonus Culture

The heavy reliance on bonuses has been a defining feature of Wall Street compensation for decades, going back to the days when investment banks were privately held partnerships. Such firms kept fixed costs under control by keeping base salaries low and paying most of the compensation in the form of cash bonuses that varied with profitability. This basic structure remained intact when the investment banks went public, but the cash bonuses were replaced with a combination of cash, restricted stock, and stock options.

The primary way that such structures might encourage excessive risk taking is through asymmetric rewards and penalties, that is, high rewards for superior performance but no real penalties for failure. Financial services firms provide significant penalties for failure in their cash bonus plans by keeping salaries below competitive market levels, so that earning a zero bonus represents a penalty. Indeed, much of the outrage over bonuses in financial services reflects the fact that, in most industries, a "bonus" connotes an extraordinary reward for extraordinary performance added on top of generous above-market salaries. But, the facts are that salaries in financial service firms represent a small portion of total compensation and the "bonuses" are not bonuses on top of normal salaries, but are rather a fundamental part of competitive compensation. Take away the bonuses, and the banks will have to raise salaries or find other ways to pay, or they will lose their top talent.

Table 1 shows that bonuses for Chief Executive Officers (CEOs) in companies receiving TARP funding declined substantially from 2007 to 2008. The sample is based on all companies in the S&P 500, S&P MidCap 400, and S&P SmallCap 600 in which the same executive served as CEO in both 2007 and 2008. Average CEO bonuses in 36 TARP-recipient companies fell 84.3% from over $2.3 million in 2007 to only $363,082 in 2008. In contrast, CEO bonuses

Murphy, Kevin J. United States Congress, June 11, 2009.

in 23 financial services firms not receiving TARP funds fell by only 13%, while CEO bonuses in 684 other non-TARP firms fell by 9.9%.

[The same pattern holds] for all proxy-named executives (typically the four highest-paid executives in addition to the CEO). Average bonuses for 170 executives in TARP-recipient companies fell by 82%, compared to a 24% decline for 119 executives in financial services not receiving TARP funding, and a 13% decline for 3,454 executives in non-TARP non-financial firms.

In addition to cash bonuses, executives and senior managers in financial services receive much of their compensation in the form of restricted stock and options, and these instruments also provide strong penalties for failure. . . . The average value of the CEO's restricted stockholdings also declined dramatically in 2008, falling over 80% from $6.8 million in 2007 to only $1.3 million at the end of 2008.

The statistics . . . understate the losses incurred by individual CEOs, since they are based only on CEOs serving continuously through 2007 and 2008 and ignore losses realized by CEOs losing their jobs as a consequence of the crisis. Moreover, these statistics only include firms that continued to operate at the end of 2008, thus ignoring losses at Bear Stearns, Lehman Brothers, Washington Mutual, Wachovia, Countrywide, and other casualties of the crisis. . . .

Given the penalties for poor performance inherent in both cash and equity incentive plans, there is nothing inherent in the current structure of compensation in financial service firms that lead to obvious incentives to take excessive risks. To the extent that the firms, indeed, took such risks, we need to look beyond the compensation structure to explain it. However, there are valid reasons to be concerned about excessive risk taking in future years. First, most of the stock options held by financial services executives by the end of 2008 were well out-of-the-money, which provides the type of asymmetric rewards and penalties that can lead to risk taking. Even more troublesome is the concept of "Too Big to Fail" guarantees applied to the financial service firms that essentially operate in-house hedge funds with hedge-fund-style incentive arrangements. If the government is very clear that there is no "Too Big to Fail" guarantee, there is no need for government oversight. But, if the guarantee is offered or implied there are massive problems with monitoring and restraining executives from taking excessive risks. Assuming that "Too Big to Fail" survives as a policy, it is critical that boards enforce strong internal penalties for risk-management failures.

Risk and Performance Measurement

Another way that compensation can lead to risk taking is through inappropriate performance measures. For example, consider mortgage brokers paid for writing loans rather than writing loans that the borrowers will actually pay back. In the years leading up to its dramatic collapse and acquisition by JPMorgan Chase at fire-sale prices, Washington Mutual rewarded its brokers for writing loans with little or no verification of the borrowers' assets or income, and paid especially high commissions for selling more-profitable adjustable-rate mortgages.[2] In the end, WaMu got what it paid for, and similar scenarios were being played out at Countrywide Finance, Wachovia, and scores of smaller lenders who collectively were not overly concerned about default risk as long as home prices kept increasing and as long as the lenders could keep packaging and selling their loans to Wall Street. But, home prices could not continue to increase when prices were being artificially bid up by borrowers who could not realistically qualify for or repay their loans. The record number of foreclosures in 2008, and the associated crash in home values, helped send the US economy (and ultimately the global economy) into a tailspin.

A solution to this performance-measurement problem is to pay people to write "good loans" and penalize them for writing "bad loans." The challenge is identifying a good loan without waiting up to 30 years to find out whether the loan is actually repaid. The answer involves basing bonuses on subjective assessments of loan quality. Unfortunately, most current and proposed regulations go in the opposite direction and require that bonuses be based solely on objective measures of performance, such as the quantity (rather than the quality) of loans. These regulatory demands reflect a suspicion that boards and managements will be unable to make and enforce the required subjective assessments, thus substituting the judgment of government for the business judgment of directors. This is a dangerous path to go down.

Table 1

Comparison of 2007 and 2008 Bonuses for CEOs of TARP and Non-TARP Recipients

	TARP Recipients	Non-TARP Banks	Other Non-TARP Companies
Number of CEOS	36	23	684
Average 2007 Bonus	$2,307,430	$1,809,640	$1,641,880
Average 2008 Bonus	$363,082	$1,573,910	$1,479,360
Change in Bonus from 2007 to 2008	−$1,944,348 (−84.3%)	−$235,730 (−13.0%)	−$162,520 (−9.9%)

Notes: Sample includes executives in S&P 500, S&P MidCap 400, and S&P Small Cap 600 Firms who held the title of Chief Executive Officer in both 2007 and 2008. Compensation data from S&P's Execu Comp database. TARP recipients include companies receiving money from the TARP as of May 7, 2009, extracted from http://www.usatoday.com/money/economy/tarp-chart.htm. Non-TARP banks defined as companies with SIC codes between 6020 and 6211 and include commercial banks, savings institutions, mortgage banks, and security and commodity brokers. Bonuses include discretionary bonuses and payments under non-equity incentive plans.

Fixing Compensation: Is Regulation the Answer?

Compensation practices in financial services can certainly be improved. For example, cash bonus plans in financial services can be improved by introducing and enforcing bonus banks or "clawback" provisions for recovery of rewards if and when there is future revision of critical indicators on which the rewards were based or received. Several banks, including Morgan Stanley, UBS, and Credit Suisse, have introduced plans with clawback features over the past several months, and I applaud these plans as moves in the right direction.

Bonus plans in financial services can also be improved by ensuring that bonuses are based on value creation rather than on the volume of transactions without regard to the quality of transactions. Measuring value creation is inherently subjective, and such plans will necessarily involve discretionary payments based on subjective assessments of performance.

Compensation practices in financial services can undoubtedly be improved through government oversight focused on rewarding value creation and punishing value destruction. However, it is highly unlikely that compensation practices can be improved through increased government rules and regulations. Indeed, Washington has a long history of attempts to regulate executive pay that have systematically created unanticipated side effects that have generally led to higher pay levels and less-efficient incentives. Consider, for example, the following case studies:

Golden Parachutes and Section 280(G)

In 1982, Bendix CEO William Agee launched a hostile takeover bid for Martin Marietta, which in turn made a hostile takeover bid for Bendix. Bendix ultimately found a "white knight" and was acquired by Allied Corp., but only after paying CEO Agee $4.1 million in a Golden Parachute payment. The payment sparked outrage in Congress, which quickly introduced Section 280(G) of the tax code, imposing severe personal and corporate tax penalties on golden parachute payments exceeding three times the executive's average recent compensation.

Ironically, although Section 280(G) was meant to reduce the generosity of parachute payments, the government action increased such payments: the new rules were followed by the introduction of golden parachutes in hundreds of companies that previously had no change-in-control agreements. Moreover, Section 280(G) triggered the proliferation of "employment agreements" for CEOs and other top-level executives in most large firms since the mid-1980s. Section 280(G) applies only to severance payments contractually tied to changes of control. Individual employment agreements typically provide for severance payments for all forms of terminations without cause, including (but not limited to) terminations

following control changes. Therefore, companies could circumvent the Section 280(G) compensation limitations (at a potentially huge cost to shareholders) by making payments available to all terminated executives, and not only those terminated following a change in control.

Unreasonable Compensation and Section 162(m)

The controversy over CEO pay became a major political issue during the 1992 US presidential campaign. After the 1992 election, president-elect Clinton re-iterated his promise to disallow deductions for all compensation above $1 million for all employees. Concerns about the loss of deductibility contributed to an unprecedented rush to exercise options before the end of the 1992 calendar year, as companies urged their employees to exercise their options while the company could still deduct the gain from the exercise as a compensation expense. In anticipation of the loss of deductibility, large investment banks accelerated their 1992 bonuses so that they would be paid in 1992 rather in 1993. In addition, several publicly traded Wall Street firms, including Merrill Lynch, Morgan Stanley, and Bear Stearns, announced that they [would] consider returning to a private partnership structure if Clinton's plan were implemented.

By February 1993, President Clinton backtracked on the idea of making all compensation above $1 million unreasonable and therefore non-deductible, suggesting that only pay "unrelated to the productivity of the enterprise" was unreasonable. In April, details of the considerably softened plan began to emerge. As proposed by the Treasury Department and eventually approved by Congress, Section 162(m) of the tax code applies only to public firms and not to privately held firms, and applies only to compensation paid to the CEO and the four highest-paid executive officers as disclosed in annual proxy statements (compensation for all others in the firm is fully deductible, even if in excess of the million-dollar limit). More importantly, Section 162(m) does not apply to compensation considered "performance-based" for the CEO and the four highest paid people in the firm.

Academic research has concluded that Section 162(m) has contributed to the increase in executive compensation. First, since compensation associated with stock options is generally considered "performance-based" and therefore deductible, Section 162(m) helped fuel the option explosion in the 1990s. Second, while there is some evidence that companies paying base salaries in excess of $1 million lowered salaries to $1 million following the enactment of Section 162(m), many others raised salaries that were below $1 million to exactly $1 million. Finally, since discretionary bonuses are not considered performance based (and therefore subject to the $1 million cap), companies were encouraged to replace their discretionary plans with overly generous and less-effective formula-based plans.

Deferred Compensation and Section 409(A)

Enron, like many other large companies, allowed mid-level and senior executives to defer portions of their salaries and bonuses through the company's non-qualified deferred compensation program. When Enron filed for Chapter 11 bankruptcy protection in December 2002, about 400 senior and former executives became unsecured creditors of the corporation, eventually losing most (if not all) of the money in their accounts. However, just before the bankruptcy filing, Enron allowed a small number of employees to withdraw millions of dollars from their deferred compensation accounts. The disclosure of these payments generated significant outrage (and lawsuits) from Enron employees who lost their money, and attracted the ire of Congress.

As a direct response to the Enron situation, Section 409(A) was added to the Internal Revenue Code as part of the "American Jobs Creation Act of 2004." In essence, the objectives of Section 409(A) were to limit the flexibility in the timing of elections to defer compensation in nonqualified deferred compensation programs, to restrict withdrawals from the deferred accounts to pre-determined dates (and to prohibit the acceleration of withdrawals), and to prevent executives from receiving severance-related deferred compensation until six months after severance. Section 409(A) imposes taxes on individuals with deferred compensation as soon as the amounts payable under the plan are no longer subject to a "substantial risk of forfeiture." Individuals failing to pay taxes in the year the amounts are deemed to no longer be subject to the substantial forfeiture risk owe a 20% excise tax and interest penalties on the amount payable (even if the individual has not received or may never receive any of the income).

Section 409(A) restricts compensation committees from offering many incentive arrangements that are in the best interest of shareholders. For example, while restricted shares and traditional stock options (i.e., options with an exercise price equal to the market price on the date of grant) are exempt from the guidelines, discount options (i.e., options with an exercise price below the market price on the date of grant) are subject to the new rules. Such options are often in the interest of shareholders, especially when employees "purchase" the discount options through explicit salary reductions or outright cash exchanges.

In each of the above cases, the regulations resulted in less-effective compensation arrangements and imposed large costs on shareholders. Part of the problem is that regulation—even when well-intended—inherently focuses on relatively narrow aspects of compensation allowing plenty of scope for costly circumvention. An apt analogy is the Dutch boy using his fingers to plug holes in a dike, only to see new leaks emerge. The only certainty with pay regulation is that new leaks will emerge in unsuspected places, and that the consequences will be both unintended and costly. I therefore strongly recommend that the Committee consider carefully this history before inevitably repeating the mistakes of the past. . . .

Notes

1. This testimony is based in part on my joint work with Michael C. Jensen to be published in *CEO Pay and What to Do About It: Restoring Integrity to Both Executive Compensation and Capital-Market Relations* (forthcoming, Harvard Business School Press, 2010).
2. See Peter S. Goodman and Gretchen Morgenson, "By Saying Yes, WaMu Built Empire on Shaky Loans," *New York Times* (December 27, 2008).

KEVIN J. MURPHY holds the Kenneth L. Trefftzs Chair in Finance in the Marshall School of Business at the University of California. He obtained his PhD in economics from the University of Chicago. He serves as an associate editor of both the *Journal of Financial Economics* and the *Journal of Corporate Finance*.

EXPLORING THE ISSUE

Should the Compensation of Executives Be Subject to Government Regulation?

Critical Thinking and Reflection

1. How appropriate is it to make income evaluations based on the notions of worth and value rather than on economic theory?
2. Is it likely that analysts in future generations will assess the public's scorn of TARP as unjustified? Explain.
3. What moral issues emerge in a discussion of "too big to fail" guarantees?
4. Is it reasonable to conclude that regulation will stifle innovation? Why or why not?

Is There Common Ground?

The financial crisis that erupted in 2007 drew contemptuous attention to the activities on Wall Street, but this was hardly the first time the finance industry had been looked upon with both suspicion and disdain. In countless works of literature and film, ultra-wealthy executives have long been characterized as greedy (even amoral or downright evil) exploiters of the hard-working middle class. So why did the unfolding reports on this modern global crisis evoke such emotional shock?

Perhaps it was because fictional accounts can be enjoyed for their seemingly over-the-top portrayals and moralizing messages. But there was no entertainment value when the grave realities of Wall Street began spilling out into the actual lives of the actual people whose livelihoods and homes were slipping away in calamitous numbers. Not only were Americans feeling crippled by the reckless practices of the finance industry, they were feeling duped by forces of insatiable (and apparently remorseless) greed.

Even those with opposite responses to the question of federally regulated executive compensation can agree that the devastating consequences of excessive risk taking are real and that measures both remedial and preventive must be taken. Although the nature and method of accountability may be disputable, an environment of financial stability and trust is a shared goal.

Create Central

www.mhhe.com/createcentral

Additional Resources

Boeri, Tito, Claudio Lucifora, and Kevin J. Murphy, *Executive Remuneration and Employee Performance-Related Pay: A Transatlantic Perspective* (Oxford University Press, 2013)

Griffith-Jones, Stephany, Ocampo, José Antonio, and Stiglitz , Joseph E. (eds.), *Time for a Visible Hand: Lessons from the 2008 World Financial Crisis* (Oxford University Press, 2010)

Hallock, Kevin F. and Murphy, Kevin J. (eds.), *The Economics of Executive Compensation* (Edward Elgar Publishing, 1999)

Stiglitz, Joseph E., *Freefall: America, Free Markets, and the Sinking of the World Economy* (Norton, 2010)

Internet References . . .

Joseph E. Stiglitz

www.josephstiglitz.com

New York Times: "Executive Pay"

http://topics.nytimes.com/top/reference/timestopics/subjects/e/executive_pay

U.S. Department of the Treasury: "Financial Stability"

www.treasury.gov/initiatives/financial-stability/

U.S. Securities and Exchange Commission: "Executive Compensation"

www.sec.gov/answers/execomp.htm

ISSUE

Has the Supreme Court Made It Possible for Corporations to Buy Elections?

YES: Mary G. Wilson, from "Testimony before the U.S. House of Representatives Committee on House Administration" (February 3, 2010)

NO: Steven M. Simpson, from "Testimony before the U.S. House of Representatives Committee on House Administration" (February 3, 2010)

Learning Outcomes

After reading this issue, you will be able to:

- Describe the duties of the Federal Election Committee (FEC).
- Discuss the relevance of the 1907 Tillman Act to current concerns.
- Identify the provisions of the 2002 Bipartisan Campaign Reform Act ("McCain–Feingold").
- Provide a brief profile of the League of Women Voters.
- Form an opinion on the legality and ethics of *Citizens United v. FEC*.

ISSUE SUMMARY

YES: Mary G. Wilson, the president of the League of Women Voters, believes that the Supreme Court's decision in *Citizens United v. FEC* that allows corporations to spend unlimited amounts of money in elections was "fundamentally wrong and a tragic mistake." She calls upon Congress to enact legislation that will reverse this decision.

NO: Steven M. Simpson, the senior attorney at the Institute for Justice, supports the Supreme Court's decision. In making his case, he argues that the decision does not reverse 100 years of precedent; the decision does not mean corporations will buy elections; and the decision recognizes that corporations must be protected under the free speech First Amendment.

Running for an elected office is no easy task. Candidates must be willing to subject themselves to careful scrutiny by members of their own party and then to even more critical examination by the opposition. A candidate must develop a platform and then be able to articulate that platform to various groups of voters. Depending on the office, a candidate must also have funds to pay for polls, for campaign office space, and for professional consultants. A candidate must be willing to engage in a variety of activities to raise funds including luncheons, dinners, and personal solicitations. The candidate with ample personal financial resources can choose to spend their own funds.

While the personal toll of a campaign is difficult to measure, spending is measured. This is especially true of federal elections for the House, the Senate, and the presidency. In 1975, the Federal Election Commission (FEC) was created; its duties are to disclose campaign finance information, enforce the provisions of the law such as the limits and prohibitions on contributions, and oversee the public funding of presidential elections. The information collected by the FEC is available to the public. Disclosure of financial information in state and local elections is governed by state and local legislation.

Some of the information about campaign spending is, to many people, simply shocking. Consider some of the information in the 2010 election (at the time of this writing only spending through October 13, 2010, was available). In order to retain his post, Senator Russ Feingold (D) of Wisconsin spent over $16 million but lost his seat to Ron Johnson, who spent less than $3 million. But the amount spent by Senator Feingold pales in comparison to what Republican candidate Linda McMahon spent in a losing bid for an open Senate seat in Connecticut: at least $42 million with almost all of it her own money. Perhaps the most glaring example of campaign spending was represented by former eBay chief executive Meg Whitman in her unsuccessful bid to succeed Arnold Schwarzenegger as governor of California: she is reported to have spent a combined $142 million in both the primary and the general elections.

These data suggest that while money is an essential part of elections, outspending an opponent does not ensure success. Still many people are concerned about the connections between money and political success and between money, political influence, and possible political corruption. This concern dates back to 1907 when the Tillman Act, banning direct corporate contributions, was passed. A number of federal election laws have been passed since then, limiting the amount that could be given to candidates, who could give money to candidates, the kinds of ads that could be financed, and the type of disclosure that the ads must contain. A number of these laws have been tested in the courts. This issue concerns one such law and its adjudication by the Supreme Court.

In the *Citizens United v. Federal Election Commission* case, the Supreme Court overturned the "electioneering communications" provisions of the 2002 Bipartisan

Campaign Reform Act (also known as McCain–Feingold). McCain–Feingold prohibited all corporations and unions from airing a communication that mentioned a candidate in a period preceding an election—30 days for primary elections and 60 days for general elections. Citizens United, a nonprofit organization, had wanted to run television ads promoting a documentary film critical of then Senator Hillary Clinton. In its 5–4 decision, released on January 21, 2010, the Supreme Court found in favor of Citizens United and thus overturned the electioneering provision of McCain–Feingold. One interpretation of the decision was that now corporations and labor unions are allowed to make unlimited election expenditures but no direct campaign contributions in support of political candidates.

In her testimony, Attorney Mary G. Wilson argues that the Court's decision was "fundamentally wrong and a tragic mistake" and asks that Congress pass new legislation to restore the old order. Attorney Steven M. Simpson supports the Court's decision, stating, "we should follow the Court's own wise counsel."

YES   Mary G. Wilson

Testimony before the U.S. House of Representatives Committee on House Administration

The League of Women Voters is a nonpartisan, community-based political organization that has worked for 90 years to educate the electorate, register voters, and make government at all levels more accessible and responsive to citizens. Organized in more than 850 communities and in every state, the League has more than 150,000 members and supporters nationwide. The League has been a leader in ensuring that democracy works for all citizens and in seeking campaign finance reform at the state, local, and federal levels for more than three decades.

Mr. Chairman, there is one overriding message I hope the Committee will take away from this hearing: With the 2010 elections fast approaching, Congress must pass and send to the President legislation governing corporate and union spending that will take effect immediately.[1] Waiting until after the 2010 elections is simply not a viable option. We urge you to craft legislation so it can be passed by both houses of Congress and be signed by the President by Memorial Day.

The Supreme Court decision in *Citizens United v. FEC* now allows corporations to spend unlimited amounts of money to support or oppose candidates at every level of government. This throws out the protections against direct corporate and union spending in elections that have served our democracy for decades. It has given the green light for corporations, including foreign corporations, to intervene directly in elections—from the local school board or zoning commission to Congress and the President of the United States—taking the power away from voters. And it has set the stage for corruption to skyrocket out of control—now that the Court has allowed unlimited corporate and union expenditures, the power of well-paid lobbyists linked with those interests will greatly increase.

Right now, the stakes are very high. We must act to protect open, honest government and a healthy democracy.

In days since the Court's decision, we have heard from citizens around the country who are deeply concerned about the direction the Court is moving and the effects this case will have on our elections and our government. They want to know what they can do to respond to the decision. Since it is unusual for us to hear from people about a Supreme Court decision, we believe this response shows a broader concern among the public. It reinforces the need for you to act. We have also heard from state Leagues and others asking how they can counteract the decision at the state level since, as you know, the Court's decision invalidates the laws of many states.

The Court's decision in *Citizens United* upends basic campaign finance law. It changes the foundation on which decades of congressional enactments on money in elections are built. Such a fundamental change, with perhaps more coming as the Court considers other cases, requires a strong and considered response from Congress and the Executive. We believe such responses are essential, and we support a wide variety of approaches. But we do not expect that legislation to be adopted this year can address every possible issue. We want to reemphasize that some steps are vital to govern the conduct of the 2010 elections.

Disclosure

After *Citizens United*, we urgently need enhanced disclosure. This is the most basic step toward protecting the role of the voter in making decisions in elections. It now seems possible for corporations, and perhaps unions, to secretly provide funds that another corporation uses to intervene in an election through independent expenditures. This is simply unacceptable. Voters need information about the sources of funding for the charges and countercharges that come during elections. That is one key way that voters test the accuracy of campaign statements and is essential if the "free and open marketplace of ideas" is to function properly. This is especially true in the case of huge expenditures that could drive out other political speech.

The Court pointed in the direction of enhanced disclosure when it said that disclosure is important to "providing the electorate with information." It also supported disclaimer requirements "so that the people will be able to evaluate the arguments to which they are being subjected." We couldn't agree more.

The League of Women Voters supports strong disclosure requirements for both those who receive election funds and those who provide such funds. For example, if corporation A receives significant funds from corporation B, and subsequently makes an election expenditure, then

Wilson, Mary G. United States Congress, February 3, 2010.

corporation A should disclose both its own expenditure and the contribution from corporation B, and corporation B should disclose its contribution to corporation A.

Thus, a trade association or other corporation that receives funds should have to disclose all the funds going into its treasury if it makes or contributes to election expenditures. And all corporations that provide funds to the trade association or corporation should also have to disclose on their own behalf. The only exception should be if the entity uses a segregated account for these monies. In that case, only the funds provided to the corporation's segregated account would be disclosed, both by the corporation and by the ones providing funds.

The issue of corporate intermediaries is one the Congress should address quickly and fully. It should not be possible for a corporation to avoid disclosure and disclaimers if it provides significant sums to another corporation which then provides funds to a third corporation that makes independent expenditures. We do not believe this type of disclosure should be avoided even if one of the corporations calls such payments a "membership" fee.

Corporations should have the responsibility for providing disclosure to the public through disclaimers and the Internet, directly to their stockholders or members, and to the Federal Election Commission and the Securities and Exchange Commission.

Disclaimers on public communications should be required for every corporation that provides funds above a certain amount directly or indirectly to an election expenditure. The Court clearly approved of disclaimers in *Citizens United,* and remarked that "With the advent of the Internet, prompt disclosure of expenditures can provide shareholders and citizens with the information needed to hold corporations and elected officials accountable for their positions and supporters."

We believe that disclosure should be cumulative so that the public and stockholders can get a full picture of the corporation's entire election activity. In other words, there should be a listing of all candidates, amounts spent in each candidate election, total amounts expended during the reporting period, and amounts and identities for funds provided to others who make election expenditures.

Do No Harm

After providing enhanced disclosure, the next most important step for Congress is to do no further harm. A decision as far-reaching in its implications as *Citizens United* will provoke a number of proposals that, we believe, could make our election system and government processes worse. Some will call for increasing or doing away with contribution limits to candidates. Others will probably support changes in limits on contributions to and from PACs. There will likely be calls to allow corporations and unions once again to make huge contributions to the political parties, effectively repealing the soft money ban in BCRA. There may even be those who call for unlimited corporate and union contributions to candidates.

The League of Women Voters strongly urges you not to do any of these things. We need fair elections, not greater involvement of big money in elections and government. Each of these steps would increase corruption or the appearance of corruption. We are also concerned that they would distort our political processes and undermine shareholder protections, the Supreme Court's rationale in *Citizens United* notwithstanding.

There are a number of other concepts which we support for moving forward in the post-*Citizens United* context. I would like to mention them, and, in some cases, make a few comments.

Corporate Governance

We support the concept that shareholders should approve election expenditures by corporations, as well as other possible reforms to corporate governance in the campaign finance context. The Court recognized the importance of disclosure to corporate governance, thereby setting the stage for additional shareholder involvement. The Court said, "Shareholders can determine whether their corporation's political speech advances the corporation's interest in making profits. . . ."

In large, for-profit corporations, the mechanisms for achieving shareholder approval or disapproval will need special attention because large amounts of stock are held in mutual funds, pension and retirement funds (including government entities) and in other forms that don't reflect the interests of the underlying owners or beneficiaries. Nonprofit corporations, including large ones such as health plans and hospitals, also raise a number of issues. We will look carefully at proposals for enhanced corporate governance.

Foreign Corporations

The Court's decision in *Citizens United* clearly opens the door for independent expenditures by foreign corporations in American elections. Indeed the rationale that only *quid pro quo* corruption can justify government limitations on corporate expenditures would obviously apply to foreign corporations. And in disparaging any anti-distortion rationale, the Court seems to undercut limitations based on the identity of the corporation.

Still, we urge Congress to carefully consider blocking election spending by foreign corporations. The obvious example of course is that of the corporation owned by a foreign government. Beyond that, issues arise as to what constitutes a foreign corporation and what form of regulation might be appropriate in each case.

Governments

We believe it is entirely inappropriate for government to intervene in elections. Thus, those corporations that have substantial governmental involvement, particularly financial involvement, should be barred from making independent election expenditures. The Congress will have to address a number of issues in determining which corporations have the requisite involvement. We believe that several approaches might work. Corporations that have received substantial funds (through TARP, for example) or have government guarantees deserve attention. Certainly government pension and insurance funds are another example. We believe that corporations receiving government contracts above a certain level raise issues of excessive government involvement or the potential for corruption.

Connections with Lobbyists

After *Citizens United*, every member of Congress who receives a visit from a lobbyist for a corporation knows that the corporation can make unlimited expenditures in his or her election. Surely this is a recipe for corruption. The process is corrupted even if the threat is not made or the spending is not carried out. Lawmakers will change their behavior because of the potential for unlimited expenditures. We urge Congress to explore methods to deal with this issue. Surely the anti-corruption rationale should provide a basis for regulation. The problem extends not just to registered lobbyists (after all, the lobby disclosure laws were designed for disclosure rather than regulatory purposes) but includes the actions of corporate officers and others who control corporate expenditures.

At the same time, we support additional regulation of bundling by lobbyists and increased disclosure of lobbying activities.

Coordination

Though the FEC has yet to develop acceptable anti-coordination rules following enactment of BCRA, it is worth looking at tighter controls to ensure that "independent" expenditures by corporations and unions are truly independent.

Public Financing

As a long-time supporter of clean money in elections, the League of Women Voters supports enactment of congressional public financing and repair and updating of the presidential public financing system. Enhanced small contributions through a fair elections system would provide candidates with clean funds, challenging both corruption and the appearance of corruption in our electoral system. We urge Congress to enact such legislation.

Conclusion

The League of Women Voters believes that the Court's majority decision in *Citizens United v. FEC* was fundamentally wrong and a tragic mistake. The majority mistakenly equated corporate free speech rights with those of natural persons. And the majority confused associations of individuals with corporations. But this is the decision of the Court. Even though we believe it will be overturned eventually, both in the judgment of history and in the law, Congress needs to respond now, recognizing its own authority and responsibility to uphold the Constitution.

Fair and clean elections, determined by the votes of American citizens, should be at the center of our democracy. We urge Congress to act quickly, but also deliberately, in addressing the Court's decision.

Note

1. While the issues surrounding corporate and union activity are not always the same, many of the recommendations with regard to corporations may apply to unions as well.

Mary G. Wilson is an attorney who has worked in the areas of estate planning, litigation, regulatory compliance, commercialization and privatization, corporate and environmental law, and employment law. She is a partner in the law firm Aungier & Wison, P.C. At the time of her testimony, she was serving as the 17th president of the League of Women Voters of the United States.

Steven M. Simpson

→**NO**

Testimony before the U.S. House of Representatives Committee on House Administration

The Supreme Court's decision in *Citizens United*, which struck down restrictions on corporate spending on speech during elections, has once again ignited a controversy over money in politics. Supporters of stringent campaign finance laws are claiming that the decision will lead to a flood of corporate money in elections, that it will destroy democracy,[1] that corporations will buy elections,[2] and that the decision is an example of conservative judicial activism[3] and the worst decision since *Dred Scott*.[4]

All of these claims are vastly overblown. Not only is *Citizens United* not an activist decision, it is based on fundamental First Amendment principles on which courts have relied for decades. Twenty-six states allow corporations to spend money on independent speech during elections. Corporations have not managed to buy elections in these states, nor have these states become hotbeds of corruption. In short, in assessing the impact of *Citizens United* we should follow the Court's own wise counsel and not let rhetoric obscure reality.

Toward that end, I offer the following responses to some of the most prominent myths about *Citizens United*.

Myth 1: *Citizens United* Is an Activist Decision That Reverses 100 Years of Precedent

Citizens United is based on enduring First Amendment principles, nearly all of which were announced or reaffirmed in *Buckley v. Valeo* over thirty years ago. Then, as now, the Court recognized that political speech is at the core of the First Amendment's protections.[5] Then, as now, the Court rejected the notion that government may attempt to equalize all voices, either directly, by silencing some voices to make room for others, or indirectly, by restricting the funds that may be devoted to speech.[6]

Indeed, the roots of these principles date back to the founding era. James Madison described the right to free speech as "the right of freely examining public characters and measures . . . which has ever been justly deemed, the only effectual guardian of ever other right."[7] Echoing this view, the Court stated in *Citizens United* that "[s]peech is an essential mechanism of democracy, for it is the means to hold officials accountable to the people."[8]

The Court recognized, as did the Founders, that special interests—or "factions" in the Founders' words—might try to influence the course of government. But for the Court, as for the Founders, limiting freedom of speech would be like eliminating air to prevent fire.[9] "Factions will necessarily form in our Republic, but the remedy of 'destroying the liberty' of some factions is 'worse than the disease.' . . . Factions should be checked by permitting them all to speak . . . and by entrusting the people to judge what is true and what is false."[10]

To sum up the point, "If the First Amendment has any force, it prohibits Congress from fining or jailing citizens, or associations of citizens, for simply engaging in political speech."[11]

Critics of *Citizens United* have said that it was "activism" for the Court to hold that corporations receive the benefit of the First Amendment protections. But, as the Court noted, it has protected freedom of speech for corporations for decades.[12] While it is true that bans on corporate contributions to candidates have been in place for nearly a century, *Citizens United* involved a ban on corporate *independent expenditures*. Congress did not ban corporate independent expenditures until 1947.[13] President Truman vetoed the ban, in part, because he saw it as a "dangerous intrusion on free speech,"[14] but Congress overrode the veto.

It was not until 1990, in *Austin v. Michigan Chamber of Commerce*, that the Supreme Court squarely addressed the ban on corporate independent expenditures in candidate elections.[15] Although the Court had previously ruled in *First National Bank of Boston v. Bellotti* that a state could not prevent a corporation from spending money on independent advocacy during ballot-issue elections,[16] in *Austin* the Court reversed course and upheld the ban by a narrow 5-4 vote, inventing a new rationale for limiting speech—the alleged "corrosive and distorting effects of immense aggregations of wealth that are accumulated with the help

Simpson, Steven M. United States Congress, February 3, 2010.

of the corporate form."[17] This "anti-distortion" rationale had never been discussed before and was inconsistent with *Buckley*'s holding that "the concept that government may restrict the speech of some elements of our society in order to enhance the relative voice of others is wholly foreign to the First Amendment."[18]

Thus, *Austin* was the outlier, and in overturning it and the portion of *McConnell v. FEC* that relied on it, the Supreme Court was returning to core First Amendment principles. As the Court itself noted in *Citizens United*, deference to Congress cannot extend to laws that violate the First Amendment.[19] Nor is this the first time the Court has overruled prior precedent in modern times. In *Brown v. Board of Education*,[20] for instance, the Court rejected the idea of "separate but equal" it had adopted in *Plessy v. Ferguson*.[21] In *West Virginia State Board of Education v. Barnette*, the Court held that public schools could not compel students to salute the American Flag and recite the Pledge of Allegiance, overruling a decision handed down a mere three years earlier.[22] And, in recent years, the Supreme Court in *Lawrence v. Texas*[23] refused to follow its earlier decision in *Bowers v. Hardwick*[24] despite that decision's seventeen-year pedigree.

Myth 2: Under *Citizens United*, Corporations Will Buy Elections

Corporations can no more buy elections with political advertising than they can buy market share with commercial advertising. If they could, we would all be driving American cars and drinking New Coke; Michael Huffington would have long since been elected Senator and Ross Perot would be President. While it is certainly true that money is necessary to win a campaign, that simply does not translate into victory for the biggest spender.[25] The examples of failed political campaigns that spend millions are as numerous as failed advertising blitzes in the commercial realm.

In fact, the evidence that even direct contributions to candidates cause corruption of the political process is weak at best. Evidence from the political science literature suggests that campaign contributions made directly to candidates have very little to no discernable impact on public policy, let alone any undue or corrupt influence.[26] Furthermore, in the only empirical study of which I am aware that examines the effects on the appearance of corruption of limits on direct contributions to candidates, the authors found that contribution limits do not improve citizens' view of government.[27] To date, there have been no scientific studies that attempt to explore the relationship between independent expenditures—by corporations or anyone else—and political corruption. However, 26 states allow corporations to make independent expenditures, but they have not become hotbeds of corruption nor have corporations managed to buy their elections.[28]

But worse than the factual errors implicit in this claim is the negative view of American voters that it betrays. According to this view, voters are incapable of thinking for themselves. Instead, they passively accept whatever thoughts and views they happen to see in slick advertising campaigns. But this is contrary to the central assumption of the First Amendment. As the Court put it in *Citizens United*, "[t]he First Amendment confirms the freedom to think for ourselves."[29] That freedom means that citizens get to decide whom to listen to and citizens get to decide how and when to speak, what message to convey, and what means to use to convey it.

Corporate spending does not buy elections; it buys speech. That speech seeks to convince voters to vote one way or another. For those who do not agree with that speech, the First Amendment again provides the answer: "[I]t is our law and our tradition that more speech, not less, is the governing rule."[30]

Corporations do not speak with one voice any more than individuals do. There are nearly six million corporations in this nation, most of them quite small. Allowing them to speak and to provide their unique views and information during elections is not an aberration that will lead to corruption; it is precisely what the First Amendment was designed to do.

Myth 3: Corporations, Unlike People, Have No Free Speech Rights

It is true that corporations are not people. But they are made up of people, like every other association—from partnerships, to marriages, to neighborhood groups, to nonprofits, and all the way up to the *New York Times*. The First Amendment protects the right of association just as it protects the freedom of speech. If individuals have the right to speak, then they have the right to join with others to speak, whether they join with one person or 10,000. The Court in *Citizens United* recognized that corporations must be protected under the First Amendment because corporations are associations of individuals, and because nothing in the First Amendment exempts particular associations simply because they adopt the corporate form.[31] In that respect, *Citizens United* is not a corporate speech case; it is a case that recognizes the importance of the right of association along with the right to freedom of speech.

It is important to note that the federal campaign-finance laws treat all groups in essentially the same manner. Any group of two or more persons that raises or spends more than $1,000 and has the primary purpose of influencing elections is a "political committee" and is subject to the same restrictions as a corporation.[32] It must register as a political committee and comply with the same burdensome regulations that apply to corporate PACs, including limitations on the source and amounts of funds it may devote to speech.[33] The FEC and campaign-finance reform groups have taken the same approach to unincorporated groups as they have to corporations, and have argued that they must register as PACs and comply with the same onerous restrictions that apply to PACs in order to speak.[34] In short, the notion that supporters of campaign finance laws are particularly concerned about corporations is false. They want to prevent *all* groups from spending unregulated funds on independent speech during elections.

Critics of *Citizens United* respond that the laws did not prohibit corporations from speaking, they simply required them to speak through political committees. But this ignores the very real burdens of political committee status. As the Supreme Court noted, the FEC has adopted 568 pages of regulations, 1278 pages of explanations and justifications of those regulations, and 1771 advisory opinions since 1975.[35] These rules define and regulate 71 distinct entities and 33 different types of speech.[36] Ninety-one of these rules, spanning over 100 pages of the federal register, apply to political committees.[37] Political committees must register with the FEC, appoint a treasurer, and forward all receipts to the treasurer within days of their receipt. They must keep detailed records of all funds received and all expenditures made, they must file detailed reports to the FEC disclosing all activities on either a monthly or quarterly basis.[38] Those who operate committees out of their homes or offices must determine the value of the space, utilities, and overhead being allocated to the committee and properly account for and disclose that information to the FEC. Even terminating a political committee requires the FEC's permission.

It is no exaggeration to say that the campaign-finance laws rival the tax code in their complexity.[39] Indeed, last week during oral argument in *SpeechNow.org v. FEC*, I had the surreal experience of debating with several judges on the D.C. Circuit about whether the regulations that apply to groups organized under section 527 of the tax code are more burdensome than the regulations that apply to political committees under the campaign-finance laws. Reasonable minds can disagree on that question, but it ought not be debatable that if Americans come to regard speaking out as equivalent to filing their income tax returns, a lot fewer of them will bother trying to speak out at all.

Conclusion

In today's world, speaking effectively to large numbers of people requires large amounts of money and often some sort of organization. Money and associations are not simply important to political speech, they are indispensable to it. While it is probably true that the Founders could not have imagined the immense corporations that exist today, there is probably little about our world that the Founders could have imagined. But that fact should no more define the reach of our voices than it should limit the scope of our knowledge or the technologies we use to expand it. As Chief Justice Roberts said in his concurring opinion in *Citizens United*, "The First Amendment protects more than just the individual on a soapbox and the lonely pamphleteer."[40] And as the Court stated, "the First Amendment protects speech and speaker."[41] That applies whether

the speaker is an individual or a group and whether they use a quill pen, a printing press, or the Internet. That the Supreme Court understands that is cause for celebration.

Notes

1. "With a stroke of the pen, five Justices wiped out a century of American history devoted to preventing corporate corruption of our democracy." Statement of Fred Wertheimer, President, Democracy 21, Supreme Court Decision in Citizens United Case Is Disaster for American People and Dark Day for the Court (Jan. 21, 2010), *available at* http://democracy21.org.

2. "The bottom line is, the Supreme Court has just predetermined the winners of next November's election. It won't be the Republicans or the Democrats and it won't be the American people; it will be Corporate America." *GOP Doesn't Run 2010 Census, But Hopes to Count Your Money*, The Post Standard (Syracuse, N.Y.), Jan. 24, 2010, at A9 (quoting Sen. Charles E. Schumer (D–N.Y.)).

3. "The Supreme Court's 5-4 decision holding that corporations and unions can spend unlimited amounts of money in election campaigns is a stunning example of judicial activism by its five most conservative justices." Erwin Chemerinsky, Dean, University of California, Irvine School of Law, Op-Ed, Conservatives embrace judicial activism in campaign finance ruling, L.A. Times, Jan. 22, 2010, *available at* http://articles.latimes.com/2010/jan/22/opinion/la-oe-chemerinsky22-2010jan22.

4. "This is the most irresponsible decision by the Supreme Court since the *Dred Scott* decision over a hundred years ago." Rep. Alan Grayson (D–FL), *Countdown with Keith Olbermann* (MSNBC television broadcast Jan. 21, 2010), *available at* http://www.msnbc.msn.com/id/3036677/ns/msnbc_tv-countdown_with_keith_olbermann#34984984.

5. *Citizens United v. FEC*, No. 08-205, slip op. at 33 (Jan. 21, 2010) ("Political speech is 'indispensable to decisionmaking in a democracy, and this is no less true because the speech comes from a corporation rather than an individual.'") (quoting *First Nat'l Bank of Boston v. Bellotti*, 435 U.S. 765, 777 (1978)).

6. *Citizens United*, slip op. at 34 ("The First Amendment's protections do not depend on the speaker's 'financial ability to engage in public discussion.'") (quoting *Buckley v. Valeo*, 424 U.S. 1, 49 (1976)).

7. James Madison, Virginia Resolutions Against the Alien and Sedition Acts, (Dec. 21, 1798), reprinted in James Madison Writings 590 (Jack N. Rakove ed., 1999).

8. *Citizens United*, slip op. at 23; *see also id.* ("The right of citizens to inquire, to hear, to speak, and to use information to reach consensus is a precondition to enlightened self-government and a necessary means to protect it."); *id.* at 24 ("The First Amendment protects speech and speaker, and the ideas that flow from each.").

9. *Id*. at 39 (quoting THE FEDERALIST No. 10, at 130 (J. Madison) (B. Wright ed. 1961)).
10. *Citizens United*, slip op. at 39.
11. *Id*. at 33.
12. *Id* at 25–26.
13. Section 314, 61 Stat. 159 (June 23, 1947).
14. Message from the President of the United States at 9, H.R. Doc. No. 80-334 (1947).
15. Prior to 1990, the closest the courts came to addressing the ban on corporate independent expenditures was in *United States v. International Union Auto Workers*, 352 U.S. 567 (1957). But in that case, as Professor Allison Hayward notes, the Court "declined to reach the issue of whether . . . prosecution would violate the union's constitutional rights." Revisiting The Fable Of Reform, 45 Harv. J. on Legis. 421, 463 (2008).
16. 435 U.S. 765 (1978).
17. 494 U.S. 652, 660 (1990).
18. 424 U.S. 1, 49 (1976).
19. *Citizens United*, slip op. at 45; *see also id*. at 12 ("It is not judicial restraint to accept an unsound, narrow argument just so the Court can avoid another argument with broader implications."); *id*. at 4 (Roberts, C.J., concurring). ("It should go without saying, however, that we cannot embrace a narrow ground of decision simply because it is narrow; it must also be right.").
20. 347 U.S. 483 (1952).
21. 163 U.S. 537 (1896).
22. 319 U.S. 624 (1943) (overruling *Minersville School District v. Gobitis*, 310 U.S. 586 (1940)).
23. 539 U.S. 558 (2003).
24. 478 U.S. 186 (1986).
25. Gary C. Jacobson, *The Effect of the AFL-CIO's "Voter Education" Campaigns on the 1996 House Elections*, 61 J. OF POL. 185, 186 (1999) ("We also have abundant evidence that money, by itself, does not defeat incumbents. Only in combination with potent issues and high-quality challengers do even the best financed campaigns have a decent chance of succeeding.").
26. Stephen Ansolabehere, Rebecca Lessem & James Snyder, *Why Is There So Little Money in U.S. Politics?*, 17 J. ECON. PERSP. 105 (2003).
27. David Primo & Jeffrey Milyo, *Campaign Finance Laws and Political Efficacy: Evidence from the States*, 5 ELECTION L.J. 23 (2006).
28. Supplemental Brief of Amicus Curiae Chamber of Commerce of The United States of America in Support of Appellant at 8-12, *Citizens United v. FEC*, No. 08-205 (Jan. 21, 2010).
29. Slip op. at 40.
30. *Citizens United*, slip op. at 45.
31. *Id*. at 25.
32. *See* 2 U.S.C. § 431(4).
33. *See Citizens United*, slip op. at 21–23.
34. *See* Brief for the Federal Election Commission at 43, *SpeechNow.org v. FEC*, No. 09-5342 (D.C. Cir. Dec. 15, 2009).
35. *Citizens United*, slip op. at 18.
36. *Id*.
37. *See* 11 C.F.R. parts 1-2-106, 110, 113, 116.
38. *Citizens United*, slip op. at 21–22.
39. *See N.C. Right to Life, Inc. v. Leake*, 525 F.3d 274, 296 (4th Cir. 2008) ("For the regulator's hand, once loosed, is not easily leashed. The Code of Federal Regulations, or its state equivalent, is no small thing. It is no unfounded fear that one day the regulation of elections may resemble the Internal Revenue Code, and that impossible complexity may take root in the very area where freedom from intrusive governmental oversight should matter most.").
40. Slip op. at 1 (Roberts, C.J., concurring).
41. *Id*. at 24.

STEVEN M. SIMPSON is a senior attorney at the Institute for Justice, self-described as the nation's only libertarian public interest law firm. He is a graduate of New York Law School and a member of the bar of New York, New Jersey, and the District of Columbia.

EXPLORING THE ISSUE

Has the Supreme Court Made It Possible for Corporations to Buy Elections?

Critical Thinking and Reflection

1. If it is inaccurate to suggest that people buy into the messages of slick advertising, then why are billions upon billions of dollars spent every year on the slick advertising of consumer products?
2. In what ways do the complexities of the FEC's regulations on political committees assure (or inhibit) an adherence to the First Amendment?
3. Explain why corporations are, or are not, constitutionally entitled to the rights of free speech.
4. What makes "enhanced disclosure" fundamental to the position held by the League of Women Voters?

Is There Common Ground?

On its most obvious level, the question presented here can only be answered in the most polar context of either "yes" or "no." In most respects, Wilson and Simpson have presented viewpoints to prove that, and yet if we are willing to look beyond the surface, we can find at least some degree of common ground.

Perhaps the most clearly expressed observation shared by both sides is that, although money is a campaign necessity, the candidate who spends the most money is not necessarily the winner. Also implied is a shared regard for the Supreme Court's authority, the value of campaign regulations, and the cultivation of an informed electorate.

Additional Resources

Clements, Jeffrey D., *Corporations Are Not People: Why They Have More Rights Than You Do and What You Can Do About It* (Berrett-Koehler Publishers, 2012)

Dranias, Nick, *Citizens United v. Federal Election Commission: A Case for Limiting Campaign Finance Regulations* (Goldwater Institute, 2010)

U.S. Congress House of Representatives Committee on Government Reform and Oversight, *Federal Election Commission Enforcement Actions: Foreign Campaign Contributions* (Ulan Press, 2011)

Create Central

www.mhhe.com/createcentral

Internet References . . .

Bloomberg Businessweek: "Will the Federal Election Commission Ever Work Again?"

www.businessweek.com/articles/2013-05-02/will-the
-federal-election-commission-ever-work-again

Daily Finance: "The Ten Biggest Corporate Campaign Contributors in U.S. Politics"

www.dailyfinance.com/2010/10/13/the-10-biggest
-corporate-campaign-contributors-in-u-s-politics

Gallup Politics: "Public Agrees with Court: Campaign Money Is 'Free Speech'"

www.gallup.com/poll/125333/Public-Agrees-Court
-Campaign-Money-Free-Speech.aspx

ISSUE

Should the United States Stop All New Offshore Drilling for Oil?

YES: Michael F. Hirshfield, from "Testimony before the U.S. House of Representatives Committee on Natural Resources" (May 27, 2010)

NO: Michelle Michot Foss, from "Testimony before the U.S. House of Representatives Committee on Natural Resources" (May 27, 2010)

Learning Outcomes

After reading this issue, you will be able to:

- Describe the consequences of the 2010 BP drilling-rig explosion in the Gulf of Mexico.
- Deliberate over the benefits versus the risks of offshore drilling.
- Identify the particular vulnerabilities of the Arctic.
- Discuss the options of renewable energy sources.

ISSUE SUMMARY

YES: Michael F. Hirshfield, the Oceana vice president and chief scientist, believes that offshore drilling is a "dirty and dangerous business." He argues that the *Deepwater Horizon* drilling disaster is not a one-time occurrence: in 2007 alone there were 39 blowouts worldwide. Among other things, he calls on Congress to "suspend all approvals, activities, and processes—other than current production—related to offshore drilling."

NO: Michelle Michot Foss, the University of Texas energy economist, provides estimates of the consequences of stopping oil and gas exploration and production. Among other things, such a ban would increase energy costs to consumers by an annual average rate of 5 percent and lead to a decrease in jobs in energy-intensive industries by 13 million by the year 2030. She believes there are "outstanding and almost immeasurable benefits associated with the discovery and utilization of oil and natural gas resources in our deep water provinces in the U.S. and around the world."

On April 20, 2010, British Petroleum's (BP) *Deepwater Horizon* drilling rig in the Gulf of Mexico exploded. The explosion killed 11 platform workers and injured 17 others. With the explosion an oil leak developed. In spite of a number of efforts to stop the oil flow, the leak lasted for 3 months, releasing an estimated 5 million barrels of oil. Besides those killed and injured, the oil spill caused widespread physical damage both to marine and wildlife habitats as well as extensive damage to the fishing and tourism industries in the Gulf areas of Louisiana, Mississippi, Alabama, and Florida.

The costs associated with the oil spill are varied and significant. Some are easy to measure while others are not. According to an early November 2010 report by the *Wall Street Journal* (http://blogs.wsj.com/source/2010/11/02/no-closure-yet-on-bp-oil-spill-costs/), BP has taken almost $40 billion in pretax charges because of the oil spill. Besides these out-of-pocket costs to BP, there is the cost to BP stockholders in the form of reduced dividends and a reduced price for BP stock. BP eliminated its dividends for the second and third quarters of 2010 and has scheduled a review of its dividend policy for February 2011. As of November 7, 2010, BP's stock price was at $42.63 with a 52-week high and low of $62.38 and $26.75, respectively (see http://www.wikinvest.com/stock/BP_(BP)). But the costs imposed on others must be considered. For example, on April 30, 2010, the White House suspended all new domestic offshore drilling pending the completion of investigations of the *Deepwater Horizon* accident. The suspension was lifted on October 12, 2010, but the result of the 5-month suspension period meant less economic activity for the oil exploration industry, with losses in income for labor and profits for firms. Operators of BP gas stations, many of which are not company owned, reported sales declines ranging up to 40 percent, a decline attributed to backlash against the company. In addition, *Deepwater Horizon* is also blamed for the decline in real estate values along the Gulf coast. The decline in economic activity as well as the decline in property values posed problems for state and local governments with declines in revenues associated with reduced income, sales, and property tax collections.

The accident also resurrected the controversy regarding offshore drilling. Environmentalists have long opposed such activity. They have always feared the kind of accident so dramatically highlighted by the *Deepwater Horizon* accident. They would argue that the damage done to the ecosystem—the Gulf waters, the Gulf shores, the marine life, the animal life—will extend far into the future and will never be fully known or repaired. Expanding offshore oil production simply postpones the inevitable transition the United States must make from reliance on nonrenewable fossil fuels to the use of renewable energy sources like wind and solar power. The proponents of offshore drilling counter with several arguments. First, such activity will lead to energy independence. Simply put, relying on domestic offshore oil production reduces the need to import oil and reduces the possibility that foreign oil producers will "hold the United States hostage." The second argument is that domestic oil production expands economic activity, with major economic benefits going to American workers and American business firms.

As might be expected, there were calls for investigations into the accident. The investigations were designed to serve several purposes. The first purpose was to ascertain why the explosion occurred so that steps could be taken to prevent similar accidents in the future. The second purpose was to assess the blame, to determine who was responsible for accident. The third purpose was to reassess the country's offshore drilling policies. Both the Senate and the House held hearings, and the readings presented here are drawn from those held in the House. Energy economist Michelle Michot Foss argues in support of offshore oil drilling, among other things because we need to replenish resource endowments. Scientist Michael F. Hirshfield is against offshore drilling; he believes that *Deepwater Horizon* "is a clear testament that offshore drilling is a dirty and dangerous business."

Michael F. Hirshfield

Testimony before the U.S. House of Representatives Committee on Natural Resources

Introduction

. . . The ongoing Deepwater Horizon drilling disaster is a clear testament that offshore drilling is a dirty and dangerous business, one that threatens jobs, both in the fishery and tourism industry, and also one that threatens public health and the health of marine ecosystems.

Oceana testified in front of the House Natural Resources committee twice last year on this very issue. . . . In both instances, Oceana stated clearly and for the record that we oppose the expansion of offshore oil and gas drilling.

Today, we echo that call and take it a step further: we must suspend all pending approvals and ban all new drilling in the Outer Continental Shelf indefinitely. In place of expanded offshore oil and gas activities, the United States should begin the transition to a clean energy economy. By pursuing carbon-free alternatives, such as offshore wind and solar energy, combined with conservation and fuel efficiency improvements such as those contemplated by President Obama's announcement last week, the [United States] can step away from the frenzied pursuit of offshore drilling, which has demonstrably put our vital ocean ecosystems at risk. The United States should promote clean energy industries that will allow us to finally break our fossil fuel addiction, stimulate our economy, and become an exporter of energy technology. And by doing so, we can stop placing the profit interests of the oil industry above those of the fishing industry, the tourism industry, human health and well being, and marine ecosystems.

Lessons from the Deepwater Horizon Drilling Disaster

The Deepwater Drilling Disaster in the Gulf of Mexico is a tragedy for the families of the workers killed, the ocean ecosystem, and coastal economies. It clearly illustrates to us that the business of offshore drilling is dirty and dangerous. . . .

Our oceans give essential protein to nearly half the world's population. United States recreational and commercial fisheries combined supply over 2 million jobs.

Coastal tourism provides 28.3 million jobs and annually generates $54 billion in goods and services. More drilling means more oil spills, more lost jobs, more contaminated beaches, and more ecosystem destruction. Our marine ecosystems and the communities that depend on them are threatened by the short- and long-term toxic effects of oil.

Oil spills happen. These spills range from small, steady leaks to large catastrophic blowouts and they occur at every stage in oil production from the exploration platform to the oil tanker to the pipeline and storage tanks. The impacts to fish and wildlife and coastal communities are numerous and well documented. To date, the Deepwater Drilling Disaster has pumped millions of gallons of toxic oil into the Gulf of Mexico. . . .

Staff of the National Marine Fisheries Service, the National Ocean Service, and the U.S. Fish and Wildlife Service have all publicly expressed concerns about the movement of oil and oil dispersal contaminants to upland habitats and their effect on estuarine and freshwater habitats. . . .

Both onshore and open ocean species of birds are vulnerable to the impacts of oil. Depending on where the oil reaches shore, beach nesters, such as terns and plovers, and marsh dwellers are vulnerable. Even if oil doesn't end up in nesting habitat, other indirect impacts could result, such as effects on food supply.

Much of the wildlife impact will remain unseen. Oil can have long-term effects on feeding, reproduction, and overall health of the animal. Also, put simply, many of the carcasses simply will not wash ashore. Nevertheless, we are now beginning to see the first images of seabirds, sea turtles, and other species affected by oil. Unfortunately, these images, and the harm to ocean life that they portray, will be continuing for the foreseeable future.

The economic impacts on the Gulf Region's commercial and recreational fisheries could be staggering. Gulf fisheries are some of the most productive in the world. In 2008, according to the National Marine Fisheries Service, the commercial fish and shellfish harvest from the five U.S. Gulf states was estimated to be 1.3 billion pounds valued at $661 million. The Gulf also contains four of the top seven fishing ports in the nation by weight and eight of

Hirshfield, Michael F. United States Congress, May 27, 2010.

the top twenty fishing ports in the nation by dollar value. Commercially important species and species groups in the Gulf of Mexico include blue crab, stone crab, crawfish, groupers, menhaden, mullets, oyster, shrimp, red snapper, and tunas. . . .

The Benefits of Offshore Drilling Are Not Worth the Risks

While the oil industry clearly stands to benefit from offshore drilling, we all bear the risk. In this case, BP has transferred a tremendous amount of risk to residents of the Gulf coast in exchange for no clear benefits. Although offshore oil and gas production can have tremendous impacts on marine life, it will not contribute significantly to lower prices at the pump or energy independence.

Offshore Drilling Provides No Relief from High Gasoline Prices and Will Not Create Energy Independence

Additional offshore oil drilling will not lower gas. In 2009, the United States Department of Energy (DOE) estimated that by 2030, gasoline prices would be only three pennies less than if previously protected ocean areas remained closed.

The U.S. Department of Energy [has predicted] that at peak production in 2030 drilling in the Atlantic, Pacific and Eastern Gulf of Mexico would produce 540,000 barrels a day, which would account for 2.5 percent of daily energy demand in the United States. Thus, regardless of the oil produced offshore, the United States will still import the vast majority of its oil from other countries. The increased production will not diminish this dependence or prices at the pump significantly. The United States Department of Energy (DOE) estimates that even if we opened all offshore areas to drilling, the U.S. would still import about 58% of its oil supply. Currently, about 62% of the crude oil supplied to the United States comes from foreign sources, with the top two suppliers being Canada and Mexico. The United States simply does not have enough domestic oil to reduce its dependence on imports, much less to fulfill its demand.

The only way to become truly energy independent is to end our addiction to oil. The best way to eliminate foreign oil dependence is to eliminate dependence on all oil by developing alternative sources, rapidly switching to plug-in and electric vehicles and phasing out oil consumption in other portions of our economy like home heating and electricity generation.

Additionally, the development of offshore wind energy off of the East Coast and Great Lakes could create thousands of jobs. Europe already has 19,000 people employed in the offshore wind industry, and the European Wind Energy Association expects nearly 300,000 to be employed by the offshore wind industry by 2030. We should be demanding, and our energy policy should be promoting, similar job growth here in the United States. It has been estimated that a $1 million investment in energy efficiency and renewables creates three times the number of jobs created if that same $1 million was invested in the oil industry.

The plain facts speak for themselves—expanded drilling will not lower gas prices or make us energy independent. The Deepwater Drilling Disaster illustrates that the harm posed by oil and gas activities in the Outer Continental Shelf dramatically outweighs any perceived benefits that can be gained by expanding drilling.

Oil and Gas Activities Have Tremendous Impacts on Marine Life

Accidents inevitably accompany all stages of offshore production, and these accidents can be catastrophic. We are now seeing in the Gulf of Mexico that there is no available technology or capability to respond to a spill, particularly a gusher of the magnitude we are witnessing in the Gulf. . . .

The Deepwater Drilling Disaster is not an isolated incident, and offshore oil drilling remains extremely dangerous. Since 2006, the United States Minerals Management Service (MMS) has reported at least 21 offshore rig blowouts, 513 fires or explosions offshore, and 30 fatalities from offshore oil and gas activities in the Gulf of Mexico. Additionally, in 2007 the MMS reported that from 1992 to 2006 there were 5,671 wells drilled, and 39 blowouts. It is important to note that these blowouts occurred at a variety of depths and in a variety of environments. A blowout is not a rare occurrence, and it can happen anywhere, not just in the deep waters of the Gulf of Mexico.

Once a spill occurs, little can be done to clean it up. According to the National Academy of Sciences, "No current cleanup methods remove more than a small fraction of oil spilled in marine waters, especially in the presence of broken ice." We have been drilling in the Gulf of Mexico for more than 60 years. Although we are using the latest advances in drilling technology, pushing the limits of the physical environment, the Deepwater Drilling Disaster shows that we still lack the technology and planning to effectively respond to large oil spills. As Robert Bea, a professor at U.C. Berkeley and former Shell employee, stated, "we are still chasing it around with Scott towels."

Industry would have us believe that the process of offshore oil and gas extraction is completely benign. Consider this statement made by the American Petroleum Institute in a 2009 letter to the Committee on Natural Resources:

> Over the past 40 years, improved practices and equipment have enabled the industry to significantly strengthen its offshore environmental performance and meet or exceed federal regulatory requirements.

Or these by David Rainey, Vice President, Gulf of Mexico Exploration BP America Inc., in his testimony to the Senate Energy and Natural Resources Committee on November 19, 2009.

Advances in drilling technologies and production systems have been significant. They include extended reach drilling, drilling in deeper waters, and to greater depths. These advances enable more production while reducing environmental impacts and allowing for efficient use of existing facilities and infrastructure.

Many of the technology examples discussed . . . have enabled a robust track record of environmental stewardship and can reduce or even eliminate the visual 'footprint' of offshore energy operations.

But offshore drilling isn't safe just because the industry says it is. We can all see with our own eyes that there are limits to the oil industry's accident prevention capability—whether they are technological or managerial limits, the industry simply cannot guarantee safe operation.

As Oceana's Jeff Short, one of the world's experts on the chemistry of oil and its impacts, stated in his testimony at that same Senate Committee hearing in November, 2009:

Oil development proposals in the marine environment are often presented and discussed as engineering challenges, without sufficient regard for the complexity of the environment in which they would occur, or the often dubious assumptions implicit in assessments of environmental risks and cleanup and mitigation technologies. Oil spill contingency plans are treated as exercises in damage control, taking for granted that not all damage can be controlled, and based on the faulty assumption all potential outcomes are adequately understood, predictable, and manageable. The truth of the matter is that our understanding of how oil behaves in the environment, the ways it affects organisms, and how well response and mitigation measures actually work in the field is still largely unknown.

The Deepwater Drilling Disaster shows us that current technology and regulation cannot prevent what we now know is inevitable—a major spill of oil into the marine environment, and one which is to date beyond our ability to control.

The Arctic Is Particularly Vulnerable—And Response Capability Is Nonexistent

The risks from these activities are particularly acute in the Arctic, where the oceans play a critical role in the culture of Native peoples[;] there is little available response, rescue, or cleanup capability, and little information about the environment or impacts from oil development is available.

Because there is a significant lack of information, both from [W]estern science and documented local and traditional knowledge of Arctic peoples, it is impossible to ensure that exploration drilling will not harm the health of Arctic marine ecosystems or opportunities for the subsistence way of life. Managers do not have the baseline information needed to conduct quantitative risk assessments of activities or, if a spill were to occur, assess impacts to hold companies accountable for damages. This lack of information is evident in the cursory and general environmental reviews that have been conducted and the errant generalizations that the Minerals Management Service (MMS) has made.

Further, response, rescue, and cleanup capabilities are virtually nonexistent for the challenging conditions in Arctic waters, which can include sea ice, stormy seas, extreme cold temperatures, and long periods of darkness. There is no demonstrated capability to clean up spilled oil in icy waters. The nearest Coast Guard response and rescue vessels would be nearly 1,000 miles away, and the Coast Guard has stated publicly that it could not respond to a spill. Particularly given the fact that we must dedicate all available resources to limiting damage in the Gulf of Mexico, it would be irresponsible to allow parallel risky activities in Arctic waters. . . .

The events surrounding the Deepwater Drilling Disaster provide significant new information that requires the Minerals Management Service (MMS) to reanalyze Shell's drilling plans. The new information goes to the heart of the decision to approve Shell's plans, and accordingly the approval of any drilling should be suspended pending reconsideration of the environmental analysis in light of the *Deepwater Horizon* spill.

Shell has made efforts to distinguish its proposals from the Gulf tragedy. It is clear, however, that the same technologies and standards that failed so tragically in the Gulf have been or will be applied in the Arctic. . . . Given the obvious deficiencies and commitment to wholesale reevaluation of our oil and gas program, there is no reason to allow Shell to take these risks with our Arctic resources. The Deepwater Horizon was an exploration well, just like those proposed by Shell for this summer. . . .

It Is Time to Kick the Habit and Move to a Clean Energy Economy

It is clearly time for a bold Congressional effort to transition America into its much needed clean energy future. In doing so, Congress should focus in part on clean sources of ocean energy such as wind, solar, and geothermal power. The Deepwater Drilling Disaster shows us that now, more than ever, our oceans and the communities that rely on them on a daily basis need a clean energy future. Future generations of Americans deserve oil free beaches and oceans that are an abundant source of food, wildlife, and clean energy.

The Deepwater Drilling Disaster presents us with a glimpse of what our oil addiction is doing to our country. It is costing us jobs, [destroying valuable] natural resources and distracting us from developing innovative new technologies that can empower us both by lighting our homes and stimulating our economies.

The United States Department of Energy has projected that we can generate 20% of electricity demand from renewables by 2030. Offshore wind could provide 20% of this amount. Supplying even 5 percent of the country's electricity with wind power by 2020 would add $60 billion in capital investment in rural America, provide $1.2 billion in new income for farmers and rural landowners, and create 80,000 new jobs. This effort has started, as the United States added enough wind power in 2007 alone to provide electricity to more than a million homes.

Let's stop pretending that offshore drilling lowers the price of gasoline. A more effective way to bring down the price of gasoline—without the risks of catastrophic environmental and economic damage—is to raise fuel economy standards for new cars and trucks sold in the United States, as called for last week by President Obama. Making cars that get 35.5 miles per gallon of gas, as federal regulations will require, will save a dollar per gallon by 2030. Compare this with the 3 cents a gallons savings the EIA says drilling all our offshore oil reserves will bring over that same period. We should be working as rapidly as possible to electrify our transportation and home-heating systems, using electricity provided by carbon-free sources like wind and solar.

Congress could make tremendous progress in creating a new energy economy right now by passing legislation that would stimulate this process. For example, setting a Renewable Electricity Standard (RES) would cut harmful carbon emissions while creating jobs and saving consumers' money, reducing costs for utilities and consumers. A strong RES, such as mandating that 25% of electricity should be generated from renewable sources by 2025, can stimulate domestic investment in new renewable energy throughout the nation, creating jobs and income in rural areas, as well as in the high tech and manufacturing sectors. An RES would reduce the need to drill for onshore and offshore natural gas or to build new supporting infrastructure for these activities such as drilling rigs, pipelines, terminals, and refineries.

It is critical that Congress continue to promote legislation that provides direct and substantial investment in clean energy component manufacturing to ensure that an adequate supply chain for goods essential to the renewable energy industry is created in the U.S. This legislation must direct federal funding for clean energy manufacturers to retool their facilities and retrain their workers to develop, produce, and commercialize clean energy technologies.

Recommendations

And so, today, on behalf of Oceana, I ask you to take three important steps that will steer our country in the right direction toward energy independence based on renewable, carbon-free energy sources and lasting protections for our coastal and marine environments. . . .

Immediately and Indefinitely Suspend All Approvals, Activities, and Process—Other Than Current Production—Related to Offshore Drilling

It is imperative to allow sufficient time for the President's commission and other investigative bodies to complete their investigations of the failures that led to the ongoing BP blowout and to apply the lessons learned from this disaster to prevent such a tragedy from ever happening again. For that reason, we must immediately suspend all approvals, activities, and processes—other than current production—related to offshore drilling. That suspension should remain in place while the independent review called for by the administration takes place and all changes recommended by it are implemented. All approvals already granted must be re-evaluated based on the new information gathered by the commission and using any new processes recommended.

The most immediate and dramatic need is to suspend approval for drilling in the Arctic Ocean. The Minerals Management Service approved Shell's plans to drill exploration wells in the Chukchi and Beaufort Seas this summer. For the same reasons, proposals to open areas off the east coast of the United States must be put on hold indefinitely. We should not be considering opening new areas to leasing when it is clear that we cannot control companies that own leases on currently open areas. . . .

Ban New Offshore Drilling in the Outer Continental Shelf (OCS) and Permanently Protect All Areas Currently Closed to Leasing

Since 1982, Congress and the President banned oil and gas leasing on much of our coasts. Those moratoria were allowed to lapse amidst the rancor of political campaigning in the last three years. Those protections should be restored and made permanent. This year's catastrophic disaster in the Gulf of Mexico illustrates that a ban on new drilling is essential to ensuring that a similar fate does not befall our other coasts, which, like the Gulf of Mexico, support important national assets in the form of valuable coastal economies and marine environments. As disturbing as this catastrophe has been for all of us, we need to make sure it never happens again. Congress should exercise its authority to permanently ban drilling offshore.

Finally, Congress Must Continue to Pursue Legislation That Provides for a More Efficient, Clean, Carbon-Free, Energy Future that Emphasizes the Development of Renewable Energy

By providing incentives for investments in clean energy such as offshore wind, we could achieve the goals outlined above and possibly more. We could generate more energy, at a lower cost, from Atlantic offshore wind farms than from drilling all the oil in the Atlantic OCS areas. East Coast offshore wind electricity generating potential could supplant 70% of the East Coast's fossil-fuel generated electricity supply. Providing this quantity of clean energy could cut 335 million metric tons of carbon dioxide emissions annually—while limiting the risk of exposure to highly volatile energy expenses and creating three times as many jobs as offshore oil and gas development.

Summary

We must dramatically change course and move forward toward a future in which we rely upon affordable, carbon-free, renewable energy and end our dependence on oil.

A "teachable moment" is upon us. What will we learn from the Deepwater Drilling Disaster? Ultimately, it is imperative for the United States to shift toward a future in which we rely upon affordable, carbon-free, renewable energy; one in which our oceans and the environment are healthy, and one that ensures our freedom from oil dependency. Part of this effort must include an emphasis on development of carbon-free technologies, including wind and solar power, in conjunction with improved energy efficiency. . . .

Michael F. Hirshfield is the senior vice president for North America and chief scientist for Oceana, a global ocean conversation organization. Among other positions he has held, he served as the director of the Chesapeake Bay Research and Monitoring Division for the Maryland Department of Natural Resources. He holds a PhD in zoology from the University of Michigan.

Michelle Michot Foss

➡ **NO**

Testimony before the U.S. House of Representatives Committee on Natural Resources

. . . On April 29, 2004, I presented testimony before the House Subcommittee on Energy and Air Quality on *Ultradeep Water Research and Development: What Are the Benefits?* I know that there are astounding and almost immeasurable benefits associated with the discovery and utilization of oil and natural gas resources in our deepwater provinces in the US and around the world. There are astounding and almost immeasurable benefits associated with oil and gas production from all of our onshore basins. These benefits are hugely difficult to replace—thus the intensity of debate in our country and worldwide about how we will best meet our energy needs into the future. The size, scope, diversity, inventiveness, determination and diligence of our oil and gas enterprises, from smallest to largest, and the men and women who work in them are attributes that other countries strive to emulate. We know this from direct experience. Finally, to meet and move beyond this current challenge will require thoughtful, careful, sincere stewardship from all facets of industry, government and civic leadership. That is where the American people need to concentrate our efforts.

The charter for these oversight hearings is broad. Domestic oil and gas production plays a vital role in our economy, ranging from domestic energy and economic security to myriad, rich scientific benefits. Future sustainability of the industry must be assured. I present four key points for the Committee's consideration.

We Have Large Resource Endowments, but Our Reserves Must Be Replenished.

Of critical importance is replenishment, the ability to convert resources to proven reserves and replace the oil and gas that we consume each year. Using publicly available data from the US Energy Information Administration (USEIA), the productivity of America's vast oil and gas industry base is easily demonstrated. Since the beginning of last century, Americans consumed 197 billion barrels of domestically produced crude oil even as the industry continued to find and add reserves, resulting in a 2008 reserve base that was orders of magnitude larger than known proved reserves in 1900. In similar fashion, our known, proven stocks of natural gas have increased as domestic production and consumption surged following World War II. With recent successes in our continental shale gas basins, drilling in the Gulf of Mexico deep shelf and deep water plays, we expect proved natural gas reserves to remain robust. Overall, on a barrel of oil equivalent basis, the US remains the largest producer and reserve holder in the world. Looking further ahead to energy frontiers, the same methane hydrate crystals that impeded containment of oil from the Macondo well drilled by Deepwater Horizon could offer a potential, clean fossil fuel source well beyond any time horizon we can imagine.

Domestic Reserve Replenishment Is Linked to Economic Benefits

Replenishment of US reserves of crude oil and natural gas generates economic benefits as domestic exploration and production proceeds. Availability, conversion and delivery of these energy resources provide competitively priced energy supplies fostering economic development and income growth.

Prior to the Deepwater Horizon incident, the National Association of Regulatory Utility Commissioners (NARUC), acting as an umbrella organization for many collaborating organizations and companies, released a major review, *Analysis of the Social, Economic and Environmental Effects of Maintaining Oil and Gas Exploration and Production Moratoria on and Beneath Federal Lands*. The analysis for the NARUC committee was undertaken by SAIC and the Gas Technology Institute using the USEIA's National Energy Modeling System (NEMS). I and many others served as external advisors for the moratoria study effort. The final report is available via www.naruc.org.

This study effort focused on questions regarding federal lands that are subject to various restrictions or for which policies are not formulated to provide access for drilling. *However, importantly for these hearings, the data in this new study can provide insights on energy availability, cost and economic consequences of policy and/or regulatory actions that would limit or ban domestic oil and gas development.* Key findings were as follows.

- A review of all available data and information for both moratoria and non-moratoria areas suggests that the natural gas resource base is estimated to increase by 132 trillion cubic feet (Tcf) onshore and 154 Tcf offshore (excluding parts of Alaska as detailed in the final report); the offshore crude oil resource base is estimated to increase by 37 billion barrels of oil (Bbo, excluding parts of Alaska); the onshore crude oil resource base is estimated to increase by 6 Bbo for the Arctic National Wildlife Refuge (ANWR), with no estimated increase in the Lower-48 resource base. With these additions, GTI estimates the current resource base to increase from 1,748 Tcf to 2,034 Tcf for gas and from 186 Bbo to 229 Bbo for oil. The increases are driven by two primary factors: the increased shale gas activity and development successes, and an increase in resource estimates for the currently restricted offshore areas to better reflect the impact of new technology and successes in the currently available and developed offshore areas.
- The study committee and advisors tested a number of scenarios (to 2030) associated with keeping moratoria in place, and which provide some guidance should domestic oil and gas drilling decline.
  - Domestic crude oil production projected to decrease by 9.9 billion barrels, or nearly 15 percent per year, on average.
  - OPEC imports projected to increase by 4.1 billion barrels, or roughly 19 percent per year on average, resulting in increased cumulative payments to OPEC of $607 billion ($295 billion on a net present value or "NPV" basis).
  - Domestic natural gas production projected to decrease by 46 Tcf or 9 percent per year on average.
  - Net natural gas imports (both as liquefied natural gas or LNG and as pipeline deliveries) projected to increase by nearly 15.7 Tcf or almost 75 percent.
  - Employment in energy intensive industries projected to decrease by nearly 13 million jobs, an average annual decrease of 0.36 percent.
  - Energy prices projected to be higher: annual average natural gas prices increase by 17 percent; annual average electricity prices increase by 5 percent; annual average motor gasoline prices increase by 3 percent. More renewables would be used adding to the higher cost of delivered energy.
  - Real disposable income projected to decrease cumulatively by $2.34 trillion ($1.16 trillion NPV or $4,500 per capita), an annual average decrease of 0.65 percent.
  - Energy costs to consumers projected to increase cumulatively by $2.35 trillion ($1.15 trillion

NPV or $3,700 per capita), an annual average increased cost of 5 percent.
  - Import costs for crude oil, petroleum products, and natural gas are projected to increase cumulatively by $1.6 trillion ($769 billion NPV), an annual average increased cost of over 38 percent.
  - Gross domestic product (GDP) projected to decrease cumulatively by $2.36 trillion ($1.18 trillion NPV), an annual average decrease from the base case of 0.52 percent.

Using 2007 data, PriceWaterhouseCoopers estimated that the more than nine million employees, $558 billion in labor income and $1 trillion in total value added by the domestic oil and gas industry, constituted more than 5 percent of US total employment, more than 6 percent of US total labor income and more than 7 percent of US total value added, respectively. However, this study did not account for the GDP effects of utilizing oil and gas in our energy systems as inputs to other goods and services, nor did PWC attempt to measure the GDP impact of goods manufactured from oil and gas feedstocks or economic effects of exporting these goods. Finally, PWC did not attempt to estimate economic benefits of US oil and gas industry investments abroad, or the total contribution in taxes, royalties and other fees paid by the oil and gas industry to all government jurisdictions as well as public (including federal) and private mineral owners. All of these benefits would push the total economic value of the US industry into the trillions of dollars and a substantial chunk of US GDP.

Of great concern is the impact on livelihoods associated with my home state's commercial and recreational fisheries and seafood businesses. A widely quoted estimate of the value of Louisiana's seafood industry is $3 billion. This is vital to the coastal communities and families that depend on these activities. But even more vital and much, much larger are the employment, income and tax revenue benefits associated with Louisiana's and the Gulf Coast region's oil and gas businesses. To understand the full scale of negative consequences and social displacement that could result from a sharp drop in drilling activity, one has only to investigate the outcomes from the collapse in oil prices during the mid-1980s. In that instance, the total effect of lost jobs and income in the states that host oil and gas industry activity along with home and commercial mortgage foreclosures and subsequent collapse of the savings and loan industry shaved roughly one percent from US GDP growth.

We know and understand very well the distribution of oil and gas resources and proved reserves around the world, the extent of sovereign government control over access and development, and the structure and role of national oil companies. While we support free and open international trade in oil, natural gas and other critical raw materials, US domestic production is our best hedge against global oil and gas geopolitical risk. Indeed, outside of the US, many other nations view our access policies and existing limitations on drilling and replenishment as hoarding our own supplies while draining those of others. Meaningful efforts to sustain our domestic industry over the long term and meaningful policy signals that we intend to continue replenish our reserves in a consistent manner would send one of the most impressive foreign policy signals we could engineer, as well as serving as a moderating force on global commodity prices.

Finally, oil and gas exploration and production activity serves up amazing, and humbling, lessons about the earth, its history and biology, physical and chemical properties and the forces that drive our planet. Offshore oil and gas exploration in particular both consumes and produces advances in science and technology that extend from global positioning to advanced composites and other lightweight materials. These are the immeasurable but absolutely necessary benefits that emanate from the industry and its workforce.

The Impact of Energy Costs, Including Costs of Alternatives, Is Very Real

Any reduction in US oil and gas production and consequent upward pressure on energy prices will impact households. Middle and lower income households are particularly vulnerable because energy costs are a larger share of their disposable income. It is these households that are most susceptible to energy price shocks. Indeed, in our view, given all available data, we feel that the national recession incorporated classic energy price shock components—extraordinarily high oil prices, combined with several years of generally rising energy costs as the US economy expanded rapidly—stretched these households to the breaking point. Borrowers from this population, no longer able to meet their obligations, in all likelihood triggered the first wave of mortgage foreclosures.

While we are optimistic about some alternative energy technologies being pursued, the reality is that costs of alternatives—including the cost of public subsidies which far too often is discounted or ignored—are high. Timing and "scalability" of low energy density options are uncertain. The law of unintended consequences plays out in large and visible new land use impacts; introduction of new and profound environmental risks (for instance "dead zones," like that in the Gulf of Mexico, are expanding due in large part to more intense cultivation and use of fertilizers for biofuels production); and security implications associated with critical non-fuel minerals requirements. This last consideration represents a distinct trade-off and risk associated with rapid acceleration of alternative energy and advanced grid technologies that we have not nearly begun to explore.

Future Sustainability of the Oil and Gas Industry Must Be Assured

The domestic US oil and gas industry has repeatedly shown an ability to absorb and deploy advanced technologies in order to progress to the next frontier of discoveries.

To sustain the oil and gas technology pathway, a number of variables must be considered.

- Finding and lifting costs and the economics of exploration and production are susceptible to, and underlie, cycles in commodity prices. Low prices send signals to producers that demand is low and supply surpluses exist. Drilling is reduced. Low prices stimulate demand, reducing excess supplies and pushing prices up. Drilling resumes. Investment decisions for oil and gas projects involve time—the larger the project, the longer the lead times. Companies must be able to manage through price cycles and adverse business conditions in order to replace reserves and be positioned to meet future demand. In a world of fast growing emerging markets and complex international geopolitics these challenges can be extreme. The oil and gas industry is a major contributor of tax revenue across all levels of government. Imposing new obligations for taxes and royalties that are rigid and not market responsive will hinder replenishment with all concomitant economic impacts.

- Environment and safety protections must be at the forefront and solutions must be flexible, adaptable, innovative and appropriate to the problem at hand. This is not a matter of regulatory oversight as we know it. As the industry progresses into new frontiers new mechanisms for assuring environment and safety protocols are needed, supported by data and analysis and bolstered by technologies that encompass real-time information and rapid deployment, not least to manage the public cost and burden of regulatory oversight. Remote logistics arrangements are needed for crisis management in frontier locations. Smooth management processes are essential. Most crucial is that we have the patience, in a trying time, to understand the sources and causes of failure and evaluate best practice future actions for prevention before engaging in wholesale restructuring and redirection of our regulatory apparatus.

- Finally, public education is essential. Very little is understood about the oil and gas industries in general. From a mass polity point of view, offshore operations, especially those in deeper waters and more remote locations, truly are akin to moon shots. Hydrocarbons in marine environments need to be better understood, both in terms of natural occurrence—the source of 70 to 80 percent of concentrations—and mitigation when accidents happen. In sum, public education on US energy sources, technologies, needs and choices could be better served.

The industry overall will be better off as lessons are learned from the Deepwater Horizon accident and new practices and technologies are developed and deployed. This will be a powerful tribute to both the lives lost and the lives saved as the industry progresses.

MICHELLE MICHOT FOSS is the chief energy economist and the head of the Center for Energy Economics, Bureau of Economic Geology, Jackson School of Geosciences, University of Texas. She has over 25 years' experience in energy and environmental research and consulting. She holds a PhD degree in political science from the University of Houston.

EXPLORING THE ISSUE

Should the United States Stop All New Offshore Drilling for Oil?

Critical Thinking and Reflection

1. If Foss is incorrect in her contention that "U.S. domestic production is our best hedge against global oil and gas geopolitical risk," then what *would* be our best hedge against such?
2. Why should the vulnerability of the Arctic be of particular concern when it is one of the least inhabited places on Earth?
3. Since the BP tragedy, do you think most Americans would rather invest in alternative energy than in offshore oil drilling, even if consumer costs may be higher? Explain.
4. Given the proven capabilities of modern technology, why have alternative, renewable energy sources been so slow in becoming established as primary energy options?

Is There Common Ground?

Both sides of this issue agree that the BP incident in the Gulf of Mexico was a devastating tragedy and that such an incident should never happen again. Both sides concur that the environment and safety protections must be at the forefront of all energy exploration and production and that the public's education on energy concerns is essential.

However, to assess such concurrence as common ground is a fairly thin argument. In virtually every respect essential to the issue of offshore oil drilling, the YES and NO perspectives are, especially in terms of risks versus benefits, immovably opposed to one another.

Create Central

www.mhhe.com/createcentral

Additional Resources

Devereux, Steve, *Drilling Technology in Nontechnical Language* (PennWell Corp., 2012)

Freiwald, André and J. Murray Roberts (eds.), *Cold-Water Corals and Ecosystems* (Springer, 2005)

Kaiser, Mark J. and Brian F. Snyder, *The Offshore Drilling Industry and Rig Construction in the Gulf of Mexico* (Springer, 2013)

Mostofizadeh, Kambiz, *Arctic Black Gold* (Mikazuki Publishing House, 2012)

Turley, A. J., *The Simple Truth: BP's Macondo Blowout* (The Brier Patch, 2012)

Internet References . . .

CBC News: "Imperial, BP Pitch Arctic Drilling to Northerners"

www.cbc.ca/news/canada/north/imperial-bp-pitch
-arctic-drilling-to-northerners-1.914459

Financial Post: "Gulf Coast Drilling Comes Roaring Back Three Years After BP Spill"

http://business.financialpost.com/2013/07/17/gulf
-coast-drilling-comes-roaring-back-three-years-after
-bp-spill/?__lsa=a69e-e14c

Oceana: "The Promising Future of Offshore Wind Power"

http://oceana.org/en/blog/2013/09/the-promising
-future-of-offshore-wind-power

Yahoo! Finance: "BP Battles for Billions in New Gulf Trial Phase"

http://finance.yahoo.com/news/bp-battles-billions
-gulf-trial-091746038.html

ISSUE

Are Health Savings Accounts Working Effectively?

YES: American Benefits Council, from "Statement before the Subcommittee on Health of the House Committee on Ways and Means" (May 14, 2008)

NO: Linda J. Blumberg, from "Statement before the Subcommittee on Health of the House Committee on Ways and Means" (May 14, 2008)

Learning Outcomes

After reading this issue, you will be able to:

- Provide a brief history of the establishment of health savings accounts (HSAs) in the United States.
- Give an identifying description of the American Benefits Council.
- Comment on the growth in HSA usage from 2004 to 2008.
- Describe the difference between flexible spending accounts (FSAs) and health savings accounts (HSAs).
- Discuss the implications of high deductibles in health coverage.

ISSUE SUMMARY

YES: The American Benefits Council, a national trade association, believes that "HSAs are working as intended" for the vast majority of the 6.1 million Americans covered by "HSA-eligible plans."

NO: Linda J. Blumberg, Urban Institute research associate, identifies a number of problems associated with medical care and argues that "HSAs are not the solutions to these pressing national concerns."

Evaluations of the health care sector of the U.S. economy usually take one of two approaches. In one approach, analysts and commentators point to the advances in health care produced by the U.S. economy: miracle drugs, path-breaking surgical procedures, new diagnostic machinery, and so on. This approach suggests that American medicine is the best in the world. The second approach takes a cost–benefit position and yields a less optimistic assessment. The analysts and commentators using this approach note that the United States spends more on health care than any other country in the world, an estimated 15 percent of gross domestic product. But the results are considered mediocre at best: 36 countries have both lower infant mortality rates and higher life expectancy than the United States (see GeographyIQ at http://www.geographyiq.com/index.htm).

While the analysts and commentators may be undecided about the right approach for the evaluation of the health care sector, most would agree that the sector does not operate as efficiently as it should. In particular, they point to health insurance and the extensive use of third-party payment of health expenses, arguing that even with deductibles and coinsurance, there is little incentive for the typical health care consumer to "comparison shop." In short, there would be a bigger bank for the medical buck if health care consumers had more incentive to spend their health care dollars in the same way they spend their dollars on housing, on automobiles, and on computers— seeking out low-cost providers and using medical health care resources only when they are needed. The question, then, is how to create these incentives and induce greater efficiency in the health care sector.

The Bush administration promotes one answer: health savings accounts (HSAs). These accounts were created on December 8, 2003, when President Bush signed the Medicare Prescription Drug, Improvement, and Modernization Act. How do HSAs work? First, a consumer must purchase an inexpensive health insurance plan that has a high deductible. Then the consumer can open an HSA account at a financial institution, contributing a particular amount to the account. Initially the limit on the amount that could be contributed to an HSA was 100 percent of the insurance's deductible. This was changed in 2006, and in 2008 the cap was $5,800 for family policies and $2,900 for a single person. These contributions are done on a tax-preferred basis. Withdrawals from the account are tax-exempt if they are spent on out-of-pocket medical expenses, and unused funds can be rolled over from one year to the next. If the money is withdrawn from an HSA and not spent on medical expenses, it is subject to income tax and a 10 percent penalty. The tax and penalty do not apply for persons 65 and older. As described by the U.S. Treasury:

> You own and control the money in your HSA. Decisions on how to spend the money are made

by you without relying on a third party or a health insurer. You will also decide what types of investments to make with the money in your account in order to make it grow.

The debate on HSAs did not end with their creation in 2003. This issue examines alternative evaluations of the effectiveness of HSAs and suggestions for change. The American Benefits Council supports HSAs, while Linda J. Blumberg offers a number of criticisms.

YES ←

Statement before the Subcommittee on Health of the House Committee on Ways and Means

The American Benefits Council (the "Council") appreciates the opportunity to submit this written statement to the Subcommittee regarding the increasing utilization and effectiveness of health savings accounts ("HSAs") and high deductible health plans ("HDHPs"). The Council is a national trade association representing principally Fortune 500 companies and other organizations that either sponsor or administer health and retirement benefit plans covering more than 100 million Americans.

HSAs are a fairly new health coverage option for American families, having been established by Congress in 2003 as part of the Medicare Modernization Act. Nevertheless, for millions of Americans, HSAs have already become an important tool in securing essential health coverage for themselves and their families. Early data from the Government Accountability Office ("GAO") and other third parties is encouraging, indicating that HSAs are working as intended for the vast majority of Americans who use them. HSA/HDHP arrangements can provide vital "first-dollar" medical coverage for accountholders (and their spouses and qualifying dependents), while utilizing important cost-sharing principles to help lower health coverage costs generally for individuals and employers alike. It is critical that we allow this important new health care option to fully develop and that we permit comprehensive data to be collected on the role it can play in providing quality health care at an affordable price. Any actions to apply new restrictions or burdens on this option would be premature and would risk eliminating a health care tool already being successfully used by millions of Americans.

The following is a summary of our comments:

- Health savings accounts have become an increasingly important tool for millions of Americans in securing lower cost, high-quality medical coverage. Recent data compiled by GAO indicates that an estimated 6.1 million Americans were covered by HSA/HDHP arrangements as of January 2008.
- Early data and testimony before the Subcommittee on May 14, 2008, indicate that the vast majority of HSAs include comprehensive "first-dollar" preventive care coverage and that HSAs can succeed in reducing health care costs for American families,

while also resulting in increased wellness and quality of care.

- Recent data strongly indicates that participants have sufficient HSA assets to meet actual out-of-pocket expenses under HDHPs, and (i) HSA withdrawals are being used principally for current-year qualified medical expenses, and (ii) HSAs, rather than being used primarily by high-income individuals as a tax shelter, are being used by individuals at a broad range of income levels. For example, one survey found that 45% of all HSA enrollees in 2005 had annual incomes of $50,000 or less, and there are good reasons to believe that this percentage may be even higher today.
- Current rules regarding HSA substantiation are consistent with the treatment afforded other special purpose accounts and health tax provisions. As discussed below, there are *numerous* instances under the Internal Revenue Code ("Code") where amounts withdrawn from a special purpose account are *not* subject to mandatory third-party FSA-like substantiation rules. Similarly, the general approach toward health expenditures under federal tax law does *not* require third-party substantiation for an individual to obtain a specific income tax deduction or other tax-favored treatment.
- Imposing third-party substantiation requirements on HSAs is not appropriate, will increase costs for HSA accountholders and limit options for health coverage at a time when such options should be expanded. The Council urges members of the Subcommittee, and members of Congress more generally, to oppose the imposition of third-party substantiation requirements on HSAs, such as the requirements included in H.R. 5719 (the "Taxpayer Assistance and Simplification Act of 2008").

HSAs Are an Increasingly Important Component to Many American Families' Health Coverage

Recent data compiled by GAO indicates that the number of Americans covered by HSA-eligible plans increased from 438,000 in September 2004 to an estimated 6.1 million in

January 2008.[1] This represents a 1,400% increase in their use in just over three years. Moreover, a recent study by America's Health Insurance Plans ("AHIP") found that HSA-usage increased by 35% in the 12-month period from January 2007 to January 2008.[2] American families and workers are indisputably turning to HSAs in increasing numbers to help control their ever-rising health coverage costs.

Early data also indicates that the increased use of HSAs is broad-based. Specifically, recent survey data by AHIP indicates that of those individuals covered by HSAs, 30% were in the small group market, 45% in the large group market, and 25% in the individual market.[3] In addition, it is very significant that the greatest growth in the HSA/HDHP market is in the small plan market, where health care coverage has been a constant public policy challenge.[4]

HSAs Can Reduce Health Costs and Improve Quality of Care

In this era of ever-rising health care costs—costs that continue to well outpace general inflation as measured by the Consumer Price Index ("CPI")—American workers and their employers continue to look for ways to help rein in these costs without negatively affecting health standards and quality of care. As Michael Chernew, Professor of Health Care Policy for Harvard Medical School, testified, cost sharing can reduce excess utilization and health expenditures generally, and HSA/HDHP coverage utilizes certain cost-sharing principles like upfront deductibles and copayments to help reduce excess utilization.[5]

Testimony from Wayne Sensor, CEO of Alegent Health, also provides a first-hand example of how HSA/HDHP coverage can both reduce costs *and* lead to increased health standards and quality of care. Specifically, Mr. Sensor testified that "there is a significantly higher level of engagement among those participants [in one of our HSA plans]." He stated that HSA participants "consume more preventive care than any other plan we offer," and that "[m]ore than 45% of HSA participants completed their health risk assessments, compared to just 16% in our PPO plan." On top of all of this, he noted that "[f]rom 2006 to 2007, the cost trend in our two HSA plans declined a full 15%!"[6]

Mr. Sensor's testimony is supported by findings from another study performed by HealthPartners. This study found that the cost of care for participants in HSAs and health reimbursement arrangements ("HRAs") was 4.4% lower than for those individuals with traditional low-deductible coverage.[7] The study also found that the cost savings did not impair the standard of care and that the utilization of preventive care services and medication for chronic illness was equivalent to that of individuals covered under more traditional low-deductible plans.

Data Indicates HSA/HDHP Coverage Utilizes Important "First-Dollar" Preventive Care Coverage

As Mr. Sensor's first-hand experience at Alegent Health demonstrates, HSA/HDHP coverage, if structured correctly, can achieve its intended result—providing quality care to Americans and their families at reduced costs. One component of successful HSA/HDHP coverage appears to be the inclusion of "first-dollar" preventive care coverage. A survey by AHIP last year showed that recommended preventive care is covered on a "first-dollar" basis by the vast majority of HSA/HDHP products.[8] Overall, the survey found that 84% of HSA/HDHP plans purchased in the group and individual markets provide "first-dollar" coverage for preventive care. Specifically, nearly all HSA plans purchased in the large group market (99%) and small group market (96%) provide "first-dollar" coverage, while 59% of HSA/HDHP policies sold on the individual market include such coverage.[9]

The AHIP survey also found that among those HSA/HDHP policies offering "first-dollar" coverage for preventive care, 100% provide coverage for adult and child immunizations, well-baby and well-child care, mammography, Pap tests, and annual physical exams. Nearly 90% of the policies provide "first-dollar" coverage for prostate screenings and more than 80% offer "first-dollar" coverage for colonoscopies.[10]

Early Data Strongly Indicates That Participants Have Sufficient HSA Assets to Meet Actual Out-of-Pocket Expenses Under HDHPs

AHIP's most recent census data indicates that HSA enrollees had an average account balance for 2007 of approximately $1,380 and withdrew on average $1,080 to reimburse qualified medical expenses, including those expenses not otherwise covered under their HDHP.[11] Additionally, early findings indicate that many employers are contributing substantial amounts to their employees' HSAs. Specifically, GAO reports that of those small and large employers that made contributions to HSAs in 2007, the average annual contribution totaled $806.[12]

The Council views these early findings as very encouraging. One criticism of HSAs has been that accountholders cannot contribute a sufficient amount to an HSA on an annual basis to meet their actual out-of-pocket expenses. This is due in large part to the fact that the maximum HSA contribution limit is almost certainly significantly less than the plan's maximum out-of-pocket limit (for example, for 2008, the maximum HSA contribution limit was $2,800 for self-only coverage and $5,900 for family coverage, but the maximum out-of-pocket limit for HDHPs was $5,600 and $11,200, respectively). Notwithstanding this fact, the data indicates that American families have been able to utilize their HSAs to effectively meet their out-of-pocket liability under the HDHP. This is very welcome news as it suggests that HSA/HDHPs meet both the cost and coverage needs of the average American family.

Data Indicates That HSAs Are *Not* Being Used As Tax Shelters by High-Income Individuals

The early data from GAO and AHIP is also encouraging for another reason. Contrary to concerns by some that HSAs would be used primarily by high-income individuals as an IRA-like retirement savings vehicle, the data indicates that HSAs are being used by both lower- and higher-income individuals principally to meet current year health costs.

With respect to the specific income levels of those individuals who are currently utilizing HSAs, available data for the 2005 tax year indicates that nearly 50% of all HSA enrollees had annual incomes of less than $60,000. Specifically, the recent GAO report indicates that 41% of HSA tax filers for 2005 had annual incomes below $60,000.[13] Similarly, a survey by eHealthInsurance, an online broker of health insurance policies, found that 45% of all HSA enrollees in 2005 had annual incomes of $50,000 or less.[14] The same survey found that 41% of HSA purchasers were not covered by health insurance during the preceding six months.[15]

Notably, the findings for the 2005 tax year may fail to accurately reflect current trends in HSA usage and may, in fact, understate the percentage of low- and middle-income HSA enrollees. This is because, as part of the Medicare Modernization Act, Congress allowed participants in early HSA-like accounts, called Medical Savings Accounts ("MSAs"), to convert these accounts into HSAs. Because MSAs generally were only available to self-employed individuals and small business owners—persons who on average would likely have higher incomes than the average American worker—the data for 2005 may well underestimate the number of low- and middle-income individuals who are currently enrolled in HSA/HDHP coverage.

Recent data from AHIP indicates that for 2007, HSA enrollees withdrew on average 80% of their annual contributions to reimburse current-year qualified medical expenses. Moreover, the GAO report states that "average contributions and average withdrawals generally increased with both income and age."[16] Thus, although higher-income individuals on average contributed more to their HSAs in a given year, they also withdrew more contributions during the same year. These early findings, when taken together, are very encouraging because they indicate that that HSAs are *not* being used primarily by higher-income individuals as a retirement savings vehicle or tax-shelter, but rather are being used by both lower- and higher-income individuals to obtain essential current-year health care coverage.

Lastly, some have pointed to the early data indicating that all HSA account balances are not "spent down" on an annual basis (as is frequently the case with FSAs given the "use-it-or-lose-it" rule) as evidence that HSAs are being used inappropriately as a tax savings vehicle. Such critiques fail to recognize the mechanics of HSA/HDHP coverage in light of the statutory contribution limits and potential out-of-pocket expenses. As noted above, in the vast majority of instances, the HSA participant's potential out-of-pocket exposure under the related HDHP can be as much as 200% of the maximum HSA annual contribution. Thus, to the extent that accountholders do not withdraw all of their HSA contributions in the same year (*i.e.,* as necessary to meet health expenditures), this should be viewed as positive from a public policy perspective. This is because any remaining account balance at year-end will help ensure that accountholders have sufficient HSA assets to meet potential out-of-pocket expenses under the HDHP plan in later years.

Available Data Indicates That HSA Monies Are Being Used for Qualified Medical Expenses

The early data, as compiled by GAO, suggests that amounts withdrawn from HSAs are being used by accountholders for qualified medical expenses. The GAO report states that "[o]f the HSA funds that were withdrawn in 2005, about 93 percent were claimed for qualified medical expenses."[17] Moreover, recent statements by a Treasury Department representative before the Ways and Means Committee indicate that 8.4% of all HSA accountholders list at least some of their HSA distributions as nonqualified taxable distributions.[18]

Under current rules, amounts withdrawn from HSAs that are not used for qualified medical expenses are subject to substantial negative tax consequences. Specifically, such amounts are subject to income tax at the accountholder's marginal tax rate as well as an additional 10% penalty tax. To the extent that an accountholder fails to accurately report taxable withdrawals, he or she would likely also be subject to various accuracy-related penalties and additions for the underpayment of income tax, as well as related interest.

The early data indicates that accountholders are using their HSAs as intended—primarily to reimburse qualified medical expenses not otherwise covered under the HDHP. Moreover, where amounts are withdrawn and are not used to reimburse qualified medical expenses, the data indicates that accountholders are correctly reporting such amounts as subject to income taxation under the current rules.

Current Rules Regarding HSA Substantiation Are Consistent with Other Special Purpose Accounts and Health Tax Provisions

Some persons have suggested that the treatment of HSAs under federal tax law—specifically the lack of a third-party substantiation requirement—is unparalleled and otherwise unique to HSAs. Such assertions are not correct. There are *numerous* instances under the Code where amounts withdrawn from a special purpose account are *not* subject to mandatory third-party FSA-like substantiation rules, such as with respect to withdrawals from 529 college saving plans or withdrawals from IRAs *in connection with a qualifying first-time home purchase.* . . .

With respect to the treatment of medical expenses more generally under federal tax law, it is HRAs and FSAs—rather than HSAs—that are in fact the exception to the rule. This is because, as with HSAs, the general approach towards health expenditures under federal tax law does not require that a taxpayer obtain third-party substantiation of qualifying medical expenses in order to obtain a specific income tax deduction or other tax-favored treatment.

One example of this can be found under Code section 162(l), which allows self-employed persons to take an above-the-line deduction for qualified medical care. In order to avail oneself of the deduction under this provision, the self-employed individual must certify on his or her annual income tax return the amount that he or she paid for qualified health insurance during the respective tax year. As with HSAs, no third-party substantiation is required under federal tax law, although the taxpayer remains subject to accuracy-related penalties and additions under federal tax law. . . .

Imposing Third-Party Substantiation Requirements on HSAs Will Increase Costs and Limit Americans' Options for Health Care Coverage

. . . At a time when Americans continue to struggle to afford their health care coverage and/or secure appropriate coverage, imposing third-party substantiation rules would impose additional costs and burdens on HSA providers and accountholders. These additional costs could operate to limit the attractiveness and efficacy of HSAs.

Americans' options for health coverage need to be expanded at this time, not limited, and imposing third-party substantiation could negatively affect the use and/or effectiveness of HSAs. Moreover, given the relative newness of HSAs generally and the encouraging early data indicating that such substantiation is unnecessary, the Council opposes the imposition of third-party substantiation rules in connection with HSAs.

Conclusion

HSAs were never intended to be a comprehensive answer to all of America's health care problems. Rather, HSAs were designed to be one important option for American families seeking lower-cost but high-quality comprehensive coverage. As the GAO report makes clear, for a significant percentage of American families, HSAs have become an integral part of their health coverage and, thus, should not be curtailed at this time.

More than ever before, Americans need good health coverage options. For a significant segment of American families, HSA/HDHP coverage meets this need by providing lower-cost, high-quality coverage. Moreover, as noted above, early data is encouraging and suggests that for the vast majority of HSA participants, HSA/HDHP coverage is operating as intended by Congress. But early data is just that—"early." It is critical, therefore, that we allow this new health care option to develop without additional burdens or restrictions. The Council believes that there is no justification for changes that could curtail the use and/or effectiveness of HSAs. Otherwise, we risk taking away from millions of American families a vital tool in securing affordable, quality health care coverage.

Notes

1. *Health Savings Accounts (HSAs) and Consumer Driven Health Care: Cost Containment or Cost-Shift? Hearing Before the Subcomm. on Health of the H. Comm. on Ways and Means, 110th Cong.* (2008) (statement of John E. Dicken, Director of Health Care, Government Accountability Office).
2. *Health Savings Accounts (HSAs) and Consumer Driven Health Care: Cost Containment or Cost-Shift? Hearing Before the Subcomm. on Health of the H. Comm. on Ways and Means, 110th Cong.* (2008) (statement of America's Health Insurance Plans) (hereinafter "AHIP").
3. *See* AHIP, *supra.*
4. *See* Id.
5. *Health Savings Accounts (HSAs) and Consumer Driven Health Care: Cost Containment or Cost-Shift? Hearing Before the Subcomm. on Health of the H. Comm. on Ways and Means, 110th Cong.* (2008) (statement of Michael E. Chernew, Ph.D., Professor of Health Care Policy, Harvard Medical School).
6. *Health Savings Accounts (HSAs) and Consumer Driven Health Care: Cost Containment or Cost-Shift? Hearing Before the Subcomm. on Health of the H. Comm. on Ways and Means, 110th Cong.* (2008) (statement of Wayne Sensor, CEO, Alegent Health).
7. *Consumer Directed Health Plans Analysis*, HealthPartners, October 2007.
8. *See* AHIP, *supra.*
9. *See* Id.
10. *Id.*
11. *See* Id. *See also Health Savings Accounts: Participation Increased and Was More Common Among*

Individuals with Higher Incomes, GAO-08-474R (April 2008), at 8 (stating that in 2005, the average HSA contribution was $2,100, with the average withdrawal being approximately $1,000).

12. *See* Id. at 9 (*citing* Kaiser Family Foundation and Health Research and Educational trust, *Employer Health Benefits: 2007 Annual Survey* (Menlo Park, Calif., and Chicago, Ill.: 2007). It should also be noted that in a study conducted by Mercer during the same period which covered only large employers, the average contribution was $626. *Id.* at 9.

13. *Id.* at 6.

14. *See* AHIP, *supra* (citing eHealthInsurance survey findings).

15. *See* Id.

16. *See* GAO, *supra*, at 8.

17. *See* Id. at 9.

18. *April 9, 2008 Mark-up of H.R. 5719 by the Subcomm. on Health of the H. Comm. on Ways and Means, 110th Cong.* (2008) (comment by Thomas Reeder, Benefits Tax Council, Dept. of Treasury) (as reported by *Congressional Quarterly*).

AMERICAN BENEFITS COUNCIL is a national trade association representing principally *Fortune* 500 companies and other organizations that either sponsor or administer health and retirement benefit plans covering more than 100 million Americans.

Linda J. Blumberg

Statement before the Subcommittee on Health of the House Committee on Ways and Means

...Thank you for inviting me to share my views on Health Savings Accounts (HSAs) and their implications for cost containment and the distribution of health care financing burdens. The views I express are mine alone and should not be attributed to the Urban Institute, its trustees, or its funders.

In brief, my main points are the following:

- The related issues of a large and growing number of uninsured Americans and the escalating cost of medical care create problems of limited access to necessary medical care for millions of Americans, financial hardship for many households, and severe budgetary pressures on the public health care safety net as well as on federal and state government. However, HSAs are not the solutions to these pressing national concerns.

- HSAs provide additional subsidies to the people most likely to purchase health insurance even in the absence of no subsidy at all—those with high incomes. As income and marginal tax rates increase, the value of the tax exemption associated with contributions to HSAs and the interest, dividends, and capital gains earned on HSA balances grows as well. Because most of the uninsured have low incomes and get little or no value from tax exemptions, the subsidies are very poorly targeted for expanding coverage.

- Because of the highly skewed nature of health care spending—the highest-spending 10 percent of the population accounts for 70 percent of total health expenditures—cost containment strategies that do not deal substantially with the high users of health care services will not have a significant effect on overall spending. . . .

- To the extent that high-deductible plans raise costs for higher-cost users, their use of medical services may fall. But there are no provisions to help these patients choose the services most important to their health, so reductions in care could lead to expensive, catastrophic health consequences in the long run. Moreover, patients' ability to compare health care providers on the basis of cost and quality is extremely limited. As a consequence, high-deductible plans and HSAs have a limited ability to make patients better value shoppers.

- Because high-deductible plans with or without HSAs place greater financial burdens on frequent users of medical care than do comprehensive policies (policies with lower out-of-pocket maximums and possibly broader sets of covered benefits), they tend to attract healthier enrollees. This selection can raise costs for the less healthy. The higher-cost insured population remaining in comprehensive coverage will tend to see their premiums rise as the healthy peel off into high-deductible/HSA plans. Unless the costs of these high users of care are spread more broadly by manipulating premiums across plan types or through regulation or subsidization, this dynamic will make coverage less affordable for those with the greatest medical needs.

- Despite lower premiums compared with comprehensive plans, high-deductible/HSA plans have so far failed to attract many low-income uninsured individuals and families. In addition to the fact that they get little tax benefit, they often do not have assets to cover the high deductibles—and have decided that they are better off remaining uninsured. The "one size fits all" high-deductible policy under the HSA legislation is flawed since, for example, a $2,200 deductible could be financially ruinous for a low-income family, while the same deductible could have virtually no cost-containment impact for a high-income family.

- Roughly half of those with HSA-compatible, high-deductible policies do not open HSAs (GAO 2008), despite the tax advantages of doing so. Two-thirds of employers offering single coverage through high-deductible/HSA combinations report making no contribution to the HSAs of their workers (Kaiser Family Foundation/Health Research and Education Trust 2007). As a consequence, low-income or high health-care-need workers with no choice of coverage but a high-deductible/HSA plan are likely to be exposed to much larger out-of-pocket financial burdens than they would be under a comprehensive policy, since employers are not, by and large, offsetting these higher deductibles with cash contributions to HSAs. Presented with the option of making varying contributions to HSAs as a function of worker income or health status, employers are highly unlikely to do so.

Blumberg, Linda J. Illinois House of Representatives, May 14, 2008.

- At present, the legal use of HSAs is far more tax favored than is any other health or retirement account. Contributions, earnings, and withdrawals for HSAs can be tax free, if spending is health related. However, there is no mechanism in place, other than being subjected to a general tax audit, to verify that spending out of HSA balances is actually being done for medical purposes. Medical Flexible Spending Accounts (FSAs), a much more widely used tax-advantaged account for paying out-of-pocket medical costs, do have verification mechanisms in place that add very little to the costs of the plans. H.R. 5917 would prevent the illegal use of HSAs as a general tool of tax evasion.

Background

Between 2000 and 2006, employer-based health insurance premiums grew by 86 percent, compared with 20 percent for worker earnings and 18 percent for overall inflation (Kaiser Family Foundation and Health Research and Educational Trust 2006). By 2006, the number of uninsured had increased to 18 percent of the total nonelderly population in the United States, and a third of the nonelderly population with incomes below 200 percent of the federal poverty level were uninsured (Holahan and Cook 2007). Health Savings Accounts have been one approach some policymakers have embraced to address these dual and growing problems.

While high-deductible plans have been available in the nongroup market for many years, the 2003 Medicare Prescription Drug, Improvement, and Modernization Act (MMA) included provisions to provide a generous tax incentive for certain individuals to seek out high-deductible health insurance policies with particular characteristics. . . .

Individuals (and families) buying these policies either through their employers or independently in the private nongroup insurance market can make tax-deductible contributions into an HSA. Funds deposited into the accounts are deducted from income for tax purposes, and any earnings on the funds accrue tax free, and are not taxed as long as they are used to cover medical costs. Contributions can be made by employers, individuals, or both. In 2006, Congress removed the requirement that annual deposits into HSAs be capped at the level of the plan's deductible, and instead provided a fixed statutory limit for annual contributions. . . .

HSAs were intended to encourage more cost-conscious spending by placing more of the health care financing burden on the users of services, as opposed to having them incorporated in the shared financing inherent in insurance coverage.

What Makes HSAs Attractive?

As a consequence of the structure of the tax subsidy and the shift of health care spending to out-of-pocket costs, these accounts are most attractive to high-income people and those with low expected health care expenses. The tax subsidy provided for HSA participants is greatest for those in the highest marginal tax bracket and is of little or no value to those who do not owe income tax. Clemans-Cope (forthcoming) demonstrated that 70 percent of the nonelderly uninsured have family incomes below 200 percent of the federal poverty level, and that only 16 percent of uninsured adults fall into the 20 percent or greater marginal tax bracket. A $5,800 HSA contribution, the maximum permitted under the law, would generate a tax reduction of $2,030 to a household in the top income tax bracket. The value of the tax benefit would be less than half as much for a moderate-income family. And it would be worth much less if the family could not afford to contribute very much into the account. For those whose incomes are so low that they have no income tax liability, the subsidy is worth nothing. However, HSA contributions made by an employer, as opposed to by an individual, will decrease even a low-income worker's payroll tax liability, resulting in a modest tax savings.

Higher-income individuals are also better able to cover the costs of a high deductible, should significant medical expenses be incurred. Jacobs and Claxton (2008) showed that uninsured households have substantially lower assets than do the insured. As a consequence, high-deductible policies are unlikely to provide the uninsured with sufficient financial access to medical care in the event of illness or injury.

Additionally, those who do not expect to have much in the way of health expenses will be attracted to HSAs by the ability to accrue funds tax free that they can use for a broad array of health-related expenses that are not reimbursable by insurance (e.g., non-prescription medications, eyeglasses, cosmetic surgery). Those without substantial health care needs may also be attracted to HSAs because they can be effectively used as an additional IRA, with no penalty applied if the funds are spent for non-health-related purposes after age 65. Young, healthy individuals may even choose to use employer contributions to their HSAs for current non-health-related expenses, after paying a 10 percent penalty and income taxes on the funds—a perk unavailable to those enrolled in traditional comprehensive insurance plans.

These expectations have been borne out in the enrollment experience of HSAs (United States Government Accountability Office [US GAO] 2008). The GAO analysis found that the average adjusted gross income of HSA participants was about $139,000 in 2005, compared with $57,000 for all other tax filers. They also found that average contributions to HSAs were more than double the average withdrawals, suggesting that either HSA participants were not high users of medical services or they used these accounts purely as investment vehicles—or both.

The incentive structure and the findings strongly indicate that HSAs and their associated tax subsidies are health care spending vehicles that are poorly targeted to the population most in need—the low-income and those with above average medical needs.

The Cost Containment Implications of the Health Care Spending Distribution

The distribution of health care spending is highly skewed, meaning a small percentage of the population accounts for a large share of total health care spending. The top 10 percent of health care spenders spend 70 percent of health care dollars, while the bottom 50 percent of spenders account for only 3 percent of those dollars (Berk and Monheit 2001). As a consequence, significantly decreasing health care spending will require substantially lowering the spending associated with high users of medical services, ideally, while not decreasing quality of care. However, the high-deductible/HSA plan approach is not well designed for lowering the spending of the high-cost population in a manner that does not negatively affect their health.

Cost savings can be manifested through two mechanisms: a decline in the amount of services per episode of care due to an increase in marginal price, or a decline in the number of episodes of care due to an increase in the average price. For those who are generally healthy and would not have annual spending that exceeded the high deductibles associated with HSA compatible plans, the increased marginal price of out-of-pocket medical care could have some impact on their use (Newhouse 1993, 2004). Incentives to curtail unnecessary services are strongest for these individuals. However, our analysis of the Medical Expenditure Panel Survey—Household Component showed that only 3 percent of total health care spending is attributable to those who spend below the minimum required deductibles. Consequently, there is little room for systemwide cost savings among this population since their spending accounts for so little of the overall expenditures.

For those who are unhealthy and who, with comprehensive insurance coverage, would spend above these higher deductibles, a number of scenarios are possible. Those who do not face significantly higher out-of-pocket maximums relative to their previous plan would not have any additional cost containment incentives. Those who face significantly higher out-of-pocket maximums under the new high-deductible/HSA plans would face a higher average price of medical care, and could reduce their spending as a consequence. However, research has demonstrated that the reductions in their spending would occur as a consequence of their reducing the number of episodes of their care, as opposed to reducing the cost of an episode once initiated (Newhouse 1993, 2004). In other words, they would decide not to initiate a contact with a medical professional for financial reasons, with potentially serious consequences for their health and for the long-term costs of their care. Two studies (Fronstin

and Collins 2005; Davis et al. 2005) have found that HSA participants were more likely to report missed or delayed health services and not filling prescriptions due to cost. These problems were greater for those with lower incomes or worse health.

Paradoxically, high-cost individuals are not likely to curtail unnecessary services before reaching the high deductible, as might be desired. That is because the lion's share (80 percent) of health care spending for high-cost users of care is attributable to their spending that is incurred once those higher deductible levels are surpassed (Clemans-Cope forthcoming). . . .

While a number of studies have found that modest one-time savings of between 4 to 15 percent might be anticipated from conversion to high-deductible/HSA plans, they do not imply that such a change would have a significant impact on the rate of growth of medical spending. This is because medical spending growth is driven largely by the increased use of, and intensity of, technologies and services for people with high health care needs (Newhouse 2004). So while increased cost sharing can be used to lower the frequency of health care provider visits, it does not lower the costs per episode once an episode of care occurs.

Other, more promising avenues exist for achieving significant cost savings in our health care system. These include, among others,

- coordinated approaches to evaluation of cost-effectiveness and efficacy of new and existing technologies/procedures/medications combined with new regulatory and pricing strategies to target resources to the most cost-effective options;
- increasing the use of preventive care and chronic-care or high-cost case management strategies;
- payment reform and development of purchasing strategies that promote the consistent delivery of care in the most efficient and appropriate setting;
- administrative cost-saving strategies, including development of effective information technology infrastructure.

While many of these avenues require significant upfront investment in infrastructure, research, analysis, or experimentation, they are substantially more likely to yield systemwide savings without compromising access to and quality of care for the high-need population.

Implications of HSAs for the High Medical Need Population

The most significant premium savings accruing to high-deductible/HSA plan enrollees likely occur by altering the mix of individuals who purchase coverage of different types. By providing incentives for healthy individuals and groups to purchase HSA-compatible plans, insurance risk pools can be further segmented by health status. The average medical costs of those purchasing the HSA plans will be substantially lower if the high-risk population is left in more traditional comprehensive plans. As the average cost of those in the comprehensive plans increases, so does the premium associated with the coverage. In the extreme risk segmentation circumstance, premiums for comprehensive coverage may increase so much that maintaining that type of coverage is no longer financially viable. . . .

Without some type of intervention by government or employers to spread health care risk more broadly, the practical effect of high-deductible/HSA plans is that the most vulnerable populations (the sick and low-income) are left bearing a greater burden of their health expenses. The extent to which this is a preferred societal outcome should be explicitly debated, as it is the primary impact of a move toward high-deductible/HSA plans.

The Ability of Patients to Be Good Value Shoppers

Theoretically, placing a greater share of the health care financing burden on the individual users of health care should create incentives for greater price/quality comparisons and more cost-effective medical decisions. However, the ability of the patients to engage in such comparison shopping is extremely limited in the current private insurance context. As Ginsburg (2007) describes, effective comparison of services on price occurs only in the context of non-emergency care, services that are not complex, bundled prices for services, consistent quality across providers, and only after an appropriate diagnosis has been made. Situations that meet such criteria eliminate a great deal of the medical care within the system. In addition, confidentiality agreements between providers and insurers prevent the providers from being able to give patients actual prices, as opposed to ranges that are generally not useful for comparison purposes. Traditionally, patients have relied upon their insurers to guide their provider decisions by choosing an efficient provider network on their behalf.

Enforcement of HSA Legal Requirements

As noted earlier, spending by those under 65 years of age out of HSA accounts is tax advantaged only if that spending is for medical purposes. If HSA funds are used for nonmedical purposes, a nonelderly individual would be required to pay taxes on the withdrawal in addition to a 10 percent penalty. However, currently, there is no administrative mechanism in place to verify that spending from HSAs is in fact being used for medical purposes. Unless an individual HSA participant is subjected to an IRS audit, there are no checks on the type of spending being done. Given that any individual's likelihood of an audit is very low, this lack of verification creates an easy mechanism for evading taxes. This problem is amplified by the increase in allowable annual contributions to HSAs and the fact that such contributions can now exceed the associated insurance plan's annual deductible.

Flexible spending accounts (FSAs) are employment-related accounts that allow users to deposit pretax dollars into accounts that can then be drawn down during the year to pay for medical expenses. The permissible medical expenses are defined broadly, including out-of-pocket costs for care that is or is not part of the account-holder's insurance policy, just like HSAs. There are a number of differences between FSAs and HSAs (e.g., unused FSA balances are forfeited at the end of the year, they do not earn income, and they do not require health insurance plan participation), but the only relevant difference for this discussion is that withdrawals from FSAs are verified by the account administrators to be medical-related expenses that comply with the FSA law. . . .

The insurance industry complains that imposing such verification on HSAs would eliminate their cost saving potential by imposing new and onerous administrative costs. However, the administrative costs of FSAs, which would be directly comparable with that of HSAs for this purpose, are actually very low. In fact, overall FSA administrative costs, which include payment of claims (a function which HSAs already perform and is included in their current administrative costs) as well as verification of the appropriateness of claims, are about $5.25 per member per month ($63 per member per year).[1] However, much of the administrative tasks associated with FSAs are not applicable to HSAs, and the cost of adding adjudication of claims to the HSAs would be about $2 per member per month according to the third-party administrator of such plans that we contacted. If an additional cost of $24 per member would substantially reduce or eliminate the cost savings associated with HSAs, as some contend, then that is clear evidence that there is currently little to no cost savings associated with participating in those plans today.

Such an increment to administrative costs associated with these plans is clearly a very small price to pay to ensure that the law is being complied with and individuals are not using HSAs merely as a personal tax dodge.

Conclusion

HSAs are a highly tax-advantaged savings vehicle that is most attractive to people with high incomes and those with low expected use of health care services. As such, they are unlikely to significantly decrease the number of uninsured, who often have low incomes and neither benefit significantly from the tax advantages nor have the assets necessary to cover the large deductibles associated with the plans. Their ability to reduce systemwide spending is also very limited. The plans have the potential to increase segmentation of health care risk in private insurance markets, unless employers set premiums to offset the healthier selection into the plans or government subsidizes the higher costs associated with the remaining comprehensive coverage market.

To date, HSAs have been less popular than their advocates envisioned, making up only about 2 percent of the health insurance market (US GAO 2008). Thus, their negative ramifications on populations with high medical needs have probably been limited. However, efforts to expand enrollment in these plans through further tax incentives, for example, could place growing financial burdens on those least able to absorb them, leading to increasing effective barriers to medical care for the low income and the sick and potentially increasing the net number of uninsured.

References

Berk, Marc and Alan Monheit. 2001. "The Concentration of Health Expenditures Revisited," *Health Affairs*, 20:204–213.

Clemans-Cope, Lisa. Forthcoming. "Short- and Long-term Effects of Health Savings Accounts." Working paper prepared for The Urban Institute–Brookings Institution Tax Policy Center.

Davis, K., Doty, M. M. and Ho, A. 2005. "How High Is Too High? Implications of High-Deductible Health Plans." The Commonwealth Fund, April.

Fronstin, Paul and S. R. Collins. 2005. "Early Experience with High-Deductible and Consumer-Driven Health Plans: Findings from the EBRI/Commonwealth Fund Consumerism in Health Care Survey," Employee Benefit Research Institute and the Commonwealth Fund, December.

Ginsburg, Paul B. 2007. "Shopping for Price in Medical Care." *Health Affairs*, March/April; 26(2): w208–w216.

Holahan, John and Allison Cook. 2007. "Health Insurance Coverage in America: 2006 Data Update." Henry J. Kaiser Family Foundation. . . .

Jacobs, Paul D. and Gary Claxton. 2008. "Comparing the Assets of Uninsured Households to Cost Sharing Under High-Deductible Health Plans." *Health Affairs.* web exclusive, April 15, 2008, pp. w214–w221.

Henry J. Kaiser Family Foundation/Health Research and Educational Trust (Kaiser/HRET) Survey of Employer-Sponsored Health Benefits, 2006. . . .

Henry J. Kaiser Family Foundation/Health Research and Educational Trust (Kaiser/HRET) Survey of Employer-Sponsored Health Benefits, 2007. . . .

Newhouse, J. P., 2004. "Consumer-Directed Health Plans and the RAND Health Insurance Experiment." *Health Affairs* Volume 23(6): 107–113.

Newhouse, J. P. and the Insurance Experiment Group. 1993. *Free for All? Lessons from the Rand Health Insurance Experiment.* Cambridge, MA: Harvard University Press.

United States Government Accountability Office (US GAO). 2008. Health Savings Accounts: Participation Increased and Was More Common Among Individuals with Higher Incomes. April 1. GAO-08-474R.

Note

1. From personal communication with third-party administrators providing administrative services for FSAs and consumer-directed health plans.

LINDA J. BLUMBERG is the principal research associate at The Urban Institute. She holds a PhD in economics from the University of Michigan.

EXPLORING THE ISSUE

Are Health Savings Accounts Working Effectively?

Critical Thinking and Reflection

1. Identify and describe, by way of your own appraisal, these two things: the greatest virtue of HSAs and the worst flaw of HSAs.
2. Is it significant to the debate that Blumberg repeatedly expresses concern over the large and growing number of uninsured Americans while the Council never once mentions the word "uninsured"? Explain.
3. How might Blumberg's overall assessment of HSAs be modified if all employers made HSA contributions?
4. How essential to the examination of health care reform is a consideration of the consumer's right to "comparison shop"? Why?

Is There Common Ground?

The debate presented here on the efficacy of health savings accounts (HSAs) is one not based on hostile polarity, so there is indeed common ground on which rational discussion could be established. The foremost agreement is that America's health care sector does not operate as efficiently as it should. Another shared perspective is the critical need to establish policies that lessen the health-cost burdens of Americans.

Although the respective assessments of the effectiveness of HSAs are clearly in opposition, the core arguments on both sides reflect an appreciation for the serious interest that all Americans, on all economic levels, have in personal and family health care issues, as well as for the consumer's right to "comparison shop." Neither side has attempted to trivialize anyone's entitlement to adequate health care services, but a concerted position on how best (and most equitably) to address America's health care inadequacies is far from being realized.

Create Central

www.mhhe.com/createcentral

Additional Resources

Cohn, Jonathan, *Sick: The Untold Story of America's Health Care Crisis—And the People Who Pay the Price* (HarperCollins, 2007)

Driskill, Edie Milligan, *The Pocket Idiot's Guide to Health Savings Accounts* (Alpha, 2006)

Emerick, Tom, and Al Lewis, *Cracking Health Costs* (Wiley, 2013)

Parks, Dave, *Health Care Reform Simplified: What Professionals in Medicine, Government, Insurance, and Business Need to Know* (Apress, 2012)

Internet References . . .

American Academy of Actuaries: "FAQs on HSAs"

www.actuary.org/pdf/health/hsa_oct07.pdf

CNN Money: "Getting the Most Out of an HSA Plan"

http://money.cnn.com/2008/03/24/pf/HSA_questions
.moneymag/index.htm

Indystar: "Health Savings Accounts Won't Work for Poor People"

www.indystar.com/article/20130919/OPINION10
/309190063/Health-savings-accounts-won-t-work
-poor-people

ISSUE

Should NBC and Comcast Be Allowed to Merge?

YES: Brian L. Roberts and Jeff Zucker, from "Testimony before the U.S. Senate Judiciary Committee, Subcommittee on Antitrust, Competition Policy, and Consumer Rights" (February 4, 2010)

NO: Mark Cooper, from "Testimony before the U.S. Senate Judiciary Committee, Subcommittee on Antitrust, Competition Policy, and Consumer Rights" (February 4, 2010)

Learning Outcomes
After reading this issue, you will be able to: • Provide brief background summaries for both NBC and Comcast.   • Identify the federal approval requirements for an NBC–Comcast merger.   • Define the essence of the Clayton Antitrust Act of 1914.   • State the meaning of "MVPD."

ISSUE SUMMARY

YES: Company presidents Brian L. Roberts (Comcast) and Jeff Zucker (NBC) support the merger of their companies; they believe the merged firm "will benefit consumers and will encourage much needed investment and innovation in the important media sector."

NO: Consumer Federation of America Research Director Mark Cooper opposes the merger because it will give the merging firms "the incentive and ability to not only preserve and exploit the worse aspects of the current market, but to extend them to the future market."

On December 3, 2009, the Comcast and General Electric (GE) corporations announced the proposed merger of GE's NBC Universal unit (old NBCU) with Comcast's Entertainment Group. The new entity, referred to as the new NBCU, would be valued at approximately $30 billion, with Comcast owning 51 percent and GE owning the remaining 49 percent. Consistent with its majority ownership position, Comcast would be the manager of the new company. The merger is self-described as a vertical combination (as opposed to horizontal or conglomerate merger) with the old NBCU component seen as a content provider and the Comcast component viewed as the distributor of that content. The proposed merger requires the federal approval of both the Justice Department (DOJ) and the Federal Communications Commission (FCC).

In order to understand the merger, some background on the involved companies is helpful. Comcast began as a cable system operator in Tupelo, Mississippi, in 1963 with 1,200 subscribers. Its early growth took the path of horizontal mergers; it was based on the acquisition of other cable operators including all or portions of Group W Cable, Storer Communications, Maclean Hunter, and Jones Intercable (horizontal mergers). The company reports that as of September 30, 2010, it has 22.9 million cable customers. But Comcast is more than a cable operator; it also provides entertainment and communication products. Again as of September 30, 2010, the company served 16.7 million high-speed Internet customers and 8.4 million voice customers. Comcast also owns several cable channels including E!, the Style Network, the Golf Channel, VERSUS, and 11 sports networks. It operates in 39 states and in the District of Columbia. Comcast has major holdings in the Philadelphia Flyers of the National Hockey League and in the Wells Fargo Center multipurpose arena in Philadelphia. The merger will not include Comcast's cable business.

NBC was formed in 1926 as the first major broadcast network in the United States. Ownership was divided into three parts: 50 percent to Radio Corporation of America

(RCA), 30 percent to GE, and 20 percent to Westinghouse. GE was subsequently forced by the government to sell its interest in NBC. GE reacquired NBC when it purchased RCA in 1986 (conglomerate merger) for $6.4 billion. Old NBCU was formed in May 2004 with the merger of GE's NBC and Vivendi Corporation's Universal Entertainment, with GE owning 80 percent. GE assumed complete ownership in 2009 by purchasing the remaining 20 percent of old NBCU from Vivendi. Old NBCU describes itself as the world leader in the "development, production, and marketing of entertainment news and information." Its activities are divided into four different areas: a television group that includes ownership of stations in major cities like New York, Los Angeles, Chicago, and Philadelphia; a film group that includes Universal Pictures; a digital media group that includes NBC.com and CNBC.com; and a parks and resorts group that includes Universal Parks and Resorts.

As for GE, the parent of old NBCU, it describes itself as a global infrastructure, finance, and media company. Besides old NBCU, its various companies produce a variety of goods and services including jet engines, kitchen appliances, light bulbs, medical technologies, and wastewater treatment facilities.

While the Comcast–old NBCU merger was proposed late in 2009, as of this writing it has yet to be consummated. The explanation is that the merger requires regulatory approval. The DOJ is evaluating the merger in the context of the nation's antitrust laws. Under the Clayton Antitrust Act of 1914, mergers are prohibited if they substantially lessen competition or if they tend to create a monopoly. Critics of the merger argue that the merger will, among other things, reduce head-to-head competition in areas such as local news, sports, and advertising. On the other hand, the FCC, which regulates interstate and international communications by radio, television, wire, satellite, and cable, will examine the merger from a broader public interest perspective. Elements to be considered in this perspective include, among other things, diversity and localism.

In the first reading, CEOs Brian L. Roberts and Jeff Zucker make the case for the merger. They believe the merger will strengthen rather than weaken competition, will support public interest, and will provide benefits for consumers. Research Director Cooper opposes the merger. He argues the merger will allow the biggest to get bigger and will result in higher prices and fewer choices for consumers.

YES

Brian L. Roberts and Jeff Zucker

Testimony before the U.S. Senate Judiciary Committee, Subcommittee on Antitrust, Competition Policy, and Consumer Rights

Mr. Chairman, and Members of the Subcommittee, we are pleased to appear before you today to discuss Comcast Corporation's ("Comcast") planned joint venture with General Electric Company ("GE"), under which Comcast will acquire a majority interest in and management of NBC Universal ("NBCU"). . . .

The new NBCU will benefit consumers and will encourage much-needed investment and innovation in the important media sector. How will it benefit consumers? First, the new venture will lead to increased investment in NBCU by putting these important content assets under the control of a company that is focused exclusively on the communication and entertainment industry. This will foster enhanced investment in both content development and delivery, enabling NBCU to become a more competitive and innovative player in the turbulent and ever changing media world. Investment and innovation will also preserve and create sustainable media and technology jobs. Second, the transaction will promote the innovation, content, and delivery that consumers want and demand. The parties have made significant commitments in the areas of local news and information programming, enhanced programming for diverse audiences, and more quality educational and other content for children and families. And finally, Comcast's commitment to sustain and invest in the NBC broadcast network will promote the quality news, sports, and local programming that have made this network great over the last 50 years. . . .

The new NBCU will advance key policy goals of Congress: diversity, localism, innovation, and competition. With Comcast's demonstrated commitment to investment and innovation in communications, entertainment, and information, the new NBCU will be able to increase the quantity, quality, diversity, and local focus of its content, and accelerate the arrival of the multiplatform, "anytime, anywhere" future of video programming that Americans want. Given the intensely competitive markets in which Comcast and NBCU operate, as well as existing law and regulations, this essentially vertical transaction will benefit consumers and spur competition, and will not present any potential harm in any marketplace.

NBCU, currently majority-owned and controlled by GE, is an American icon—a media, entertainment, and communications company with a storied past and a promising future. At the heart of NBCU's content production is the National Broadcasting Company ("NBC"), the nation's first television broadcast network and home of one of the crown jewels of NBCU, NBC News. NBCU also has two highly regarded cable news networks, CNBC and MSNBC. In addition, NBCU owns Telemundo, the nation's second largest Spanish-language broadcast network, with substantial Spanish-language production facilities located in the United States. NBCU's other assets include 26 local broadcast stations (10 NBC owned-and-operated stations ("O&Os"), 15 Telemundo O&Os, and one independent Spanish-language station), numerous national cable programming networks, a motion picture studio with a library of several thousand films, a TV production studio with a library of television series, and an international theme park business.

Comcast, a leading provider of cable television, high-speed Internet, digital voice, and other communications services to millions of customers, is a pioneer in enabling consumers to watch what they want, when they want, where they want, and on the devices they want. Comcast is primarily a distributor, offering its customers multiple delivery platforms for content and services. Although Comcast owns and produces some cable programming channels and online content, Comcast owns relatively few national cable networks, none of which is among the 30 most highly rated, and, even including its local and regional networks, Comcast accounts for a tiny percentage of the content industry. The majority of these content businesses will be contributed to the joint venture. The distribution side of Comcast (referred to as "Comcast Cable") is not being contributed to the new NBCU and will remain under Comcast's ownership and control.

The proposed transaction is primarily a *vertical* combination of NBCU's content with Comcast's multiple distribution platforms. Antitrust law, competition experts, and the FCC have long recognized that vertical combinations can produce significant benefits. Experts and the FCC also have found that vertical combinations with limited horizontal issues generally do not threaten competition.

Roberts, Brian L.; Zucker, Jeff. U.S. Senate, February 4, 2010.

The transaction takes place against the backdrop of a communications and entertainment marketplace that is highly dynamic and competitive, and becoming more so every day. NBCU—today and post-transaction—faces competition from a large and growing roster of content providers. There are literally hundreds of national television networks and scores of regional networks. These networks compete not only with each other but also with countless other video choices—both for consumers' attention and for distribution on various video platforms. In addition, content producers increasingly have alternative outlets available to distribute their works, free from any purported "gatekeeping" networks or distributors. . . .

Competition is fierce among distributors as well. Consumers in every geographic area have multiple choices of multichannel video programming distributors ("MVPDs") and can obtain video content from many non-MVPDs as well. In addition to the local cable operator, consumers can choose from two MVPDs offering direct broadcast satellite ("DBS") service: DirecTV and Dish Network, which are now the second and third largest MVPDs in America, respectively. Verizon and AT&T, along with other wireline overbuilders, are strong, credible competitors, offering a fourth MVPD choice to tens of millions of American households and a fifth choice to some. Indeed, as competition among MVPDs has grown, Comcast's nationwide share of MVPD subscribers has steadily decreased (it is now less than 25 percent, a share that the FCC has repeatedly said is insufficient to allow an MVPD to engage in anticompetitive conduct). . . .

Consumers can also access high-quality video content from myriad other sources. Some households continue to receive their video through over-the-air broadcast signals, which have improved in quality and increased in quantity as a result of the broadcast digital television transition. Millions of households purchase or rent digital video discs ("DVDs") from one of thousands of national, regional, or local retail outlets, including Walmart, Blockbuster, and Hollywood Video, as well as Netflix, MovieCrazy, Café DVD, and others who provide DVDs by mail. High-quality video content also is increasingly available from a rapidly growing number of online sources that include Amazon, Apple TV, Blinkx, Blip.tv, Boxee, Clicker.com, Crackle, Eclectus, Hulu, iReel, iTunes, Netflix, Sezmi, SlashControl, Sling, Veoh, Vevo, Vimeo, VUDU, Vuze, Xbox, YouTube, and many more. These sites offer previously unimaginable quantities of professionally-produced content and user-generated content that can be accessed from a variety of devices, including computers, Internet-equipped televisions, videogame boxes, Blu-ray DVD players, and mobile devices. In addition, there is a huge supply of user-generated video content, including professional and quasi-professional content. . . .

The combination of NBCU and Comcast's content assets under the new NBCU—coupled with management of the new NBCU by Comcast, an experienced, committed distribution innovator—will enable the creation of new pathways for delivery of content to consumers on a wide range of screens and platforms. The companies' limited shares in all relevant markets, fierce competition at all levels of the distribution chain, and ease of entry for cable and online programming ensure that the risk of competitive harm is insignificant. Moreover, the FCC's rules governing program access, program carriage, and retransmission consent provide further safeguards for consumers as do the additional public interest commitments made by the companies to the FCC.

At the same time, the transaction's public interest benefits—particularly for the public interest goals of diversity, localism, competition, and innovation—are substantial. Through expanded access to outlets, increased investment in outlets, and lower costs, the new venture will be able to increase the amount, quality, variety, and availability of content more than either company could on its own, thus promoting *diversity*. This includes content of specific interest to minority groups, children and families, women, and other key audience segments. . . .

In addition, Comcast and NBCU have publicly affirmed their continuing commitment to free, over-the-air broadcasting. Despite a challenging business and technological environment, the proposed transaction has significant potential to invigorate NBCU's broadcasting business and expand the important public interest benefits it provides to consumers across this country. . . .

Moreover, combining Comcast's expertise in multiplatform content distribution with NBCU's extensive content creation capabilities and video libraries will not only result in the creation of more and better programming—it will also encourage investment and innovation that will accelerate the arrival of the multiplatform, "anytime, anywhere" future of video programming that Americans want. This is because the proposed transaction will remove negotiation friction that currently inhibits the ability of Comcast to implement its pro-consumer vision of multiplatform access to quality video programming. Post-transaction, Comcast will have access to more content that it can make available on more outlets, including the new NBCU's national and regional networks and Comcast's cable systems, video-on-demand ("VOD") platform, and online platform. . . .

The past is prologue: Comcast sought for years to develop the VOD business, but it could not convince studio distributors—who were reluctant to permit their movies to be distributed on an emerging, unproven platform—to provide compelling content for VOD. This caution, though understandable in light of marketplace uncertainty, slowed the growth of an innovative and extremely consumer-friendly service. Comcast finally was able to overcome the contractual wrangling and other industry resistance to an innovative business model when it joined with Sony to acquire an ownership interest in Metro-Goldwyn-Mayer ("MGM"). This allowed Comcast to "break the ice" and obtain access to hundreds of studio movies that Comcast could offer for free on VOD. Thanks to Comcast's extensive efforts to foster the growth of this new technology, VOD has gone on to become extremely popular. . . .

The formation of the new NBCU will remove negotiation impediments by providing Comcast with control of a rich program library and extensive production capabilities that Comcast can use to develop novel video products and services that will be offered to consumers across an array of distribution platforms. There is every reason to believe that the transaction proposed here will create a pro-consumer impetus for making major motion pictures available sooner for in-home, on-demand viewing and for sustainable online video distribution—which, as the FCC has observed, will help to drive broadband adoption, another key congressional goal.

As noted above, the risk of competitive harm in this transaction is insignificant. Viewed from every angle, the transaction is pro-competitive.

First, combining Comcast's and NBCU's programming assets will give rise to no cognizable competitive harm. Comcast's national cable programming networks account for only about three percent of total national cable network advertising and affiliate revenues. While NBCU owns a larger number of networks, those assets account for only about nine percent of overall national cable network advertising and affiliate revenues. In total, the new NBCU will account for only about 12 percent of overall national cable network advertising and affiliate revenues. The new NBCU will rank as the fourth largest owner of national cable networks, behind Disney/ABC, Time Warner, and Viacom—which is the same rank that NBCU has today. Because both the cable programming market and the broader video programming market will remain highly competitive, the proposed transaction will not reduce competition or diversity, nor will it lead to higher programming prices to MVPDs or consumers or higher advertising prices.

Even after the transaction, approximately six out of every seven channels carried by Comcast Cable will be unaffiliated with Comcast or the new NBCU.

Second, Comcast's management and ownership interests in NBCU's broadcast properties raise no regulatory or competitive concern. While Comcast will own both cable systems and a stake in NBC owned and operated broadcast stations in a small number of Designated Market Areas ("DMAs"), the FCC's rules do not prohibit such cross-ownership, nor is there any policy rationale to disallow such relationships. The prior cross-ownership prohibitions have been repealed by actions of Congress, the courts, and the FCC. . . .

Third, the combination of Comcast's and NBCU's Internet properties similarly poses no threat to competition. There is abundant and growing competition for online video content. Although Comcast operates a video site, called Fancast, and NBCU holds a 32 percent, non-controlling interest in Hulu, a site that provides access to certain online video content, the leader in online viewing

(by far) is Google (through YouTube and other sites it has built or acquired), with nearly 55 percent of online video viewing. This puts Google well ahead of Microsoft, Viacom, and Hulu (all of which are in low- or mid-single digits) and even farther ahead of Fancast (currently well below one percent). There are countless other sites that provide robust competition and near-infinite consumer choice. . . .

Finally, a vertical combination cannot have anti-competitive effects unless the combined company has substantial market power in the upstream (programming) or downstream (distribution) market, and such circumstances do not exist here. As noted, the video programming, video distribution, and Internet businesses are fiercely competitive, and the proposed transaction does not reduce that competition. The recent history of technology demonstrates that distribution platforms are multiplying, diversifying, and increasingly rivalrous. . . .

In any event, there is a comprehensive regulatory structure already in place, comprising the FCC's program access, program carriage, and retransmission consent rules, as well as an established body of antitrust law that provides further safeguards against any conceivable vertical harms that might be presented by this transaction.

Although the competitive marketplace and regulatory safeguards protect against the risk of anticompetitive conduct, the companies have offered an unprecedented set of commitments to provide assurances that competition will remain vibrant. Moreover, the companies have offered concrete and verifiable commitments to ensure certain pro-consumer benefits of the transaction. In addition to the commitment to continue to provide free, over-the-air broadcasting, mentioned previously, the companies have committed that following the transaction, the NBC O&O broadcast stations will maintain the same amount of local news and information programming they currently provide, and will produce an additional 1,000 hours per year of local news and information programming for various platforms. . . .

Comcast will commit voluntarily to extend the key components of the FCC's program access rules to negotiations with MVPDs for retransmission rights to the signals of NBC and Telemundo O&O broadcast stations for as long as the FCC's current program access rules remain in place. Of particular note, Comcast will be prohibited in retransmission consent negotiations from unduly or improperly influencing the NBC and Telemundo stations' decisions about whether to sell their programming, or the terms and conditions of sale, to other distributors. . . .

The companies also have committed that Comcast will use its On Demand and On Demand Online platforms to increase programming choices available to children and families as well as to audiences for Spanish-language programming. . . .

As Comcast makes rapid advances in video delivery technologies, more channel capacity will become available. So Comcast will commit that, once it has completed its digital migration company-wide (anticipated to be no later than 2011), it will add two new independently owned and operated channels to its digital line-up each year for the next three years on customary terms and conditions. . . .

We have proposed that these commitments be included in any FCC order approving the transaction and become binding on the parties upon completion of the transaction. A summary of the companies' commitments is attached to this statement.

In the end, the proposed transaction simply transfers ownership and control of NBCU from GE, a company with a very diverse portfolio of interests, to Comcast, a company with an exclusive focus on, and a commitment to investing its resources in, its communications, entertainment, and information assets. This transfer of control, along with the contribution of Comcast's complementary content assets, will enable the new NBCU to better serve consumers. The new NBCU will advance key public policy goals: diversity, localism, competition, and innovation.

Competition, which is already pervasive in every one of the businesses in which the new NBCU—and Comcast Cable—will operate, provides abundant assurance that consumer welfare will be not only safeguarded but increased. Comcast and NBCU will succeed by competing vigorously and fairly. . . .

BRIAN L. ROBERTS is the chairman and chief executive officer of Comcast Corporation. He received his undergraduate degree from the Wharton School at the University of Pennsylvania. Comcast, founded by his father in Tupelo, Missisippi, in 1963, serves over 23 million cable customers in 39 states and the District of Columbia.

JEFF ZUCKER is the president and chief executive officer of NBC Universal. He received his undergraduate degree from Harvard University. He has spent his entire career at NBC and has served in a variety of positions before reaching his current position in 2007. He is a five-time Emmy Award winner.

Mark Cooper

NO

Testimony before the U.S. Senate Judiciary Committee, Subcommittee on Antitrust, Competition Policy, and Consumer Rights

... The merger of Comcast and the National Broadcasting Company (NBC) is a hugely complex undertaking, unlike any other in the history of the video marketplace. Allowing the largest cable operator in history to acquire one of the nation's premier video content producers will radically alter the structure of the video marketplace and result in higher prices and fewer choices for consumers. The merging parties are already among the dominant players in the current video market. This merger will give them the incentive and ability to not only preserve and exploit the worst aspects of the current market, but to extend them to the future market.

Comcast has sought to downplay the impact of the merger by claiming that it is a small player in comparison to the vast video universe in which it exists. It has also glossed-over the fact that this merger involves the elimination of actual head-to-head competition. Finally, it has argued that existing protections and public interest promises will prevent any harms that might result from the merger. All three claims are wrong.

Neither Comcast's regurgitation of market shares and counts of outlets and products nor its public interest commitments begin to address the fundamental public policy questions and competitive issues at stake in this merger. Nor can the merger of these companies be viewed separately from the products they sell. NBC and Comcast do not sell widgets. They sell news and information and access to the primary platforms American use to receive this news and information. Control over production and distribution of information has critical implications for society and democracy. As a consequence, the merger of these two media giants reaches far beyond the economic size of the merging parties to the very content consumers receive and how they are permitted to access it.

Finally, if the size and scope of this merger is not sufficient to give you pause, the past actions of the acquiring party should. Comcast has raised cable rates for consumers every year and is among the lowest ranked companies in terms of customer service. Comcast is the frequent subject of program access complaints of competing video providers as well as of discriminatory carriage complaints by independent programmers. Finally, Comcast is on record lying to a federal agency regarding whether they blocked Internet users' access to a competing a video application for anti-competitive purposes. These past practices do not bode well for future competition if Comcast is allowed to acquire NBC. Further, Comcast's lack of candor in past proceedings cast[s] doubt on the prudence of relying on Comcast's voluntary public interest commitments as a means of addressing the anti-consumer impacts of this merger.

The goal of mega-mergers such as this is to cut costs and increase revenues. The most direct path to those outcomes are firing workers and raising prices. Cutting jobs is hardly a laudable goal in the current environment, but the primary "synergy" that mergers produce is the ability to reduce employment by sharing resources between the commonly-held companies. To expect the opposite to happen here based on the evidence-free assertions of Comcast would be foolhardy. Simply put, this merger is about higher prices, fewer choices, and lost jobs.

The Biggest Gets Bigger (and Stronger)

Comcast is the nation's largest cable operator, largest broadband service provider and one of the leading providers of regional cable sports and news networks. NBC is one of only four major national broadcast networks, the third largest major owner of local TV stations in terms of audience reach, an icon of local and national news production and the owner of one of a handful of major movies studios.

As large as Comcast is nationally, it is even more important as a local provider of video services. Comcast is a huge entity in specific product markets. It is the dominant multi-channel video programming distributor (MVPD) in those areas where it holds a cable franchise, accounting, on average for over half of the MVPD market. It is the dominant broadband access provider in the areas where it has a cable franchise, accounting for over half of that market. This dominance of local market distribution platforms is the source of its market power. The merger will eliminate competing distribution platforms in some of its markets and will give Comcast control over strategic assets to preserve and expand its market power in all of its markets.

Broadcasters and cable operators are producers of goods and services that compete head-to-head, including local news, sports, and advertising. In addition, NBC and Comcast are also suppliers of content and distribution platforms, which are goods and services that complement one another. In both roles there is a clear competitive rivalry between them. For example, in providing complementary services, broadcasters and cable operators argue about the price, channel location and carriage of content. The merger will eliminate this natural rivalry between two of the most important players in the multi-channel video space, a space in which there are only a handful of large players.

These anticompetitive effects of the merger are primarily what antitrust practice refers to as horizontal effects. They are likely to reduce competition in specific local markets—head-to-head competition in local video markets, head-to-head competition for programming viewers, head-to-head competition for distributions platforms. The merger will raise barriers to entry even higher through denial and manipulation of access to programming and the need to engage in two-stage entry. The merger will increase the likelihood of the exercise of existing market power within specific markets, and will increase the incentive and ability to raise prices or profits.

The fact that some of the leverage is brought to bear because of the link to complementary products (i.e. is vertical in antitrust terms), should not obscure the reality that the ultimate effects are on horizontal competition in both the distribution and programming markets. The merger would dramatically increase the incentive and ability of Comcast to raise prices, discriminate in carriage, foreclose and block competitive entry and force bundles on other cable systems. The merger enhances the ability of Comcast to preserve its position as the dominant local MVPD, reinforce its ability to exercise market power in specific cable or programming markets and extend its business model to the Internet.

We raise these concerns about the merger based on eight specific anticompetitive effects that the merger will have on the video market. . . .

Higher Prices, Fewer Choices, Less Competition

(1) This merger will reduce choice and competition in local markets. The merging parties currently compete head-to-head as distributors of video content, in local markets. Because broadcasters own TV stations, they compete with cable in local markets for audiences and advertisers—especially in the production and distribution of local news, and local and political advertising. This merger eliminates this head-to-head competition in 11 major markets where NBC owns broadcast stations and Comcast operates a cable franchise. These 11 markets account for nearly a quarter of U.S. TV households.

This merger also eliminates a competitor for local and political advertising. In fact, in 2006 NBC told the Federal Communications Commission that local cable operators present the single biggest threat to broadcasters in terms of securing local and political advertising.[1] Now that NBC is looking to merge with Comcast, the potential elimination of this local competition has been conveniently ignored. But federal authorities cannot and should not ignore the fact that a merger between Comcast and NBC is likely to cause a significant decline in competition in local advertising markets and excessive domination by the merged company. Not only will advertisers lose an important option, but the merger will be to the detriment of other local broadcasters—particularly smaller, independent ones—who are already facing ad revenue declines in an economic downturn. A stand-alone broadcaster will not be able to offer package deals and volume discounts for advertising across multiple channels the way that Comcast/NBC will be able to do post-merger. That means other local broadcasters will have less money to produce local news and hire staff. To compete, rival broadcasters will have two options: fire staff and reduce production of local news and information; or consolidate in order to compensate for market share lost to the new media mammoth.

(2) This merger removes an independent outlet and an independent source of news and information. These two companies compete in the video programming market, where Comcast's regional sports and news production compete with NBC's local news and sports production. By acquiring NBC, Comcast's incentive to develop new programming would be reduced. Instead of continuing to compete to win audience, it just buys NBC's viewers. Where two important entities were producing programming, there will now be one.

(3) The merger will eliminate competition between Comcast and NBC in cyberspace. NBC content is available online in a variety of forms and on different websites and services. Most prominently, of course, NBC is a stakeholder in Hulu—an online video distribution portal that draws millions of viewers. Comcast has put resources into developing its own online video site—"Fancast"—where consumers can find content owned by the cable operator. The merger eliminates this nascent, head-to-head competition.

Moreover, Comcast is the driving force behind the new "TV Everywhere" initiative. This collusive venture—which we believe merits its own antitrust investigation—would tie online video distribution of cable content to a cable subscription and pressure content providers to restrict or refrain from online distribution outside of the portal. This is a disaster for video competition. The proposed merger strengthens Comcast's hand in this scheme by increasing their market power in both traditional and online video distribution. Comcast is clearly attempting to control the distribution of the video content it makes available on the web by restricting sales exclusively to Comcast cable customers. It does not sell that content to non-Comcast customers. By contrast, NBC has exactly the opposite philosophy—or at least it did. Through Hulu, NBC is competing for both Comcast and non-Comcast customers by selling video online that is not tied to cable. NBC also has incentives to make its programming available in as many points of sale as possible. Merger with Comcast will put an end that pro-competitive practice.

(4) The merger will provide Comcast with greater means to deny rivals access to Comcast-controlled programming. Comcast already has incentive to undermine competing cable and satellite TV distributors by denying them access to critical, non-substitutable programming, or by extracting higher prices from competitors to induce subscribers to switch to Comcast. Post-merger it will have a great deal more content to use as an anticompetitive tool. Comcast has engaged in these anticompetitive acts in the past and by becoming a major programmer it will have a much larger tool to wield against potential competitors. Moreover, Comcast has opposed, and is currently challenging in court, the few rules in place that would prevent it from withholding its programming from competing services.

(5) The merger will provide greater incentive for Comcast to discriminate against competing independent programmers. Comcast already has a strong incentive to, and significant track record of, favoring its own programming over the content produced by others with preferential carriage deals. Post-merger it will have a lot more content to favor. The current regulatory structure does not appear sufficient to remedy the existing problem and cannot be expected to address the resulting post-merger threat to independent programmers. The econometric analysis of program carriage indicates there is a great deal of discrimination occurring already. The fact that the FCC is continually trying to catch up with complaints of program carriage discrimination is testimony to the existence of the problem and the inability of the existing rules to correct it.

(6) The merger will stimulate a domino effect of concentration between distributors and programmers. The new combination will create a major asymmetry in the current cartel model in the cable industry. It brings together a large cable provider with a huge stable of must-have programming *and* the largest wireline broadband platform in America. Very likely, this will trigger more mergers and acquisitions because it changes the dynamics of the market. But there will be no positive competitive outcomes resulting from this change.

This merger signals that the old, anticompetitive game is still on—but with a twist. Like all other cable operators, Comcast has never entered the service territory of a competing multi-channel video program provider, allowing everyone to preserve market power and relentlessly raise prices. But Comcast's expanded assets and especially its new leverage over the online video market will give it a substantial edge against its direct competitors in its service territory. The likely effect of the merger will be for other cable distribution and broadband companies to muscle up with their own content holdings to try and offset Comcast's huge advantage. In other words, there is only one way to deal with a vertically integrated giant that has must-have content and control over two distribution platforms—you have to vertically integrate yourself. This merger would send a signal to the industry that the decades old game of mutual forbearance from competition will be repeated but at the next level of vertical integration that spills over into the online market. Watch for AT&T and Verizon to be next in line for major content acquisitions. When that happens, it will be extremely difficult for any company that is merely a programmer or merely a distributor to get into the market. Barriers to entry to challenge vertically integrated incumbents will be nearly unassailable. The only option may be a two-stage entry into both markets at the same time—which is an errand reserved only for the brave and the foolish.

(7) By undermining competition, this merger will result in higher prices for consumers. Comcast already raises its rates every year for its cable subscribers, and prices are likely to rise further after the merger. By weakening competition, Comcast's market power over price is strengthened, but there are also direct ways the merger will push the price to consumers up. Comcast will have the opportunity and incentive to charge its competitors more for NBC programs and force competitors to pay for less desirable Comcast cable channels in order to get NBC programming—those added costs will mean bigger bills for cable subscribers. Furthermore, the lack of competitive pressure that has failed to produce any appreciable downward pressure on cable rates since 1983, will not discipline Comcast from raising its own rates.

(8) This merger will result in higher prices for consumers through the leveraging of "retransmission rights." Through its takeover of local NBC broadcast stations, Comcast will also gain special "retransmission consent rights," which allow stations to negotiate fees for cable carriage of broadcast signals. These rights will enable Comcast to leverage control over must-have local programming and larger bundles of cable channels to charge competing cable, telco and satellite TV providers more money for content. Additionally, once Comcast acquires a broadcaster, it will have the means and incentive to raise retransmission rights payments for NBC-owned stations. This will be reinforced by two factors. First, as the owner of NBC, Comcast profits from the retransmission payments it receives and does not lose from the retransmission payments it makes, which are passed through to consumers. Second, Comcast can charge competitors more for local NBC programming, and will be able to exploit asymmetric information. Cable operators do not publish what they pay for retransmission; broadcasters do not publish what they get. Because of Comcast's superior bargaining power, it will ask for more and pay less.

A Comcast/NBC Merger Should Not Be Allowed to Proceed

The merger has so many anti-competitive, anti-consumer, and anti-social effects that it cannot be fixed. Comcast's claim that FCC oversight will protect the public is absurd. The challenges that this merger poses to the future of video competition cannot be ignored, or brushed aside by reliance on FCC rules that have yet to remedy current problems and, thus, are ill-equipped to attend to the increased anticompetitive means and incentives that will result from Comcast's acquisition of NBC. The FCC rules have failed to break the stranglehold of cable to-date; there is no reason to believe they will be better able to tame the video giant that will result from this merger.

Further, any suggestion that the public interest commitments Comcast has made will solve these problems is misguided. Temporary band-aids cannot cure long-term structural injuries. Comcast's promises lack substance and accountability. More importantly, the commitments do not begin to address the anticompetitive effects of the merger. Many of Comcast's commitments amount to little more than a promise to obey the law. Where they go beyond current law, they largely fall within the company's existing business plans. Anything beyond that is meager at best, and in no way substitutes for the localism and diversity that a vigorously competitive industry would produce.

Over the past quarter century there have been a few moments when a technology comes along that holds the possibility of breaking the chokehold that cable has on the multi-channel video programming market, but on each occasion policy mistakes were made that allowed the cable industry to strangle competition. This is the first big policy moment for determining whether the Internet will function as an alternative platform to compete with cable. If policymakers allow this merger to go forward, the prospects for a more competition-friendly, consumer-friendly multi-channel video marketplace will be dealt a severe setback.

I urge policymakers to think long and hard before they allow a merger that gives the parties incentives to harm competition and consumers, while increasing their ability to act on those incentives. This hearing should be the opening round in what must be a long and rigorous inquiry into a huge complex merger of immense importance to the American people. It should be the first step in a review process that concludes the merger is not in the public interest and should not be allowed to close.

Note

1. NBC Media Ownership Comments, FCC Docket 06-121 (filed Oct. 2006).

Mark Cooper is the director of research of the Consumer Federation of America. He holds a PhD from Yale University. He is a former Yale University and Fulbright Fellow. He has written a book dealing with media and democracy and digital communication, and another titled *Cable Mergers and Monopolies*.

EXPLORING THE ISSUE

Should NBC and Comcast Be Allowed to Merge?

Critical Thinking and Reflection

1. How have antitrust issues related to media competition changed since the enactment of the Clayton Antitrust Act in 1914?
2. Why is it appropriate (or not so) for corporate mergers to come under the scrutiny of government in a free, capitalist society?
3. Is the persuasiveness (or even the credibility) of the "YES" argument compromised by the fact that it is presented only by the presidents of the two companies in question? How so?
4. The NBC–Comcast merger did in fact occur in January 2011, and Comcast became the sole owner in March 2013—so, has the Clayton Antitrust Act been violated? Explain.

Create Central

www.mhhe.com/createcentral

Additional Resources

Baker, C. Edwin, *Media Concentration and Democracy: Why Ownership Matters* (Cambridge University Press, 2007)

Hanson, Ralph E., *Mass Communication: Living in a Media World* (CQ Press, 2013)

Manishin, Glenn B., et al., *Recent Developments in Antitrust Law* (Aspatore Books, 2013)

Internet References . . .

Bloomberg: "Merger Made Comcast Strong, U.S. Web Users Weak"

www.bloomberg.com/news/2012-12-25/merger-made
-comcast-strong-u-s-web-users-weak.html

Huffington Post: "Comcastrophe: Comcast/NBC Merger Approved

www.huffingtonpost.com/josh-silver/comcastrophy
-comcastnbc-m_b_810380.html?view=print&
comm_ref=false"

www.huffingtonpost.com/josh-silver/comcastrophy
-comcastnbc-m_b_810380.html

Politico: "Comcast Merger Helps Consumers"

www.politico.com/news/stories/1210/46081.html

Unit 2

Macroeconomic Issues

UNIT

Macroeconomic Issues

*T*he economy incorporates the behavior of different groups, including consumers, businesses, and the government, to produce a wide variety of goods and services. One very large component of the American economy is health care. Major health care legislation was passed recently, and it will affect this important part of the economy for years to come. The government affects the economy in other ways as well: in its efforts to reduce unemployment, the way consumers interact with the firms that provide financial services, the minimum wage workers receive, and immigration. But consumers, when they act as voting citizens, select the political officials who pass the laws. These interactions are reflected in each of the issues and help underscore the importance of the issues.

ISSUE

Is Obamacare a Disaster for the Economy?

YES: Kathryn Nix, from "Top 10 Disasters of Obamacare," Heritage Foundation *WebMemo* #2848 (March 30, 2010)

NO: John Holahan, from "Will Health Care Reform Hurt the Economy and Increase Unemployment?" *Timely Analysis of Immediate Health Policy Issues* (August 2010)

Learning Outcomes

After reading this issue, you will be able to:

- Identify the official name of the health care act known widely as Obamacare.
- Cite the percentage of Republican votes against Obamacare in the 111th Congress.
- Explain what is meant by the "doc fix."
- Discuss the background of U.S. health care reform efforts dating back to Theodore Roosevelt.
- Consider the cost-containment effects of Obamacare.

ISSUE SUMMARY

YES: Heritage Foundation Researcher Kathryn Nix identifies 10 major problems with Obamacare (the Patient Protection and Affordable Care Act). Among other things, she argues that the legislation will hinder growth, increase the federal deficit, place new burdens on state governments, and, at the same time, discriminate against low-income workers.

NO: John Holahan, the director of the Health Policy Center at the Urban Institute, argues that Obamacare is "not likely to have a significant direct effect on the U.S. economy or on employment." More specifically, he states that state and local governments as well as small businesses should benefit from the legislation.

On March 23, 2010, President Barack Obama signed the Patient Protection and Affordable Care Act (PPACA) into law. Thus ended, at least for the remainder of the 111th Congress, one of the most heated and divisive debates in our nation's history. The extent of the controversy can be captured in several different ways. One way is the votes in the Senate and the House: the Senate vote was 60 to 39 with all the Republicans voting against, while the House vote was 219 to 212 with all 178 Republicans voting against; that is, every Republican in the Senate and the House voted against the bill. The controversy was also represented in the 2010 midterm elections with many House and Senate Republican candidates running on the promise to repeal Obamacare; that is, the arguments about health care reform will resume in the 112th Congress.

The general background of the health care debate is fairly well known. The United States spends more, relatively and absolutely, on health care than any other country in the world and, by a number of measures of health care status,

produces, at best, mediocre results. On the spending side, total health care expenditures in 2008 were estimated by the Centers for Medicare & Medicaid Services (CMS) at $2.3 trillion; this represented $7,681 for every person in the country and accounted for 16.2 percent of gross domestic product (GDP). CMS was projecting growth to 17.3 percent of GDP for 2009 and 19.3 percent of GDP by 2019. In terms of supplying these expenditures, CMS estimated that 23 percent came from businesses, 31 percent from households, 3 percent from private sponsors, and 42 percent from governments. With respect to health care results, the two measures used most frequently, especially by critics of the American health care system, are infant mortality (probability of dying by age 1 per 1,000 live births) and life expectancy. According to the World Health Organization, in 2008 the U.S. infant mortality rate (both sexes) stood at 7, a rate below that of other advanced economies including the United Kingdom (5), Spain (4), Sweden, (2), and Japan (2). In 2008, the U.S. life expectancy (at birth, both sexes) stood at 78 years, again below that of economies similar to the United States including the United Kingdom (80), Spain (81), Switzerland (82), and Japan (83).

Efforts to make significant changes in the way health care is provided date back to President Theodore Roosevelt and call for universal coverage. At that time, there were efforts during the presidency of Franklin Roosevelt to include publicly funded health programs in the Social Security legislation. President Harry Truman called for universal health care in 1949. Significant change did occur during the 1960s when President Johnson successfully pushed for Medicare and Medicaid. President Richard Nixon called for comprehensive health insurance in 1974. President Clinton produced a major health care plan in the 1990s but was unsuccessful in moving it through Congress. President George W. Bush supported legislation that achieved a major extension of Medicare—a prescription drug plan for the elderly and the disabled.

During the 2008 election campaign, both candidates pushed for health care changes. Senator John McCain's plan centered on the use of tax credits that would be of major assistance for individuals and families who did not have employer-provided health insurance. Then Senator Obama's proposal included the call for a National Health Insurance Exchange that included a government option. Others including America's Health Insurance Plan (AHIP is a national association representing approximately 1,300 health insurance companies) made their own proposals.

There was extensive debate and controversy as health care legislation worked its way through the 111th Congress. Various interest groups resorted to a variety of actions, including advertising and public demonstrations in an effort to shape the legislation to their ends. But the enactment of PPACA has not ended the debate and the controversy. State governments are suing to have the legislation declared unconstitutional. The new Republican House majority in the 112th Congress is expected to seek repeal of the legislation. Critics and supporters trade barbs as well as detailed analysis to support their positions. The selections here take a broad view of PPACA and provide representative samples of the arguments being made. Issue 8 in this volume takes a more narrow view, concentrating on the cost ramifications of PPACA.

YES

Kathryn Nix

Top 10 Disasters of Obamacare

President Obama recently signed gargantuan health care legislation into law that will have major ramifications for every man, woman, and child in the United States. This newly enacted law originates from the Senate health care bill (the "Patients Protection and Affordability Act") and a sidecar reconciliation bill that originated in the House. Between these two bills are countless provisions that grow federal spending, increase burdensome taxes, and put federal rules and regulations between Americans and control over their health care.

Outlined here are the 10 major ways in which the Left's so-called health care reform will hurt Americans.

1. New Spending Grows the Federal Deficit
The Congressional Budget Office (CBO), the official score-keeper for Congress, sets the projected cost of the health care package from 2010 to 2019 at $940 billion, reducing the deficit by $138 billion.[1] Unfortunately, the true cost of the new law will be far greater.

The CBO is proficient at its work, but it is required to score legislative proposals based on assumptions about the future behavior of Congress—not according to its more likely behavior. The authors of this legislation took advantage of this in crafting the language of the bill, employing several budgetary gimmicks to make it appear cheaper.

These include omitting cuts to Medicare provider payment rates, known as the "doc fix," double-counting savings from Medicare and the CLASS Act, indexing benefits to general inflation rather than medical inflation, and delaying the expensive provisions of the bill. When these costs are accounted for, the new law is more likely to cost closer to $2.5 trillion.[2] Such levels of spending will not only negate any projected deficit reduction but [also] increase the federal deficit further than would prior law.

2. Bending the Cost Curve in the Wrong Direction
The provisions of the legislation aimed at reducing health care spending are reactionary, addressing the symptoms rather than the root causes of growth in spending.[3] Instead of reducing spending in health care, the bill will increase overall health spending in the U.S. by $222 billion between now and 2019.[4]

In addition, CBO reports that premiums in the non-group market will increase by 10–13 percent as a result of the bill.[5]

3. New Taxes and Mandates Hinder Economic Growth
The new law requires employers who do not offer insurance deemed adequate by the federal government to pay a fine of $2,000 for every employee, exempting the first 30 employees. Employers forced to pay this penalty will have to reduce wages, cut jobs, or rely more heavily on part-time workers. Any of these options will be bad for the economy.[6]

The health care package also taxes investment income as a means to provide additional revenue to pay for the bill. The tax will discourage investment in the U.S. economy, thereby decreasing capital and reducing the potential for economic growth.

Heritage Foundation analysts Karen Campbell, Ph.D., and Guinevere Nell found that this tax, at President Obama's proposed rate of 2.9 percent, would reduce household disposable income by $17.3 billion a year.[7] The rate included in new law is 3.8 percent, so the actual effects are likely to be even more dramatic.

4. Regulations Grow Government Control over Health Care
The new law empowers the Department of Health and Human Services (HHS) to define a required benefits package that every health plan in America must include. Moreover, the law now allows the federal government to dictate the prices that insurers set through new age rating regulations and medical-loss ratio requirements.

The bill also opens the door for a de facto public option by creating government-sponsored national health plans to compete against private health plans in the health insurance exchanges the states are required to establish. The national health plans would be administered by the Office of Personnel Management (OPM), which currently runs the Federal Civil Service and also administers the Federal Employees Health Benefits Program, which serves federal workers and retirees.[8] OPM would make the rules for these government-sponsored plans.

Because of this difference in regulatory authority, it would be very easy for the OPM-administered health plans to secure an unfair advantage against other plans in the state insurance exchanges. The reason: They will not be subjected to the exact same rules and regulations that are set by HHS for private health insurers. This could result in a gaming of the system in favor of the government-sponsored health plans. It is also possible that the government-sponsored health plans could be protected from insolvency through taxpayer bailouts. [9] Government-sponsored enterprises are usually "too big to fail."

5. Expanding Broken Entitlement Programs

Under the new law, Medicaid will be extended to all Americans who fall below 133 percent of the federal poverty level. This is one of the primary means through which coverage is increased among the uninsured. According to CBO, of the 32 million newly insured in 2019, half will receive their coverage from Medicaid.[10]

As it stands, Medicaid is a low-quality, poorly functioning program that fails to meet the needs of the Americans it serves. In most states, Medicaid beneficiaries have great difficulty finding a doctor who will treat them at the program's low reimbursement rates and are more likely than the uninsured to rely on emergency rooms for care. Heritage Foundation Health Policy Fellow Brian Blase reports that, following an expansion of Tennessee's Medicaid program, health outcomes in Tennessee actually deteriorated and Tennessee's mortality rate declined at a much slower rate than surrounding states that did not expand their Medicaid programs.[11]

6. Burdening State Budgets

The reconciliation bill ensures that the federal government will cover the expansion of Medicaid benefits in all 50 states until 2017. Federal matching rates will decrease from 100 percent in 2017 to 93 percent in 2019, resting permanently there. Moreover, the 100 percent federal match rate does not include administrative costs, which Heritage analyst Ed Haislmaier finds will accrue a cost to the states of $9.6 billion between 2014 and 2019.[12]

The health care reconciliation bill further adds to several states' new costs by changing Medicaid funding formulas. The new law would increase payments for primary care providers to match Medicare payment rates. In the initial years of the expansion, the federal government will provide 100 percent of the funding. However, after two years, federal funding for increases in provider payment rates will end, leaving states to either find a way to pick up the cost or go back to lower reimbursement rates. This provision would thus only temporarily solve the problems Medicaid beneficiaries have finding primary care, instead digging an even bigger financial hole for the states, whose budgets are already in the red due to decreasing revenues.[13]

7. Neglecting Medicare

Medicare is due to become insolvent in 2016, and long-term unfunded liabilities exceed $38 trillion.[14] To address this, Medicare provider payment rates are scheduled to decrease annually according to the Sustainable Growth Rate. However, Congress votes to suspend these cuts every year, as it is a well-known fact that severe cuts in provider payments would result in many physicians refusing to see Medicare patients altogether.

Congress did not include a permanent way to repeal and pay for the cuts to physician reimbursement rates in their health care bills. Instead, they added a similar and even more unlikely "fix" to create savings in Medicare: more than half a trillion dollars in cuts to the program. These include billions in cuts to the popular Medicare Advantage program, which creates savings for seniors and gives them more options and control over their care. These savings—assuming they ever occur—will be used not to extend the solvency of the Medicare program but to fund the new entitlement programs that are now law.

8. Creates Discrimination Against Low-Income Workers

The employer mandate requires employers to offer a federally defined level of insurance or pay a fine. Moreover, even if an employer does offer insurance but their low-income employees qualify and elect to enter the health exchange instead, the employer will pay a $3,000 penalty for each employee who makes this choice. This is in addition to the cost of offering insurance.

In several cases, depending on the proportion of an employer's workforce that comes from low-income families, it would be more beneficial for employers to drop coverage altogether rather than pay for the increased penalty for employees in the exchange. This creates an incentive for employers to avoid hiring workers from low-income families, hurting those who need jobs the most.[15]

9. Exchange Eligibility Creates Inequity

The new law will create generous subsidies for Americans to purchase insurance in the newly created health exchanges. However, these subsidies will be available only to those who fall between 133 and 400 percent of the federal poverty level and are not offered federally defined sufficient assistance by their employer to purchase health insurance. All other Americans—including those in the very same income bracket—will not get subsidies but will instead rely only on the current tax exclusion for employer-sponsored insurance for federal assistance to purchase coverage. For workers with comparable incomes, the difference between this and the generous subsidy to buy insurance in the exchange will be thousands of dollars.[16]

The federal government will thus create a gross inequity between Americans making similar incomes. It is unlikely that this will be tolerated for long by the American public, which will instead demand that the subsidies be made more equitable. However, doing so will add enormously to the cost of the government overhaul of the health care system.

10. Questions of Constitutionality

The new law requires all Americans to purchase health insurance or pay a penalty. This represents an unprecedented extension of congressional power—never before has the federal government required Americans to purchase a good or service as a stipulation of being a lawful citizen.[17]

The health care overhaul also diminishes the federalist system upon which the U.S. was founded, which grants certain powers to the states in order to limit those of the federal government. The new law undermines state authority through the individual mandate to purchase insurance, a mandate to expand Medicaid (a state–federal joint program), and several new federal regulations of the insurance industry.

The End of the Beginning

These disasters are only the beginning of the vast effects the President's health care overhaul will have on the U.S. As bits and pieces of the law are implemented, its effects on states, businesses, and Americans of every ilk will become manifest. Congress and the American people should not view passage of the liberals' health care package as the end of the debate on reform. Rather, the long and tedious journey toward restoring personal control over health care dollars and decisions is just beginning.

Notes

[1] Congressional Budget Office, "H.R. 4872, Reconciliation Act of 2010," March 18, 2010, at http://www.cbo.gov/ftpdocs/113xx/doc11355/hr4872.pdf (March 29, 2010).

[2] James C. Capretta, "Obamacare Will Break the Bank, Not Reduce the Deficit," The Foundry, March 18, 2010, at http://blog.heritage.org/2010/03/18/obamacare-will-break-the-bank-not-cut-the-deficit/.

[3] Jason Fodeman and Robert A. Book, "Bending the Curve': What Really Drives Health Care Spending," Heritage Foundation *Backgrounder* No. 2369, February 17, 2010, at http://www.heritage.org/Research/Reports/2010/02/Bending-the-Curve-What-Really-Drives-Health-Care-Spending.

[4] Richard S. Foster, Chief Actuary, Centers for Medicare and Medicaid Services, "Estimated Financial Effects of the 'Patient Protection and Affordable Care Act,' as Passed by the Senate on December 24, 2009," January 8, 2010, at http://www.cms.hhs.gov/ActuarialStudies/Downloads/SPPACA 2010-01-08.pdf (March 29, 2010).

[5] Congressional Budget Office, "An Analysis of Health Insurance Premiums Under the Patient Protection and Affordable Care Act," November 30, 2009, at http://www.cbo.gov/ftpdocs/l07xx/doc10781/11-30-Premiums.pdf (March 29, 2010).

[6] John Ligon and Robert A. Book, "The House Health Fix: Even Higher Tax Penalties for Employers," Heritage Foundation *WebMemo* No. 2837, March 19, 2010, at http://www.heritage.org/Research/Reports/2010/03/The-House-Health-Fix-Even-Higher-Tax-Penalties-for-Employers.

[7] Karen Campbell and Guinevere Nell, "The President's Health Proposal: Taxing Investments Undermines Economic Recovery," Heritage Foundation *WebMemo* No. 2817, February 25, 2010, at http://www.heritage.org/Research/Reports/2010/02/The-Presidents-Health-Proposal-Taxing-Investments-Undermines-Economic-Recovery.

[8] Robert Moffit and Kathryn Nix, "The Public Health Plan Reincarnated: New—and Troubling—Powers for OPM," Heritage Foundation *Backgrounder* No. 2364, January 21, 2010, at http://www.heritage.org/Research/Reports/2010/01/The-Public-Health-Plan-Reincarnated-New-and-Troubling-Powers-for-OPM.

[9] The Honorable Linda Springer, Donald Devine, the Honorable Dan Blair, and Robert Moffit, "The Office of Personnel Management: A Power Player in America's Health Insurance Markets?" Heritage *Lecture* No. 1145, January 20, 2010, at http://www.heritage.org/Research/Lecture/The-Office-of-Personnel-Management-A-Power-Player-in-Americas-Health-Insurance-Markets.

[10] Congressional Budget Office, "H.R. 4872, Reconciliation Act of 2010."

[11] Brian Blase, "Obama's Proposed Medicaid Expansion: Lessons from TennCare," Heritage Foundation *WebMemo* No. 2821, March 3, 2010, at http://www.heritage.org/Research/Reports/2010/03/Obamas-Proposed-Medicaid-Expansion-Lessons-from-TennCare.

[12] Edmund Haislmaier, "Expanding Medicaid: The Real Costs to the States," Heritage Foundation *WebMemo* No. 2757, January 14, 2010, at http://www.heritage.org/Research/Reports/2010/01/Expanding-Medicaid-The-Real-Costs-to-the-States.

[13] Dennis Smith, "Medicaid Expansion Ignores States' Fiscal Crises," Heritage Foundation *WebMemo* No. 2744, January 5, 2010, at http://www.heritage.org/Research/Reports/2010/01/Medicaid-Expansion-Ignores-States-Fiscal-Crises.

[14] See Boards of Trustees, Federal Hospital Insurance and Federal Supplementary Medical Insurance Trust Fund, "2009 Annual Report," May 12, 2009, at http://www.cms.hhs.gov/ReportsTrustFunds/downloads/tr2009.pdf (March 29, 2010).

[15] Ligon and Book, "The House Health Fix."

[16] James C. Capretta, "The Senate Health Care Bill's 'Firewall' Creates Disparate Subsidies," Heritage Foundation *WebMemo* No. 2730, December 11, 2009, at http://www.heritage.org/Research/Reports/2009/12/The-Senate-Health-Care-Bills-Firewall-Creates-Disparate-Subsidies.

[17] Randy Barnett, Nathaniel Stewart, and Todd Gaziano, "Why the Personal Mandate to Buy Health Insurance Is Unprecedented and Unconstitutional," Heritage Foundation *Legal Memorandum* No. 49, December 9, 2009, at http://www.heritage.org/Research/Reports/2009/12/Why-the-Personal-Mandate-to-Buy-Health-Insurance-Is-Unprecedented-and-Unconstitutional.

KATHRYN NIX is a research assistant in the Center for Health Policy Studies at the Heritage Foundation. She was also a research assistant at the Center for Eukaryotic Structural Genomics at the University of Wisconsin. She holds a bachelor's degree from the University of Wisconsin and has also studied at l'Institut Catholique de Paris.

John Holahan **NO**

Will Health Care Reform Hurt the Economy and Increase Unemployment?

The Patient Protection and Affordable Care Act (PPACA) provides for a major expansion of health insurance coverage through Medicaid expansions and tax credits. The cost of the expansion is offset by cuts in Medicare payment rates and new taxes and penalties. Despite fears expressed by some in the political arena, health reform is not likely to have a significant direct effect on the U.S. economy or on employment. The changes in spending and taxes in health reform generally have offsetting effects and are simply too small relative to the overall size of the economy, to have much of an impact.

Over the six-year period, 2014–2019, the Congressional Budget Office (CBO) estimated net new federal spending on health care (over and above reductions in spending by Medicare and other government programs) to be about $439 billion.[1] The projected gross domestic product (GDP) over this period is about $116 trillion; thus, new spending would amount to almost 0.4 percent of GDP. Over the entire 2010–2019 period, new spending on health care (net of reductions in current payments) would be roughly the same while the GDP would be $178 trillion; over this period, spending would be 0.2 percent of GDP. Using a different modeling approach and considering spending from all sources, the Centers for Medicare and Medicaid Services (CMS) actuaries estimated the increase in national health expenditures to be $311 billion over 10 years, less than 0.2 percent of 10 years of GDP.[2]

Offsetting Effects

This does not mean that there will not be important effects on individual sectors of the economy. The expansion of health insurance coverage will lead to an increase in spending ($938 billion over 10 years, mostly from 2014 to 2019) and demand for labor in the health sector. It should also increase the use of medical equipment, new technologies and pharmaceuticals, and will likely lead to wage and salary increases in the health sector. Health reform is partially financed through spending reductions in Medicare and other government programs ($511 billion).[3] These reductions will have the opposite effect, that is, reduce the demand for labor and the purchase of services and equipment in health care sector. The net effect,

however, will be positive, higher net spending in the health care sector.

On the other hand, the net new spending will be financed through various taxes on insurers, medical device and pharmaceutical manufacturers, and earned and unearned income of individuals with incomes above $200,000 ($250,000 for couples). The increased taxes on health care providers and insurers could mean higher prices for drugs, medical devices and insurance premiums, which could mean reduced demand for drugs and medical devices and, thus, fewer jobs in those sectors. These effects are likely to be small, as discussed below.

PPACA also includes an excise tax on high-cost insurance plans; the new tax is expected to increase federal revenues by $32 billion in 2018 and 2019 and increasing amounts thereafter.[4] The higher excise tax is likely to lead people to choose less comprehensive health insurance plans that presumably will have higher cost-sharing requirements than the plans people would purchase in the absence of the new tax. Thus, the government will either obtain revenue directly from the excise tax or from income taxes on the higher wages and salaries that will result as employers pay less for health insurance. The penalties paid by individuals who do not sign up for coverage and employers that do not offer coverage will yield another $69 billion in revenues.[5] The increased taxes, penalties, and higher out-of-pocket expenses (from less comprehensive coverage) will reduce the discretionary income individuals and families have to spend on other goods and services, which could consequently reduce the demand for labor in various sectors.

The increased payroll taxes on those with incomes above $200,000 will have a small effect on demand for goods and services because only a very small population will be affected, and the wealthiest people are the least likely to change their buying behavior as a consequence of a new tax. The same is true for the tax on unearned income and its effect on investment decisions. The estimated revenue from the taxes on payroll and unearned income is only $210 billion; again, this is over an eight-year period in which cumulative GDP is $148 trillion (0.19 percent of GDP).

The ultimate result is that the economic impact of coverage expansions, reductions in current Medicare and other government spending, and new taxes are largely offsetting. There is actually more in offsets and new revenues than in new spending, and thus a small reduction in the deficit ($143 billion). The overall effect on gross domestic product will be extremely small. Given that the health sector is one of the more labor-intensive sectors in the U.S. economy, health care reform could result in a small aggregate increase in employment. There are many other forces that will have a much greater impact on economic activity over the 10-year period than health reform.

Cost Containment

The efforts to contain costs will have the opposite effect. To the extent that the cost containment efforts are successful, they will reduce the growth in health care costs. This will reduce incomes in the health care sector, as well as the demand for labor, but will increase the discretionary income that individuals and families have. Thus, if the efforts are successful, there will be additional spending outside the health sector that will increase the demand for labor in other sectors.

Successful cost containment will have other economic effects as well. One will be to reduce the growth in spending on Medicare and, after the initial expansion, Medicaid. This reduces the taxes or borrowing the federal government has to undertake to finance these programs. The Council of Economic Advisers has argued that containing costs of the two large federal programs would reduce the federal budget deficit, increase national savings, keep interest rates lower, and increase economic growth.[6] The CBO and the Joint Tax Committee both project the excise tax on high-cost insurance plans to reduce the growth rate of annual health care costs by 0.5 percentage points per year once implemented.[7] Curtailing the growth of health care costs would mean lower costs for businesses and individuals. The Council of Economic Advisers has estimated that reducing the growth in health care costs by 1 percentage point per year would result in a GDP 4 percent higher by 2030.[8] This would occur because of a higher national savings rate, more capital formation, and higher output. Faster growth in GDP would mean more jobs, lower unemployment, and higher family incomes.

State and Local Governments

State and local governments will also benefit from reduced spending on state-funded indigent care programs and uncompensated care resulting under reform because of increased coverage. Medicaid enrollment will increase, but states will bear only a small share of the new Medicaid spending.[9] State and local taxes could thus be lowered, or states could redirect resources to education and infrastructure projects.

New Taxes and Innovation

Concerns have been raised that the taxes on drugs and medical device manufacturers could adversely affect innovation and discovery of new pharmaceuticals and technologies. This seems unlikely to be a serious concern because the new revenues in these industries from expanded coverage would considerably exceed the new taxes. The "fees" on drug manufacturers would amount to $27 billion between 2012 and 2019. When compared with projected prescription drug spending of almost $3 trillion between 2012 and 2019, the amount of the assessment is less than 1 percent of prescription drug spending over this period. These fees could be passed onto insurers, in which case drug manufacturers would suffer no loss in net revenues; this of course depends on drug companies' ability to negotiate with insurers. There is certain to be more demand for prescription drugs because of the expanded coverage. We estimate an increase in prescription drug revenues from expanded coverage of about $65 billion between 2014 and 2019, a considerably greater amount than the new fees.[10] Not all of this would mean higher profits for pharmaceutical manufacturers (a share of new revenues goes to wholesalers and retail outlets) but the new revenues should easily exceed the new taxes, if in fact the manufacturers do bear them in the end.

The same argument can be made for medical device manufacturers, though the excise tax imposed on this industry will be somewhat greater as a percentage of spending on medical devices. Nonetheless, increased spending by newly insured people under reform will largely offset the negative effects of taxes. Thus, incentives for medical device manufacturers to innovate and create new products should be relatively unaffected by the new excise taxes. If the number of uninsured would have grown in the absence of reform, demand for medical devices would have declined. To the extent that expanded coverage means increased demand, the incentives for innovation in this area are at best increased and at least unchanged.

Impact on Small Business

Some have argued that penalties in the law for not offering coverage to workers who end up receiving government subsidies will hurt small businesses. This argument ignores the fact that small businesses (with fewer than 50 workers) will be exempt from any such penalties. The Council of Economic Advisers has estimated that insurance premiums for small businesses will fall considerably because of access to coverage through exchanges.[11] This will increase the competitiveness of small firms in the marketplace, increase entrepreneurship, and provide workers with greater incentives to work in small businesses.

The vast majority of businesses that are not exempt from the penalties under PPACA already provide coverage to their employees. In 2008, 97 percent of employers with 50 or more employees offered health insurance to their workers.[12] While a few businesses with more than 50 workers may have to provide coverage for the first time or pay a penalty if their workers obtain exchange-based subsidies, in the long run, much of the cost of coverage will be passed onto workers in the form of lower wages; the economic effects of this should be unimportant in practice, given the small number of employers affected. Some firms will not be able to pass the cost of coverage back to workers because of minimum wage laws. This could reduce profitability, or alternatively, could lead to reduced employment. Again, this is unlikely to affect the economy significantly because the increased spending on health insurance will mean a corresponding increase in the demand for labor in the health sector. In addition, some small firms will likely cease offering coverage, potentially leading to increases in wages and salaries. Overall, the impact on small businesses should be positive given the availability of lower-cost plans and the significant commitment to cost containment reflected in the law.

Other Effects

Health reform will affect the overall economy in other ways, but these effects are also likely to be quite small. First, health reform will reduce "job lock," that is, the tendency for individuals to stay in a given job to retain their health insurance. Because health reform will allow for considerably more flexibility in the movement from job to job, it will make the labor market more efficient and increase economic productivity. Second, to the extent that health reform improves health in the long term, as is expected, it should increase labor supply by reducing disability and worker absenteeism, improve learning, and increase workers' productivity. These effects, however, should take a considerable period of time and will probably have a relatively small impact on the economy.

Conclusion

PPACA is unlikely to have a major aggregate effect on the U.S. economy primarily because the changes in spending and taxes are quite small relative to the size of the economy; moreover, most of the effects offset each other. Increased spending will increase the demand for health services and the demand for labor in health sector. Cuts in Medicare and cost-containment provisions will have opposite effects. The net effect on employment is likely to be slightly positive because the health sector is labor-intensive. New taxes on insurers and medical device and pharmaceutical manufacturers could have adverse effects on those industries except for the fact that coverage expansion should provide new revenues well in excess of the new tax obligations. Cost-containment efforts, if successful, should reduce the growth in spending on Medicare and eventually on Medicaid, which would reduce the taxes or borrowing the federal government has to undertake. Cost containment that reduces the federal budget deficit would result in faster economic growth, more employment, and higher family incomes. The impacts on small businesses are likely to be insignificant, because most small businesses will be exempt from any penalties. Most firms affected by potential penalties (those employing 50 or more workers) already provide health insurance. Overall, small businesses should benefit from the availability of lower-cost plans and efforts to increase competition and contain costs within exchanges.

Notes

1. Congressional Budget Office, "Letter to the Honorable Nancy Pelosi Providing Estimates of the Spending and Revenue Effects of the Reconciliation Proposal" (Washington, DC: Congressional Budget Office, March 20, 2010).
2. Centers for Medicare and Medicaid Services, Office of the Actuary, "Estimated Financial Effects of the 'Patient Protection and Affordable Care Act'" (Baltimore, MD: Centers for Medicare and Medicaid Services, 2010).
3. Congressional Budget Office, "Letter to the Honorable Nancy Pelosi," 2010.
4. Congressional Budget Office, "Letter to the Honorable Nancy Pelosi," 2010.
5. Congressional Budget Office, "Letter to the Honorable Nancy Pelosi," 2010.
6. Council of Economic Advisers, the Executive Office of the President, "The Economic Case for Health Care Reform" (Washington, DC: Council of Economic Advisers, 2009).
7. Council of Economic Advisers, the Executive Office of the President, "The Economic Case for Health Care Reform: Update" (Washington, DC: Council of Economic Advisers, 2009).
8. Council of Economic Advisers, "Update," 2009.
9. J. Holahan and I. Headen, "Medicaid Coverage and Spending in Health Reform: National and State-by-State Results for Adults at or below 133% FPL" (Kaiser Commission on Medicaid and the Uninsured, 2010).
10. We derived an estimate of the growth in prescription drug spending due to increases in coverage as follows: Assuming drug spending remains constant as a share of expenditures by insured persons, we estimate about $300 in additional prescription drug spending by each of those who would gain insurance coverage under reform in 2014. Assuming the same growth rate for personal health care spending as currently projected in the National Health Accounts, and using CBO estimates of the reduction in the number of uninsured, we would predict that the prescription drug spending would increase by about $65 billion between 2014 and 2019.

11. Council of Economic Advisers, Executive Office of the President, "The Economic Effects of Health Care Reform on Small Businesses and Their Employees" (Washington, DC: Council of Economic Advisers, 2009).
12. Agency for Healthcare Research and Quality, Center for Financing, Access, and Cost Trends, "Percent of Private-Sector Establishments That Offer Health Insurance by Firm Size and Selected Characteristics: United States, 2008" (Rockville, MD: Agency for Healthcare Research and Quality, 2008), http://www.meps.ahrq.gov/mepsweb/data_stats/summ_tables/insr/national/series_1/2008/tia2.pdf.

JOHN HOLAHAN is the director of the Urban Institute's Health Policy Research Center. He holds a PhD in economics from Georgetown University. His research focuses on state health policy and issues of federalism and health.

EXPLORING THE ISSUE

Is Obamacare a Disaster for the Economy?

Critical Thinking and Reflection

1. Does extreme party division over controversial legislation make it easier or more difficult for Americans to be objective in their own assessments? Explain.
2. Given that health care is something that essentially everyone needs, why has the provision of such evolved into one of the most heated and divisive issues in our history?
3. How might Obamacare lead to employment, wage, and salary increases in the health sector?
4. Consider the "top 10 disasters of Obamacare" cited by Nix, and discuss how many (and which ones) seem irrefutably disastrous.

Is There Common Ground?

Logic dictates that common ground is the point from which opposing sides can examine the possibility of compromise. At its best, common ground can facilitate what is for the common good. The subject of health care for Americans has never been without its common ground—certainly no politician has ever suggested depriving citizens of health services, and no American wants to be so deprived. What's more, there has long been a fairly unifying sentiment that the inequity of health care coverage among Americans is a real problem, especially as medical costs continue to escalate.

Yet the debate on health care reform in the United States has wavered between simmering and raging for more generations than any living person can recall. The positions presented here regarding Obamacare are stark reminders of how divisive the subject can be. Although the common ground may remain intact, the respective arguments of Kathryn Nix (anti-Obamacare) and John Holahan (pro-Obamacare) clearly demonstrate that we are still a long way from using it to facilitate a compromise-driven plan for the common good.

Create Central

www.mhhe.com/createcentral

Additional Resources

Blackman, Josh, *Unprecedented: The Constitutional Challenge to Obamacare* (PublicAffairs, 2013)

Gruber, Jonathan, *Health Care Reform: What It Is, Why It's Necessary, How It Works* (Hill and Wang, 2011)

Haines, Ronald, *Obamacare Explained* (CreateSpace Independent Publishing Platform, 2013)

Turner, Grace-Marie, et al., *Why ObamaCare Is Wrong for America* (HarperCollins, 2011)

Internet References . . .

Bangor Daily News: "Supreme Court Ruling Caps Century of Debate over How to Get Medical Care for All"

http://bangordailynews.com/2012/06/28/politics/supreme-court-ruling-caps-a-century-of-american-debate-over-how-to-get-medical-care-for-all/

CNN Politics: "Latest House Bid Fails as Bitter Back-and-Forth over Government Shutdown Rages"

www.cnn.com/2013/10/01/politics/government-shutdown/index.html

HealthCare.gov: "How Does the Health Care Law Protect Me?"

www.healthcare.gov/how-does-the-health-care-law-protect-me/

ISSUE

Will Health Reform's Pilot Programs Lead to the Control of Health Care Costs?

YES: Atul Gawande, from "The Health-Care Bill Has No Master Plan for Curbing Costs. Is That a Bad Thing?" *The New Yorker* (December 14, 2009)

NO: Alain C. Enthoven, from "Would Reform Bills Control Costs? A Response to Atul Gawande," *Health Affairs* (December 22, 2009)

Learning Outcomes

After reading this issue, you will be able to:

- Discuss the improvements in U.S. agriculture through the trial and error of pilot programs.
- Explain why Enthoven calls Gawande's agriculture analogy "inapt."
- Address the topic of health-insurance exchanges.
- Identify and give a brief profile of the legislation known as PPACA.

ISSUE SUMMARY

YES: Atul Gawande, a surgeon, an associate professor in the Department of Health Policy and Management at the Harvard School of Public Health, who served as a senior health policy advisor in the White House from 1992 to 1993, argues that the transformation of American agriculture began with a pilot program, and the numerous pilot programs to test ways to curb costs and improve quality contained in the health care legislation could similarly transform health care.

NO: Alain C. Enthoven, an economist and a professor emeritus at Stanford University's Graduate School of Business, who served as a consultant to the Carter administration and researched unsustainable growth in national health expenditures and costs of health insurance and market-based universal health insurance in the United States, responds that Gawande's analysis is flawed and the agriculture analogy is "inapt"—while farmers wanted better crops and "generally welcomed or tolerated pilots to show the better ways," the "Medical Industrial Complex does not want such pilots and often strangles them in the crib."

There are many who believe that the primary goal of health care reform in the United States is—or should be—the control and the reduction of costs of its health care delivery system. The different ways that this could be done, and have been proposed in the debate toward the new legislation, have been, are being, and will most likely continue to be argued, contested, debated, resisted, and lobbied for, as advocates seek to advance their views and demonstrate the superiority of the measures they favor over the measures approved by others. It is pointed out that there is a lack of clear consensus about how to contain health costs in America.

The Patient Protection and Affordable Care Act (PPACA) contains several provisions to reduce costs and improve quality. However, as Stephen Zuckerman of the Urban Institute states, these provisions are not as well tested as are the limits on Medicare payments that will offset half the costs of the expanding coverage to about 34 million more Americans by 2019. One of the provisions to contain costs in the new law is health insurance exchanges, believed by some to have the potential to grow into a very powerful mechanism for cost control. Through these exchanges, individuals would buy insurance from providers who would comply with basic coverage standards. Zuckerman notes that the exchanges could promote competition among plans based on price and quality.

Another element of cost containment is an excise tax on high-cost health plans that is scheduled to go into effect in 2018: CBO projected the biggest cost containment and revenue effects to occur in the decade thereafter. The tax controls premium growth, giving employers an incentive to reduce the generosity of benefits (cost simulators estimate that wages would then grow more quickly).

Another measure, delivery system and payment reforms, would move the system away from rewarding providers for more services toward one that reduces waste, slows spending growth, and rewards quality care. The provisions under this head include development of Accountable Care Organizations (ACOs) responsible for the cost and quality of care delivered to a subset of traditional Medicare beneficiaries. CBO projected that this provision will save Medicare $4.9 billion. Some provisions aimed at improving efficiency could contain costs in the future, although CBO did not expect savings from them during the first 10 years of reform. One such program is a national pilot program on payment bundling in Medicare—one payment for *all* services provided during an episode of care as opposed to payments for individual services. Another program is for development of value-based purchasing for hospitals and physicians.

PPACA also provides for the Independent Payment Advisory Board to slow Medicare and private spending growth. The Board would recommend Medicare spending cuts in years in which per capita Medicare growth exceeded the increase in an average of two price indices. Its recommendations would become law unless Congress passed an alternative proposal to achieve the same budgetary savings. CBO estimated that this provision would save Medicare $15.5 billion between 2015 and 2019.

Additionally, the new health care law puts greater emphasis on prevention and wellness programs. PPACA also seeks broader efforts to reduce waste, fraud, and abuse: CBO projected a fall in spending of $2.9 billion and an increase in revenue of $0.9 billion over 10 years.

A number of people look to the many pilot programs provided for in the health care legislation as having the most significant promise of cost control and cost reduction. Many others do not agree with this view, favoring other approaches. The selections here isolate this one element in the debate over the effect of the reforms on health care costs in the United States.

Will Health Reform's Pilot Programs Lead to the Control of Health Care Costs?

91

YES

Atul Gawande

The Health-Care Bill Has No Master Plan for Curbing Costs. Is That a Bad Thing?

Cost is the spectre haunting health reform. For many decades, the great flaw in the American health-care system was its unconscionable gaps in coverage. Those gaps have widened to become graves—resulting in an estimated forty-five thousand premature deaths each year—and have forced more than a million people into bankruptcy. The emerging health-reform package has a master plan for this problem. By establishing insurance exchanges, mandates, and tax credits, it would guarantee that at least ninety-four percent of Americans had decent medical coverage. This is historic, and it is necessary. But the legislation has no master plan for dealing with the problem of soaring medical costs. And this is a source of deep unease.

Health-care costs are strangling our country. Medical care now absorbs eighteen percent of every dollar we earn. Between 1999 and 2009, the average annual premium for employer-sponsored family insurance coverage rose from $5,800 to $13,400, and the average cost per Medicare beneficiary went from $5,500 to $11,900. The costs of our dysfunctional health-care system have already helped sink our auto industry, are draining state and federal coffers, and could ultimately imperil our ability to sustain universal coverage.

What have we gained by paying more than twice as much for medical care as we did a decade ago? The health-care sector certainly employs more people and more machines than it did. But there have been no great strides in service. In Western Europe, most primary-care practices now use electronic health records and offer after-hours care; in the United States, most don't. Improvement in demonstrated medical outcomes has been modest in most fields. The reason the system is a money drain is not that it's so successful but that it's fragmented, disorganized, and inconsistent; it's neglectful of low-profit services like mental health care, geriatrics, and primary care, and almost giddy in its overuse of high-cost technologies such as radiology imaging, brand-name drugs, and many elective procedures.

At the current rate of increase, the cost of family insurance will reach twenty-seven thousand dollars or more in a decade, taking more than a fifth of every dollar that people earn. Businesses will see their health-coverage expenses rise from ten percent of total labor costs to seventeen percent. Health-care spending will essentially devour all our future wage increases and economic growth. State budget costs for health care will more than double, and Medicare will run out of money in just eight years. The cost problem, people have come to realize, threatens not just our prosperity but our solvency.

So what does the reform package do about it? Turn to page 621 of the Senate version, the section entitled "Transforming the Health Care Delivery System," and start reading. Does the bill end medicine's destructive piecemeal payment system? Does it replace paying for quantity with paying for quality? Does it institute nationwide structural changes that curb costs and raise quality? It does not. Instead, what it offers is . . . pilot programs.

This has provided a soft target for critics. "Two thousand seventy-four pages and trillions of dollars later," Mitch McConnell, the Senate Minority Leader, said recently, "this bill doesn't even meet the basic goal that the American people had in mind and what they thought this debate was all about: to lower costs." According to the Congressional Budget Office, the bill makes no significant long-term cost reductions. Even Democrats have become nervous. For many, the hope of reform was to *re-form* the health-care system. If nothing is done, the United States is on track to spend an unimaginable ten trillion dollars more on health care in the next decade than it currently spends, hobbling government, growth, and employment. Where we crave sweeping transformation, however, all the current bill offers is those pilot programs, a battery of small-scale experiments. The strategy seems hopelessly inadequate to solve a problem of this magnitude. And yet—here's the interesting thing—history suggests otherwise.

At the start of the twentieth century, another indispensable but unmanageably costly sector was strangling the country: agriculture. In 1900, more than forty percent of a family's income went to paying for food. At the same time, farming was hugely labor-intensive, tying up almost half the American workforce. We were, partly as a result, still a poor nation. Only by improving the productivity of farming could we raise our standard of living and emerge as an industrial power. We had to reduce food costs, so that families could spend money on other goods, and resources could flow to other economic sectors. And we had to make farming less labor-dependent, so that more of the population could enter non-farming occupations and support economic growth and development.

America's agricultural crisis gave rise to deep national frustration. The inefficiency of farms meant low crop yields, high prices, limited choice, and uneven quality. The agricultural system was fragmented and disorganized, and ignored evidence showing how things could be done better. Shallow plowing, no crop rotation, inadequate seedbeds, and other habits sustained by lore and tradition resulted in poor production and soil exhaustion. And lack of coordination led to local shortages of many crops and overproduction of others.

You might think that the invisible hand of market competition would have solved these problems, that the prospect of higher income from improved practices would have encouraged change. But laissez-faire had not worked. Farmers relied so much on human muscle because it was cheap and didn't require the long-term investment that animal power and machinery did. The fact that land, too, was cheap encouraged extensive, almost careless cultivation. When the soil became exhausted, farmers simply moved; most tracts of farmland were occupied for five years or less. Those who didn't move tended to be tenant farmers, who paid rent to their landlords in either cash or crops, which also discouraged long-term investment. And there was a deep-seated fear of risk and the uncertainties of change; many farmers dismissed new ideas as "book farming." . . .

The United States did not seek a grand solution. Private farms remained, along with the considerable advantages of individual initiative. Still, government was enlisted to help millions of farmers change the way they worked. The approach succeeded almost shockingly well. The resulting abundance of goods in our grocery stores and the leaps in our standard of living became the greatest argument for America around the world. And, as the agricultural historian Roy V. Scott recounted, four decades ago, in his remarkable study "The Reluctant Farmer," it all started with a pilot program.

In February, 1903, Seaman Knapp arrived in the East Texas town of Terrell to talk to the local farmers. He was what we'd today deride as a government bureaucrat; he worked for the United States Department of Agriculture. Earlier in his life, he had been a farmer himself and a professor of agriculture at Iowa State College. He had also been a pastor, a bank president, and an entrepreneur, who once brought twenty-five thousand settlers to southwest Louisiana to farm for an English company that had bought a million and a half acres of land there. Then he got a position at the U.S.D.A. as an "agricultural explorer," travelling across Asia and collecting seeds for everything from alfalfa to persimmons, not to mention a variety of rice that proved more productive than any that we'd had. The U.S.D.A. now wanted him to get farmers to farm differently. And he had an idea.

Knapp knew that the local farmers were not going to trust some outsider who told them to adopt a "better" way of doing their jobs. So he asked Terrell's leaders to find just one farmer who would be willing to try some "scientific" methods and see what happened. The group chose Walter C. Porter, and he volunteered seventy acres of land where he had grown only cotton or corn for twenty-eight years, applied no fertilizer, and almost completely depleted the humus layer. Knapp gave him a list of simple innovations to follow—things like deeper plowing and better soil preparation, the use of only the best seed, the liberal application of fertilizer, and more thorough cultivation to remove weeds and aerate the soil around the plants. The local leaders stopped by periodically to confirm that he was able to do what he had been asked to.

The year 1903 proved to be the most disastrous for cotton in a quarter century because of the spread of the boll weevil. Nonetheless, at the end of the season Porter reported a substantial increase in profit, clearing an extra seven hundred dollars. He announced that he would apply the lessons he had learned to his entire, eight-hundred-acre property, and many other farmers did the same. Knapp had discovered a simple but critical rule for gaining cooperation: "What a man hears he may doubt, what he sees he may possibly doubt, but what he does himself he cannot doubt."

The following year, the U.S.D.A. got funding to ramp up his activities. Knapp appointed thirty-three "extension agents" to set up similar demonstration farms across Texas and into Louisiana. The agents provided farmers with technical assistance and information, including comparative data on what they and others were achieving. As experience accrued, Knapp revised and refined his list of recommended practices for an expanding range of crops and livestock. The approach proved just as successful on a larger scale.

The program had no shortage of critics. *Southern Farm Magazine* denounced it as government control of agriculture. But, in 1914, after two years of stiff opposition, Congress passed the Smith–Lever Act, establishing the U.S.D.A. Cooperative Extension Service. By 1920, there were seven thousand federal extension agents, working in almost every county in the nation, and by 1930 they had set up more than seven hundred and fifty thousand demonstration farms.

As Daniel Carpenter, a professor of government at Harvard, points out, the demonstration-farm program was just one of a hodgepodge of successful U.S.D.A. initiatives that began as pilots. Another was devoted to comparative-effectiveness research: experimental stations were established—eventually, in every state—that set about determining the most productive methods for growing plants and raising livestock. There was a pilot investigation program, which, among other things, traced a 1904 fruit-decay crisis in California to cuts in the fruit from stem clippers and the fingernails of handlers (and, along the way, introduced modern packing methods industry-wide). The U.S.D.A.'s scientific capabilities grew into the world's greatest biological-discovery machine of the time. . . .

What seemed like a hodgepodge eventually cohered into a whole. The government never took over agriculture, but the government didn't leave it alone, either. It shaped a feedback loop of experiment and learning and encouragement for farmers across the country. The results were beyond what anyone could have imagined. Productivity went way up, outpacing that of other Western countries. Prices fell by half. By 1930, food absorbed just twenty-four percent of family spending and twenty percent of the workforce. Today, food accounts for just eight percent of household income and two percent of the labor force. It is produced on no more land than was devoted to it a century ago, and with far greater variety and abundance than ever before in history.

This transformation, though critical to America's rise as a superpower, involved some painful dislocations: farms were consolidated; unproductive farmers were winnowed out. As the historian Sally Clarke, of the University of Texas at Austin, has pointed out, it's astonishing that the revolution took place without vast numbers of farm foreclosures and social unrest. We cushioned the impact of the transformation—with, for instance, price supports that smoothed out the price decline and avoided wholesale bankruptcies. There were compromises and concessions and wrong turns. But the strategy worked, because United States agencies were allowed to proceed by trial and error, continually adjusting their policies over time in response not to ideology but to hard measurement of the results against societal goals. Could something like this happen with health care?

There are, in human affairs, two kinds of problems: those which are amenable to a technical solution and those which are not. Universal health-care coverage belongs to the first category: you can pick one of several possible solutions, pass a bill, and (allowing for some tinkering around the edges) it will happen. Problems of the second kind, by contrast, are never solved, exactly; they are *managed*. Reforming the agricultural system so that it serves the country's needs has been a process, involving millions of farmers pursuing their individual interests. This could not happen by fiat. There was no one-time fix. The same goes for reforming the health-care system so that it serves the country's needs. No nation has escaped the cost problem: the expenditure curves have outpaced inflation around the world. Nobody has found a master switch that you can flip to make the problem go away. If we want to start solving it, we first need to recognize that there is no technical solution.

Much like farming, medicine involves hundreds of thousands of local entities across the country—hospitals, clinics, pharmacies, home-health agencies, drug and device suppliers. They provide complex services for the thousands of diseases, conditions, and injuries that afflict us. They want to provide good care, but they also measure their success by the amount of revenue they take in, and, as each pursues its individual interests, the net result has been disastrous. Our fee-for-service system, doling out separate payments for everything and everyone involved in a patient's care, has all the wrong incentives: it rewards

doing more over doing right, it increases paperwork and the duplication of efforts, and it discourages clinicians from working together for the best possible results. Knowledge diffuses too slowly. Our information systems are primitive. The malpractice system is wasteful and counterproductive. And the best way to fix all this is—well, plenty of people have plenty of ideas. It's just that nobody knows for sure.

The history of American agriculture suggests that you can have transformation without a master plan, without knowing all the answers up front. Government has a crucial role to play here—not running the system but guiding it, by looking for the best strategies and practices and finding ways to get them adopted, county by county. Transforming health care everywhere starts with transforming it somewhere. But how?

We have our models, to be sure. There are places like the Mayo Clinic, in Minnesota; Intermountain Healthcare, in Utah; the Kaiser Permanente health-care system, in California; and Scott & White Healthcare, in Texas, that reliably deliver higher quality for lower costs than elsewhere. Yet they have had years to develop their organizations and institutional cultures. We don't yet know how to replicate what they do. Even they have difficulties. Kaiser Permanente has struggled to bring California-calibre results to North Carolina, for instance. Each area has its own history and traditions, its own gaps in infrastructure, and its own distinctive patient population. To figure out how to transform medical communities, with all their diversity and complexity, is going to involve trial and error. And this will require pilot programs—a lot of them.

Pick up the Senate health-care bill—yes, all 2,074 pages—and leaf through it. Almost half of it is devoted to programs that would test various ways to curb costs and increase quality. The bill is a hodgepodge. And it should be.

The bill tests, for instance, a number of ways that federal insurers could pay for care. Medicare and Medicaid currently pay clinicians the same amount regardless of results. But there is a pilot program to increase payments for doctors who deliver high-quality care at lower cost, while reducing payments for those who deliver low-quality care at higher cost. There's a program that would pay bonuses to hospitals that improve patient results after heart failure, pneumonia, and surgery. There's a program that would impose financial penalties on institutions with high rates of infections transmitted by health-care workers. Still another would test a system of penalties and rewards scaled to the quality of home health and rehabilitation care.

Other experiments try moving medicine away from fee-for-service payment altogether. A bundled-payment provision would pay medical teams just one thirty-day fee for all the outpatient and inpatient services related to, say, an operation. This would give clinicians an incentive to work together to smooth care and reduce complications. One pilot would go even further, encouraging clinicians to band together into "Accountable Care Organizations" that take responsibility for all their patients' needs, including prevention—so that fewer patients need operations in the first place. These groups would be permitted to keep part of the savings they generate, as long as they meet quality and service thresholds.

The bill has ideas for changes in other parts of the system, too. Some provisions attempt to improve efficiency through administrative reforms, by, for example, requiring insurance companies to create a single standardized form for insurance reimbursement, to alleviate the clerical burden on clinicians. There are tests of various kinds of community wellness programs. The legislation also continues a stimulus-package program that funds comparative-effectiveness research—testing existing treatments for a condition against one another—because fewer treatment failures should mean lower costs.

There are hundreds of pages of these programs, almost all of which appear in the House bill as well. But the Senate reform package goes a few U.S.D.A.-like steps further. It creates a center to generate innovations in paying for and organizing care. It creates an independent Medicare advisory commission, which would sort through all the pilot results and make recommendations that would automatically take effect unless Congress blocks them. It also takes a decisive step in changing how insurance companies deal with the costs of health care. In the nineteen-eighties, H.M.O.s tried to control costs by directly overruling doctors' recommendations (through requiring pre-authorization and denying payment); the backlash taught them that it was far easier to avoid sicker patients and pass along cost increases to employers. Both the House and the Senate bills prevent insurance companies from excluding patients. But the Senate plan also imposes an excise tax on the most expensive, "Cadillac" insurance plans. This pushes private insurers to make the same efforts that public insurers will make to test incentives and programs that encourage clinicians to keep costs down.

Which of these programs will work? We can't know. That's why the Congressional Budget Office doesn't credit any of them with substantial savings. The package relies on taxes and short-term payment cuts to providers in order to pay for subsidies. But, in the end, it contains a test of almost every approach that leading health-care experts have suggested. (The only one missing is malpractice reform. This is where the Republicans could be helpful.) None of this is as satisfying as a master plan. But there can't be a master plan. That's a crucial lesson of our agricultural experience. And there's another: with problems that don't have technical solutions, the struggle never ends.

Recently, I spoke with the agricultural extension agent for my home town, Athens, Ohio. His name is Rory Lewandowski. He is fifty-one and has been the extension agent there for nine years. He grew up on a Minnesota dairy farm and got a bachelor's degree in animal science and agronomy from the University of Minnesota and a master's degree in agronomy from the University of Wisconsin. He spent most of his career in farm education, including eight years in Bolivia, where, as a volunteer for the Mennonite Central Committee, he created demonstration farms in an area where the mining economy had collapsed. . . .

I'd caught Lewandowski in his office on a Saturday. He routinely puts in sixty-five to eighty hours a week at his job. He has a five-week small-ruminant course for sheep and goat producers; a ten-week master-gardener course; and a grazing school. His wife, Marcia, who has written two knitting books, handles registration at the door. He sends out a monthly newsletter. He speaks with about half the farmers in the county in the course of a year.

Mostly, the farmers come to him—for guidance and troubleshooting. He told me about a desperate message that a farmer left him the other day. The man's spinach plants had been afflicted with downy mildew and were collapsing. "He said he was going to lose his whole crop by the weekend and all the markets that he depended on," Lewandowski said. He called the farmer back and explained that the disease gets started with cooler temperatures and high humidity. Had the farmer been using overhead watering?

Yes, he said, but he had poked around the Internet and was thinking about switching to misting.

Not a good idea. "That still leaves too much moisture on the leaf," Lewandowski said. He recommended that the farmer switch to drip irrigation and get some fans in his greenhouse, too.

The farmer said that he'd thought about fans but worried that they would spread the spores around.

They will, Lewandowski said. "But you need wetness on the leaves for four to six hours to get penetration through the leaf cuticle," he explained. If the plants were dried out, it wouldn't be a problem. "You've got to understand the biology of this," he said to me.

He doesn't always understand the biology himself. He told me about a beef farmer who had been offered distiller's grain from a microbrewery and wanted to know whether he could feed it to his cows. Lewandowski had no idea, but he called the program's beef extension expert and got the answer. (Yes, with some limits on how much he put in a ration.) A large organic farm called with questions about growing vegetables in high tunnels, a relatively new innovation that the farm had adopted to extend its growing season. Lewandowski had no experience with this, but an extension agent in Wooster, Ohio, was able to supply information on what had worked best elsewhere.

"You have to be able to say, 'I don't know, but I can figure that out for you,'" Lewandowski said. . . .

I asked him if he has had any victories. All the time, he said. But he had no illusions: his job will never end.

Cynicism about government can seem ingrained in the American character. It was, ironically, in a speech to the Future Farmers of America that President Ronald Reagan said, "The ten most dangerous words in the English language are 'Hi, I'm from the government, and I'm here to help.'" Well, Lewandowski is from the government, and he's here to help. And small farms in Athens County are surviving because of him. What he does involves continual improvisation and education; problems keep changing, and better methods of managing them keep emerging—as in medicine.

In fact, when I spoke with Lewandowski about farming in Athens, I was struck by how much it's like the health-care system there. Doctors typically work in small offices, with only a few colleagues, as in most of the country. The hospital in Athens has less than a tenth the number of beds that my hospital in Boston has. The county's clinicians could do much more to control costs and improve quality of care, and they will have to. But it will be an ongoing struggle.

My parents recently retired from medical practice in Athens. My mother was a pediatrician and my father was a urologist. I tried to imagine what it would be like for them if they were still practicing. They would be asked to switch from paper to electronic medical records, to organize with other doctors to reduce medical complications and unnecessary costs, to try to arrive at a package price for a child with asthma or a man with kidney stones. These are the kinds of changes that everyone in medicine has to start making. And I have no idea how my parents would do it.

I work in an academic medical group in Boston with more than a thousand doctors and a vastly greater infrastructure of support, and we don't know the answers to half these questions, either. Recently, I had a conversation with a few of my colleagues about whether we could accept a bundled payment for patients with thyroid cancer, one of the cancers I commonly treat in my practice as a surgeon. It seemed feasible until we started thinking about patients who wanted to get their imaging or radiation done elsewhere. There was also the matter of how we'd divide the money among the surgeons, endocrinologists, radiologists, and others involved. "Maybe we'd have to switch to salaries," someone said. Things were getting thorny. Then I went off to do an operation in which we opened up about a thousand dollars' worth of disposable materials that we never used.

Surely we can solve such problems; the reform bill sets out to find ways that we can. And, in the next several years, as the knowledge accumulates, I suspect that we'll

need our own Seaman Knapps and Rory Lewandowskis to help spread these practices county by county.

We'll also need data, if we're going to know what is succeeding. Among the most important, and least noticed, provisions in the reform legislation is one in the House bill to expand our ability to collect national health statistics. The poverty of our health-care information is an embarrassment. At the end of each month, we have county-by-county data on unemployment, and we have prompt and detailed data on the price of goods and commodities; we can use these indicators to guide our economic policies. But try to look up information on your community's medical costs and utilization—or simply try to find out how many people died from heart attacks or pneumonia or surgical complications—and you will discover that the most recent data are at least three years old, if they exist at all, and aren't broken down to a county level that communities can learn from. It's like driving a car with a speedometer that tells you only how fast all cars were driving, on average, three years ago. We have better information about crops and cows than we do about patients. If health-care reform is to succeed, the final legislation must do something about this.

Getting our medical communities, town by town, to improve care and control costs isn't a task that we've asked government to take on before. But we have no choice. At this point, we can't afford any illusions: the system won't fix itself, and there's no piece of legislation that will have all the answers, either. The task will require dedicated and talented people in government agencies and in communities who recognize that the country's future depends on their sidestepping the ideological battles, encouraging local change, and following the results. But if we're willing to accept an arduous, messy, and continuous process we can come to grips with a problem even of this immensity. We've done it before.

ATUL GAWANDE is a general and endocrine surgeon at Brigham and Women's Hospital in Boston and the associate director of the Center for Surgery and Public Health. He is also an associate professor at the Harvard School of Public Health and an associate professor of surgery at Harvard Medical School. He has written on medical matters for both the *New Yorker* and *Slate* magazines.

Alain C. Enthoven

→ **NO**

Would Reform Bills Control Costs? A Response To Atul Gawande

Atul Gawande, MD, is one of the best medical writers of our time. I subscribed to the *New Yorker* just so I could read him. I reached eagerly for my Dec. 14, 2009 *New Yorker* when I heard he had an article there[1]. I was deeply disappointed. What worries me is that his article will be used to support a political campaign to gloss over the failure of proposed legislation to significantly moderate health expenditure growth.

Gawande acknowledges that the cost of health care "... will essentially devour all our future wage increases and economic growth. The cost problem, people have come to realize, threatens not just our prosperity but our solvency." "So what does the reform package do about it? ... Does it institute nationwide structural changes that curb costs and raise quality? It does not. Instead what it offers is ... pilot programs."

Gawande goes on the recount the history of how the Agricultural Extension service did research, developed pilots to test the results, persuaded farmers to try the pilots, and sparked the agricultural revolution that so benefited the US economy in the first half of the 20th century. And he goes on to suggest that the many pilot programs for health care improvement proposed in the Senate bill could lead to a similar result and transform American health care.

His analysis is deeply flawed.

The Farmers Were Willing Partners; The Medical Industrial Complex Is Not

First, the agriculture analogy is inapt. In the case of early 20th century agriculture in the United States, the Agricultural Extension Service was working with the winds of market incentives at its back, helping it to move forward. That is, the Extension Service was helping farmers to do exactly what farmers wanted to do—if only they had the necessary information about what works—that is, innovate to improve quality, productivity and profits. The Department of Agriculture's goals and the farmers' incentives were aligned.

That is not the case in medicine today. Physicians complain that doing the right thing costs them money.

The incentives in today's dominant payment model are oriented to doing more, spending more, using more complex methods when simpler methods would do just as well for the patient. I recall the chancellor of a famous academic medical center complaining: "We introduced innovations that saved thousands of dollars in patient care and the result was that we lost the dollars in revenue."

Virginia Mason Clinic[2] in Seattle offered a well-publicized example. Stopping the wasteful practice of doing an MRI on every lower back patient cost them a lot of revenue and drove the diagnosis and treatment of back pain from very profitable to being a loser. I doubt they'll ever want to do that again.

Second, Gawande got it wrong about pilots. In agriculture, the farmers wanted better crops and generally welcomed or tolerated pilots to show the better ways. The Medical Industrial Complex does not want such pilots and often strangles them in the crib. For example, nothing lasting and significant came of the pilot to reward people for getting their heart bypass surgery at regional centers of excellence. I don't remember the details of how it died, but I believe it was tried and went nowhere. No doubt every hospital thought it was a center of excellence and wanted to be so rewarded.

Another more recent example is durable medical equipment. David Leonhardt had an excellent article in the *New York Times* on June 25, 2008 called "High Medicare Costs Courtesy of Congress[3]." Someone had sold the good idea that prices of durable medical equipment should be determined by competition, and there was a provision in law for pilots to test competition. The industry lobbied hard to stop it and promulgated scare stories. "Grandma won't get her oxygen." Leonhardt recounts how Democratic and Republican leaders got together and postponed the pilot—and, I suspect, postponed it forever. There were proposals to test health plan competition, fought off by the industry of course. So this is not a fertile political environment for pilots. In fact, one of the most important lessons that has come out of the current "reform" process is the enormous power of the medical industrial complex and their large financial contributions and armies of lobbyists to block any significant cost containment.

Moreover, we do have some excellent and outstanding prototypes of better care at less cost. Gawande and the President name them: the Mayo Clinic[4], Kaiser

Permanente[5], Intermountain Healthcare, Geisinger[6], Scott and White, etc. So if they are so great, why haven't they proliferated and taken over America?—a question I have been hearing and answering for at least 30 years.

I wrote a paper called "Curing Fragmentation with Integrated Delivery Systems" for a June 2008 Harvard Law School conference[7], soon to appear in a book by Oxford Press[8]. Briefly, in the first half of the 20th Century, the medical profession went all out to strangle these group practices with many reprehensible anti-competitive tactics. The Supreme Court found[9] that organized medicine had violated the Sherman [A]ct when trying to destroy the Group Health Association. When Russell V. Lee founded the Palo Alto Clinic, the Santa Clara County Medical Society expelled him[10], and his expulsion had significant negative consequences for his malpractice insurance and hospital privileges. Organized medicine got laws passed to outlaw "the corporate practice of medicine".

Then came World War II with the well-known story of how exemption of health benefits from [w]age and [p]rice controls and income taxes put health insurance into employers' hands. And, for various reasons, most employers don't offer choices of health insurers, blocking competitive market entry by the health plans affiliated with medical groups. Or, if they do offer choices, employers like the state of Massachusetts pay 80–100% of the premium for the plan of the employee's choice, thus depriving efficient plans the opportunity to market their superior cost-effectiveness. On the other hand, a few employers like the University of California, Stanford—and, I believe, Harvard—as well as the states of Wisconsin and California offer choices and a fixed dollar contribution so that efficient systems can reach the market and sell their superior cost-effectiveness. In these employment groups, large majorities usually choose efficient integrated delivery systems. That experience ought to be replicated across America.

As I listened to the President and read Gawande's citation of the iconic delivery systems, I thought "I wish they would ask themselves what it is about this health insurance market that prevents the Hondas and Toyotas of medical care from winning out." There is an answer. If America wants 1,000 pilot projects to blossom and grow into significant improvements in health care delivery, it must reform its system based on the principles of competition and wide, responsible, informed, individual consumer choice of health plans. Experience shows that people will join if they get to keep the savings.

No Time to Wait

The third major flaw in Gawande's analysis is that we do not have time to wait for the decades it took for the agricultural revolution to happen. In 2009, health care is draining the federal budget some $1.15 trillion, which accounts for most of the federal deficit of $1.4 trillion. (This includes the revenue loss from the exclusion of employer contributions from taxable incomes.) Worse yet, that amount is keyed to the growth in National Health Expenditures, growing some 2.7% per year faster than non-health care GDP. The track we are on is feeding soaring deficits. So President Obama and Budget Director Peter Orzag have been right in saying that we must reform health care to get expenditures under control.

The tragedy is that the two laws working their way through Congress do practically nothing to slow health expenditures, except for the excise tax on high cost plans (a good and important idea) and pilots. The excise tax would be a lot more effective if it were accompanied by a system to assure people choices so that they could respond to the incentive in the tax.

Health care expenditures are now doing great damage to our society's future, crowding out education, infrastructure, criminal justice and research, all of which are important for health in the long run. This will make it much harder to pay for projects intended to mitigate greenhouse gasses and climate change as well as to pay for the military forces needed to deny Al Qaeda safe havens from which to plan attacks.

This is a nation founded on a tax revolt, and Americans' tolerance for taxes is low. The case for more taxes is not helped by the obvious and generally acknowledged wastefulness in the health care system (which government now pays most of) or by the obvious failure of public schools to do their job. And of course, health care's contribution to the national debt is burdening future generations and risking our fiscal future.

The American people are being deceived. We are being told that health expenditure must be curbed, therefore "reform is necessary." But the bills in Congress, as Gawande acknowledges, do little or nothing to curb the expenditures. When the American people come to understand that "reform" was not followed by improvement, they are likely to be disappointed. Our anguish is only intensified by the fact that the Republicans are no better at fiscal responsibility, probably worse as they demagogue reasonable attempts to limit expenditures.

Congress is sending the world an unmistakable signal that it is unable or unwilling to control health expenditures and the fiscal deficit. That is not going to make it easier to sell Treasury bonds on international markets. I fear this will lead to higher interest rates.

The Way Forward

What should be done? I explained it in my "Consumer Choice Health Plan" articles[11] in the 1978 *New England Journal of Medicine*. The idea is also in a recent report by the Committee for Economic Development[12] (CED). The general idea is for government to pay everyone's way into the purchase of an efficient or low-cost health plan, meeting standards in their state or region but no more; if people want something that costs more, they must pay the difference with their own net after-tax dollars. Additionally, the creation of exchanges that broker multiple choices of health plans would drive the delivery system to produce better value through consumer choice and competition.

Of course, this cannot be done in one stroke. Incremental steps are needed. One of the best legislative expressions of this was the Managed Competition Act[13] (MCA) of 1992 and 1993 sponsored by Conservative Democratic congressmen Cooper, Andrews and Stenholm. Briefly, create exchanges (then called Health Plan Purchasing Cooperatives, the same idea) in every state, require all employment groups up to 100 employees to buy through the exchange (to continue to qualify for the tax exclusion), cap the tax exclusion at the price of the low-priced plan in the exchange, and use the savings to subsidize health insurance for low-income people. The Congressional Budget Office[14] estimated that the number of uninsured below the poverty line would decline from 15 million to 4 million, and National Health Expenditures would be reduced below the baseline projection.

The Committee for Economic Development report starts out like the MCA and describes a smooth transition rolling out exchanges to successively larger employment groups until all employees have the benefits of choice and competition to serve them. The bi-partisan Wyden-Bennett "Healthy Americans Act"[15] is built on the same principles. In the late 1990s, the bi-partisan Commission on the Future of Medicare[16] proposed a similar idea to convert Medicare to defined contributions or "premium support" payments and offer multiple choices of competing alternative plans. Victor Fuchs and Ezekiel Emanuel[17] proposed a similar concept. In all these cases, cost conscious individuals would limit expenditure growth by choosing plans offering the most value for money.

Notes

[1] An article there: http://www.newyorker.com/reporting/2009/12/14/091214fa_fact_gawande.
[2] Virginia Mason Clinic: http://content.healthaffairs.org/cgi/content/abstract/26/4/w532.
[3] High Medicare Costs Courtesy of Congress: http://www.nytimes.com/2008/06/25/business/25leonhardt.html.

[4] Mayo Clinic: http://content.healthaffairs.org/cgi/content/abstract/hlthaff.28.2.w173.
[5] Kaiser Permanente: http://content.healthaffairs.org/cgi/content/abstract/28/2/323.
[6] Geisinger: http://content.healthaffairs.org/cgi/content/abstract/27/5/1235.
[7] June 2008 Harvard Law School conference: http://www.law.harvard.edu/programs/petrie-flom/PDFs/OUR%20FRAGMENTED%20HEALTH%20CARE%20SYSTEM%20.pdf.
[8] A book by Oxford Press: http://www.oup.com/us/catalog/general/subject/Law/HealthMedicalLaw/?view=usa&sf=toc&ci=9780195390131.
[9] Supreme Court found: http://supreme.justia.com/us/317/519/case.html.
[10] expelled him: http://www.fresh-thinking.org/docs/workshop_090108/Commentary_A_Enthoven.pdf.
[11] Consumer Choice Health Plan articles: http://content.nejm.org/cgi/content/abstract/298/12/650.
[12] Report by the Committee for Economic Development: http://www.ced.org/images/newsroom/2009/hcexchanges121609.pdf.
[13] Managed Competition Act: http://www.archive.org/details/hr3222managedcom00unit.
[14] Congressional Budget Office: http://www.cbo.gov/doc.cfm?index=5009&type=0.
[15] Wyden-Bennett "Healthy Americans Act": http://thomas.loc.gov/cgi-bin/bdquery/z?d111:S391.
[16] Commission on the Future of Medicare: http://thomas.loc.gov/medicare/.
[17] Victor Fuchs and Ezekiel Emanuel: http://www.robert-h-frank.com/PDFs/Emanuel-Fuchs.NEJM.3-24-05.pdf.

ALAIN C. ENTHOVEN is the Marriner S. Eccles professor of public and private management, emeritus, and a senior fellow, emeritus, Freeman Spogli Institute for International Studies at Stanford University. He is a fellow of the American Academy of Arts and Sciences. Since 1980, his teaching has been focused on health care. He holds degrees in economics from Stanford, Oxford, and the Massachusetts Institute of Technology.

EXPLORING THE ISSUE

Will Health Reform's Pilot Programs Lead to the Control of Health Care Costs?

Critical Thinking and Reflection

1. During the early twentieth century, in what ways were the Department of Agriculture's goals and the farmers' incentives aligned?
2. Does an understanding of successful pilot programs necessarily shed valuable light on how to model and/or conduct other pilot programs? Why or why not?
3. Are there ways in which the goals of the medical industry could be aligned with the goals of heath reformers? Explain.
4. How is efficiency helped or hindered by employers who offer choices and fixed-dollar contributions in their health insurance plans?

Is There Common Ground?

Gawande asks us first to consider how America's agriculture was transformed (even rescued) through a series of pilot programs, and then to see the useful parallels to today's pilot programs for health reform. Enthoven's essay is a direct response, pointing out why the agriculture analogy simply does not fit.

In that the very purpose of Enthoven's argument is to counter Gawande's entire premise, common ground is not an essential feature. But on a more peripheral level, we would have to recognize that Enthoven does not disagree about the positive effects of pilot programs on U.S. agriculture, so it is at least somewhat feasible that Gawande could present a point that Enthoven might consider applicable to health reform. Even if that is an unlikely scenario, there is little doubt that the two share an interest in the complex issue of controlling health care costs in the United States, and that both are compelled to find reform approaches that will work.

Create Central

www.mhhe.com/createcentral

Additional Resources

Enthoven, Alain, *Health Care, the Market and Consumer Choice* (Edward Elgar Publishing, 2012)

McCan, Robert L., *Citizen's Guide to Health Care Reform: Understanding the Affordable Care Act Paperback* (CreateSpace Independent Publishing Platform, 2012)

United States Government Congress, *The Patient Protection and Affordable Care Act PPACA: "Obama Care"* (CreateSpace Independent Publishing Platform, 2010)

Internet References . . .

Chief Executive.net: "Controlling Health Care Costs"

http://chiefexecutive.net/controlling
-health-care-costs

New York Times Economix: "Controlling Health Care Spending, Revisited"

http://economix.blogs.nytimes.com/2013/08/16
/controlling-health-care-spending-revisited/?_r=0

Washington Post Wonkblog: "This Is Why Controlling Health-Care Costs Is Almost Impossible"

www.washingtonpost.com/blogs/wonkblog
/wp/2013/08/21/this-is-why-controlling-health
-care-costs-is-almost-impossible/

ISSUE

Did the American Recovery and Reinvestment Act of 2009 Create Jobs?

YES: Josh Bivens, from "Testimony before the U.S. House of Representatives Budget Committee" (July 14, 2010)

NO: Veronique de Rugy, from "Testimony before the U.S. House of Representatives Budget Committee" (July 14, 2010)

Learning Outcomes

After reading this issue, you will be able to:

- Explain why the 2007–2009 recession deserves the name "Great Recession."
- Identify the two interrelated factors that were at work to make the Great Recession so severe.
- Debate the effectiveness of the American Recovery and Reinvestment Act (ARRA).
- Define the term "multiplier effect."

ISSUE SUMMARY

YES: Josh Bivens of the Economic Policy Institute argues that the American Recovery and Reinvestment Act (ARRA) was badly needed, it worked, it was cheap, and that another similar effort is needed.

NO: Veronique de Rugy of George Mason University believes that ARRA, in spite of claims made on its behalf, "appears to have lost money by destroying growth."

According to the National Bureau of Economic Research, the nonprofit, nongovernment arbiter of U.S. business cycles, the economy's latest recession began in December 2007 and lasted for 18 months, ending in June 2009. The economic downturn was the steepest of the 11 recessions the U.S. economy has experienced since the Great Depression of the 1930s. For this reason, it is now referred to as the Great Recession. There are several reasons why the latest contraction is worthy of the title. First, at 18 months the length of the Great Recession was 2 months longer than any of the other 10 recessions. Second, the unemployment rate rose from 4.4 percent in May 2007 to a recession high of 10.1 percent in October 2009 (unemployment typically decreases only after the rest of the economy begins to improve) with the number of unemployed persons rising from 6.8 million to 15.6 million. Third, real gross domestic product fell from $13.4 trillion in the third quarter of 2007 to $12.8 trillion in the second quarter of 2009, a loss of almost 4.5 percent in total production. To make matters worse, the recovery since the official end of the Great Recession has been described as anemic at best.

What made the Great Recession so severe? Two interrelated factors were at work: the collapse of the housing bubble with a significant decline in housing prices and a sharp contraction in the construction industry combined with financial distress as a number of financial markets and financial firms experienced illiquidity and insolvency. The breadth and depth of the economic problems brought forth a multipronged governmental response. The Bush administration proposed and Congress passed the Emergency Economic Stabilization Act that included the Troubled Assets Relief Program (most often referred to as the bank bailout bill). In addition, the Federal Reserve took both conventional and unconventional actions, reducing interest rates to record lows and providing funds to banks and other financial organizations. Even after the end of the recession, the Federal Reserve continued to engage in expansionary monetary policy with what is called quantitative easing, that is, the purchase of agency securities, mortgage-backed securities, and longer-term treasury securities.

The Obama administration came into power in January 2009 in the latter part of the Great Recession when unemployment rates were still rising and the end of the recession was nowhere in sight. They decided that a stimulus package was necessary with government remedying the lack of private demand with a combination of tax cuts and spending increases. The stimulus package was the top priority of the new administration and the Democratically controlled House and Senate. The official name of the stimulus package was the American Recovery and Reinvestment Act (ARRA), and President Obama signed it into law on February 17, 2009, less than a month after his inauguration. The final version of ARRA did not receive any Republican votes in the House, and only three Republican votes were cast in its favor in the Senate. The Obama administration described ARRA as "the largest countercyclical fiscal action in American history."

The stimulus package was estimated at $787 billion and was divided into two parts: $281 billion of tax cuts and increased spending of $506 billion. The tax cuts, including the Making Work Pay tax credit, a homebuyer tax credit, a $70 billion adjustment to the alternative minimum tax, and expansion of the earned income tax credit were primarily directed to individuals. Business tax cuts included an extension of bonus depreciation that reduced taxes on new investment and tax credits for renewable energy pro-

duction. The increased spending was spread over a variety of programs, including $45 billion in aid to local school districts, $28 billion in highway and bridge construction, $40 billion in extended unemployment benefits, and a one-time payment of $250 to seniors, veterans, and people with disabilities.

As indicated by the votes in the House and the Senate, ARRA was controversial. For example, the Republicans favored a greater emphasis on tax cuts and less reliance on increased spending. Some individuals were concerned about the impact of ARRA on the federal government's deficit and debt. Still others worried that the efforts to reduce unemployment and return the economy to a path of economic growth would be unsuccessful. Some who took this position believed the stimulus was too small to have much of an impact, while others, like de Rugy in her testimony, pointed to empirical evidence regarding spending multipliers. Bivens, although he supports additional stimulus efforts, believes ARRA was successful.

YES  Josh Bivens

Testimony before the U.S. House of Representatives Budget Committee

In assessing the economic impact of the American Recovery and Reinvestment Act (ARRA, the Recovery Act henceforth) there are essential four arguments I'd like to make today:

- First, the Recovery Act was needed, and badly. The American economy at the end of 2008 and the beginning of 2009 was essentially in freefall and all other policy tools that had been tried had little effect in arresting the decline.
- Second, it worked as advertised. It has created almost 5 million fulltime equivalent jobs and kept the unemployment rate from sitting well over 11% today. Unfortunately, the economic crisis that it was meant to address called for much stronger medicine than the Recovery Act by itself could provide.
- Third, it was cheap. While the sticker-price of the Recovery Act (estimated at $787 billion when passed) is often characterized in press accounts as enormous, it was less than half as large as the full-cost of the tax cuts enacted during the 2000s, smaller than the cost of wars in Iraq and Afghanistan, and, most importantly, small relative to the economic shock it was meant to absorb. Further, because it spurred economic activity and tax collections and reduced the need for safety net spending, its net budgetary impact was likely less than half the $787 billion amount.
- Fourth, lessons learned from the passage of the Recovery Act should be heeded: More fiscal support should be provided to prop up the economy and spur a genuine recovery in the jobs-market. While the Recovery Act worked as advertised and the economy today would be worse off if it had not been passed, unemployment still sits at 9.5% today and will surely rise above 10% over the coming year, returning to pre-recession levels only several years from now unless more fiscal support is provided.

It Was Needed

The root of the current recession is simple to identify: the bursting of the housing bubble and its fallout. Between 1997 and 2006, the real price of homes in the U.S. economy, which had been roughly flat for many decades, almost doubled. Given that the stock of housing in the

U.S. is enormous, this led to a huge increase in wealth. Because so few influential economists correctly pointed out that this wealth increase was sure to be ephemeral, U.S. households began borrowing against the value of their homes to support current consumption. When the housing bubble popped, these same households realized that meeting long-run wealth targets (planning for retirement or sending their kids to college) could no longer be financed out of rising housing wealth, so they began saving. As households began saving, businesses, seeing a threat to new sales, stopped investing to expand their own capacity.

This negative shock to private sector spending was enormous—between the end of 2006 and the beginning of 2009, the private sector went from borrowing 3.6% of GDP to saving 5.6% of GDP. This 9.2% swing in private sector spending was a larger economic shock than the one that led to the Great Depression. . . .

Luckily, the U.S. economy is different now than compared to the 1930s. In particular, today's economy has a larger public sector and one that contains many "automatic stabilizers"—including progressive tax collections that fall more rapidly than private sector incomes and safety net spending (like unemployment insurance and food stamps and Medicaid) that provides increased transfers to households when the economy slows. These automatic stabilizers kicked in as private spending slowed. This led to a purely mechanical rise in the deficit—roughly $329 billion of the increase in the deficit between 2007 and 2009 can in fact be attributed to this purely mechanical effect of automatic stabilizers, according to the Congressional Budget Office.

And this large increase in the deficit was a very good thing. The increase in public spending power leaned hard against the rapid decline in private spending power, and contributed to keeping the economy from entering another Depression.

Of course, the increase in the deficit was not the only thing that helped support the economy—at the same time the Federal Reserve was aggressively fighting the downturn by cutting interest rates and supplying liquidity to the financial sector.

Still, automatic stabilizers and Federal Reserve action were not enough to forestall a rapid economic deterioration. By February 2009, the economy had seen monthly

Bivens, Josh. United States Congress, July 14, 2010.

Did the American Recovery and Reinvestment Act of 2009 Create Jobs?

103

job-loss that averaged 653,000 in each of the past 6 months, despite the fact that the short-term interest rates controlled by the Federal Reserve had been below 1% for 21 months. . . .

In short, because the primary tool that national policymakers use to fight recessions—lowering short-term interest rates—had been rendered ineffective, something else had to be done. This something was the Recovery Act, a deficit-financed combination of a roughly equal measure of tax cuts, transfer payments and direct government grants to support demand for goods and services and blunt the recession.

It should be remembered that the size and composition of the Recovery Act was a compromise. Many, including myself, thought the overall size of the package would be too small to bring the economy back to recovery without further action. Many (also including myself) also thought tax cuts had too large a weight in the final package and that many of them (particularly the fix to the alternative minimum tax, or AMT) were ill-suited for short-term stimulus. Because of these compromises on the size and composition of the Act, many believed that it would not be sufficient by itself to provide the economic boost needed to get the American job market back to health in an acceptably rapid time frame.

All this said, passage of the Recovery Act was a serious response to the nation's economic crisis, and even with its somewhat-compromised composition, its forecasted impact was large—the best estimates were that it would create between 2 [and] 4 million jobs and boost GDP by roughly 5% over the first 2 years of its implementation.

It Worked

And this estimate has been spot-on. For those most convinced by appeals to authority let's start with what private sector macroeconomic forecasters say about the Recovery Act. These are, remember, people whose salary relies on being closer than their competitors in forecasting economic trends. As a group, they are in near-universal agreement that the Recovery Act added roughly 3 percent to GDP by the end of June and that it created or saved between 2 [and] 3 million jobs. The non-partisan Congressional Budget Office (CBO) concurs, calculating that the Recovery Act contributed between $240 billion [and] $645 billion to the economy by the end of June, creating or saving up to 5.3 million full-time equivalent jobs and keeping the unemployment rate up to 2 points lower than it would have been in the absence of the Act.

There are a number of factors that explain the near-unanimity among forecasters who have examined the impact of ARRA.

First, it is firmly in line with what mainstream economic theory teaches is the likely effect of deficit-financed tax cuts, transfers and spending in an economy that has high unemployment even in the presence of rock-bottom interest rates (i.e., is in a liquidity trap). The effect of increasing deficits to finance tax cuts, transfers and spending in a *healthy* economy is ambiguous and there are many complications to assessing it. However, in a liquidity trap these complications fade away and the impact of these policy maneuvers become quite straightforward; they unambiguously push the economy closer to its potential, lowering the unemployment rate.

Second, the timing of the Recovery Act coincides perfectly with the halt in the downward spiral of both economic output and employment.[1] In the 6 months before the Act began paying out funds, gross domestic product *contracted* at a 5.9% annualized rate while in the 6 months after its passage the economy *grew* at a 0.75% annualized rate. In the first 3 months of 2010 it grew at an annualized rate of 2.7%. In the 6 months before the Recovery Act took effect, average monthly employment declined by 653,000 while in the 6 months after its passage it's average declines fell nearly in half to 369,000. In the first 6 months of this year average monthly employment has actually grown by 147,000. . . .

Third, the turnaround in GDP growth between the 6 months before and the 6 months after the passage of the Recovery Act was driven predominantly by a reversal in consumer spending. This portion of GDP (accounting for almost 70% of the total) contracted by 1.25% in the 6 months before the Act and actually grew by 0.95% in the [6] months after the Act's passage. Contrary to most descriptions of the Recovery Act, this is actually exactly what one would have expected if it was working. Two-thirds of the Act's provisions (the tax cuts and transfer payments) go directly to boosting the purchasing power of households, not in directly purchasing goods and services for the government. This boost to household disposable income helped to arrest the steep fall in consumer spending. . . .

This evidence—the preponderance of opinion of macroeconomic forecasters, the timing of the Recovery Act taking effect and the reversal of the downward spiral in the middle of 2009, and the very large footprint of the Recovery Act provisions on personal disposable income and its correlation with consumer spending—adds up to an overwhelming case that the Recovery Act worked as advertised.

Essentially, without it, GDP would be $600 billion lower today, there would be 3 million fewer jobs in the economy, and the unemployment rate would be nearly 2% higher even with fewer Americans in the labor force. While there remains much to be done to make sure that all Americans looking for a job have a decent chance of finding one, it is clear that we would be digging out of a much deeper hole today had the Recovery Act not passed.

It Was Cheap

Besides a general misunderstanding about its effectiveness, the primary resistance to providing more fiscal stimulus to today's economy, even in the face of historically high unemployment, is concerns about the federal budget deficit. This section will argue that in the context of the nation's *actual* challenge concerning the national debt—budget deficits that are forecast to rise in coming decades even during periods of healthy economic growth—the costs of the Recovery Act and further fiscal support to the economy are minimal. It further argues that a broader view of the Act's costs—not just its cost in terms of the federal budget but in terms of *overall* economic opportunity costs—show that these costs are actually negative; that is, the Act resulted in greater, not less, private investment and employment.

It is clear that the country faces long-run budget challenges that will require policy action in coming decades. A close look at the economics, however, shows that these budget challenges have nothing to do with the Recovery Act that was passed nor would they be appreciably exacerbated at all if more fiscal support was provided to the economy today.

For example, the Recovery Act added between 0.1% [and] 0.2% to the long-run (50-year) fiscal gap.[2] If one is a true budget pessimist and believes that the alternative fiscal scenario identified by CBO in their latest report on the long-run budget outlook is a good forecast of the most likely trajectory of deficits (I'm not, for the record, such a pessimist), then this would imply that the Recovery Act was responsible for less than about 1–2% of the long-run fiscal gap facing the country.

The reason for this non-effect of the Recovery Act on long-run budget challenges is simple: the Act is temporary and the main drivers of long-run deficits remain rising health care costs and low revenues as a share of GDP.

Another reason why the Recovery Act was cheap (and why further fiscal action aimed at spurring the economy would be cheap) is that its headline cost ($787 billion in the case of Recovery Act) is actual[ly] far greater than its actual net impact on the budget deficit. Because the Recovery Act saved jobs and wage incomes, it generated new tax revenue. And because it kept people working, it kept them out of public safety net programs.

Say that the overall multiplier of the Recovery Act was 1.25—this is the boost to total GDP per dollar increase in the deficit. The more effective parts of the Act (extensions of unemployment insurance and other safety net programs and investments in the nation's infrastructure and aid to fiscally strapped state and local governments) actually have multipliers significantly higher than this, but because the Recovery Act also included items like the AMT fix that provided very little bang-for-buck, the overall multiplier was lower. Given a multiplier of 1.25, the $600 billion in Recovery Act spending that is set to occur before the end of calendar year 2010 will result in GDP that is higher by roughly $750 billion by the end of this year.

Other data from the Congressional Budget Office suggests that each $1 increase in GDP relative to potential yields a $0.35 decrease in the deficit as revenues rise and spending falls. Multiplying the $750 billion in extra output by this $0.35 indicates that the economic activity spurred by the Recovery Act actually recoups just under $330 billion—*more than half* the headline price tag of $600 billion. In short, well-designed policies aimed at spurring economic activity come with a built-in and significant offset to their total costs.

This exercise also drives home the importance of designing stimulus packages well. Take the high and low-end of Recovery Act provisions in terms of bang-for-buck provided by Moody's Economy.com. If the entire Act consisted of provisions with a bang-for-buck as low as that provided by corporate tax cuts or providing the opportunity of businesses to "carryback" past losses against future taxes, the budget offset provided by the Act would be less than $80 billion. If instead the entire Act consisted of provisions with bang-for-buck comparable to safety net expansions and infrastructure spending, the budget offset approaches $400 billion. Simple design of stimulus packages can make their final impact on the deficit differ by literally hundreds of billions of dollars. Besides just not providing effective stimulus, the less well-designed parts of the Act should have been excluded on the basis of fiscal responsibility. . . .

Besides having a minimal impact on the stock of outstanding national debt, the Recovery Act was financed in an economic context of historically low long-term interest rates for government debt. These low rates are no fluke—they are low precisely because private spending and borrowing are at historic lows (i.e., the recession). Further fiscal support could also be financed at very low rates, as excess capacity and little competition for loanable funds continue to characterize the economy. Additionally, upward interest rate pressure stemming from Federal Reserve actions is extremely unlikely, given both the weakness of the overall economy and their stated intention to keep rates low until the economy has begun a robust recovery.

While low interest rates contribute much to the relative cheapness of the Recovery Act, they also provide the clearest indication that the Act is also cheap in its broader economic opportunity costs. The most well-pedigreed argument against increasing budget deficits in healthy economies is the fear that increased government borrowing causes interest rates to rise as public demand competes with private demand for fixed savings of households and businesses. These rising interest rates spurred by growing deficits result in private investment "crowding out" private capital formation, and the lower value of the private capital stock leads to lower future growth. When economic commentators make arguments disparaging the ability of the Recovery Act (or government spending of any kind) to create jobs, they generally make variants of this crowding-out argument.

The general failure of interest rates to rise in response to the increase in budget deficits, and to the Recovery Act in particular, is a prime piece of evidence that no crowding out of private investment is occurring, making the Recovery Act not just cheap, but essentially free in terms of its overall economic opportunity cost.[3] This is, again, not unexpected. Economic theory teaches that increased public borrowing during a liquidity trap does not crowd-out private sector activity. . . .

It is worth stressing this "crowding out" mechanism, given that many Recovery Act detractors have pointed to very low rates of overall investment as some sign that private activity is being stunted by increased public sector activity. The textbook presentation of the effects of fiscal policy *requires* higher interest rates as the mechanism through which private investment may be stunted by increased public borrowing in a healthy economy. Without the rise in interest rates, there is no way to link increased public borrowing and lower private investment.

Some commentators, having neither theory nor evidence on their side in making the argument that increased public spending must by definition reduce private spending, have done the economic equivalent of banging the table—insisting that vague concerns about "uncertainty" spurred by the economic policy actions of the administration explain the reduction in private investment. This is supremely unconvincing, for a few reasons.

First, there is no particular reason to think that private investment is actually abnormally low at the moment. Numerous academic studies suggest that the prime determinant of private investment is in fact the simple state of the economy. Given that we are just emerging from the steepest and longest recession in post World War II history, it is far from surprising that investment spending is low.

Further, the capacity utilization rate (think of this as the employment rate of factories instead of people) reached historic lows in the past year. With current capacity far from being fully utilized, why would businesses seek to spend money to build more of this capacity? Finally, it should be remembered that investment in structures, both residential and non-residential, is an important component (just under half) of overall investment. Given the massive overbuilding in the residential housing sector for the past decade and the sharply rising vacancy rates in commercial real estate, it is again hard to imagine why businesses would seek to expand investments in structures. . . .

Second, there is very little evidence that economic uncertainty of any kind provides a the kind of sharp shock to private investment that would explain the very large fall-off in investment that characterized the worst phases of the last recession.[4]

Lastly, given that overall economic activity is a prime determinant of private investment and that the Recovery Act assuredly spurred greater activity, it is very likely that the Recovery Act actually "crowded in" private investment—actually made the fall-off in private investment *less steep* than it would have been absent the Act's effects. Evidence for this can be seen in a number of papers that find very large multiplier effects of fiscal support when an economy is a liquidity trap.[5]

It Should Be Repeated

So, while the Recovery Act saved the U.S. economy from a worse economic fate—today's economic fate is still poor. Today's unemployment rate stands at 9.5% and a series of economic overhangs—the overhang of average hours decline, the overhang of the "missing labor force" (the 2 million workers who withdrew from the labor force since the recession began and who will certainly return looking for work in coming years), and the overhang of business and consumer debt that will keep spending in both sectors cautious in coming years—mean that, absent further support to the economy, it will take an agonizingly long time to bring it down to levels seen before the recession began. For example, the Congressional Budget Office (CBO) has forecast the unemployment rate will average 6.3% in 2013—this is higher than the peak rate reached during the recession and jobless recovery in the early 2000s recession. . . .

Further, even this grim forecast for unemployment assumes the economy grows consistently in the next couple of years. Given recent headwinds that have picked up steam in the past few months, even this cannot be assured. The most recent monthly employment situation demonstrated that the pace of private-sector hiring has decelerated and wages actually fell in inflation-adjusted terms. State and local spending has actually contracted in each of the past 3 quarters—only the 4th time in the post-war period that this has happened. . . .

Economic data in the form of rapidly decelerating prices and wages is also sending strong signals that excess capacity in the economy is threatening to grow again. Essentially all indicators of overall price pressure in the economy show rapidly decelerating price growth, and several show outright deflation (falling prices) in recent months. . . .

Perhaps most distressing, the boost to growth provided by the Recovery Act is actually fading—and fast. The current quarter (the third quarter of 2010) is probably the last time the Act will contribute 1% to annualized GDP growth. By the last quarter of this year, it will be contributing next to nothing. Given that GDP growth in the past 3 quarters would have likely been zero without the influence of Recovery Act spending—it seems clear that more support is needed to provide the bridge to the period where private incomes and spending can generate economic growth on their own.

Conclusion

The Recovery Act worked just as advertised, creating nearly 5 million full-time equivalent jobs in the economy when such growth was desperately needed. However, the bulk of its effect has passed—and millions of jobs remain desperately needed.

It seems amazing now, but 30 months ago Congress acted quickly to pass a $160 billion stimulus package to avoid the prospect of unemployment rising from 5 to 6%. The unemployment rate now stands at 9.5% and further fiscal support does not seem to be forthcoming. This testimony tried to make the case that there is no *economic* reason to believe things have so changed in the past 30 months as to make further fiscal support unwise.

The fiscal support provided by the Recovery Act was needed, effective, and cheap. Further support is clearly needed and, if structured well, could be very effective and cheap as well.

References

Bachmann, Ruediger and Steffen Elstner and Eric Sims (2010). "Uncertainty and Economic Activity: Evidence from Business Survey Data." Working Paper.

Eggerston, Gauti (2009). "What fiscal policy is effective at zero interest rates?" *Federal Reserve Bank of New York Staff Report*, No. 402, November 2009.

Hall, Robert (2009). "By How Much Does GDP Rise if the Government Buys More Output?" *Brookings Papers on Economic Activity*, 2009, 2, pp. 183–231.

Woodford, Michael (2009). "Simple Analytics of the Government Expenditure Multiplier." Working Paper. Columbia University.

Notes

1. In what follows I date the effect of the Recovery Act as beginning April 1, 2009. While it was passed in late February and some money was spent before this, April 2009 is the first month that saw significant amounts of money being spent.
2. The fiscal gap is a short-hand measure of the long-run fiscal imbalance. Essentially, it tells one how much some combination of tax increases and/or spending cuts (expressed as a share of GDP), enacted immediately, would be needed to close the long-run budget deficits.
3. There is an additional channel through which increasing federal budget deficits in a healthy economy can lead to slower domestic income growth—if the increased borrowing spurred by them leads to greater borrowing from foreign investors. Very few (if any) detractors of the Recovery Act have made the argument that this has happened—and correctly so. The mechanism for this channel to work would have to be a rise in the trade deficit. But, the trade deficit fell significantly over the course of this recession.
4. See Bachman, Elstner and Sims (2010) for the very low short-run impacts of business uncertainty on investment.
5. See Eggerston (2010), Woodford (2009) and Hall (2009) for representatives of this finding.

JOSH BIVENS is a macroeconomist with the Economic Policy Institute. He is the author of *Everybody Wins Except for Most of Us: What Economics Teaches About Globalization*. He holds a PhD degree in economics from the New School for Social Research.

Veronique de Rugy

Testimony before the U.S. House of Representatives Budget Committee

Since the Great Recession began in December 2007, employment has shrunk by 7.5 million jobs,[1] long-term unemployment is higher now than in any previous recession,[2] and real GDP has plummeted to 2006 levels.[3] The understandable temptation to take action in time of recession however should not lead lawmakers to take counterproductive actions. On February 13, 2009, President Obama signed into law the American Recovery and Reinvestment Act (ARRA) at a cost of $787 billion with the promise that it would "create or save" 3.5 million jobs over the next two years, mostly in the private sector.[4] What's more, based on a study by Christina Romer, the Chairman of the Council of Economic Advisors, and Jared Bernstein, the administration claimed that without the Recovery Act unemployment rate would reach 8.8 percent while with the Act it would immediately start declining.[5]

Since the president signed the stimulus package into law, the U.S. economy has shed another 2.5 million jobs and the unemployment rate has climbed to 9.7 percent from 7 percent, higher than the White House predicted it would have reached even *without* the stimulus.

While the stimulus may have appeared to have been a wise investment when it was made, it was really no wiser than a junk-rated mortgage-backed security: though the stimulus claimed a good rate of return, in reality it appears to have lost money by destroying growth. At best, it shifted jobs from privately funded to publicly funded ones.

Promises, Promises

The stimulus bill draws on the views of economist John Maynard Keynes. In Keynesian thought, a fall in economic demand causes a fall in spending. Since one person's spending is someone else's income, a fall in demand makes a nation poorer. When that poorer nation prudently cuts back on spending, it sets off yet another wave of falling income. So a big shock to consumer spending or business confidence sets off waves of job losses and layoffs.

Can anything stop this cycle? Keynesians say yes: government spending can take the place of private spending during a crisis. If the government increases its own spending, it will create new employment. These new workers should consume more, and businesses should then buy more machines and equipment to meet the government's and the revitalized public's demands.

This increase in gross domestic product is what economists call *the multiplier effect*. It means that one dollar of government spending will end up creating *more* than a dollar of new national income.

The Theory of Multipliers

It is difficult to get solid evidence on the economy's response to changes in government spending. Direct reporting measures—such as those employed by Recovery .gov, the U.S. government's website for tracking stimulus spending—capture the direct and observable effects of government spending on economic activity. These measures can be helpful, but they fail to account for the indirect, less-easily observable effects of government spending. To capture the big-picture effect of government spending, economists turn to the *spending multiplier*.

As explained above, the *multiplier effect* or *spending multiplier* refers to the idea that an initial amount of government spending leads to a change in the activity of the larger economy. In other words, an initial change in the total demand for goods and services (what economists term aggregate demand) causes a change in total output for the economy that is a multiple of the initial change. For example, if the government spends one dollar and, as a result of this spending, the economy (as expressed by the Gross Domestic Product, or GDP) grows by $2, the spending multiplier is 2. . . .

The Spending Multiplier Debates

The theory sounds pat, but economists have been debating aspects of government spending multipliers for years. One crucial debate centers on how to measure a multiplier's value. Some economists find spending multipliers that are smaller than 1.[6] Other economists, however, assert that spending multipliers are much larger.[7] Still others argue that multipliers can't even be credibly measured.[8]

Another debate surrounds the implications of spending multipliers. For Keynesians, consumption is the ultimate goal of government spending, and even with a multiplier smaller than 1, spending can still increase GDP. Thus Keynesians argue that, during a recession, when

de Rugy, Veronique. United States Congress, July 14, 2010.

people tend to save their money rather than investing it in the private market,[9] a small increase in GDP is better than nothing.

Simple Keynesian macroeconomics assumes that in times of high unemployment, the government is better than the private market at guiding idle resources to create economic output. Government spending puts unemployed labor and capital to work at zero social cost.[10] . . .

A New Classical understanding of the multiplier starts with the idea that government spending has some social cost (i.e. a rise in government spending requires a fall in other parts of GDP, such as consumption and investment). As such, the value of the public projects (bridge construction or roads) needs to justify that social cost. This view doesn't assume that an increase in consumption at any cost is a good thing: if the multiplier's value is less than 1, then government spending has crowded out the private investment and spending that would have otherwise happened.

Even government spending where the multiplier is higher than 1 could still be a poor use of taxpayer dollars. For instance, though $1 in government spending could lead to a GDP boost of $1.50 in the short run, it could also make it harder to solve the longer-term debt problem.

The Data of Defense

So what is the historical value of the multiplier in the United States? A new study by Harvard professor Dr. Robert Barro and Charles Redlick answers this question in details by using defense spending as a proxy for overall government spending.[11]

First, the economists explain that in order to understand the effects of government spending on the economy, one must know how much of the economic change is due to government spending and how much is due to other factors. Unfortunately, it is impossible to figure this out with general government spending since the level of government spending often expands and contracts along with the economy.[12] . . .

However, they argue that there is a useful, much more isolated proxy for overall government spending: defense spending. Using defense spending as a proxy has several advantages.[13] First, government does not set defense spending levels based on the state of the economy. Non-economic factors drive defense spending. Second, changes in defense spending are very large and include sharply positive and negative values. . . . Finally, the historical data on defense spending covers periods of high unemployment. . . .

Moreover, studying the effects of defense spending on the economy gives the best-case scenario of the spending-multiplier effect of government spending on the economy because defense spending leads to economic growth in ways that general government spending does not. For example, in times of war, the government mandates the increased production of particular goods, and the scarcity of domestic labor due to military enlistment and resources also forces economic resources to go to innovative and productive uses that did not exist before the war.[14]

Barro and Redlick's research estimates that the multiplier for changes in defense spending that people think will be temporary—spending for the Iraq war, for example—is between 0.4 and 0.5 at the time of the spending and between 0.6 and 0.7 over two years. If the change in defense spending becomes permanent, then these multipliers increase by 0.1 to 0.2.[15] Over time, this is a maximum multiplier of 0.9. Thus even in the government's best-case spending scenario, *all* of the estimated multipliers are significantly less than one. This means greater government spending crowds out other components of GDP, particularly investment.

In addition, they calculate the impact on the economy if the government funds the spending with taxes. They find that the tax multiplier—the effect on GDP of an increase in taxes—is –1.1. This means that if the government raises taxes by $1, the economy will shrink by $1.1. When this tax multiplier is combined with the effects of the spending multiplier, the overall effect is negative. Barro and Redlick write that, "Since the tax multiplier is larger in magnitude than the spending multipliers, our estimates imply that GDP declines in response to higher defense spending and correspondingly higher tax revenue."[16] Thus, they conclude that greater government spending financed by tax increases hurts the economy.

More Data

Other economists have also calculated defense spending multipliers of less than or equal to 1.[17] Economists Bob Hall and Susan Woodward recently examined spending increases from World War II and the Korean War and found that the government spending multiplier is about 1.[18] Economist Valerie Ramey's work on how U.S. military spending influences GDP gives a multiplier estimate of 1.2 in the short term, but in the long term, she finds that consumer and business spending fall after a rise in government purchases, offsetting the initial effect of the government spending.[19]

In a recent blog post over at Neighborhood Effects, my colleague Matt Mitchell reports on a number of peer-reviewed studies have also examined the relationship between government size, somehow measured, and economic growth.

Here is a sample: Barro (1991 and 1989); Folster and Henrekson (2001); Romero-Ávila and Strauch (2008); Afonso and Furceri (2008); Chobanov and Mladenova (2009); Roy (2009); and Bergh and Karlsson (2010). Each of these studies finds a strong, statistically significant, negative relationship between the size of government and economic growth.

What about the short run? Here again the evidence seems weak at best. Consider new research by Harvard's Robert Barro and Charles

Redlick. They find that for every dollar the government spends on the military (read: takes out of the private economy), the economy gains just 40 to 70 cents. Spending a dollar to obtain 40 to 70 cents does not a good deal make. Or consider another study by Harvard's Laruen Cohen, Joshua Coval and Christopher Malloy. They rely on the fact that the federal government tends to spend more money in districts whose congressional members are chairs of powerful committees than in districts whose members are just rank-and-file. They find that firms actually cut capital expenditures by 15 percent following the ascendency of a congressman to the chairmanship. Moreover, firms seem to scale back employment and experience declines in sales.[20]

Job Creating or Just Job Shifting?

It's obvious that the government can hire people. But how many of these jobs will be taken by people already working in the private sector? This is a statistic that desperately needs to be calculated. After all, if most stimulus jobs are taken by people just switching over from privately funded jobs to publicly funded ones, that hurts any short-run Keynesian stimulus effect. In fact, in the last year, some people *have* switched from private to public sector jobs. According to the *Boston Globe*, these people were willing to take a cut in pay because they valued the security and fringe benefits of a government job.[21] Every worker who switches to a government job for the good benefits hurts the Keynesian story.

In a 2007 paper, economists Quadrini and Trigari posed another important question: if a government routinely hires more workers during a recession, will the unemployed intentionally stay unemployed longer, in hopes of getting a good government job?[22] Since government jobs and stimulus-funded Davis-Bacon prevailing wage jobs tend to have high wages and good benefits, there might be a strong incentive for unemployed workers to search a bit longer before settling for a private-sector job. In a simulation, Quadrini and Trigari found that when government spending stimulates the economy during a recession, it makes the typical recession worse. Many of the unemployed stay unemployed a few weeks longer, in the hopes of finding a high-paying, secure, stimulus-funded job. Common sense for an unemployed worker—searching for the best job possible—means a longer recession for all of us. So the Quadrini/Trigari multiplier isn't just zero: It's *negative*, even in the short run.

If stimulus jobs paid market wages rather than high Davis-Bacon wages, this would be less of a problem, but a problem it is.[23] And it's a problem that only points in one direction: a smaller multiplier. Perhaps it won't push the short-run multiplier down to zero (or less than zero) but a multiplier between zero and one starts to sound much more plausible. And if that's the case, then fiscal "stimulus" grows the government at the cost of shrinking the private sector.

Why Does It Matter?

Getting the multiplier wrong has big consequences when understanding the effects of fiscal stimulus on the economy. The government uses multipliers to estimate the widely cited projections of unemployment, job creation, and economic output. In the time leading up to the passage of the ARRA, Council of Economic Advisors (CEA) economists Christina Romer and Jared Bernstein used spending multipliers greater than 1 to promote the economic effects of the fiscal stimulus package.[24] In the months following the implementation of this package, the Congressional Budget Office (CBO) used estimates of a spending multiplier between 1.0 and 2.5,[25] relying on macroeconomic models that ignore the possibility that the growth of the economy may be affecting the level of government spending and not the reverse.[26] By extrapolating from these multipliers, CBO and CEA have made important projections about the effects of fiscal stimulus on the economy. These projections, however, have been largely wrong.

For example, in their January 2009 report,[27] Romer and Bernstein used multipliers of between 1.0 and 1.55 to determine the effect of the proposed stimulus spending (then $775 billion) would have on GDP and job creation. They assumed that each 1 percent increase in real GDP would create an additional 1 million jobs. Based on that assumption and their estimated spending multiplier, they estimated that the fiscal stimulus would create 3.5 million jobs by the end of 2010. While we cannot be certain how many jobs would have been lost or created without a stimulus package, we do know that since February 2009, 2.55 million jobs have been lost.[28]

The Worst-Possible Stimulus

Leaving the multiplier debate aside, there are other important reasons why the stimulus bill will have deleterious consequences for the economy. The Recovery Act took the form of increased government spending through federal and state bureaucracies, going to areas such as education, infrastructure, and energy spending.

For months now then, the stimulus bill has routed the bulk of the stimulus money through various government bureaucracies. As economist Keith Hennessey explains, this spending will be "*inefficient*—It will be inefficient in two senses. The spending represents the policy preferences of legislators (and all their ugly legislative deals and compromises), rather than the choices of hundreds of millions of Americans who presumably know better how they would like money spent on them. The spending will also be wasteful, and we are starting to see signs of this in the press."[29]

The spending is also occurring very slowly. According to the recovery.org data, 16 months after the adoption of the Recovery Act, agencies, firms, and citizens spent some $190 billion in grants and contracts—that is a mere 60 percent of discretionary spending in the bill (highways, mass transit, energy efficiency, broadband, education, state aid).[30] And only $20 billion in additional spending was reported during the last quarter of the 2010 for which the data is available. Congress has expended most of the $267 billion for set aside for entitlement spending (food stamps, unemployment, and Medicare refundable tax credits), but the bulk of that sum went to Medicaid spending, which flows to the states, not into the private economy. Spending in states defers, not mitigates, the economic impact of the recession. By extending unsustainable spending programs, this spending has simply prolonged the lag time until needed spending adjustments occur, not created jobs. . . .

Stimulus Facts

Using the tens of thousands of stimulus recipient reports published on Recovery.gov each quarter and economic and political data from the Bureau of Labor Statistics, the Census Bureau, GovTrack.us, and others, I am writing a series of quarterly reports that put this aggregate information into a larger context.

I am about to release the third of that series. Today I would like to highlight some preliminary findings based on this data. (The data and results presented here encompass the first quarter of the calendar year 2010 reports of Recovery Act contracts and grants only. The complete dataset used for this report will be available for download at Mercatus.org when the full report is released at the end of July 2010.)

First, in the third quarter for which Recovery.gov reports are available, federal agencies awarded over 69,717 contracts and grants. Total spending reached over $192.2 billion. That is roughly $22 billion more reported received than in the previous quarter. At that rate, the government should be done awarding stimulus dollars by 2020. In other words, the money is being spent very slowly.

Second, the total number of jobs the stimulus has created or saved is claimed to be 679,814. However, it is hard to know what these jobs represent since the administration recently changed how it counts jobs. According to the new rules, the administration no longer keeps a cumulative tally of jobs created and saved by the stimulus. Instead, it posts only a count of jobs for each quarter. Also, instead of counting only created and saved jobs, it counts any person who works on a project funded with stimulus money—even if that person never lost his or her original job.[31]

These changes highlight the near impossibility of accounting for how many jobs were saved by the (expenditure or allocation of) stimulus funds, but what we do know from these numbers is that of the 679,814 jobs reported created or saved, four times as many of these jobs were in the public rather than the private sector.

- Total jobs "created or saved" in public entities: 550,749
- Total jobs "created or saved" in private entities: 127,306

Third, the average cost of each job created or saved is $282,000. However, the average cost per private sector job created or saved is over $647,000.

Fourth, controlling for the percentage of the district employed in the construction industry, which is often used as a proxy for the vulnerability to recession of a district, the preliminary results find no statistical correlation between all relevant unemployment indicators and the allocation of funds. This preliminary result, which is similar to the ones in the two previous reports, suggests that unemployment, at least thus far, has not been the factor leading the awards. Also, I found no correlation between other economic indicators, such as income, and stimulus funding. As the main argument for enacting the $787 billion stimulus bill was that if government spends money where it is the most needed, that expenditure would create jobs and trigger economic growth, one would have expected the government would invest relatively more money in districts that have the highest unemployment rates and less money in districts with lower unemployment rates. Such does not appear to be the case.

Conclusion

The understandable temptation to take action in time of recession should not lead lawmakers to take counterproductive actions. Economists have shown that stimulus by government spending is not productive, and Barro and Redlick's data show that the CBO's multiplier overestimates the return on government spending almost by a factor of two.

What's more, the stimulus's effect on job creation is unclear. Did it create productive jobs? Is the stimulus money simply funding public jobs for some who had jobs in the private sector but switched over for reasons of security? Is the stimulus simply funding pay raises that would have happened stimulus money or not? Is the stimulus money simply funding jobs that existed and were not at risk?

Unfortunately, we cannot know. In fact, a recent report by the Government Accountability Office highlights that Recovery.gov is not transparent and the data displayed on it doesn't promote the transparency agenda of the Obama administration.[32]

If stimulus funds are a bad investment, is there anything Congress can do to help the economy? A few years ago, Christina and David Romer looked at the impact of tax cuts on the economy and concluded that the tax multiplier is about three: a dollar of tax cuts raises GDP by about three dollars.[33] Their finding suggests that the economy might get more bang for the buck with tax cuts rather than spending hikes.

Notes

1. Statistics from the Bureau of Labor Statistics National Current Employment Statistics survey at http://bls.gov. Job loss calculated by author

using non-farm payroll employment change from December 2007 to June 2010.

2. Randy Ilg, "Long-Term Unemployment Experience of the Jobless," *Issues in Labor Statistics*, Summary 10-05 (2010).

3. Author's calculation based on data from NIPA Table 1.1.6. *Real Gross Domestic Product, Chained Dollars* from the Bureau of Economic Analysis.

4. Barack Obama, "Address to Joint Session of Congress" (speech, The United States Capitol, Washington, D.C., February 24, 2009), http://www .whitehouse.gov/the_press_office/remarks-of-president -barack-obama-address-to-joint-session-of-congress/.

5. Christina Romer and Jared Bernstein, "The Job Impact of the American Recovery and Reinvestment Plan," news release, January 9, 2009.

6. Robert Barro, "Government Spending Is No Free Lunch," *Wall Street Journal*, January 22, 2009, http:// online.wsj.com/article/SB123258618204604599.html.

7. For estimates of multipliers greater than 1, see Marianne Baxter and Robert G. King, "Fiscal Policy in General Equilibrium," *American Economic Review* 83, no. 3 (1993): 315–334; Christina Romer, Jared Bernstein, "The Job Impact of the American Recovery and Reinvestment Plan," news release, January 10, 2009, and Andrew Mountford and Harald Uhlig, "What Are the Effects of Fiscal Policy Shocks" (working paper no. *14551*, National Bureau of Economic Research, December 2008).

8. Murray Rothbard, "Money and Its Purchasing Power," in *Man, Economy and State, With Power and Market*, http://mises.org/rothbard/mes/chap11a.asp.

9. Michael Woodford, "Simple Analytics of the Government Expenditure Multiplier" (working paper, Columbia University, January 27, 2010), 43, http:// www.columbia.edu/~mw2230/G_ASSA.pdf.

10. Another way to think of this is that there is something wrong with the price system. To learn more about why this is not the case in a world with rational actors, see Robert Barro, "Long-term contracting, sticky prices, and monetary policy," *Journal of Monetary Economics* 3, no. 3 (July 1977): 305–316.

11. Robert Barro and Charles Redlick, "Macroeconomic Effects from Government Purchases and Taxes" (working paper, Mercatus Center at George Mason University, Arlington, VA, 2010).

12. Zvi Hercowitz and Michel Strawczynski, "Cyclical Ratcheting in Government Spending: Evidence from the OECD," *The Review of Economics and Statistics* 86, no. 1 (February 2004): 353–361 and Graciela L. Kaminsky, Carmen M. Reinhart, and Carlos A. Végh, "When It Rains, It Pours: Procyclical Capital Flows and Macroeconomic Policies," *NBER Macroeconomics Annual* 19, (2004): 11–53.

13. The use of defense spending as an exogenous shock to study the effect of government spending has been explored in-depth in Roberto Perrotti, "In Search of the Transmission Mechanism of Fiscal Policy," (working paper 13143, National Bureau of Economic Research). In addition, it has been used

as an econometric tool to study the effects of fiscal stimulus on the economy in a number of studies, including Olivier Blanchard and Roberto Perotti, "An Empirical Characterization of the Dynamic Effects of Changes in Government Spending," *Quarterly Journal of Economics* 107, no. 4 (November 2002): 1329–1368 and Miguel Almunia and others, "From Great Depression to Great Credit Crisis: similarities, differences and lessons" *Economic Policy* 25, no. 62 (2010): 219–265, among others.

14. Robert Barro and Charles Redlick, "Macroeconomic Effects from Government Purchases and Taxes," 32.

15. Ibid, 44.

16. Ibid, 29.

17. See Olivier Blanchard and Roberto Perotti, "An Empirical Characterization of the Dynamic Effects of Changes in Government Spending and Taxes on Output," and Robert E. Hall, "By How Much Does GDP Rise if the Government Buys More Output?" *Brookings Papers on Economic Activity*, forthcoming.

18. Bob Hall and Susan Woodward, "Measuring the Effect of Infrastructure Spending on GDP," in *Financial Crisis and Recession*, http://woodwardhall .wordpress.com/2008/12/11/measuring-the-effect-of -infrastructure-spending-on-gdp/.

19. Valerie Ramey, "Identifying Government Spending Shocks: It's All in the Timing," unpublished, University of California San Diego, October 2009.

20. Matt Mitchell, "Why This Isn't a Time to Worry That Government Is Spending Too Little," Neighborhood Effects, June 30, 2010. http://neighborhoodeffects .mercatus.org/2010/06/30/why-this-isnt-a-time-to-worry -that-government-is-spending-too-little/

21. Megan Woolhouse, "Now hiring, your Uncle Sam," *Boston Globe*, May 30, 2009, http://www .boston.com/jobs/news/articles/2009/05/30/unlike_rest_ of_us_federal_government_is_hiring_a_lot/.

22. Quadrini and Trigari, (2007) "Public Employment and the Business Cycle," http://www-rcf.usc .edu/~quadrini/papers/PublicEmployPap.pdf, later published in *Economic Inquiry*.

23. Indeed, if government jobs paid market wages, then recessions would be a great time to build roads and hospitals at a much lower cost than usual: Taxpayers could save money, hiring employees who were waiting for the private-sector to improve.

24. Christina Romer and Jared Bernstein, "The Job Impact of the American Recovery and Reinvestment Plan," 12.

25. Congressional Budget Office, *Estimated Impact of the American Recovery and Reinvestment Act, January 2010 through March 2010* (Washington, DC: Congressional Budget Office, May 2010), http://www .cbo.gov/ftpdocs/115xx/doc11525/05-25-ARRA.pdf.

26. Ibid, Appendix. For an example of models operating under similar assumptions, see R. C. Fair, "Estimated Macroeconomic Effects of the U.S. Stimulus Bill," unpublished, Yale University, March 2010.

27. Christina Romer and Jared Bernstein, *The Job Impact of the American Recovery and Reinvestment Act* (January 9, 2009), http://otrans.3cdn.net/45593e8ecbd339d074_l3m6bt1te.pdf.

28. Authors' calculations using data from the Bureau of Labor Statistics, *Employment, Hours, and Earnings from the Current Employment Statistics Survey*, total change in nonfarm payroll employment, January 2009 to June 2010.

29. Keith Hennessey, "Will the Stimulus Come Too Late," June 3, 2009. http://keithhennessey.com/2009/06/03/will-the-stimulus-come-too-late/print/

30. Congressional Budget Office, Implementation Lags of Fiscal Policy: http://www.cbo.gov/ftpdocs/102xx/doc10255/06-02-IMF.pdf.

31. For example: When Chrysler reported a $53 million contract to build 3,000 government vehicles last fall, it listed zero jobs because it used existing employees to fill the orders. But under the new rules, those workers would have counted. Also, now recipients can count pay raises as stimulus jobs as long as they are counted as fractions of a job.

32. Government Accountability office, "Increasing the Public's Understanding of What Funds Are Being Spent on and What Outcomes Are Expected," May 2010. http://www.gao.gov/highlights/d10581high.pdf full report: http://www.gao.gov/new.items/d10581.pdf.

33. Christina D. Romer and David H. Romer, "The Macroeconomic Effects of Tax Changes: Estimates Based on a New Measure of Fiscal Shocks," (working paper, University of California–Berkeley, March 2007), http://www.econ.berkeley.edu/~cromer/RomerDraft307.pdf.

VERONIQUE DE RUGY is a senior research fellow at the Mercatus Center at George Mason University. She has also held positions with the American Enterprise Institute and the Cato Institute. She holds a PhD degree in economics from the University of Paris–Sorbonne.

EXPLORING THE ISSUE

Did the American Recovery and Reinvestment Act of 2009 Create Jobs?

Critical Thinking and Reflection

1. Should the worthiness of ARRA be weighed solely on monetary statistics? Explain.
2. How might the presence of "automatic stabilizers" in the 1930's economy have alleviated some of the grief of the Great Depression?
3. Is the stimulus bill a good example of applying Keynesian economics? Why or why not?
4. Why have "spending multipliers" generated debate among economists for years?

Is There Common Ground?

The only common ground in this debate seems to be the acknowledgment of what has come to be known as the Great Recession. Yes, it really happened, and, yes, it was really a bad period of economic distress. And, yes, measures toward recovery are still to be pursued and maintained.

But the specific question that frames the argument here is whether the American Recovery and Reinvestment Act of 2009 created jobs. To answer this, Bivens and de Rugy both rely on statistical analysis, but their respective assessments (based on different selected sets of data) do not intersect, which is why Bivens's answer is as clearly "Yes" as de Rugy's is clearly "No."

Create Central

www.mhhe.com/createcentral

Additional Resources

Bivens, Josh, *Failure by Design: The Story Behind America's Broken Economy* (ILR Press, 2011)

Hart, Rupert, *Guide to the Stimulus: The Definitive Desk Reference to the American Recovery & Reinvestment Act 2009* (CreateSpace Independent Publishing Platform, 2013).

U.S. Department of Transportation, *Office of Inspector General Audit Report: ARRA Job Data Reporting for FAA Programs—Lessons Learned for Improving Accuracy and Transparency for Future* (BiblioGov, 2013).

Internet References . . .

Congressional Budget Office

www.cbo.gov/publication/41374

Economic Policy Institute

www.epi.org/publication/ib343-obama-romney-job-growth/

Ohio State University, Department of Economics

http://web.econ.ohio-state.edu/dupor/arra10_may11.pdf

ISSUE

Do American Consumers Need a Financial Protection Agency?

YES: **Janis Bowdler**, from "Testimony before the U.S. House of Representatives Committee on Financial Services" (September 30, 2009)

NO: **Bill Himpler**, from "Testimony before the U.S. House of Representatives Committee on Financial Services" (September 30, 2009)

Learning Outcomes

After reading this issue, you will be able to:

- Identify the difference between revolving and non-revolving credit.
- Define the concept that economists refer to as "information asymmetry."
- Name several federal consumer protection laws.
- Discuss the potential economic effects of Consumer Financial Protection Agency (CFPA)—both favorable and unfavorable.

ISSUE SUMMARY

YES: Janis Bowdler, the deputy director, Wealth-Building Policy Project, National Council of La Raza, supports the creation of a Consumer Financial Protection Agency (CFPA). She identifies three specific ways in which existing regulatory agencies have failed consumers, including the failure to create and promote tools that will allow consumers to make "true apples-to-apples comparisons" of credit products. She and her organization believe a new agency is needed to redress these failures, and it would be a strong vehicle for improving the way financial markets serve their Latino clients.

NO: Bill Himpler, the executive vice president of the American Financial Services Association, opposes the creation of a CFPA. His argument takes several forms, including the fact that finance companies are already heavily regulated at the state level. He also believes that the creation of a CFPA is likely to mean "higher prices and reduced product choice for financial services customers."

According to the Federal Reserve System (Fed), the total debt outstanding of consumers during the second quarter of 2010 was $13.5 trillion, a total that was approximately equal to the gross public debt of the federal government and larger than the outstanding debt of the nonfinancial business sector ($10.9 trillion) or the combined outstanding debt of state and local governments ($2.4 trillion). The debt of the financial sector of the economy, which is largely used to finance the borrowings of consumers, government, and nonfinancial business, stood at $14.7 trillion.

The Fed disaggregates consumer total debt into two large categories: home mortgages ($10.1 trillion) and consumer credit ($2.4 trillion). In accumulating debt, consumers borrow from a variety of different organizations including commercial banks, finance companies, mortgage companies,

credit unions, the federal government, savings institutions, and insurance companies. And the act of borrowing or taking out a loan creates a variety of financial instruments or IOUs. For example, home mortgages include fixed interest rate mortgages and variable interest rate mortgages, and each of these mortgages has various maturities and other conditions. There is also the distinction between prime and subprime mortgages. As for consumer credit, the Fed also breaks this total down into two major categories: revolving and nonrevolving. One common definition of revolving credit is that it is an arrangement with a lender that allows the borrower access to funds up to a certain limit and repayment reestablishes the availability of funds. Credit cards are the best example of revolving credit. The Fed describes nonrevolving credit as "including automobile loans and all other loans not included in revolving credit, such as loans for mobile homes, education, boats, trailers, or vacations."

Consider the situation of a representative family. It probably has a mortgage that it used to purchase its home, an outstanding car loan, unpaid balances on credit cards, and perhaps outstanding student loans. And during a lifetime, a consumer may take out several of each of these types of loans; for example, they may take out more than one mortgage because of the purchase of a different home or the refinancing of a mortgage.

What underlies the concern about consumer borrowing and calls for a Consumer Financial Protection Agency is not just the magnitude of consumer debt. Rather, it is a concern that in the process of taking out a loan, the consumer does not have the knowledge or expertise of the lender. This is a problem that economists refer to as information asymmetry: a condition in which one party to a transaction has more information than the other party and creates the possibility that the party with the greater information will take advantage of the less well-informed counter party. If information asymmetry exists, then markets are less likely to produce efficient outcomes.

The financial crisis that began in the summer of 2007 revealed a number of problems with consumer credit arrangements. There were revelations about practices of various lenders that were, although legal, considered inappropriate. For example, credit card companies did not indicate on credit card statements how long it would take the cardholder to pay off their balance if the holder only made the required minimum payment. Another example was mortgage lenders making loans that exceeded the capacity of the borrower to repay or that mortgage lenders were steering borrowers into subprime (and higher interest rate mortgages) when they qualified for a prime loan.

Congress took up the issue of abuses by organizations that lent to consumers. The credit card industry was the first to be addressed (see Issue 10 in the 14th edition of this volume) and in 2009, the Credit Card Accountability, Responsibility, and Disclosure Act (the Credit Card Act) became law. Congress did eventually pass the Wall Street Reform and Consumer Protection Act (Dodd–Frank) in 2010. This legislation creates the Bureau of Consumer Financial Protection that is housed within the Fed. The two selections presented here are excerpted testimony in hearings held before the legislation was passed. They are representative of the controversy that still exists about the consumer protection part of the legislation.

YES

Janis Bowdler

Testimony before the U.S. House of Representatives Committee on Financial Services

... **T**he economic consequences from the recession and historically high foreclosure rates are broadly and deeply felt by middle-class families nationwide, and communities of color have been hit particularly hard. Congress has a responsibility to plug the holes in a broken financial system that allowed millions of families to watch their savings and wealth evaporate and their debt skyrocket.

In my testimony today, I will discuss the structural flaws in the credit market that led to millions of families being shuffled into ill-fitting credit products. Then I will offer NCLR's feedback on the proposed CFPA, followed by recommendations.

A Broken System

Most Americans share a fundamental goal of achieving economic sustainability and wealth that they can pass to their children. To do so, they rely on financial products such as mortgages, car loans, credit cards, insurance, and retirement accounts to facilitate their upward mobility. Unfortunately, structural flaws in our financial market have resulted in unequal access to those products key to economic success and the proliferation of deceptive practices. As a result, Hispanic families routinely pay more for credit, often accompanied by risky terms. Not surprisingly, they also bear a disproportionate share of the consequences, as demonstrated by declining income, wealth, and homeownership levels.

Despite having the necessary authority and mandates, federal regulators failed to reign in the worst practices or advance policies that could have set families up for financial success. In fact, rollbacks on regulations and oversight paved the way for many troubling practices. Borrowers that were otherwise qualified for credit but considered hard-to-serve were often shut out of the market and forced to rely on inferior products. Issuers of subprime mortgage and credit frequently targeted minority communities as fertile ground for expansion, often as a *replacement* of prime products rather than a complement. Much of this lending was conducted by underregulated finance companies. In the years before the burst of the housing bubble, true market oversight was nearly impossible and gaming the system became widespread.

Under such a regime, Latino borrowers and neighborhoods fared poorly. The lack of strong oversight,

inability to identify disparate impact trends, and general inactivity to prevent deceptive practices have manifested real consequences for struggling families. Specifically, deficient oversight failed Latinos, other communities of color, and those of modest means in the following ways:

- **Access to prime products was restricted, even when borrowers had good credit and high incomes.** This most often occurred because short-term profits were prioritized over long-term gains. For instance, many Hispanic borrowers have unique profiles that creditors often consider "hard-to-serve."[1] Despite the fact that sound underwriting models and products exist that can service consumers with these characteristics, there was little incentive to sell them in the marketplace. Such models earned issuers little profit, while subprime models had streamlined underwriting processes and were easy to line with high fees and inflated interest rates. The profitability of the models was also set in part by the price that Wall Street was willing to pay for risk. As their appetite for risk grew, expensive and risky subprime credit became readily available while affordable and low-risk prime credit was restricted. In this way, expensive and risky products drove out those that were most favorable to borrowers. As a result, Latino families have paid more for credit in most market segments. They are 30% more likely to receive high-cost mortgages, nearly twice as likely as White families to have credit card interest rates over 20%, and more likely to be charged costly markups on their auto loans.

- **Disparate impact trends and practices were not properly identified, investigated, or acted upon.** Despite clear evidence that minority borrowers were paying more for credit and being steered into subprime credit when they qualified for prime, the trends went unnoticed by federal regulators. Federal analysts claimed that not enough data was available to take enforcement action against specific lenders. However, the Federal Reserve and other agencies did not exercise their authority to further investigate clear and obvious signs of trouble. For example, a recent study shows that even after controlling for percent minority, low credit scores, poverty, and median home value, the proportion of subprime loans originated at the metropolitan level correlates with racial segregation.[2] In fact, a study conducted by the Department of Housing and Urban Development (HUD) in 2000 found that *high-income* Blacks living in predominately Black neighborhoods were three times more likely to receive a subprime purchase loan than *low-income* White borrowers.[3] Simple investigations would have turned up enough information to justify new lending rules and guidance, and possibly enforcement action. In fact, in one private meeting with a major mortgage lender, NCLR discovered that the company's wholesale portfolio consisted almost entirely of Black clients and only offered high-cost loans. The company was clearly targeting minority communities with its subprime affiliate while catering to affluent White households with its retail operation. A similar practice has also been revealed by whistleblowers in *Baltimore v. Wells Fargo*, who claim that deliberate strategies were employed whereby agents would target communities of color to market subprime mortgages.[4] Other research has shown that payday lenders, "buy here pay here" auto dealers, and other fringe financial providers tend to cluster in minority and low-income communities.[5]

- **Shopping for credit was nearly impossible.** Many experts pointed to the growing complexity of credit products and many reports demonstrated that consumers lacked the information necessary to make sound decisions. Credit card, auto, and mortgage offers are not transparent, and borrowers are often unaware of the hidden costs in their loans. Few shopping tools exist that can help borrowers create true apples-to-apples cost comparisons. As a result, many borrowers forego shopping all together. According to one survey, only 7% of Hispanic consumers who carry a credit card balance report "substantial" shopping for credit, compared to 12% for similar White consumers; approximately 25% of Hispanic card users that had been denied a loan did not reapply for fear of rejection.[6] In the case of mortgage and auto loans, mortgage brokers and auto dealers serve as an intermediary between the borrower and the lender. While many borrowers believe these agents are shopping for the best deal on their behalf, they are under no legal or ethical responsibility to do so. While most consumers do not proactively shop for credit, credit issuers shop aggressively for borrowers. Roughly 5.2 billion credit card solicitations were sent to U.S. households in 2004.[7] Through the collection of consumer financial information, issuers essentially prescreen and select their customers. Meanwhile, federal regulators sat on major reforms for years that could have improved shopping, such as a revised Good Faith Estimate and other documents made available under the Real Estate and Settlement Procedures Act (RESPA) and reforms defining unfair and deceptive marketing practices. ˉ

While some would be happy to allow market forces to continue unchecked, this regulatory philosophy has had serious consequences for families and local and national economies. For example, credit card companies made over

$17 billion in penalty fees in 2006[8] and banks will make $38.5 billion in customer overdraft fees in 2009,[9] money that could otherwise be used for household expenses or savings. Subprime foreclosures are estimated to cost states and local governments $917 million in lost property tax revenue,[10] while payday lenders drain nearly $5 billion per year from the earnings of working people.[11] After reaching an all-time high, the homeownership rate for native-born Latinos has declined by nearly three percentage points in just three years.[12] As wealth and savings have eroded, families are left with no safety net for emergencies and an uncertain financial future.

Establishing Commonsense Oversight

As members of this committee seek to revamp our financial regulatory system to prevent further crisis, they must fill the gaps in oversight and accountability that left Hispanic borrowers vulnerable to steering and other unfair practices. Specifically, lawmakers must ensure that borrowers have the opportunity to be matched to credit products that truly reflect their risk of nonpayment in the most affordable terms possible. This includes improving competition and transparent shopping opportunities, promoting a viable and nonpredatory subprime market, advancing new consumer decision-making tools, and increasing product innovation to serve a wide range of credit needs. Furthermore, any reform must also establish strong market accountability. Credit markets and practices are dynamic, as are the tricks bad actors use to lure borrowers into products laced with risky and expensive features. While some argue that it is the borrower's responsibility to be on the lookout for deception, it is unreasonable to expect individual families to be able to regulate the market and, in effect, detect what the Federal Reserve did not. Lessons from the market implosion suggest that simply having good products available does not guarantee that they will reach the intended population. Bad practices often kept best practices and products at bay. The ideal regulatory structure would be able to identify and eliminate deceptive practices and enforce strong consumer protection laws.

The Consumer Financial Protection Agency (CFPA), proposed by the Obama administration and members of this committee, is the dominant policy proposal currently under consideration to address these issues. NCLR supports the creation of a new agency dedicated to consumer protection, product innovation, and equal access to financial markets. While some are pointing to recent actions by federal regulators as evidence that the necessary regulatory capacity exists, conflicts of interest prevent federal agencies from focusing expressly on the needs of consumers, especially those of color. Federal regulators missed key trends impacting Latinos and all consumers, acting only when it was too late to stop an implosion of the credit market. That said, the CFPA must be established with the authority, jurisdiction, and funding necessary to carry out to accomplish its mission. As laid out in the discussion draft of the "Consumer Financial Protection Act of 2009,"[13] the agency stands to improve market oversight in critical ways. Other aspects, however, still require strengthening.

As this committee moves forward with its deliberations, we urge you to retain the following aspects of the discussion draft:

- **Elevation of fair lending laws.** As described above, many Latino consumers were steered into subprime loans, even when they had high incomes and good credit. Had federal regulators better enforced fair lending laws, many such tactics would have been eliminated. The discussion draft authorizes CFPA to assume responsibility for overseeing the financial industry's compliance with fair lending laws currently under the jurisdiction of the federal regulators. It also explicitly incorporates civil rights into the agency's mission, as well as its structure, by establishing an Office of Fair Lending and Equal Opportunity. These additions elevate the enforcement of fair lending as a major priority within the agency. We urge lawmakers to go one step further in tasking CFPA with identifying trends and practices that have disparate impact on minority and underserved populations, and taking the steps necessary to curb such behavior.
- **Strong supervision and consumer protection rule-writing ability.** In the most recent draft, CFPA has been granted robust rule-writing authority that will allow it to consolidate enforcement of consumer protection laws and better protect financial services consumers. It also provides the agency with an independent Executive Director, which will allow the agency to stay objective in its assessments of the market. Moreover, rules issued by CFPA will not preempt stronger laws elsewhere, ensuring that no borrowers lose protection as a result of CFPA action. These provisions should not be weakened.

In addition to these provisions, NCLR has also been working closely with members of the committee to lay the groundwork for greater access to financial advice. Timely advice and information is critical to improving the way consumers make decisions, promoting wealthbuilding and preventing cycles of debt. It is not enough for CFPA to develop passive and generic materials. Instead, they must actively promote the delivery of financial counseling from trained professionals to families that need it most.

CFPA could be a strong vehicle for improving the way financial markets serve their Latino clients. However, more could be done to ensure that this new agency can fully accomplish its goals. NCLR strongly encourages Congress to strengthen or reinstate key provisions to guarantee that Hispanic consumers are well-served. Specifically:

- **Improve access to simple, prime credit products.** Ensuring that one can obtain the most favorable credit product and terms for which one qualifies

should be a principal goal of federal efforts to reform financial oversight. Provisions that would have required financial institutions and entities to offer basic, straightforward car and home loans or credit cards have been removed. This leaves a gaping hole in protections for households that struggle to connect to the most favorable products for which they qualify. CFPA must be able to promote and advance simple, standard products in the marketplace. This includes fostering innovation in product development to meet the needs of underserved communities. Borrowers should be qualified against that product first and opt for other products as necessary based on niche needs or qualifications.
- **Eliminate loopholes for those that broker financing and credit bureaus.** Cut off or underserved by many retail outlets, borrowers of color or those with modest incomes often rely on finance brokers to help them find a loan. Financing offered by auto dealerships, mortgage brokers, or real estate agents are major sources of credit that demand greater attention and oversight. Many of the worst abuses in the auto and home loan markets were at the hands of brokers and dealers. As those closest to the transaction, dealers, brokers, and agents have an extraordinary responsibility and opportunity to ensure that credit deals are fair and fitting to the borrower's circumstances. Moreover, an exemption was also made for credit bureaus. While not direct lenders, the practices of credit bureaus directly impact the quantity and quality of credit that flows to consumers. For example, credit bureaus set rules around the manner in which credit scores are calculated. Also, by making their data available to certain vendors, creditors are able to shop for consumers, limiting the information and offers made available to all. Real estate agents, brokers, auto dealers, and credit bureaus should not escape greater accountability. Committee members should ensure that they are within the jurisdiction of CFPA.
- **Reinstate community-level assessment in CFPA.** CFPA must be able to assess product offerings at a community and regional level. Without such an assessment, favorable credit products may be developed but will remain unavailable in entire neighborhoods. Subprime lenders, creditors, and fringe financial providers often target entire neighborhoods based on the demographics of the area. Their efforts are often successful because those offering more favorable products are physically absent or do not cater to the needs of local residents. With CRA removed from the jurisdiction of CFPA, there is no mechanism for promoting access to credit and eliminating abuses at the community level. To be successful, CFPA must be able to assess the delivery of products at the community level, as well as the products and industries themselves. Including CRA in the CFPA will give the agency the authority necessary to make such an assessment.

Conclusion

Poor oversight and market inefficiencies have diverted untold sums of hard-earned income and savings away from households. Rather than waste money, a sound financial market should provide opportunities to achieve financial security. NCLR supports the committee's efforts to improve market oversight and accountability with this shared goal in mind. As one of the hardest-hit communities by the current recession, Latinos stand to benefit from an improved market where credit is more equitably distributed. We support the concept of a strong, independent CFPA that can serve as a consumer watchdog and level the playing field for those of modest means. We also look forward to working with the committee and other policymakers on further reforms of the financial oversight system and credit markets.

References

1. See Janis Bowdler, *Jeopardizing Hispanic Homeownership: Predatory Practices in the Homebuying Market,* Issue Brief no. 15 (Washington, DC: National Council of La Raza, 2005).

2. Gregory D. Squires, Derek S. Hyra, and Robert N. Renner, "Segregation and the Subprime Lending Crisis" (paper presented at the 2009 Federal Reserve System Community Affairs Research Conference, Washington, DC, April 16, 2009).

3. U.S. Department of Housing and Urban Development, *Unequal Burden: Income and Racial Disparities in Subprime Lending in America.* Washington, DC, 2000.

4. Michael Powell, "Bank Accused of Pushing Mortgage Deals on Blacks," *New York Times,* June 6, 2009, http://www.nytimes.com/2009/06/07/us/07baltimore.html?_r=2&pagewanted=1&sq=wells%20fargo&st=cse&scp=2 (accessed September 29, 2009).

5. See Wei Li et al., *Predatory Profiling: The Role of Race and Ethnicity in the Location of Payday Lenders in California* (Washington, DC: Center for Responsible Lending, 2009).

6. Unpublished data from the *2004 Survey of Consumer Finances* tabulated by the Federal Reserve on behalf of NCLR.

7. Government Accountability Office, *Credit Cards: Increased Complexity in Rates and Fees Heightens Need for More Effective Disclosures to Consumers.* Washington, DC, 2006.

8. U.S. PIRG Education Fund, "A Consumer's Guide to Credit Cards" (Boston, MA: U.S. PIRG Education Fund) http://www.uspirg.org/html/Credit_Card_Booklet.pdf (accessed September 2009).

9. Reuters, "U.S. banks to make $38 billion from overdraft fees: report," August 10, 2009, http://www.reuters.com/article/newsOne/idUSTRE5790YM20090810 (accessed September 2009).

10. Majority Staff of the Joint Economic Committee, *The Subprime Lending Crisis: The Economic Impact on Wealth, Property Values and Tax Revenues, and How We Got Here.* Washington, DC, 2007, http://jec.senate.gov/archive/Documents/Reports/10.25.07OctoberSubprimeReport.pdf (accessed September 2009)

11. Center for Responsible Lending, "A 36% APR cap on high-cost loans promotes financial recovery" (Durham, NC: Center for Responsible Lending, 2009), http://www.responsiblelending.org/payday-lending/policy-legislation/congress/payday-and-the-economy.pdf (accessed September 2009).

12. Rakesh Kochhar, *Through Boom and Bust: Minorities, Immigrants and Homeownership* (Washington DC: Pew Hispanic Center, 2009).

13. Available at http://www.house.gov/apps/list/press/financialsvcs_dem/discussion_draft_of_cfpa_bill_092509.pdf (accessed September 28, 2009).

JANIS BOWDLER is the deputy director of the Wealth- Building Policy Project at the National Council of La Raza. In this position, she oversees policy analysis, research, and advocacy on issues related to housing, homeownership, wealth building, and financial services. She has an undergraduate degree from Malone College and a graduate degree from Cleveland State University.

Bill Himpler

Testimony before the U.S. House of Representatives Committee on Financial Services

... **C**hairman Frank, in light of the revisions for the CFPA that you put forth last week, I'd like to thank you for your willingness to listen and consider different perspectives on this very important proposal. At the same time, we noted that many of the revisions focus on nonbanks.

In addition, some committee members may have seen *The Washington Post's* front-page article on September 27th that defined consumer finance companies more narrowly than we do. Before I present our views on the CFPA, I'd like to take a minute to set the record straight regarding consumer finance companies and how they're currently regulated.

Finance companies come in many shapes and sizes—some are independently owned lenders that specialize in providing personal loans to consumers and small business owners; others are "captives" that provide financing for vehicles or other products manufactured by their parent companies. While I cannot speak for other institutions that may fall under the proposal's definition of nonbanks, I can assure this committee that finance companies are already heavily regulated.

In addition to being subjected to federal consumer protection laws, such as the Truth in Lending Act (TILA), Fair Credit Reporting Act (FCRA), and the Equal Credit Opportunity Act (ECOA), finance companies are licensed and regulated by the states and abide by consumer protection statutes in all of the states in which they do business.

Like banks, finance companies undergo regular and vigorous examination by state regulators. These companies have been successful at meeting the credit needs of communities in part because they are subject to oversight by state regulators who have a familiarity with local and regional situations and issues faced by lenders. This knowledge, along with their proximity, means state regulators frequently are among the first to identify emerging issues, practices, or products that may need further investigation. Though the state system has not been perfect, no one can argue that states have not aggressively fought abusive lending. In 2008 alone, state regulators took more than 7,000 mortgage enforcement actions.

After a careful review of the proposed revisions, AFSA remains opposed to the CFPA proposal. While some critics have equated our stance as being opposed to *any* changes to consumer protection regulations, this is not the case. To the contrary, AFSA strongly supports efforts by the Obama Administration and others to improve consumer protections for financial services customers—but we do have philosophical differences as to how to go about achieving this goal. We also have concerns that the revised language for the proposal could reduce—and perhaps eliminate—a critical source of consumer credit. I'll discuss this in more detail later.

To begin, let me outline four fundamental reasons for our position on the CFPA.

First, because it's based on the premise that the entire financial services industry is broken, the CFPA would try to "fix" what's still working.

Second, the CFPA is still likely to mean higher prices and reduced product choice for financial services customers even if the "plain vanilla" requirement was eliminated.

Third, we believe that more government intervention in the form of a vast, new regulator won't necessarily result in better consumer protection.

And fourth, the creation of another separate regulator would bifurcate the consumer protection and safety and soundness functions of financial regulation.

If Isn't Broke, Don't Fix It

The CFPA is based upon the notion that the entire financial services system is broken based upon what occurred in the housing market. In addition, the bill's intent is to use a "one-size-fits-all approach" and treat all financial services products the same. For instance, it makes no sense to compare terms, such as APR, for a 30-year fixed mortgage with those of a short-term installment loan used to buy a new washer and dryer.

It's important to recognize that mortgages are just one of many products within the expansive consumer lending marketplace. Many of the companies that would be subject to intensified requirements, greater restrictions and higher compliance costs under the CFPA would be those that didn't contribute to the mortgage crisis—i.e., those offering auto financing, personal loans and other types of products that enable consumers and small businesses to meet their everyday needs.

To put it another way, the lenders that weren't part of the problem will be left holding the bag. The financial

Himpler, Bill. United States Congress, September 30, 2009.

crisis took a toll on many of these institutions, such as the auto finance companies that are now struggling to obtain access to capital. Some of them may decide the compliance costs and risks associated with the CFPA are untenable, causing them to exit the market and leaving borrowers with fewer credit options.

More Government Doesn't Mean Better Consumer Protection

Supporters of the CFPA have attempted to portray it as a government watchdog that would be better able to weed out bad practices in the financial services sector than the existing federal agencies. Yet there's no guarantee this will happen—and policymakers should not be "tricked and trapped" into thinking that more bureaucracy is what's needed to improve consumer protection.

Even if it were scaled back in accordance to last week's revisions, the proposed agency still would require an immense amount of resources—as well as a restructuring of existing regulatory personnel—before it could become operational. Such an approach seems ill-advised when we already have several federal regulators with the expertise and experience to do the job.

What's more, putting an untested, inexperienced agency in charge of consumer protection for the entire financial marketplace could exacerbate existing problems, rather than reduce them. A public opinion survey conducted this summer found that 79% of Americans believe that "before creating a new agency, we should make sure we understand how it will impact the economy. Rushing to create it may cause more harm in the long run."

Consumers and Small Businesses Will Have Fewer, More Expensive Borrowing Options

If the CFPA were to become a reality, financial services customers are likely to have less borrowing flexibility even with the elimination of the "plain vanilla" requirement. The new regulator would still retain expansive rulemaking authority and the ability to determine allowable products and services, which will greatly influence the options that will be available to consumers. Financial institutions falling underneath the CFPA's jurisdiction will face considerable compliance costs that will get passed on to borrowers. In essence, this would impose a new tax on consumers at a time when they are least able to afford it.

Splitting the Prudential and Consumer Protection Functions Won't Yield Better Results

AFSA supports, and believes consumers will be better served by, a regulatory structure where prudential and consumer protection oversight is housed within a single regulator. Congress tried to separate these two intertwined functions with the Government Sponsored Enterprises (GSEs). Federal Housing Finance Agency Director James Lockhart recently cited this separation of functions as one of the primary reasons for the failure of Fannie Mae and Freddie Mac. Today, no evidence shows that a separation of prudential and consumer protection regulation will offer better results in the financial services arena—in fact, indications are to the contrary. We urge Congress to support a regulatory structure that does not separate financial products and services from the viability of the companies that offer them.

Indeed, given that the agency would be required only to "consult" with prudential regulators, it is all too likely that the agency would embark on a mission to severely restrict sound business and financial practices it perceives as not "consumer friendly."

CFPA—Economic Ramifications

For the reasons I've just explained, AFSA believes the creation of a CFPA will not fulfill the goal of improving consumer protection for financial services customers. It most certainly is not in the consumer's best interest to add layers of bureaucracy, reduce credit choices, and raise prices for financial services.

In addition, I'd also like to point out that, if the proposal were to focus on nonbanks, it could reduce—and perhaps eliminate—many finance companies, which are a critical source of credit for consumers and small businesses.

While banks play a vital role in the economy and the consumer credit market, Federal Reserve Board statistics show that the majority of non-mortgage consumer credit is provided by finance companies and others who raise funds through securitization. Finance companies have a long history of meeting the credit needs of consumers—from buying a car to get to work, to paying college costs for a son or daughter.

Today's installment lenders are a key element in supporting the country's economic health. People turn to installment lenders for a multitude of reasons. Key among these, however, is the need to access small sums to deal with unforeseen circumstances.

Take for example, an unanticipated car repair. Keeping one's vehicle in good repair is essential to allow transportation to work. Absent access to small sums over and above a wage, the repairs necessary for such transportation may not be possible, resulting in job loss. Many less-advantaged citizens in our country do not have access to the kinds of credit cards and financial offerings available to the more fortunate, and have long relied on access to small-sum installment loans to meet their credit needs. And they have proven that they can and do make good use of borrowed money, even if they sometimes struggle to demonstrate their creditworthiness to lenders.

In addition to installment lenders, auto finance companies are vitally important, especially in an economy where preserving or finding employment is foremost on the minds of many Americans. Vehicles play a critical role in sustaining employment because the majority of Americans still use them to get to work. A 2007 U.S. Census Bureau American Community Survey found that close to nine out of 10 workers drove to work in 2005, with 75% of the commuters driving alone.

It's worth noting that, while the proposed revisions to the CFPA legislation would exempt car dealers, this will be of little consequence to them. These dealers, after all, will need finance companies to provide their customers with a means to acquire cars.

Consumers are not the only ones who will feel the effects—millions of small businesses will as well. According to a September 2009 report from the U.S. Chamber of Commerce's Center for Capital Markets Competitiveness, most of the 26.7 million businesses in the United States, including the self employed, rely on credit cards, home equity loans and other sources of consumer lending to finance their business. Among the report's conclusions is that "the CFPA credit squeeze would likely result in business closures, fewer startups and slower growth."

If installment, auto and other finance companies were required to shoulder much of the compliance burden resulting from a CFPA, it undoubtedly would affect their ability to provide safe, convenient, and affordable loans—just as the economy is starting to show signs of recovery.

A More Effective Approach

AFSA does not oppose consumer protections—it embraces them. We support rational consumer protection that is regulated and enforced in a manner that allows financial services providers to plan and price for risk, to operate their businesses efficiently and safely, and promote access to a full range of credit products for Americans.

To that end, we offer the following suggestions:

1. *Improve consumer disclosures*
   We agree with Elizabeth Warren and others who have cited the need for clear, easy-to-understand disclosures for consumer credit products—but it makes no sense to create another agency when we already have an alphabet soup of regulators that can do the job.
2. *Consider alternatives to the CFPA*

The CFPA is not the only option we have for changing consumer protection. Representative Minnick, for example, is working on an alternative proposal that would have existing federal and state regulators work together on a "consumer financial protection council." Given the importance of this issue, we urge this committee to avoid rushing into solutions that, in the end, could create more harm than good.

3. *Pursue a regulatory structure that does not separate financial products and services from the viability of the companies that offer them*
   All prudential agencies should work together to coordinate on consumer protection regulation for financial products and services with the goal that the regulations be consistent and uniform.
4. *Step up enforcement of existing consumer protection laws*
   This is not to say we advocate the status quo. While the current financial regulators already have many enforcement tools at their disposal, changes are needed to enable these regulators to fully utilize these tools. This includes allocating sufficient resources and other support.
5. *Continue efforts to improve financial education*
   The President's Advisory Council on Financial Literacy and the U.S. Treasury's Office of Financial Education play important roles in working with the financial services industry and others in the private sector on financial literacy initiatives. Ultimately, an educated consumer is the best defense against fraud and unscrupulous practices.

As I said at the outset, we fully support the goal of the administration and this committee to improve the quality and effectiveness of consumer protection for all Americans. I appreciate the opportunity to testify here today and am happy to answer any questions Members may have.

BILL HIMPLER is the executive vice president of the American Financial Service Association. Prior to this position, he headed the congressional relations office of the U.S. Department of Housing and Urban Development. He holds a law degree from the Catholic University of America.

EXPLORING THE ISSUE

Do American Consumers Need a Financial Protection Agency?

Critical Thinking and Reflection

1. Is it beneficial to the consumer that there exists a great variety of different lending organizations? Why or why not?
2. If lenders are guilty of inappropriate practices and yet have done nothing illegal, who should be held most accountable: the lenders, the borrowers, or the regulatory agencies? Explain.
3. Why would it be that Hispanic families in the United States routinely pay more for credit, often accompanied by risky terms?
4. How could comparative shopping for credit products be more facilitated than it currently is?

Is There Common Ground?

In the testimonies of Bowdler and Himpler, shared objectives are not hard to find. The idea of improved consumer protection for financial-services customers is one of them. The need for easy-to-understand disclosures for consumer credit products is another. Even the contentions that vigorous and vigilant regulation is necessary and that existing regulations could and should be better enforced are common to both voices in this debate.

It is really only at the specific point from which the title question is asked—do American consumers need a financial protection agency?—that the lines are drawn. Bowdler says the failure of the existing regulatory agencies justifies the creation of a federal Consumer Financial Protection Agency. Himpler, however, believes that a heavily regulated system at the state level already exists and that a federal agency will not improve matters and may make things worse. And therein lies the essential argument between the two testimonies: similar goals, different approaches.

Create Central

www.mhhe.com/createcentral

Additional Resources

CCH Tax Law Editors, *American Recovery and Reinvestment Act of 2009: Law, Explanation and Analysis* (CCH, Inc., 2009)

Kaminsky, Graciela L., and Carmen M. Reinhart, *International Finance Discussion Papers: The Twin Crises: The Causes of Banking and Balance-of-Payments Problems* (BiblioGov, 2013)

Mishel, Lawrence, et al., *The State of Working America* (ILR Press, 2012)

Internet References . . .

AFSA

www.afsaonline.org/library/files
/AFSALetterCFPBApril2010.pdf

Huffington Post

www.huffingtonpost.com/tag/consumer-financial
-protection-agency

Mint.com

www.mint.com/blog/trends/what-the-consumer
-financial-protection-agency-means-for-you/

Washington Times

www.washingtontimes.com/news/2009/sep/15
/consumer-protection-fight-looms/

ISSUE

Should Minimum Wage and Living Wage Laws Be Eliminated?

YES: D. W. MacKenzie, from "Mythology of the Minimum Wage," Ludwig von Mises Institute (May 3, 2006)

NO: Jeannette Wicks-Lim, from "Measuring the Full Impact of Minimum and Living Wage Laws," *Dollars & Sense* (May/June 2006)

Learning Outcomes

After reading this issue, you will be able to:

- Describe "Okun's law" about the relationship between unemployment and GDP.
- Identify the apparent party lines on minimum wage laws.
- Discuss the stagnation, in nominal terms, of the minimum wage over the nine years preceding 2006.
- Cite the history of the pre–minimum-wage unemployment rate as far back as 1902.

ISSUE SUMMARY

YES: Economics instructor D. W. MacKenzie believes that eliminating minimum wage laws would "reduce unemployment and improve the efficiency of markets for low productivity labor." He also believes that the "economic case for a living wage is unfounded."

NO: Economist Jeannette Wicks-Lim stresses the ripple effects of minimum and living wage laws; these effects increase the "effectiveness" of minimum and living wage laws as "antipoverty strategies."

Congress passed the Fair Labor Standards Act (FLSA) of 1938 in the midst of the Great Depression. In one bold stroke, it established a minimum wage rate of $.25 an hour, placed controls on the use of child labor, designated 44 hours as the normal work week, and mandated that time-and-a-half be paid to anyone working longer than the normal work week. Sixty-eight years later the debates concerning child labor, length of the work week, and overtime pay have long subsided, but the debate over the minimum wage rages on.

The immediate and continued concern over the minimum wage component of the FLSA should surprise few people. Although $.25 an hour is a paltry sum compared to today's wage rates, in 1938 it was a princely reward for work. It must be remembered that jobs were hard to come by, and unemployment rates at times reached as high as 25 percent of the workforce. When work was found, any wage seemed acceptable to those who roamed the streets with no safety net to protect their families. Indeed, consider the fact that $.25 an hour was 40.3 percent of the average manufacturing wage rate for 1938.

Little wonder, then, that the business community in the 1930s was up in arms. Business leaders argued that if wages went up, prices would rise. This would choke off the little demand for goods and services that existed in the marketplace, and the demand for workers would be sure to fall. The end result would be a return to the depths of the depression, where there was little or no hope of employment for the very people who were supposed to benefit from the Fair Labor Standards Act.

Simple supply-and-demand analysis supports this view. As modern-day introductory textbooks in economics invariably show, unemployment occurs when a minimum wage greater than the equilibrium wage is mandated by law. The simplistic analysis, which assumes competitive conditions in both the product and factor markets, is predicated upon the assumptions that as wages are pushed above the equilibrium level, the quantity of labor demanded will fall and the quantity of labor supplied will increase. Wage rigidity prevents the market from clearing. The end result is an excess in the quantity of labor supplied relative to the quantity of labor demanded. The same would be true for the imposition of a living wage above the equilibrium wage.

The question that should be addressed in this debate is whether or not a simple supply-and-demand analysis is capable of adequately predicting what happens in real-world labor markets when a minimum wage or living wage is introduced or an existing minimum/living wage is raised. The significance of this is not based on idle curiosity. The minimum wage has been increased numerous times since its introduction in 1938. The current federal minimum wage of $7.25 was set in 2009. Did this minimum wage increase, and other increases before it, do irreparable harm to those who are least able to defend themselves in the labor market, the marginal workers? That is, if a minimum wage is imposed, what happens to all those marginal workers whose value to the firm is something less than the minimum wage? Are these workers fired? Do firms simply absorb this cost increase in the form of reduced corporate profits? What happens to productivity?

D. W. MacKenzie argues that eliminating the minimum wage would increase economic efficiency in the labor market for teenagers and ethnic minorities, lowering their unemployment rates. Imposition of living wages would make their unemployment rates rise higher than they are already. Jeannette Wicks-Lim focuses on the ripple effects of minimum wages and living wages, that is, how much would the wages of *other* workers increase as a result of an increase in the minimum wage? The larger the ripple effects, the stronger the case for higher wage minimums to improve the lives of the working poor.

YES ←

D. W. MacKenzie

Mythology of the Minimum Wage

Once again politicians and pundits are calling for increases in the legal minimum wage. Their reasons are familiar. Market wages are supposedly immoral. People need to earn a "living wage." If the minimum wage went up at least to $7, or better still to near $10 an hour, millions would be lifted out of poverty.[1]

The economic case against minimum wage laws is simple. Employers pay a wage no higher than the value of an additional hour's work. Raising minimum wages forces employers to dismiss low productivity workers. This policy has the largest [effect] on those with the least education, job experience, and maturity. Consequently, we should expect minimum wage laws to affect teenagers and those with less education. Eliminating minimum wage laws would reduce unemployment and improve the efficiency of markets for low productivity labor.

There are a few economists who have been leading the charge for higher minimum wages. Some of these economists have obvious ideological leanings. Economists connected with the Left-orientated Economic Policy Institute and the Clinton Administration have concocted a rational for minimum wage increases. According to these economists higher wages make employees more content with their jobs, and this leads to higher worker productivity. Thus workers will be worth paying a minimum wage once their employers are forced to pay these wages. Of course, if this were true—if employers could get higher productivity out of less educated and experienced workers by paying higher wages—they would be willing to do this without minimum wage legislation. But the economists who make this case claim to have empirical evidence that proves them right. Economists David Card and Alan Krueger have published studies of the fast food industry [indicating] that small increases in the minimum wage would cause only minor job losses, and might even increase employment slightly in some instances. These studies by Card and Krueger show only that a small increase in minimum wage rates might not cause much of an increase in unemployment. Such studies ignore the fact that the current level of minimum wages are already causing significant unemployment for some workers.

The economic case for minimum wage increases has gained some ground with public and even professional opinion. Even some free market leaning economists, like Steven Landsburg, have conceded that minimum wage increases do not affect employment significantly.[2]

Landsburg notes that critics of minimum wage laws emphasize that they have a disproportionate effect on teens and blacks. But he dismisses these critics because "minimum wages have at most a tiny impact on employment . . . The minimum wage kills very few jobs, and the jobs it kills were lousy jobs anyway. It is almost impossible to maintain the old argument that minimum wages are bad for minimum-wage workers."

Real statistics indicate that the critics of minimum wage laws were right all along. While it is true that minimum wages do not drive the national unemployment rate up to astronomical levels, it does adversely affect teenagers and ethnic minorities. According to the Bureau of Labor Statistics the unemployment rate for everyone over the age of 16 was 5.6% in 2005. Yet unemployment was 17.3% for those aged 16–19 years. For those aged 16–17 unemployment was 19.7%. In the 18–19 age group unemployment was 15.8%. Minimum wage laws do affect ethnic minorities more so than others.[3] The unemployment rate for white teens in the 16–17 age group was 17.3% in 2005. The same figures for Hispanic and black teens were 25% and 40.9% respectively. Of course, these figures decrease for older minorities. Blacks aged 18–19 and 20–24 had 25.7% and 19.9% unemployment in 2005. For Hispanics unemployment was slightly lower—17.8% at age 18–19 and 9.6% at age 20–24.

Landsburg might maintain that most of these lost jobs are lousy jobs that teens will not miss. DeLong thinks that minimum wage laws can help to avert poverty—workers who keep their jobs at the minimum wage gain much, while unemployed workers lose little. Part of the problem with this argument is that it involves arbitrary value judgments. According to mainstream economic theory, we achieve economic efficiency when markets clear because this is how we realize all gains from trade. With teen unemployment in double digits—running as high as 40.9%—it is obvious that some labor markets are not clearing. If labor market imperfections led to such levels of unemployment, economists like DeLong, Card, and Krueger would call for government intervention to correct these "market failures." Yet they find double digit teen unemployment acceptable when it derives from government intervention. Why? Because they want to use such policies to redistribute income.[4]

Mainstream economic theory lacks any basis for judging the effects of income redistribution. According to textbook economics we attain the highest level of economic efficiency when markets clear, when we realize the maximum gains from mutually advantageous trade. Income transfers benefit some at the expense of others. Economists have no scientific methods for comparing gains and losses through income transfers.[5] Once economists depart from discussing efficiency conditions and begin to speak about income redistribution, they become advocates of a political agenda, rather than objective scientists. The jobs lost to minimum wage laws might not seem worthwhile to DeLong or Landsburg, but they obviously are worthwhile to the workers and employers whom these laws affect. Why should the value judgments of a few armchair economists matter more than the interests of would be employees and employers? These jobs may be "lousy jobs," but one could also argue that these jobs are quite important because they are a first step in gaining job experience and learning adult responsibility.

A second problem with the case against minimum wages is that they affect older workers too. As already noted, workers in the 20–24 age group appear to be affected by minimum wage laws. Unemployment rates in the 25–34 age group are higher than for the 35–44 age group. The unemployment rate for blacks and Hispanics aged 25–34 were 11.1% and 5.8% in 2005. Unemployment for whites and Asians in this age group were 4.4% and 3.5%. In the 35–44 age group the unemployment rates for these four ethnicities were 7.2%., 5.1%, 4.4%, and 2.7%. A comparison of black to Asian unemployment is revealing. In the United States, Asians tend to attain higher levels of education than blacks. Thus minimum wage laws are relatively unimportant to Asian Americans. Consequently, Asians are able to attain unemployment as low as the 2–3% range. For Asians aged 16+ the unemployment rate was only 3.3% in 2005. For Asians in the 20–24 age group unemployment was 5.1%. These figures are only a fraction of the unemployment rates experienced by blacks in 2005. There is no reason why white, Hispanic, and black Americans cannot also reach the 2–3% range of unemployment.

Supporters of minimum wage laws do not realize that prior to minimum wage laws the national unemployment rate did fall well below 5%. According to the US Census, national unemployment rates were 3.3% in 1927, 1.8% in 1926, 3.2% in 1925, 2.4% in 1923, 1.4% in 1919 and 1918, 2.8% in 1907, 1.7% in 1906, and 3.7% in 1902.[6] Even today, some states have unemployment rates as low as 3%. Virginia now has an unemployment rate of 3.1%. Wyoming has an unemployment rate of 2.9%. Hawaii has an unemployment rate of 2.6%. National unemployment rates seldom drop below 5% because some categories of workers are stuck with double digit unemployment. Given these figures, it is quite arguable that minimum wage laws

keep the national unemployment rate 3 percentage points higher than would otherwise be the case.

Economist Arthur Okun estimated that for every 1% increase in unemployment GDP falls by 2.5–3%. If minimum wage laws are responsible for keeping the national unemployment rate 3 percentage points above where it would otherwise be, then the losses to minimum wage unemployment are substantial. Since Okun's law is an empirical proposition it is certainly not constant. Eliminating minimum wages might not increase GDP as much as this "law" indicates. However, the elimination of minimum wage laws would surely have a positive effect on GDP. In any case, economic theory and available data indicate that minimum wage laws do result in economic inefficiency. The implementation of a "living wage" would only increase these losses. Do proponents of living wages really want to see unemployment rates among ethnic minorities and teens climb even higher?

The economic case for a living wage is unfounded. Current minimum wage rates do create high levels of unemployment among low productivity workers. Higher "living wages" would only make these problems worse. The alleged moral case for a living wage ignores the fact that minimum wage increases adversely affect the very people whom advocates of living wages intend to help. If politicians wish to pursue sound policies, they should consider repealing minimum wage laws, especially where teens are concerned. Unfortunately, most politicians care more about political expediencies than sound economic policy. This being the case, minimum wages will increase unless public opinion changes significantly.

Notes

1. See Dreier and Candeale *A Moral Minimum Wage,* April 27, 2006 and Cauchon *States Say 5.15 too little,* April 27, 2006.
2. See *The Sin of Wages* by Steven Landsburg and *The Minimum Wage and the EITC* by J. Bradford DeLong.
3. This is likely due to the poor quality of many inner city public schools.
4. It is worth noting that Landsburg opposes redistribution via minimum wage laws.
5. This would require interpersonal comparisons of welfare. Robbins (1933) proved that such comparisons are unscientific.
6. US Bureau of the Census *Historical Statistics,* p. 135.

D. W. MACKENZIE teaches economics at the State University of New York at Plattsburgh.

Jeannette Wicks-Lim

➡ NO

Measuring the Full Impact of Minimum and Living Wage Laws

Raising the minimum wage is quickly becoming a key political issue for this fall's midterm elections. In the past, Democratic politicians have shied away from the issue while Republicans have openly opposed a higher minimum wage. But this year is different. Community activists are forcing the issue by campaigning to put state minimum-wage proposals before the voters this fall in Arizona, Colorado, Ohio, and Missouri. No doubt inspired by the 100-plus successful local living-wage campaigns of the past ten years, these activists are also motivated by a federal minimum wage that has stagnated for the past nine years. The $5.15 federal minimum is at its lowest value in purchasing-power terms in more than 50 years; a single parent with two children, working full-time at the current minimum wage, would fall $2,000 below the poverty line.

Given all the political activity on the ground, the Democrats have decided to make the minimum wage a central plank in their party platform. Former presidential candidate John Edwards has teamed up with Sen. Edward Kennedy (D-Mass.) and ACORN, a leading advocacy group for living wage laws, to push for a $7.25 federal minimum. Even some Republicans are supporting minimum wage increases. In fact, a bipartisan legislative coalition unexpectedly passed a state minimum wage hike in Michigan this March.

Minimum-wage and living-wage laws have always caused an uproar in the business community. Employers sound the alarm about the dire consequences of a higher minimum wage both for themselves and for the low-wage workers these laws are intended to benefit: Minimum wage mandates, they claim, will cause small-business owners to close shop and lay off their low-wage workers. A spokesperson for the National Federation of Independent Business (NFIB), commenting on a proposal to raise Pennsylvania's minimum wage in an interview with the Philadelphia Inquirer, put it this way: "That employer may as well be handing out pink slips along with the pay raise."

What lies behind these bleak predictions? Mark Shaffer, owner of Shaffer's Park Supper Club in Crivitz, Wisc., provided one explanation to the Wisconsin State Journal: ". . . increasing the minimum wage would create a chain reaction. Every worker would want a raise to keep pace, forcing up prices and driving away customers." In other words,

employers will not only be forced to raise the wages of those workers earning below the new minimum wage, but also the wages of their co-workers who earn somewhat more. The legally required wage raises are difficult enough for employers to absorb, they claim; these other raises—referred to as ripple effect raises—aggravate the situation. The result? "That ripple effect is going to lay off people."

Ripple effects represent a double-edged sword for minimum-wage and living-wage proponents. Their extent determines how much low-wage workers will benefit from such laws. If the ripple effects are small, then a higher minimum (or living) wage would benefit only a small class of workers, and boosting the minimum wage might be dismissed as an ineffective antipoverty strategy. If the ripple effects are large, then setting higher wage minimums may be seen as a potent policy tool to improve the lives of the working poor. But at the same time, evidence of large ripple effects provides ammunition to employers who claim they cannot afford the costs of a higher wage floor.

So what is the evidence on ripple effects? Do they bloat wage bills and overwhelm employers? Do they expand the number of workers who get raises a little or a lot? It's difficult to say because the research on ripple effects has been thin. But getting a clear picture of the full impact of minimum and living wage laws on workers' wages is critical to evaluating the impact of these laws. New research provides estimates of the scope and magnitude of the ripple effects of both minimum-wage and living-wage laws. This evidence is crucial for analyzing both the full impact of this increasingly visible policy tool and the political struggles surrounding it.

Why Do Employers Give Ripple-Effect Raises?

Marge Thomas, CEO of Goodwill Industries in Maryland, explains in an interview with The Gazette (Md.): "There will be a ripple effect [in response to Maryland's recent minimum wage increase to $6.15], since it wouldn't be fair to pay people now making above the minimum wage at the same level as those making the new minimum wage." That is, without ripple effects, an increase in the wage floor will worsen the relative wage position of workers just above it. If there are no ripple effects, workers earning $6.15 before Maryland's increase would not only see their wages fall to the bottom of the wage scale, but also to the same level as workers who had previously earned inferior wages (i.e., workers who earned between $5.15 and $6.15).

Employers worry that these workers would view such a relative decline in their wages as unfair, damaging their morale—and their productivity. Without ripple effect raises, employers fear, their disgruntled staff will cut back on hard-to-measure aspects of their work such as responding to others cheerfully and taking initiative in assisting customers.

So employers feel compelled to preserve some consistency in their wage scales. Workers earning $6.15 before the minimum increase, for example, may receive a quarter raise, to $6.40, to keep their wages just above the new $6.15 minimum. That employers feel compelled to give non-mandated raises to some of their lowest-paid workers because it is the "fair" thing to do may appear to be a dubious claim. Perhaps so, but employers commonly express anxiety about the costs of minimum-wage and living-wage laws for this very reason.

The Politics of Ripple Effects

Inevitably, then, ripple effects come into play in the political battles around minimum-wage and living-wage laws—but in contradictory ways for both opponents and supporters. Opponents raise the specter of large ripple effects bankrupting small businesses. At the same time, though, they argue that minimum-wage laws are not effective in fighting poverty because they do not cover many workers—and worse, because those who are covered are largely teens or young-adult students just working for spending money. If ripple effects are small, this shores up opponents' assertions that minimum-wage laws have a limited impact on poverty. Evidence of larger ripple effects, on the other hand, would mean that the benefits of minimum-wage laws are larger than previously understood, and that these laws have an even greater potential to reduce poverty among the working poor.

The political implications are complicated further in the context of living-wage laws, which typically call for much higher wage floors than state and federal minimum-wage laws do. The living-wage movement calls for wage floors to be set at rates that provide a "livable income," such as the federal poverty level for a family of four, rather than at the arbitrary—and very low—level current minimum-wage laws set. The difference is dramatic: the living-wage ordinances that have been passed in a number of municipalities typically set a wage floor twice the level of federal and state minimum wages.

So the mandated raises under living-wage laws are already much higher than under even the highest state minimum-wage laws. If living-wage laws have significant ripple effects, opponents have all the more ammunition for their argument that the costs of these laws are unsustainable for employers.

How Big Are Ripple Effects?

My answer is a typical economists' response: it depends. In a nutshell, it depends on how high the wage minimum is set. The reason for this is simple. Evidence from the past 20 years of changes to state and federal minimum wages suggests that while there is a ripple effect, it doesn't extend very far beyond the new minimum. So, if the wage minimum is set high, then a large number of workers are legally due raises and, relatively speaking, the number of workers who get ripple-effect raises is small. Conversely, if the wage minimum is set low, then a small number of workers are legally due raises and, relatively speaking, the number of workers who get ripple-effect raises is large.

In the case of minimum-wage laws, the evidence suggests that ripple effects do dramatically expand their impact. Minimum wages are generally set low relative to the wage distribution. Because so many more workers earn wages just above the minimum wage compared to those earning the minimum, even a small ripple effect increases considerably the number of workers who benefit from a rise in the minimum wage. And even though the size of these raises quickly shrinks the higher the worker's wage rate, the much greater number of affected workers translates into a significantly larger increase in the wage bills of employers.

For example, my research shows that the impact of the most recent federal minimum-wage increase, from $4.75 to $5.15 in 1997, extended to workers earning wages around $5.75. Workers earning between the old and new minimums generally received raises to bring their wages in line with the new minimum—an 8% raise for those who started at the old minimum. Workers earning around $5.20 (right above the new minimum of $5.15) received raises of around 2%, bringing their wages up to about $5.30. Finally, those workers earning wages around $5.75 received raises on the order of 1%, bringing their wages up to about $5.80.

This narrow range of small raises translates into a big overall impact. Roughly 4 million workers (those earning between $4.75 and $5.15) received mandated raises in response to the 1997 federal minimum wage increase. Taking into account the typical work schedules of these workers, these raises translated into a $741 million increase to employers' annual wage bills. Now add in ripple effects: Approximately 11 million workers received ripple-effect raises, adding another $1.3 billion to employers' wage bills. In other words, ripple-effect raises almost quadrupled the number of workers who benefited from the minimum-wage increase and almost tripled the overall costs associated with it.

Dramatic as these ripple effects are, the real impact on employers can only be gauged in relation to their capacity to absorb the higher wage costs. Here, there is evidence that businesses are not overwhelmed by the costs of a higher minimum wage, even including ripple effects. For example, in a study I co-authored with University of

Massachusetts economists Robert Pollin and Mark Brenner on the Florida ballot measure to establish a $6.15 state minimum wage (which passed overwhelmingly in 2004), we accounted for ripple-effect costs of roughly this same magnitude. Despite almost tripling the number of affected workers (from almost 300,000 to over 850,000) and more than doubling the costs associated with the new minimum wage (from $155 million to $410 million), the ripple effects, combined with the mandated wage increases, imposed an average cost increase on employers amounting to less than one-half of 1% of their sales revenue. Even for employers in the hotel and restaurant industry, where low-wage workers tend to be concentrated, the average cost increase was less than 1% of their sales revenue. In other words, a 1% increase in prices for hotel rooms or restaurant meals could cover the increased costs associated with both legally mandated raises and ripple-effect raises.

The small fraction of revenue that these raises represent goes a long way toward explaining why economists generally agree that minimum-wage laws are not "job killers," as opponents claim. According to a 1998 survey of economists, a consensus seems to have been reached that there is minimal job loss, if any, associated with minimum-wage increases in the ranges that we've seen.

Just as important, this new research revises our understanding of who benefits from minimum wage laws. Including ripple-effect raises expands the circle of minimum-wage beneficiaries to include more adult workers and fewer teenage or student workers. In fact, accounting for ripple effects decreases the prevalence of teenagers and traditional-age students (age 16 to 24) among workers likely to be affected by a federal minimum-wage increase from four out of ten to three out of ten. In other words, adult workers make up an even larger majority of likely minimum-wage beneficiaries when ripple effects are added to the picture.

The Case of Living-Wage Laws

With living-wage laws, the ripple effect story appears to be quite different, however—primarily because living wage laws set much higher wage minimums.

To understand why living-wage laws might generate far less of a ripple effect than minimum-wage hikes, it is instructive to look at the impact of raising the minimum wage on the retail trade industry. About 15% of retail trade workers earn wages at or very close to the minimum wage, compared to 5% of all workers. As a result, a large fraction of the retail trade industry workforce receives legally mandated raises when the minimum wage is raised, which is just what occurs across a broader group of industries and occupations when a living-wage ordinance is passed.

My research shows that the relative impact of the ripple effect that accompanies a minimum-wage hike is much smaller within retail trade than across all industries. Because a much larger share of workers in retail receive legally required raises when the minimum wage is raised, this reduces the relative number of workers receiving ripple effect raises, and, in turn, the relative size of the costs associated with ripple effects. This analysis suggests that the ripple effects of living wage laws will likewise be smaller than those found with minimum-wage laws.

To be sure, the ripple effect in the retail trade sector may underestimate the ripple effect of living-wage laws for a couple of reasons. First, unlike minimum-wage hikes, living-wage laws may have ripple effects that extend across firms as well as up the wage structure within firms. Employers who do not fall under a living-wage law's mandate but who are competing for workers within the same local labor market as those that do may be compelled to raise their own wages in order to retain their workers. Second, workers just above living-wage levels are typically higher on the job ladder and may have more bargaining power than workers with wages just above minimum-wage levels and, as a result, may be able to demand more significant raises when living-wage laws are enacted.

However, case studies of living-wage ordinances in Los Angeles and San Francisco do suggest that the ripple effect plays a smaller role in the case of living-wage laws than in the case of minimum-wage laws. These studies find that ripple effects add less than half again to the costs of mandated raises—dramatically less than the almost tripling of costs by ripple effects associated with the 1997 federal minimum-wage increase. In other words, the much higher wage floors set by living-wage laws appear to reverse the importance of legally required raises versus ripple-effect raises.

Do the costs associated with living-wage laws—with their higher wage floors—overwhelm employers, even if their ripple effects are small? To date, estimates suggest that within the range of existing living-wage laws, businesses are generally able to absorb the cost increases they face. For example, Pollin and Brenner studied a 2000 proposal to raise the wage floor from $5.75 to $10.75 in Santa Monica, Calif. They estimated that the cost increase faced by a typical business would be small, on the order of 2% of sales revenue, even accounting for both mandated and ripple-effect raises. Their estimates also showed that some hotel and restaurant businesses might face cost increases amounting to up to 10% of their sales revenue—not a negligible sum. However, after examining the local economy, Pollin and Brenner concluded that even these cost increases would not be likely to force these businesses to close their doors. Moreover, higher productivity and lower turnover rates among workers paid a living wage would also reduce the impact of these costs.

Ultimately, the impact of ripple-effect raises appears to depend crucially on the level of the new wage floor. The lower the wage floor, as in the case of minimum-wage laws, the more important the role of ripple-effect raises. The higher the wage floor, as in the case of living-wage laws, the less important the role of ripple-effect raises.

Making the Case

The results of this new research are generally good news for proponents of living- and minimum-wage laws. Ripple effects do not portend dire consequences for employers from minimum and living wage laws; at the same time, ripple-effect raises heighten the effectiveness of these laws as antipoverty strategies.

In the case of minimum-wage laws, because the cost of legally mandated raises relative to employer revenues is small, even ripple effects large enough to triple the cost of a minimum-wage increase do not represent a large burden for employers. Moreover, ripple effects enhance the somewhat anemic minimum-wage laws to make them more effective as policy tools for improving the lot of the working poor. Accounting for ripple effects nearly quadruples the number of beneficiaries of a minimum-wage hike and expands the majority of those beneficiaries who are adults—in many instances, family breadwinners.

However, ripple effects do not appear to overwhelm employers in the case of the more ambitious living-wage laws. The strongest impact from living-wage laws appears to come from legally required raises rather than from ripple-effect raises. This reinforces advocates' claims that paying a living wage is a reasonable, as well as potent, way to fight poverty.

JEANNETTE WICKS-LIM is an economist and research fellow at the Political Economy Research Institute at the University of Massachusetts–Amherst. She holds an undergraduate degree from the University of Michigan and earned her PhD in economics from the University of Massachusetts–Amherst.

EXPLORING THE ISSUE

Should Minimum Wage and Living Wage Laws Be Eliminated?

Critical Thinking and Reflection

1. Does "Okun's law" present a worthy factor in the debate over minimum and living wage laws? Explain.
2. If the "ripple effect" plays a lesser role in the case of living wage laws than in the case of minimum wage laws, why might that be?
3. Is it a reasonable prediction that employment rates for black and Hispanic teens could improve with the elimination of the minimum wage? Why or why not?
4. Why has the debate over minimum wage raged on since its inception in the Fair Labor Standards Act of 1938, while other issues addressed in that act (child labor, length of work week, overtime pay) have long ago lost their controversy?

Is There Common Ground?

Statistical analysis, which certainly can be a valuable discipline, can also be utilized by opposing points of view, to the advantage of each. Which numbers are examined and the interpretations derived from them definitely play key roles in each presentation of this debate. Not unlike many opposing analyses, the statistics cited here are clearly selected to support each side's original premise.

So, while their conclusions may be quite different, one from the other, MacKenzie and Wicks-Lim do have a shared purpose: they both believe in a strong workforce, equitable employment opportunities, and the lowest unemployment figures possible. Although they disagree on the effects that minimum wage has on these ideals, the common ground of the ideals themselves is significant.

Create Central

www.mhhe.com/createcentral

Additional Resources

Landsburg, Steven E., *The Armchair Economist: Economics and Everyday Life* (Free Press, 2012)

Pollin, Robert, et al., *A Measure of Fairness: The Economics of Living Wages and Minimum Wages in the United States* (ILR Press, 2008)

Stabile, Donald R., *The Living Wage: Lessons from the History of Economic Thought* (Edward Elgar, 2009)

Internet References . . .

David Card (Berkeley): "Minimum Wages and Employment: A Case Study of the Fast-Food Industry in New Jersey and Pennsylvania"

http://davidcard.berkeley.edu/papers/njmin-aer.pdf

The Economist: "Living-Wage Laws: Bad Welfare"

www.economist.com/blogs /democracyinamerica/2013/07/living-wage-laws

United States Department of Labor

www.dol.gov/whd/minwage/coverage.htm

ISSUE

Does Immigration Benefit the Economy?

YES: George W. Bush White House, from "Immigration's Economic Impact," *White Paper* (June 20, 2007)

NO: Steven A. Camarota, from "Testimony before the U.S. House of Representatives Committee on the Judiciary, Subcommittee on Immigration, Citizenship, Refugees, Border Security and International Law" (September 30, 2010)

Learning Outcomes

After reading this issue, you will be able to:

- Cite the George W. Bush White House's three key findings on immigration's economic impact.
- Define the term "immigration surplus."
- Enumerate the four main lessons imparted by the long-term fiscal view on immigration (per Bush).
- Recognize the formulas used to estimate wage loss.

ISSUE SUMMARY

YES: In its White Paper, the George W. Bush White House argues that immigration has a positive effect on the American economy because it increases overall economic activity, increases incomes of native-born Americans, and produces positive long-run fiscal effects.

NO: Steven A. Camarota, the director of research at the Center for Immigration Studies, argues that immigration is harmful to the economy in several different ways including wage losses for the existing population and an increase in net government costs.

The importance of immigration to the founding and development of the U.S. economy can be demonstrated in a variety of ways. First, and most obvious, one can reference the discovery of America by Columbus. Then one can conjure up the images of the *Mayflower*, the pilgrims, and Plymouth Rock. There is the poem of Emma Lazarus inscribed on the pedestal of the Statue of Liberty: "Give me your tired, your poor, your huddled masses yearning to breathe free. . . ."

All of these references are positive, pointed to with pride. But the fact remains that for most of our history immigration has been a point of controversy and frequently heated controversy. This is certainly true today with both legal and illegal immigration generating strong public and private discussion. How do we stop the flow of illegal immigrants into the country? What should we do with the illegal immigrants who are already in the country? Should we increase the flow of legal immigrants, especially those with valuable skills like scientists and engineers? Should we reduce or even eliminate the inflow of legal but unskilled immigrants? How far should we

go to fortify our borders to prevent illegal immigration? There is even talk of changing U.S. policy so that the children of illegal immigrants born in this country would not be given automatic citizenship.

Before getting into the current issue, some background and data provide context. According to the Census Bureau, the U.S. population in 2009 was 301.5 million. The Census Bureau classifies 264.7 million of these as "native," that is, individuals who were born in the United States, "in Puerto Rico, U.S. Island areas, or born abroad to American parent(s)." The remaining 36.8 million portion of the U.S. population is classified as "foreign born." The Census Bureau then divides the "foreign born" into two groups: 15.5 million naturalized citizens and 21.3 million "noncitizens" (http://factfinder .census.gov/servlet/ADPTable?_bm=y&-geo_id=01000US&-ds _name=ACS_2009_5YR_G00_&-_lang=en&-_caller=geoselect& -format). But not all the 21.3 million of the "noncitizens" are, to use the government term, "unauthorized immigrants" or what many refer to as illegal immigrants. According to the Department of Homeland Security, there were approximately 10.8 million immigrants in the United States in 2009 (http://www.dhs.gov/xlibrary/assets/statistics/publications/ois_ill_pe_2009.pdf).

But how do authorized immigrants get into the United States? First, they must obtain an immigrant visa—issued to those who intend to live and work permanently in the United States. As described by immigration services, "Having a U.S. visa allows you to travel to a port of entry, airport or land border crossing, and request permission of the Department of Homeland Security (DHS) Custom and Border Protection (CBP) inspector to enter the U.S." (http://travel.state.gov/visa/questions/what/what_4429.html).

Once the permission is secured, the next step is to obtain a Permanent Resident Card (a "green card"), which constitutes proof that an immigrant has been granted authorization to live and work in the United States on a permanent basis (http://www.usaimmigration.info/). A person with a green card then has the option of beginning the process of becoming a U.S. citizen or continuing to work and live in the United States as a noncitizen.

The government also issues nonimmigrant or temporary visas for those who come as tourists, on business, to seek medical treatment, or to engage in certain types of temporary work. Unauthorized immigrants are those individuals who enter the United States without a visa (sneaking in) or who enter with a temporary visa and then do not leave when the temporary visa expires. A study by the Pew Hispanic Center using census data estimates the number of unauthorized immigrants entering the United States in 2009 at about 300,000 (http://pewhispanic.org/reports/report.php?ReportID=126).

As noted, the debate about immigration takes place at several different levels. The selections here are concerned with legal overall immigration and whether or not such immigration helps or hurts the economy. For a debate on unskilled immigration, see Issue 12 in the 14th edition of *Taking Sides: Clashing Views on Economic Issues*. Here the George W. Bush administration argues that immigration is a net positive for the country, whereas Steven Camarota holds that while immigration may increase total production, its net effects are negative.

YES ↵

George W. Bush White House

Immigration's Economic Impact

Introduction

In 2006, foreign-born workers accounted for 15% of the U.S. labor force, and over the last decade they have accounted for about half of the growth in the labor force. That immigration has fueled U.S. macroeconomic growth is both uncontroversial and unsurprising—more total workers yield more total output. That immigrant workers benefit from working in the United States is also uncontroversial and unsurprising—few would come here otherwise.[1]

Assessing how immigration affects the well-being of U.S. natives is more complicated. This is because immigration's economic impact is complex and may play out over generations, and because not all natives are alike in terms of their economic characteristics. Even in retrospect it is not easy to distinguish the influence of immigration from that of other economic forces at work at the same time. Nor is it easy to project costs and benefits far into the future. Nonetheless, economists and demographers have made headway on many of the measurement problems. This white paper assesses immigration's economic impact based on the professional literature and concludes that immigration has a positive effect on the American economy as a whole and on the income of native-born American workers.

Key Findings

1. On average, U.S. natives benefit from immigration. Immigrants tend to complement (not substitute for) natives, raising natives' productivity and income.
2. Careful studies of the long-run fiscal effects of immigration conclude that it is likely to have a modest, positive influence.
3. Skilled immigrants are likely to be especially beneficial to natives. In addition to contributions to innovation, they have a significant positive fiscal impact.

General Points

- Immigrants are a critical part of the U.S. work-force and contribute to productivity growth and technological advancement. They make up 15% of all workers and even larger shares of certain occupations such as construction, food services

and health care. Approximately 40% of Ph.D. scientists working in the United States were born abroad. (Source: Bureau of Labor Statistics; American Community Survey)
- Many immigrants are entrepreneurs. The Kauffman Foundation's index of entrepreneurial activity is nearly 40% higher for immigrants than for natives. (Source: Kauffman Foundation)
- Immigrants and their children assimilate into U.S. culture. For example, although 72% of first-generation Latino immigrants use Spanish as their predominant language, only 7% of the second generation are Spanish-dominant. (Source: Pew Hispanic Center/Kaiser Family Foundation)
- Immigrants have lower crime rates than natives. Among men aged 18 to 40, immigrants are much less likely to be incarcerated than natives. (Source: Butcher and Piehl)
- Immigrants slightly improve the solvency of pay-as-you-go entitlement programs such as Social Security and Medicare. The 2007 OASDI Trustees Report indicates that an additional 100,000 net immigrants per year would increase the long-range actuarial balance by about 0.07% of taxable payroll. (Source: Social Security Administration)
- The long-run impact of immigration on public budgets is likely to be positive. Projections of future taxes and government spending are subject to uncertainty, but a careful study published by the National Research Council estimated that immigrants and their descendants would contribute about $80,000 more in taxes (in 1996 dollars) than they would receive in public services. (Source: Smith and Edmonston)

Evaluating the Effect of Immigration on the Income of Natives

Immigrants not only change the size of the labor force, they change the relative supplies of factors such as unskilled labor, skilled labor, and capital in the economy. U.S. natives tend to benefit from immigration precisely because immigrants are not exactly like natives in terms of their productive characteristics and factor endowments. For example, . . . in contrast to their 15% share in the total labor force, foreign-born workers accounted for much higher proportions of workers without high school degrees

From White House Release, June 20, 2007.

and of those with Ph.D. degrees (especially for those working in scientific occupations). Differences between natives and immigrants lead to production complementarities that benefit natives.

Example:

- The presence of unskilled foreign-born construction laborers allows skilled U.S. craftsmen and contractors to build more homes at lower cost than otherwise—therefore the U.S. natives' productivity and income rise.
- Thus, when immigrants are added to the U.S. labor force, they increase the economy's total output, which is split between immigrants (who receive wages) and natives (who receive wages and also earn income from their ownership of physical and human capital). Natives may also gain from having a wider variety of goods and services to consume and from lower prices for the goods and services produced by industries with high concentrations of foreign-born workers.

The "immigration surplus" is a simple and frequently cited metric of natives' total gains from immigration. The surplus accrues to native factors of production that are complemented by immigrant workers—that is, to factors whose productivity is enhanced by the presence of immigrants. In a simple model with just capital and labor (not differentiated by skill), similar in structure to that presented in the National Research Council (NRC) analysis, one can estimate this surplus as the area of a triangle defined by a downward sloping labor demand curve and the shift in labor supply attributed to immigration. Using a standard estimate of labor demand elasticity (0.3) and measures of the foreign-born share of the labor force, the current immigration surplus is about 0.28% of GDP, or roughly $37 billion per year.[2]

Although the simplicity of the "immigration surplus" approach is attractive, the implicit assumptions are numerous, and it is well understood by economists that this is not a full reckoning of immigration's influence on the economy. For example, the approach does not differentiate between different kinds of workers (by skill, experience, or nativity) and does not allow for an endogenous and positive capital market response to the change in labor supply. Because immigration changes the mix of factors in the economy, it may influence the pattern of factor prices, which in turn may induce endogenous changes in other factor supplies. Moreover, implicit in the surplus calculation is an assumed negative effect on average wages for natives—an effect that is difficult to detect in empirical studies of the U.S. wage structure.[3]

A more complex approach to measuring the influence of immigration on natives' income differentiates workers by skill, nativity, and experience and also allows for a capital accumulation response to changes in the supply of labor. In this scenario complementarities from

immigrant workers are allowed to accrue to native workers. A recent paper by Ottaviano and Peri (2006) takes such an approach to measuring the wage effects of immigration and concludes that immigration since 1990 has boosted the average wage of natives by between 0.7% and 1.8% depending on the assessment's time frame—the effect is more positive when the capital stock has had time to adjust.[4] Fully 90% of U.S. native-born workers are estimated to have gained from immigration. Multiplying the average percentage gains by the total wages of U.S. natives suggests that annual wage gains from immigration are between $30 billion and $80 billion.[5]

In both approaches described above, natives benefit from immigration because the complementarities associated with immigrants outweigh any losses from added labor market competition. Rather than focusing on average effects, special attention could be paid to the well-being of the least-skilled natives. The number of natives with less than a high school degree has declined over time, which is one reason less-skilled immigrants have been drawn into the U.S. labor force to fill relatively low-paying jobs. Even so, . . . one might expect the remaining least-skilled natives to face labor market competition from immigrants.[6] Evidence on this issue is mixed. Studies often find small negative effects of immigration on the wages of low-skilled natives, and even the comparatively large estimate reported in Borjas (2003) is under 10% for immigration over a 20-year period.[7] The difficulties faced by high school dropouts are a serious policy concern, but it is safe to conclude that immigration is not a central cause of those difficulties, nor is reducing immigration a well-targeted way to help these low-wage natives.

- Conclusion: Immigrants increase the economy's total output, and natives share in part of that increase because of complementarities in production. Different approaches to estimating natives' total income gains from immigration yield figures over $30 billion per year. Sharply reducing immigration would be a poorly targeted and inefficient way to assist low-wage Americans.

Evaluating the Fiscal Benefits and Costs

To assess the fiscal implications of immigration, it is important to take a long-term view of the process and its interaction with projected demographic and economic trends. The National Research Council (NRC) published a landmark study of immigration in 1997, including an assessment of the overall fiscal impact (incorporating taxes and benefits at all levels of government).[8] Although 10 years have passed since its publication, the volume's basic methodological lessons and empirical results are worth repeating.[9]

One key point is that "snapshot" views of immigration's fiscal impact, particularly when based on analysis of households headed by immigrants, are insufficient and potentially misleading guides to immigration's long-run fiscal impact.[10] Instead, "Only a forward-looking projection of taxes and government spending can offer an accurate picture of the long-run fiscal consequences of admitting new immigrants" (Smith and Edmonston 1997, p. 10). This approach captures the full costs and benefits of the children of immigrants. Of course, such projections must rely on assumptions about the future path of taxes and government spending as well as economic and demographic trends. From this long-run point of view, the NRC study estimated that immigrants (including their descendants) would have a positive fiscal impact—a present discounted value of $80,000 per immigrant on average in their baseline model (in 1996 dollars).[11] The surplus is larger for high-skilled immigrants ($198,000) and slightly negative for those with less than a high school degree (−$13,000). It is worth noting that the NRC's estimated fiscal cost from less-skilled workers is far smaller than some commentators have recently suggested based on less satisfactory methods.

The long-term fiscal approach imparts four main lessons: (1) although subject to uncertainty, it appears that immigration has a slightly positive long-run fiscal impact; (2) skilled immigrants have a more positive impact than others; (3) the positive fiscal impact tends to accrue at the federal level, but net costs tend to be concentrated at the state and local level; and (4) the overall fiscal effect of immigration is not large relative to the volume of total tax revenues—immigration is unlikely to cure or cause significant fiscal imbalances.

- Conclusion: Although subject to the uncertainties inherent to long-run projections, careful forward-looking estimates of immigration's fiscal effects, accounting for all levels of government spending and tax revenue, suggest a modest positive influence on average. The fiscal impact of skilled immigrants is more strongly positive.

Immigrants in the U.S. Labor Force

From the perspective of workers in many countries today, the potential income gains from migration are large. For example, Hanson (2006) measured average wages for Mexico-born men who had recently moved to the United States and compared them to the wages of similar men who were still working in Mexico.[12] The real wage ratios (that is, wages adjusted for international differences in prices) ranged from about 6-to-1 to 2-to-1 in favor of the U.S.-based workers, depending on the age and education group. Facing such large international wage differences, a worker might hope to move to the U.S. permanently or with the expectation of returning home after accumulating some savings. In this scenario the opportunity to work

abroad temporarily can help finance large purchases or investments (like a house, car, or new business) in home countries where credit markets are underdeveloped and where wealth accumulation is difficult due to low wages. Migration might also allow households to expand and diversify their income sources, thereby serving as a lifeline to a higher and more stable income level for family members who remain based in a less-developed economy. In short, the economic gains to immigrants and their families are typically quite large.

These immigrants, like those in the past, work hard to improve their lot and that of their children. Their labor force participation rate, reflecting their concentration in prime working ages, is somewhat higher than that of natives (69% versus 66% in 2006), and conditional on being in the labor force their unemployment rate is somewhat lower than that of natives (4.0% versus 4.7% in 2006).[13] Although their average income level is lower than natives', Table 1 shows that they do fairly well in comparison with natives who have similar levels of education. Immigrants have low rates of incarceration compared to natives.[14] And they are more likely to engage in entrepreneurial activity.[15] Children of Latino immigrants overwhelmingly learn English.[16] Finally, relative to natives, the children of low-education immigrants narrow much of the educational and income gap that their parents faced.[17]

- Conclusion: As in the past, immigrants evince a strong work ethic, and the children of immigrants tend to assimilate in terms of language acquisition and educational attainment.

Table 1

Median Weekly Earnings by Educational Attainment, 2006

Educational Attainment	Native-born earnings	Foreign-born earnings	Foreign earnings as % of native earnings	Foreign-born unemployment rate
All	$743	$575	77	3.6
Less than a high school diploma	462	396	86	5.1
High school graduates, no college	607	507	84	3.5
Some college, no degree	701	613	87	3.4
College graduates	1042	1024	98	2.3

Note: Wage data relate to full-time wage and salary workers aged 25 years and older. Unemployment data relate to those in the labor force aged 25 years and over.

Source: Department of Labor (Bureau of Labor Statistics).

Notes

1. This document will use "immigrant" and "foreign born" interchangeably. The terms encompass both legal and illegal migrants. Because it is difficult to determine the legal status of migrants in standard data sets, the economics literature generally assesses all foreign-born workers together.

2. Arithmetically, as a share of GDP the surplus is approximated by one-half times labor's share of income times the proportional increase in employment times the estimated wage adjustment to a supply shift of that size. Varying the assumed elasticity of labor demand changes the estimated surplus proportionally. An elasticity of 0.1 yields a surplus estimate of $12 billion, whereas an elasticity of 0.5 yields [a] surplus estimate of $62 billion. The approach is discussed at some length in chapter 4 of J. Smith and B. Edmonston (eds.), *The New Americans: Economic, Demographic, and Fiscal Effects of Immigration*, Washington DC: National Research Council, National Academy Press, 1997. The NRC's rough immigration surplus estimate was $14 billion in 1996. The larger 2006 figure here is due to a larger economy, inflation to 2006 dollars, and growth in the immigrant share of the workforce.

3. See, for instance, D. Card, "Is the New Immigration Really So Bad?" NBER Working Paper 11547 (2005) or R. Friedberg and J. Hunt, "The Impact of Immigration on Host Country Wages, Employment and Growth," *Journal of Economic Perspectives* 9 (1995): 23–44.

4. The 1.8% figure is based on Ottaviano and Peri's "median" value for the elasticity of substitution between native and foreign-born workers within education-experience groups (6.6). Varying the parameter from 5 to 10 yields long-run average wage gains ranging from 2.3% to 1.2%. See G. Ottaviano and G. Peri, "Rethinking the Effects of Immigration on Wages," NBER Working Paper 12497 (2006).

5. Total wages earned by U.S. natives were calculated using the 2005 American Community Survey.

6. Note that even within categories defined by education and experience levels, natives may have language skills and local knowledge that substantially differentiate them from immigrants.

7. G. Borjas, "The Labor Demand Curve Is Downward Sloping: Reexamining the Impact of Immigration on the Labor Market," *Quarterly Journal of Economics* 118 (2003): 1335–1374. The figure cited in the text appears on p. 1369. G. Ottaviano and G. Peri (2006), using an approach that builds directly on Borjas (2003), estimate a negative effect of only 1% to 2% for the least-skilled natives. A key methodological difference is that Ottaviano and Peri allow for imperfect substitution between immigrants and natives within education-experience cells. Card (2005) also questions whether immigrants substantially lower the wages of unskilled natives.

8. J. Smith and B. Edmonston (eds.), *The New Americans: Economic, Demographic, and Fiscal Effects of Immigration*, Washington DC: National Research Council, National Academy Press, 1997.

9. For a more recent but parallel investigation, see R. Lee and T. Miller, "Immigration, Social Security, and Broader Fiscal Impacts," *American Economic Review* 90, 2 (May 2000): 350–354.

10. For example, see R. Rector and C. Kim, "The Fiscal Cost of Low-Skill Immigrants to the U.S. Taxpayer," Washington, DC: Heritage Foundation, 2007.

11. The NRC volume estimated that the limitations on public benefits in the 1996 Personal Responsibility and Work Opportunity Reconciliation Act would raise the fiscal impact by an additional $8,000 on average. The NRC baseline model assumed that the debt–GDP ratio would be stabilized after 20 years by a 50-50 combination of falling government spending and rising taxes. The report discusses alternative scenarios and concludes that the basic results are not strongly affected by the assumed mix of adjustment of benefits versus taxes (Smith and Edmonston 1997, p. 338).

12. G. Hanson, "Illegal Migration from Mexico to the United States," *Journal of Economic Literature*, 44 (2006): 869–924.

13. http://www.bls.gov/news.release/pdf/forbrn.pdf.

14. See Anne Morrison Piehl's testimony before the U.S. House of Representatives Committee on the Judiciary, Subcommittee on Immigration, Citizenship, Refugees, Border Security, and International Law (May 17, 2007), available at http://judiciary.house .gov/media/pdfs/Piehl070517.pdf. Piehl, an economist at Rutgers University, testified that ". . . there is no empirical evidence that immigrants pose a particular crime threat. In contrast, the evidence points to immigrants having lower involvement in crime than natives. The direct evidence on crime rates shows that localities that receive large numbers of immigrants do not experience increases in relative crime rates."

15. See the Kauffman Foundation's index of entrepreneurial activity (available at www.kauffman.org).

16. See the Pew Hispanic Center/Kaiser Family Foundation 2002 National Survey of Latinos, summary results are available at: http://pewhispanic.org/files /execsum/15.pdf.

17. See D. Card, "Is the New Immigration Really So Bad?" NBER Working Paper 11547 (2005). Also See D. Card, J. DiNardo, and E. Estes, "The More Things Change: Immigrants and the Children of Immigrants in the 1940s, 1970s, and the 1990s," in G. Borjas (ed.), *Issues in the Economics of Immigration*. Chicago: University of Chicago Press, 2000.

Additional Reading

G. Borjas, *Heaven's Door: Immigration Policy and the American Economy*, Princeton: Princeton University Press, 1999.

D. Card, "Is the New Immigration Really So Bad?" NBER Working Paper 11547 (2005). http://www .nber.org/papers/w11547.

D. Card, J. DiNardo, and E. Estes, "*The More Things Change: Immigrants and the Children of Immigrants in the 1940s, 1970s, and 1990s,*" NBER Working Paper 6519 (1998). http://www.nber.org/papers/w6519.

Council of Economic Advisers, *Economic Report of the President,* Washington DC: United States Government Printing Office, 2007. Chapter 9, "Immigration." /cea/ch9-erp07.pdf.

Council of Economic Advisers, *Economic Report of the President,* Washington DC: United States Government Printing Office, 2005. Chapter 4, "Immigration." http://www.gpoaccess.gov/eop/2005/2005_erp.pdf.

G. Hanson, "Illegal Migration from Mexico to the United States," *Journal of Economic Literature,* 44 (2006): 869–924. http://irpshome.ucsd.edu/faculty/gohanson/JEL_Mexican_Immigration_0306.pdf.

R. Lee and T. Miller, "Immigration, Social Security, and Broader Fiscal Impacts," *American Economic Review* 90 (May 2000): 350–354. http://www.jstor.org/view/00028282/ap000009/00a00700/0.

G. Ottaviano and G. Peri, "Rethinking the Effects of Immigration on Wages," NBER Working Paper 12497 (2006). http://papers.nber.org/papers/w12497.

J. Passel, "The Size and Characteristics of the Unauthorized Migrant Population in the U.S.," Pew Hispanic Center, 2006. http://pewhispanic.org/files/reports/61.pdf.

J. Smith and B. Edmonston (eds.), *The New Americans: Economic, Demographic, and Fiscal Effects of Immigration,* Washington DC: National Research Council, National Academy Press, 1997.

GEORGE W. BUSH WHITE HOUSE is a website containing historical materials from the presidency of George W. Bush.

Steven A. Camarota

→ **NO**

Testimony before the U.S. House of Representatives Committee on the Judiciary, Subcommittee on Immigration, Citizenship, Refugees, Border Security and International Law

Introduction

In my very brief comments I will touch on several key issues surrounding immigration and the economy. My goal will be to clear up some of the confusion that often clouds the immigration debate. In particular, I will explain the difference between increasing the overall size of the U.S. economy and increasing the per-capita income of Americans. Finally, I will touch on the issue of immigration's impact on public coffers.

Immigration and the Size of the U.S. Economy

Immigration increases the overall size of the U.S. economy. Of this there is no question. In 2009 immigrants accounted for 15 percent of all workers. More workers and more people mean a bigger GDP. Immigrants are 15 percent of U.S. workers. They likely account for about 10 percent of GDP or more than a trillion dollars annually. However, this does not mean that the native-born population benefits from immigration. Basic economic theory shows that the overwhelming majority of this increase in economic activity goes to the immigrants themselves in the form of wages and other compensation. It is important to understand that the increase in the size of the economy is not, by itself, a benefit to the existing population. Moreover, immigrants who arrived in the last 10, 20, or 50 years are without question earning and living better on average than they would be had they remained in their home countries.

If the question is how much does the existing population benefit, then the key measure is the impact of immigration on per-capita GDP in the United States, particularly the per-capita GDP of the existing population. We can see the importance of per-capita GDP versus aggregate GDP by simply remembering that the economy of Mexico and Canada are similar in size. But this does not mean the two countries are equally rich because Mexico's population is roughly three times that of Canada's.

Benefits to Natives

There is a standard way of calculating the benefit from immigration, also referred to as the immigrant surplus, that goes to the existing population. A 1997 study by National Academy of Sciences (NAS),[1] authored by many of the top economists in the field, summarizes the formula for calculating the benefit (see pages 151–152). The NAS study updates an earlier study by the nation's top immigration economist, George Borjas of Harvard (see page 7).[2] In 2007 the President's Council of Economic Advisers (CEA) again used the same formula to estimate the benefit of immigration to Americans.[3] A blog by professor Borjas has a clear non-technical explanation of the calculation, from which I borrow heavily in this paper.[4]

The next gain from immigration can be estimated using the following formula:

Net gain from immigration as a share of GDP = $-.5$ × labor's share of income × wage elasticity × immigrant share of labor force squared.

"Labor share" refers to the percentage of GDP that goes to workers, which is usually thought to be 70 percent, the rest being capital. The immigrant share of the labor force is well known, and is currently 15 percent. "Wage elasticity" refers to the percentage change in wages from immigration increasing the size of the labor force by 1 percent. The size of the elasticity is a contentious issue. The NAS study assumed an elasticity of .3, and so will I in the calculation below. This means that each 1 percent increase in supply of labor caused by immigration reduces wages by 0.3 percent. Put a different way, if immigration increased the supply of workers by 10 percent, it would reduce the wages of American workers by 3 percent. Putting the values into the formula produces the following estimate:

$$0.24\% = -.50 \times .70 \times -0.3 \times (.15 \times .15)$$

Thus the net gain from immigration is 0.24 percent of GDP. (Expressed as decimal it is .0024.) If GDP is $14 trillion, then the net benefit would be $33 billion.

U.S. House of Representatives, September 2010.

Three important points emerge from this analysis. First, the net effect of immigration on the existing population is positive overall, though not for all workers. Second, the benefits are trivial relative to the size of the economy, less than one-quarter of 1 percent. Third, the benefit is dependent on the size of the wage losses suffered by the existing population of workers. Or put a different way, the bigger the wage loss, the bigger the net benefit. Those who contend that immigration has no impact on the wages of immigrants are also arguing, sometimes without realizing it, that there is no economic benefit from immigration.

The same model can be used to estimate the wage losses suffered [by] American workers.

> Wage loss as a fraction of GDP = − "labor's share of income" × "wage elasticity" × "immigrant share of labor force" × "native-born share of labor force."

Putting the numbers into the equation you get the following:

$$2.7\% = -0.7 \times -0.3 \times 0.15 \times 0.85$$

This is 2.7 percent of GDP, or $375 billion in wage losses suffered by American workers because of immigration. This is not trivial. There is nothing particularly controversial about this estimate and it stems from the same basic economic formula as the one above. Think of it this way: Labor is 70 percent of the economy, which is $14 trillion in total. If the elasticity is .3 and immigrants are 15 percent of the labor force, then wages will decline several percentage points (15 × .3). Thus the total wage loss must run into the hundreds of billions of dollars. If we are to accept the benefit that the model implies from immigration, then we must also accept the wage losses that the model implies.

The money that would have gone to workers as wages if there had been no immigration does not vanish into thin air. It is retained by owners of capital as higher profits or passed on to consumers in the form of lower prices. The fact that business owners lobby so hard to keep immigration levels high is an indication that much of the lost wages are likely retained by them. Also, workers who face little or no competition from immigrants will not suffer a wage loss. In fact, demand for their labor may increase and their incomes rise as a result. For example, if you are an attorney or a journalist at an English-language news outlet in the United States you face very little competition from immigrants.[5] In fact, immigration may increase your wages as demand for your occupation rises. In contrast, if you are a nanny, maid, bus boy, cook, meat packer, or construction laborer, the negative wage impact is likely to be large because immigration has increased the supply of workers in these sectors quite a bit. But overall the gain to some workers, businesses, and consumers is still slightly larger than the loss suffered by the losers; hence the tiny net benefit reported above.

Immigrant and Native Job Competition

Some may feel that there is no job competition between immigrants and native-born workers. The argument is often made, mostly by non-economists, that immigrants only do jobs Americans don't want. But analysis of all 465 occupations defined by the Department of Commerce shows that even before the current recession only four are majority immigrant. These four occupations account for less than 1 percent of the total U.S. workforce. Many jobs often thought to be overwhelmingly immigrant are, in fact, majority native-born. For example, 55 percent of maids and housekeepers are native-born, as are 58 percent of taxi drivers and chauffeurs, 63 percent of butchers and meat processors, 65 percent of construction laborers, and 75 percent of janitors. There are 93 occupations in which at least 20 percent of workers are immigrants. There are about 24 million native-born Americans in these high-immigrant occupations.[6] Thus, the argument that immigrants and natives never compete for jobs is simply incorrect. The real question is how have the poorest and the least educated American workers fared in recent decades as immigration has increased.

Deterioration at the Bottom of the Labor Market

There has been a long-term decline in wages, even before the current recession, among the less educated. Hourly wages for those who have not completed high school declined 22 percent in real terms (adjusted for inflation) from 1979 to 2007. Hourly wages for those with only a high school education declined 10 percent in real terms from 1979 to 2007.[7]

The share of less educated adults holding a job has been deteriorating for some time. This is true even before the current recession. From 2000 to 2007 the share of adult natives (ages 18 to 65) without a high school diploma holding a job fell from 54 percent to 48 percent. For those with only a high school education, the share [of] employed fell from 73 percent to 70 percent. By 2009 it was down to 43 percent for those without a high school diploma and 65 percent for those with only a high school education. There is a huge supply of less-educated people available as potential workers. In 2007, before the recession, there were more than 22 million native-born Americans (18 to 65) with no more than high school education who were not working. By 2009 that number was 26 million.[8]

If there was a tight labor market and unskilled workers really were in short supply, then we would expect that wages to rise for the less educated. We would also expect that the share of these workers holding a job would be climbing. But even before the current recession, this was not what has happening. The deterioration in wages and employment for the less educated is the kind of pattern we would expect to see as a result of immigrant competition.

Fiscal Impact of Immigration

The impact of immigration on public coffers is not directly part of a discussion on immigration and the economy. But when thinking about the overall effect of immigration on our pocketbooks, the taxes paid and services used by immigrants are important issues. It may be the most important issue. The previously mentioned National Academy of Sciences study estimated that the net fiscal drain (taxes paid minus services used) from immigrant households in 1997 was $11 to $20 billion a year. At the same time, using the same formula discussed above, the NAS study estimated a net economic benefit of $1 billion to $10 billion a year from immigration. Thus, the estimated fiscal drain was larger than the economic benefit. (Today the economic benefit and fiscal drain are larger reflecting our larger economy and government.)

It also must be remembered that there are still wage losses for less-skilled workers. The NAS study indicated that the wages of the poorest 10 percent of American workers were reduced by 5 percent as a result of immigrant-induced increases in the supply of labor.

More recent analysis indicates that the fiscal costs of immigration remain large. Census Bureau data indicate that one-third of those without health insurance in the United States are either immigrants (legal or illegal) or U.S.-born children (under 18) of immigrants. One-fourth of children living in poverty in the United States have immigrant fathers. In 2008, 53 percent of immigrant households with children used at least one major welfare program, primarily food assistance and Medicaid.[9] These fiscal costs are incurred despite immigrants' high rates of labor force participation. Their high welfare use rates and the resulting fiscal drain they create stem from the fact that a large share have relatively little education. About one-third of immigrants who arrive as adults have not graduated from high school. The modern American economy offers limited opportunities to such workers. This fact, coupled with a welfare state designed to help low-income workers with children, is the reason for the above statistics.

Conclusion

When thinking about immigration it is important to recognize that its impact on the size of the economy is not a measure of the benefit to natives. There is no question that U.S. GDP is significantly larger because of immigrant workers. However, a larger economy is entirely irrelevant to the key question of whether the per-capita GDP of natives is higher because of immigration. Efforts to measure the impact of immigration on the per-capita GDP of Americans using the standard economic model show that the benefit is trivial relative to the size of the economy. Perhaps most important, these trivial gains are the result of reduced wages for American workers in competition with immigrants. These workers tend to be the least educated and poorest already. If there is no wage reduction, then there is no economic gain. Finally, the tiny economic gain is probably entirely offset by the fiscal drain immigrants create on taxpayers.

In the end, arguments for or against immigration are as much political and moral as they are economic. The latest research indicates that we can reduce immigration without harming the economy. Doing so makes sense if we are very concerned about low-wage and less-educated workers in the United States. On the other hand, if one places a high priority on helping unskilled workers in other countries, then we should continue to allow in a large number of such workers. Of course, only an infinitesimal proportion of the world's poor could ever come to this country even under the most open immigration policy one might imagine. Those who support the current high level of immigration should at least understand that the American workers harmed by the policies they favor are already the poorest and most vulnerable.

Notes

1. Edmonston, Barry, and James Smith, Eds., *The New Americans: Economic, Demographic, and Fiscal Effects of Immigration,* Washington D.C., National Academy Press, 1997, http://books.nap.edu/open-book .php?isbn=0309063566.
2. George Borjas, "The Economic Benefits of Immigration," *Journal of Economic Perspectives* Vol. 9, No. 2, Spring 1995, http://www.hks.harvard.edu/fs /gborjas/Papers/Economic_Benefits.pdf.
3. "Immigration's Economic Impact," white paper, June 20, 2007, http://georgewbush-whitehouse .archives.gov/cea/cea_immigration_062007.html.
4. "No Pain No Gain," June 8, 1997, http://borjas.type -pad.com/the_borjas_blog/ 2007/06/index.html.
5. Steven Camarota and Karen Jensenius, "Jobs Americans Won't Do? A Detailed Look at Immigrant Employment by Occupation," Center for Immigration Studies *Memorandum,* August 2009, http://www.cis.org/illegalimmigration-employment.
6. *Ibid.*
7. Lawrence Mishel, Jared Bernstein and Heidi Shierholz, "The State of Working America 2008/2009," Economic Policy Institute, Table 3.16, p. 166.
8. All figures for employment are based on the author's calculation of employment and labor force participation from the public-use files of the Current Population Survey in the third quarters of 2000, 2007, and 2009.
9. Figures come from the March 2009 Current Population Survey, which asks about health insurance coverage and welfare use in the prior calendar year. It also asks where respondents' parents were born. Thus, indentifying the children of immigrant parents is a simple calculation.

STEVEN A. CAMAROTA is director of research at the Center for Immigration Studies and an expert in economics and demographics.

EXPLORING THE ISSUE

Does Immigration Benefit the Economy?

Critical Thinking and Reflection

1. To what degree should the children of immigrants be factored into the analysis of immigration's fiscal consequences and why?
2. Assuming it is true that "immigrants evince a strong work ethic," does that put them on par with native-born Americans, or on a higher rung of ethics? For what reasons?
3. How do the levels of education represented by American workers affect an analysis of immigration's economic impact?
4. Ultimately, are the arguments for and against immigration mostly political, moral, or economic? Explain.

Is There Common Ground?

The opposing views espoused by the George W. Bush Administration and by Steven A. Camarota may be summarized simply as "yes, immigration benefits the U.S. economy" (Bush) and "no, it does not" (Camarota). Statistics on both sides support their respective positions, but this is by no means an issue without its common ground.

Neither testimony attempts to refute such statistical evidence as to how many legal immigrants live and work in the United States, or even what the natures of those jobs are. Both arguments acknowledge the various levels of education represented by both native-born Americans and their immigrant counterparts. In addition, there is no suggestion by either side that immigration laws are unnecessary—in fact, a common regard for the importance of such is apparent.

On the issue-specific subject of domestic economics, both sides even agree that immigration may indeed increase total production, but there is a point at which the analyses diverge from shared perspectives. Whereas the Bush Administration sees such productivity as contributing to the net positive of immigration, Camarota shows how productivity is countered by other factors that generate a net negative.

Create Central

www.mhhe.com/createcentral

Additional Resources

Camarota, Steven A., *The Wages of Immigration* (Center for Immigration Studies, 1998)

Card, David, and Steven Raphael, eds., *Immigration, Poverty, and Socioeconomic Inequality* (Russell Sage Foundation, 2013)

Pollin, Robert, *Back to Full Employment* (MIT Press, 2012)

Internet References . . .

Center for Immigration Studies: "Back Where We Started: An Examination of Trends in Immigrant Welfare Use Since Welfare Reform"

www.cis.org/TrendsImmigrantWelfare-WelfareReform

Fusion: "Analysis: What Is the Economic Impact of Immigration Reform?"

http://fusion.net/justice/story/analysis-economic-impact-immigration-reform-15366

New York Times Business: "Illegal Immigrants Are Bolstering Social Security with Billions"

www.nytimes.com/2005/04/05/business/05immigration.html?ex=1270353600&en=78c87ac4641dc383&ei=5090&_r=0

Unit 3

The World Around Us

The World Around Us

*T*he issues explored in this unit are diverse. Topics such as international trade, the collapse of the housing bubble, the federal government deficits and debt, U.S. dependence on foreign oil, public education, and the distribution of income in the United States are addressed.

Selected, Edited, and with Issue Framing Material by:
Miren Ivankovic, *Anderson University*

ISSUE

Is a Fair Trade Policy Superior to a Free Trade Policy?

YES: Ngaire Woods, from "Fair Trade: The Proposer's Opening Remarks," *The Economist* (May 4, 2010)

NO: Jagdish Bhagwati, from "Fair Trade: The Opposition's Opening Remarks," *The Economist* (May 4, 2010)

Learning Outcomes

After reading this issue, you will be able to:

- Explain the strengths and weaknesses of free trade.
- Explain the strengths and weaknesses of fair trade.
- Describe barriers to trade.
- Discuss comparative advantage and trade.
- Discuss absolute advantage and trade.

ISSUE SUMMARY

YES: Ngaire Woods, international political economy professor and director of Global Economic Governance at Oxford University, feels that carefully deployed special preferences and protectionism could be used intelligently to help to catalyze growth in African countries, and to improve the lives of the bottom billion. Conversely, the dismantling of special preferences has levied some high costs.

NO: Jagdish Bhagwati, professor of economics and law at Columbia University, states that if the demand for fair trade in the sense of demanding reciprocity in openness leads to others reducing their trade barriers, that is good. But if it leads to closing of one's own, because others do not yield to such demands, that is bad.

$\mathbf{A}$s Harvard Professor Gregory Mankiw states in his *Principles of Economics* text, trade can make everyone better off. Yes, he states it *can*, not it *does*. But from the same text in Chapter 3, "Interdependence and the Gains from Trade," he elaborates on the gains that come from the specialization and the division of labor. Adam Smith talks about the gains from trade in his book *An Inquiry into the Nature and Causes of the Wealth of Nations*, which was a landmark in the analysis of trade and economic interdependence, published in 1776. According to Smith, "It is a maxim of every prudent master of a family, never to attempt to make at home what it will cost him more to make than to buy." Smith's book inspired David Ricardo, to write the *Principles of Political Economy and Taxation* in 1817. He used the example of two countries and two outputs and developed the concept of comparative advantage, which gives true meaning to gains from free trade. Ricardo was so convinced about the theory of comparative advantage that he, as a member of the British

Parliament, opposed the Corn Laws, which restricted the import of grain. The main benefit of comparative advantage is that regardless of the wealth of a particular nation, opportunity cost to make one good/service will vary among the nations. A country with a lower opportunity cost will have a comparative advantage in the production of that good/service and be able, with trade, to focus on its production, while importing a good/service in which it has higher opportunity cost. This activity is a trade, and by lowering any barriers to trade, it becomes as free as two trading partners want it to be. Each nation provides more to its citizens with the trade than without the trade. However, the factors of production that are not as efficient (high opportunity cost) will see an increase in unemployment, and this will be a problem in the short run. As the more efficient sector expands, we should see mobility of labor into that sector. How easy it is to move from an industry that makes shirts into one that makes cars or planes, which is the case in South Carolina, is hard to determine, but we know it is not easy. One sector requires low-skilled labor and the other high-skilled labor. Most likely the low-skilled labor will become unemployed and seek social help.

Thus the concept "free trade" is an objective one. The problem is when we talk about trade fairness. That is harder to measure; it is more subjective. We know that some nations subsidize certain sectors, so it becomes very difficult to engage in free trade under those conditions. Some nations are more open than others; thus, they are willing to export their products but not import as much. A country can engage in currency manipulation by devaluing its currency and making its exports more attractive than the imports. China's government manages its currency to a point that is weaker vis-a-vis other trading partners' currencies, thus making its exports very attractive in foreign markets. We also know that wages for labor differ among the nations. Theory suggests that the wages will equate in the long run, but in the short run, low-wage

nations will gain advantage, especially among labor-intensive products. And the list goes on . . . barriers like tariffs and quotas and specific industry standards are making trade less free and also less fair.

As the debate proceeds, I hope we arrive at a clearer understanding of what precisely we should understand fairer trade to mean, as well as of the ways in which trade remains unfree. What does the evidence of trade's effects on inequality within and between countries say? And how should trade's effects on things like inequality or the wages of the less skilled in rich countries be balanced against the jobs it creates for poorer workers in developing countries, as well as its less-remarked-upon but widely dispersed benefits for consumers at large? I wonder also whether fair and free ought to be seen as being in constant conflict. Perhaps both fair and free will never become one, but we hope the distance between the two can become narrower, thereby benefiting all of us.

YES ⤶

Ngaire Woods

Fair Trade: The Proposer's Opening Remarks

Trade has a pretty bad name in some quarters. "Trade robs poor people of a proper living, and keeps them trapped in poverty" writes Oxfam on its website. The Confederation of British Industry (CBI) reckon Britain lost some 250,000 jobs to China, India, eastern Europe, and other countries in the decade up to 2004. The "giant sucking sound" of jobs disappearing abroad is invoked in each American election. Others criticise the rigged rules of the trading system. Recall the raucous protests at the WTO's 1999 meeting in Seattle. There is a widely held popular view that trade is unfair.

Making trade fairer is important to avert a further public backlash against trade. It is also important so as better to reconcile trade goals with other important national goals such as environmental and social protection. Finally, the so-called free trade system needs to be made fairer so that it does not stymie competition, and crush innovation and entrepreneurship. It needs to offer a more level playing field to commercial newcomers and competitors in rich and poor countries alike.

Advocating freer trade will not resolve the unfairness of trade. Free trade is the dream of most textbook-wielding economists. But few others go much beyond the slogan. Free trade is a useful banner for traders who want access to other people's markets. "Free trade" has been used successfully by powerful countries to prise open markets to sell pharmaceuticals and banking services, and to gain access to government procurement contracts.

At home the story is different. Large firms have little appetite for free trade and competition in their own backyard. They prefer to enjoy the advantages and protections for which they have carefully lobbied. Robust competition has little appeal for those who understand that they will make more profit if they can corner the market, whether at home or abroad. The invisible hand of the market and free trade is reserved for deploying against competitors.

Making trade fairer is about addressing both outcomes and processes of trade. Fairness is not just moral pleading. It affects behavior. The fairness of outcomes has been explored in recent years by economists using a simple experiment. A player is given a sum of money to share with another. The first player can offer any portion of the money he or she likes to the other who can either accept or reject it. If the second player rejects the offer, neither player gets any money. Obviously, self-interest would

suggest that whatever is offered—whether perceived as "fair" or not—is worth the second player accepting (since it represents a net gain). Yet players offered small amounts often reject on the grounds of unfairness.

Fairness may become yet more influential. According to a recent report by *The Economist*, notions of fairness increase steadily as societies achieve greater market integration: "People from better-integrated societies are also more likely to punish those who do not play fair, even when this is costly to themselves." In international trade then, the fairness of outcomes may matter more and more not less and less.

The world expects trade outcomes to be somewhat unequal. But when Oxfam reported back in 2002 that 97% of the income generated by international trade benefits rich and middle-income countries, while 3% flows to poor countries, it made a stir. Standards of fairness had been breached.

Fairer trade rather than freer trade could change some of these outcomes. A persuasive case is made by my Oxford colleagues, Paul Collier and Tony Venables. Carefully deployed special preferences and protectionism could be used intelligently to help to catalyse growth in African countries, and to improve the lives of the bottom billion. Conversely, the dismantling of special preferences has levied some high costs.

Fairness is also important in the governance of trade. International trade negotiations have resulted in rules which open up markets mostly for the goods and services exported by rich and emerging economies, while keeping markets closed in agriculture and other goods which are the main produce of poorer countries. The rules are made in negotiations in which the powerful call the shots, and do not always do so in good faith. In the Uruguay Round of negotiations industrialised countries were perceived to have exacted precise and far-reaching commitments from developing countries, in exchange for vague promises, such as to liberalise agriculture, which they have not kept. The Doha Round keeps failing to restart, in large part because there is too little trust in the fairness of its likely outcomes, as well as the fairness of the negotiating process, something Pascal Lamy, Director-General of the WTO, is trying valiantly to change.

The enforcement of trade rules is also unfair. When countries break trade rules, they are not systematically policed. They will be caught when their actions affect countries in which business groups are organised and well resourced enough to play a key role in gathering information and financing the preparation of the case against the offender. For most small countries, bringing a case against an important trade partner is unthinkable. They could lose discretionary trade access, aid or geostrategic assistance. Were they to win, they would secure the right to apply retaliatory measures which might have little effect—a pyrrhic victory for many.

Trade needs saving. But freer trade will not do the trick. The perceived unfairness of trade leads people to press for less trade not freer trade. Fairer trade, by contrast, would bolster public support, allow a better reconciliation with national priorities such as environment and development, and could offer a more level playing field to ensure more open and vibrant competition.

PROFESSOR NGAIRE WOODS is the inaugural dean of the Blavatnik School of Government and professor of global economic governance. Her research focuses on global economic governance, the challenges of globalization, global development, and the role of international institutions. She was educated at Auckland University (BA in economics, LLB Hons in law). She studied at Balliol College, Oxford as a New Zealand Rhodes Scholar, completing an MPhil (with Distinction) and then DPhil (in 1992) in international relations. She won a Junior Research Fellowship at New College, Oxford (1990–1992) and subsequently taught at Harvard University (Government Department) before taking up her fellowship at University College, Oxford.

Jagdish Bhagwati   → **NO**

Fair Trade: The Opposition's Opening Remarks

At the outset, we have a problem of ambiguity. While we know what free trade means—we mean by it the absence of price or quantity interventions in trade that prevent the translation of world prices into domestic prices, keeping in mind that trade instruments can be decomposed into a sum of domestic policy instruments—it is a phrase that has no settled meaning in policy discourse. In fact, there are three main meanings which we can assign to it today. Fortunately, in each case, we can argue that making trade fairer will have malign effects whereas making trade freer will make us better off.

In the first meaning, often, in the United States in particular, free trade is considered unfair if other nations are less open than one's own. This notion of unfair trade was also manifest in Britain at the end of the 19th century when Germany and the United States had emerged as competitors to British hegemony. Fair trade associations grew up at the time, agitating to end Britain's unilateral free trade, much as the United States saw the demands for fair trade increased when it faced the rise of Japan in the 1980s and many feared that the principal source of relative American decline was the asymmetric closed the Japanese market. This is, of course, a recurrent theme in the United States: Japan has been replaced by China, currently prospering because its markets are considered to be closed relative to the American markets.

Now, if the demand for fair trade in the sense of demanding reciprocity in openness leads to others reducing their trade barriers, that is good. But if it leads to closing of one's own, because others do not yield to such demands, that is bad. Thus, the theory of unilateral trade and reciprocity teaches that if others open their markets when we open ours, we generally speaking get a double dividend (from opening ours and others opening theirs); that if such reciprocity does not obtain, we would still profit from our own unilateral freeing of trade; and that, in fact, if immediate reciprocity is denied, it may be prompted down the road in these initially non-liberalising nations by the demonstration of success with freer trade or the relative strengthening of pro-trade lobbies in these nations as they liberalise on their own: what I have called "induced reciprocity" (see "Going Alone," MIT Press, 2002).

In the second meaning, a more potent notion in current discourse is the notion that fair trade requires that rival producers abroad should carry the same burdens on labor (and domestic-pollution) standards as one does. If the same industry carries differential burdens across countries, and yours is greater, then free trade will harm you.

These demands, when reflecting lobbying by specific industries complaining of unfair trade because their competitors are less burdened, are misplaced since there is no reason why there should be such identity of industry standards across countries. The shadow price of domestic pollution may well be different across countries for an industry: abundant fresh air and widespread dysentery owing to polluted water in Kenya relative to the United States may legitimately mean that the polluter-pay tax be less in Kenya for air pollution and more for water pollution than in the United States.

The same goes for labor standards. Except for consensus on a very small (but possibly growing) set of universal labor standards such as the proscription of hazardous child labor, many standards will reflect local history, politics and economic circumstance. When labor unions in the United States typically ask, nonetheless, that others abroad raise their labor standards to the US standards, the argument is usually couched in terms of altruism: we are doing this for your workers. But, in truth, the argument is prompted by self-interest, that is, it is designed to raise the cost of production abroad so as to moderate competition which, it is wrongly feared, is harming one's own workers. Economists will recognise this as a form of export protectionism, as an alternative to conventional import protectionism. If a beast is charging at you, you can catch it by the horns (as with import restrictions) or you can reach behind the beast, catch it by the tail and break the charge (as with export protectionism).

Some labor groups have turned instead to asking for acceptance of the core labor conventions at ILO by a country as a requisite for freeing trade with it. Ironically, however, for several reasons, the United States has not ratified a large fraction of them. Maybe the United States will begin by suspending all its exports until all core conventions are ratified: if charity begins at home, so must trade sanctions for lack of ratification of the core conventions?

As for the third meaning, perhaps the most influential demand for fair trade today is in an altogether different sense. It derives from British charities like Oxfam and is really a demand for what economists call a just price to be paid to foreign suppliers in trade, a notion that goes back at least to Rowntree's practice of paying a higher-than-market price for cocoa beans processed into its chocolate.

This is of course a perfectly innocuous procedure, except that it turns into a form of protectionism if regular trade is sought to be eliminated in favor of fair trade. For example, retailers may be forced to carry only fair trade coffee. I believe that this is a mistake. In particular, when I pay a higher price for my fair trade coffee, I am providing a subsidy to the suppliers of this coffee vis-à-vis the market price. That may well be what I want to do as my altruistic activity. But I may want instead to use my altruistic funds on what I consider worthier causes like support of women's rights NGOs or children's nutrition. I see no reason why I should be forced to accept someone else's definition of how I should behave as an altruist.

JAGDISH BHAGWATI is university professor (economics, law, and international affairs) at Columbia University and senior fellow for international economics at the Council on Foreign Relations (CFR). He has been economic policy adviser to Arthur Dunkel, director-general of GATT (1991–93), special adviser to the UN on globalization, and external adviser to the WTO. He has served on the expert group appointed by the director-general of the WTO on the future of the WTO and the advisory committee to Secretary-General Kofi Annan on the NEPAD process in Africa, and was also a member of the Eminent Persons Group under the chairmanship of President Fernando Henrique Cardoso of Brazil on the future of UNCTAD. Recently, he has been co-chair with President Halonen of Finland of the Eminent Persons Group on Developing Countries in the World Economy. A native of India, Professor Bhagwati attended Cambridge University where he graduated in 1956 with a first in economics tripos. He then continued to study at MIT and Oxford, returning to India in 1961 as professor of economics at the Indian Statistical Institute and then as professor of international trade at the Delhi School of Economics. He returned to MIT in 1968, leaving it twelve years later as the Ford International Professor of Economics to join Columbia. He is married to Padma Desai, the Gladys and Ronald Harriman Professor of Comparative Economic Systems at Columbia University and a scholar of Russian and other former socialist countries' transition problems. They have one daughter, Anuradha Kristina.

EXPLORING THE ISSUE

Is a Fair Trade Policy Superior to a Free Trade Policy?

Critical Thinking and Reflection

1. How can a country benefit from free trade?
2. Does everyone gain from free trade? If not, how should society solve the problem of the ones that do not gain?
3. Is fair trade possible to be implemented without political influences from certain groups of the society?
4. Is there a roll for tariffs, quotas, and other barriers available to a country? Explain.
5. List several policies that can be used to enforce the fair trade and explain each.

Is There Common Ground?

Based on the work of Alston, Kearl, and Vaughn, "Is there a consensus among economists in the 1990s?" published in the *American Economic Review* in 1992, 93 percent of economists agree that tariffs and import quotas usually reduce general economic welfare. Along the same percentage numbers, economists agree that open economy policies are stimulating growth, and that trade is beneficial to the society. Most economists will support free trade policies, and the assumption is that in most instances, free trade is fair trade as well. Free markets, brand name reputation, product loyalty, etc . . . are perhaps sufficient to prevent any major deviations from fair trade. Firms that do engage in unfair trade, like labor abuse, do suffer the consequences in free markets.

Additional Resources

Littrell, Mary Ann, *Social Responsibility in the Global Market: Fair Trade of Cultural Products* (Sage, 1999)

Conti, Delia B., *Reconciling Free Trade, Fair Trade, and Interdependence: The Rhetoric of Presidential Economic Leadership,* Series in Political Communication (Praeger, 1998)

Nader, Ralph et al., *The Case Against Free Trade: GATT, NAFTA and the Globalization of Corporate Power* (North Atlantic Books, 1993)

Daly, Herman E. and Cobb Jr., John B., *For The Common Good: Redirecting the Economy toward Community, the Environment, and a Sustainable Future* (Beacon Press, 1994)

Create Central

www.mhhe.com/createcentral

Internet References . . .

Free Trade Vs. Fair Trade—Global Envision

www.globalenvision.org/library/15/834

Free Trade Vs. Fair Trade—Chron.com

http://smallbusiness.chron.com/trade-vs-fair-trade-1683.html

Free Trade versus Fair Trade

http://fairtradecoffee.org/free-trade-versus-fair-trade.html

ISSUE

Is Loan Mitigation the Answer to the Housing Foreclosure Problem?

YES: David G. Kittle, from "A Review of Mortgage Servicing Practices and Foreclosure Mitigation," statement before the House of Representatives Committee on Financial Services (July 25, 2008)

NO: Julia Gordon, from "A Review of Mortgage Servicing Practices and Foreclosure Mitigation," statement before the House of Representatives Committee on Financial Services (July 25, 2008)

Learning Outcomes

After reading this issue, you will be able to:

- Define the mortgage-related terms "subprime" and "underwater."
- Enumerate the costs to servicers when a loan is delinquent.
- Identify the functions of the HOPE NOW Alliance.
- Describe the "ripple effects" experienced in neighborhoods with foreclosed properties.

ISSUE SUMMARY

YES: Mortgage Bankers Association official David Kittle, after reviewing the cost of foreclosure and loan mitigation options, presents data to back his assertion that loan mitigation is working.

NO: Center for Responsible Lending Policy Counsel Julia Gordon stresses both the direct costs and the spillover costs of foreclosures and believes that voluntary loan modifications "have done little to stem the overwhelming tide of foreclosures."

T he American dream, or at least a large part of the American dream, is to own one's own home. The purchase of a home for all but a very few involves borrowing the money, going into debt, and acquiring a mortgage. In applying for a home mortgage loan, most prospective homeowners will get either a prime loan or a subprime loan. The former is a loan made to borrowers with good credit histories, good repayment prospects, and above-minimum down payments. A subprime mortgage loan is one made to a borrower with a poor credit history and/or with a high debt-to-income ratio (the borrower's outstanding debt is high relative to his or her income) or a high loan-to-value ratio (the amount borrowed with the mortgage is close to the value of the home being purchased). Of course, a subprime borrower has to pay a higher interest rate to compensate the lender for the higher risk he or she accepts in making a subprime loan.

Both types of mortgage loans can be made with a fixed interest rate or a variable interest rate. For the former the interest rate that the borrower pays and the lender receives stays constant over the life of the loan, while with the latter,

frequently referred to as an adjustable rate mortgage (ARM), the interest rate rises and falls (resets) over time as market interest rates rise and fall. During the housing boom, in the first half of the decade, an increasing proportion of mortgage loans consisted of subprime ARMs. So by early 2008, according to a Federal Reserve report (*A Snapshot of Mortgage Conditions with an Emphasis on Subprime Mortgage Performance,* available at http://federalreserveonline.org/pdf/MF_Knowledge _Snapshot-082708.pdf), the subprime mortgage market, whether measured by the number of loans or the value of loans, accounted for about 12 percent of the total residential mortgage markets. More specifically, the subprime portion had a value of $1.2 trillion while the total residential mortgage market was estimated at $10.1 trillion, with subprime ARMs constituting more than half of the subprime component. The total number of mortgage loans was estimated at 54.7 million, with 6.7 million subprime loans and 3.2 million subprime ARMs.

But the booming housing market of the early part of the decade came to an abrupt halt—the housing bubble burst. As interest rates increased and housing prices began to fall, borrowers had problems meeting their mortgage obligations. This was especially true for those borrowers who had used subprime ARMs to finance their home purchases. The Federal Reserve estimated that as of March 31, 2008, more than 721,000 subprime loans were in foreclosure, including 543,000 subprime ARMs. Foreclosure involves a legal process in which a lender seeks recovery of the borrower's collateral (in the case of a residential mortgage the collateral is the home being purchased by the borrower). A lender will take this action when the borrower is no longer able to meet the obligations of the mortgage agreement. Foreclosure normally means that the current market value of the property is less than the outstanding balance of the mortgage loan; otherwise the borrower would sell the property, pay off the loan, and still have something left over.

Foreclosures obviously create problems for borrowers and lenders, but the damage can and has spread to other property owners, other lending organizations, other borrowers, and local governments. With the rising tide of foreclosures, public and private action was taken. Loan mitigation is a private effort to avoid foreclosure and can take a variety of forms, including loan modification. The issue examined here is whether or not loan mitigation is working effectively in solving the problems created by the rising tide of foreclosures and the collapse of the housing market. Kittle believes loan mitigation is working while Gordon argues that it is not.

YES

David G. Kittle

A Review of Mortgage Servicing Practices and Foreclosure Mitigation

Chairman Frank, Ranking Member Bachus, Members of the Committee, I am David G. Kittle, CMB, President and Chief Executive Officer of Principle Wholesale Lending, Inc. in Louisville, Kentucky and Chairman-Elect of the Mortgage Bankers Association (MBA).[1] I appreciate the opportunity to appear before you to discuss the progress of the mortgage industry in working out troubled loans.

MBA's members strive to keep borrowers in their homes and avoid foreclosures whenever possible. Such goals serve the interests not only of borrowers, but also of our members and of the communities in which they do business. We understand the urgency of borrowers seeking the industry's assistance and our members continue to step up their foreclosure prevention programs.

Avoiding Foreclosures

None of us wants a family to lose its home, and MBA members are devoting significant time and resources to finding ways to help borrowers keep their homes. The tools used to avoid foreclosure and retain a borrower's home include forbearance and repayment plans, loan modifications, refinances and partial and advance claims. Mortgage loan servicers use short sales and deeds in lieu of foreclosure to avoid foreclosure when the borrower does not want to or cannot retain the home.

It makes good economic sense for mortgage servicers to help borrowers who are in trouble. The recent increase in mortgage delinquencies and foreclosures has brought significant attention to the costs of foreclosure to homeowners, communities and mortgage industry participants. While the impact of foreclosure upon homeowners and communities is clear to everyone, statements by some advocates and government officials indicate that confusion still exists about the impact of foreclosures upon industry participants particularly lenders, servicers and investors.

Mortgage lenders and servicers do not profit from foreclosures. In reality, every party to a foreclosure loses—the borrower, the immediate community, the servicer, mortgage insurer and investor. It is important to understand that profitability for the mortgage industry rests in keeping a loan current and, as such, the interests of the borrower and lender are mostly aligned.

As a recent Congressional Research Service paper notes, for lenders and investors, foreclosure is a lengthy and extremely costly process and, generally, a losing financial proposition.[2] While losses can vary significantly, several independent studies have found the losses to be quite significant: over $50,000 per foreclosed home[3] or as much as 30 to 60 percent of the outstanding loan balance.[4]

Risk of Loss

When a lender holds a loan in portfolio, it retains the credit risk on the loan and takes a direct loss if the loan goes to foreclosure sale. When a loan has been securitized, the investors in the mortgage securities hold the credit risk and take a direct loss to principal if the loan goes to foreclosure sale. The servicer, if different from the noteholder, also bears certain costs if the loan goes to foreclosure—most notably the loss of its servicing asset.

Once the borrower has obtained a mortgage and the originator has closed the mortgage, the main objective for the mortgage servicer is to keep the loan current. If a loan is terminated through foreclosure, the servicer does not continue to receive the servicing fee (the primary source of a mortgage company's income). The standard servicing fee for a fixed-rated Fannie Mae or Freddie Mac loan is ¼ of 1 percent of the principal balance, or $250 per annum for a typical $100,000 loan. Subprime loans generally carry a higher servicing fee because of the increased delinquency risk and costs. Minimum servicing on subprime loans is ½ of 1 percent of the principal balance. Servicers of MBS, otherwise, do not retain the principal and interest (P&I) payment the borrower makes as those amounts are passed on to the ultimate investor.

In addition to losing the servicing income for the asset, servicers must pay out-of-pocket costs when the loan is delinquent. The servicer must:

- Advance interest and principal to the investors (despite not receiving payments from the borrower);
- Advance taxes and insurance payments;
- Pay for foreclosure attorneys fees, court costs and other fees;
- Pay for bankruptcy attorneys and court costs, if applicable;
- Pay for property inspections and property preservation work (mowing the grass, boarding, rekeying, winterizing, etc.), as applicable;

Kittle, David G. Illinois House of Representatives, July 25, 2008, pp. excerpts.

- Pay for other costs including appraisals, title searches, publications, and other direct costs; and
- Pay for increased staff, contractors and other costs, such as technology costs.

To make principal, interest, tax and insurance advances, mortgage companies have to borrow the funds or use their own capital. These borrowing costs can reach into the millions of dollars per company, as many lenders experienced after Hurricane Katrina and are experiencing today.

State law dictates the foreclosure process and timeline. As a result, foreclosure costs vary significantly from state to state. In certain states, foreclosure requires court action. In these "judicial foreclosure" states, foreclosure takes longer and, consequently, is more costly. Even without a judicial foreclosure, the process is lengthy. The national average time between the first missed payment and the foreclosure sale is approximately one year.[5] After that, it may take additional time to gain possession of the property, clear the title and prepare and sell the real estate owned (REO) property.

If the loan goes to foreclosure sale, the servicer is generally not reimbursed for all its out-of-pocket, direct and indirect costs. For example, the Federal Housing Administration (FHA) only reimburses two-thirds of certain out-of-pocket expenses incurred by the servicer (e.g. foreclosure attorney fees) and sets maximums for foreclosure and bankruptcy costs and property preservation costs that often do not cover the actual expenses. In private label securities, pooling and servicing agreements (PSAs) often establish maximum payments for out-of-pocket costs incurred by the servicers. Moreover, in private label securities, servicers have higher unreimbursed carrying costs because the servicer does not receive reimbursement until it sells the REO property.

Conversely, if the loan is brought current through loss mitigation, out-of-pocket expenses generally are reimbursed through the workout plan or are separately collected by the servicer. Carrying costs are also usually reduced. Curing the delinquency allows the servicer to salvage its valuable servicing asset. Reinstatement, therefore, is far more desirable from an economic standpoint for servicers than foreclosure.

Additional Investor/ Noteholder Expenses

Investors and portfolio lenders have added incentives to avoid foreclosure. They incur additional cost and losses as owners of the note or repossessed property. Post foreclosure costs alone can account for over 40 percent of foreclosure-related gross losses.[6] The main expenses during this phase of the process are:

- **Costs of Restoring the Property**—Often homes of borrowers in financial distress fall into disrepair, requiring repairs and capital improvements to sell the property;

- **Property Maintenance**—REO properties must continue to be maintained (grass mowed, property winterized, etc.) and secured (boarded up and rekeyed to avoid break-ins, etc.) and removed of safety code violations (drain and cover pools, etc); and

- **Real Estate Commissions and Closing Costs**— Lenders typically use real estate agents, just as individuals do, to sell properties and must pay the real estate broker commissions.

The last step that creates a major expense for investors and portfolio lenders is the loss on the unpaid principal balance that occurs upon the sale of the REO property. While exceptions occur (mostly in appreciating markets), holders of REO properties do not sell them at a gain. REO properties generally do not attract top dollar, and once sale proceeds are netted against the various costs incurred during the delinquency period and foreclosure process, the investor and lender usually end up with losses.[7] These losses make up approximately 20 percent of the total costs of foreclosure. The current softness of the housing market could push this rate even higher. While private mortgage and government insurance and guarantees may offset some of these losses, coverage can be limited. Moreover, not all noteholders are protected by mortgage insurance. Subprime mortgages generally do not carry mortgage insurance.

Loss Mitigation

Mortgage companies and investors have recognized the impact of foreclosures on their bottom lines and over the last ten years have developed innovative techniques to help borrowers resume payments. These options have proven successful for the homeowner, the servicer and investor.

If a homeowner misses a payment and becomes delinquent, the mortgage servicer will attempt multiple contacts with the homeowner in order to help that borrower work out the delinquency. Servicers have several foreclosure prevention options that can get a borrower back on his or her feet, including those outlined below.

Forbearance Plan: Forbearance is a temporary agreement, which allows the homeowner to make partial or no payments for a period. The forbearance agreement is followed by a further evaluation of the loan and the homeowner's circumstance to identify if there are any permanent workout options such as a repayment plan or modification.

Repayment Plan: A repayment plan is a verbal or written agreement where a delinquent homeowner resumes making regular monthly payments in addition to a portion of the past due payments to reinstate the loan to "current" status.

Loan Modifications: Loan modifications are the next level of loss mitigation options. A loan modification is a change in the underlying loan document. It might extend the term of the loan, change the interest rate, change repayment terms or make other alterations. Often features are combined to include rate reductions and term extensions. . . .

Partial and Advance Claims: Servicers are also using partial or advance claims on government and conventional products (i.e., Fannie Mae's HomeSaver Advanced program). In a partial or advance claim, a junior lien is created in the amount of the arrearage. The loan proceeds from the newly created junior lien are used to pay the arrearage on the first mortgage, thus bringing the borrower current. . . .

Refinances: Servicers also use refinances to assist borrowers who are current, but are at risk of defaulting on the loans in the future or borrowers who are in the early stages of delinquency. FHASecure is one example of a program targeted at borrowers with adjustable rate mortgages who are unable to make payments due to an increase in rate.[8] . . .

Short Sales and Deeds in Lieu of Foreclosure: Not all borrowers want to or can stay in their homes. Some have decided to stop making mortgage payments because to do so no longer suits their economic interests.[9] Others face divorce or relocations for which the current home is no longer viable.

Borrowers who cannot maintain their home for whatever reason may still avoid foreclosure through a short sale or deed in lieu of foreclosure. In both cases, the borrower is usually relieved of the debt despite selling the house for less than the debt or delivering an asset that is worth less than the debt.

All of these loss mitigation options benefit the borrower in varying ways and servicers strive to help as many borrowers as is prudently possible.

Loss Mitigation Is Working

Our servicing members have worked aggressively to make the available tools as efficient as possible. The industry formed the HOPE NOW Alliance in an effort to approach foreclosure prevention in a coordinated fashion and to enhance communication efforts about loss mitigation opportunities with borrowers.

Servicers' actions are clearly working. HOPE NOW estimates that more than 1.7 million homeowners have avoided foreclosure because of industry efforts since July of 2007. In May 2008 alone, servicers provided approximately 170,000 at risk borrowers with repayment and modification plans. Early indications show that servicers are maintaining this pace for June.[10] Of the workout plans offered in May, approximately 100,000 were repayment plans and 70,000 were loan modifications.

Workouts are clearly outpacing foreclosures. In the first quarter of 2008, the number of repayment plans and modifications alone equaled 482,996 as compared with 198,172 foreclosure sales in the same timeframe. Servicers are also engaged in partial or advance claims, delinquent refinances, short sales and deeds in lieu of foreclosure that are not captured currently in the survey. We believe the

industry has demonstrated its willingness and commitment to help borrowers avoid foreclosure.

Let me repeat this: despite assertions to the contrary, the numbers are clear. In the first three months of this year, 482,996 families received workouts, more than twice the number of people who experienced foreclosure sales: 198,172. The industry is engaged in an historic effort to assist people in trouble, despite an unending stream of criticism that somehow our efforts are inadequate.

Obviously, the sooner a borrower in trouble can get a workout plan, the greater the chance the borrower has to avoid foreclosure and the less impact there is on the surrounding community. However, servicers cannot forgo due diligence for speed. As some have suggested, granting every borrower a loan modification simply because the borrower requests one is unwise and contrary to the servicer's contractual responsibility to investors or duty to shareholders. As prudent businesses, servicers must review the specific circumstances of the request and tailor the response to the borrower's unique circumstances. Failure to do so would also harm the borrower, as each borrower's financial situation is different, which calls for different solutions.

Lenders continue to explore ways to improve execution and responsiveness. We recognize that we can do better, and we are working to improve even more. Servicers are increasing staff, sending special mailings, making phone calls, developing Web sites, going door-to-door and using other creative means to reach out to distressed homeowners. As a normal course, servicers send numerous letters to delinquent homeowners notifying them about loss mitigation. Additionally, HOPE NOW launched an additional nationwide campaign to reach at-risk homeowners. So far, HOPE NOW members have sent approximately 1.3 million special letters. About 18 to 20 percent of homeowners receiving the HOPE NOW-coordinated letters have contacted their servicer, a 6- to 9-fold increase over the standard 2–3 percent response rate servicers have historically received.

Industry Action

Servicers have also advanced or promoted several other beneficial programs:

HOPE Hotline: The industry, through the HOPE NOW Alliance, continues to promote the Homeownership Preservation Foundation's HOPE Hotline (888-995-HOPE) which is available 24 hours a day, 7 days a weeks, and 365 days a year. There is no cost to homeowners for using the HOPE Hotline. . . . The HOPE Hotline currently has approximately 450 HUD-approved housing counselors available to assist and advise borrowers on mortgages and other debts. However, borrowers must take action. The longer the borrower waits to seek help, the less likely he or she will qualify for loss mitigation.

Streamlined Modifications: Lenders and servicers of HOPE NOW worked with the American Securitization Forum (ASF) to create a framework to more readily modify certain at-risk subprime loans securitized in the secondary market.[11] The focus of the effort has been to identify categories of borrowers with subprime hybrid adjustable rate mortgages (ARM) who can be streamlined into refinancings or modifications. . . .

Foreclosure Prevention Workshops: Members are working with government agencies, federal and state legislative offices and consumer groups to host foreclosure prevention workshops, where borrowers can meet servicers face-to-face to discuss and execute workout options. . . . In the past four months, HOPE NOW alone has connected almost 6,000 homeowners with their lender and/or a HUD-certified housing counselor at workshops in 14 different cities in California, Georgia, Illinois, Pennsylvania, Ohio, Nevada, Texas, Wisconsin, Tennessee, Florida and Indiana.

Use of Third Parties: In addition to the successful use of housing counselors, servicers are also piloting the use of other third parties, such as foreclosure attorneys, to discuss foreclosure prevention alternatives with borrowers. . . . Servicers are also employing third parties to make personal contacts with borrowers at their homes to execute loss mitigation packages.

Innovations with Counselors: The industry, through HOPE NOW and the technology provider Computer Sciences Corporation, have crafted a Web-based tool which housing counselors can use to capture critical borrower information needed to complete a workout by the servicer. . . . The software can generate a workout recommendation that is based on a particular servicer's or investor's rules and the specific borrower information.

Servicer Best Practices: Servicers working through the HOPE NOW Alliance issued guidelines last month that provide greater clarity and uniformity to the workout process. . . .

Web Sites: Servicers have also created Web sites that allow borrowers at any time of the day to learn about the loss mitigation process, educate themselves on the requirements, and download or print the financial forms and other documents necessary to initiate the workout process. . . .

Servicer Challenges

The Committee has inquired whether impediments exist that inhibit increased execution of workouts. We would like to take this opportunity to explore some of the more common reasons modifications and other workout strategies fail or are slow to complete.

Investment Properties: The options for helping borrowers who purchased homes as investments are limited. During the housing boom of the last several years, there were many speculators and investors looking to profit from price appreciation. The strength of our economy relies on the willingness of people to take risks, but risk means one does not always get his or her rewards. During this time, a majority of these properties were purchased to try to capitalize on appreciating home values or to use rents as a source of investment income, or some combination of both. With the downturn in the housing market, a number of these investors are walking away from their properties and defaulting on their loans. In the third quarter of 2007, 18 percent of foreclosure actions started were on non-owner occupied properties. Foreclosure starts for the same period for non-owner occupied properties in Arizona, Florida, Nevada and Ohio were at 22 percent.[12] . . .

Junior Liens: Many borrowers have second and third liens. If the first lienholder seeks to modify the mortgage by adding the arrearage to the balance of the loan—which is common practice to bring the loan current—or seeks to extend the maturity date, the first lienholder must get the junior lienholders to resubordinate their interests to the first lienholder. Failure to get that subordination would jeopardize the first lienholder's priority position and would likely violate the trust and pooling and servicing agreements. . . .

The June HOPE NOW Servicing Guidelines identify these limitations, but also indicate that junior lienholders who are not restricted by servicing agreements to the contrary will resubordinate their interest when:

- a refinancing does not increase the first lien principal amount by more than reasonable closing costs and arrearages and no cash is extracted by the homeowner; and
- A loan modification that lowers or maintains the monthly payment of the first lien via term extension, rate reduction and/or principal write down and no cash is extracted by the homeowner.

Recidivism: Recidivists or serial defaulters are costly to servicers and can create a barrier to repeat offers of loss mitigation. While the industry will consider revising previous modifications or repayment plans based upon true hardship, requests for multiple modifications with no intentions of honoring the terms will—and should—be rejected. Workouts are not free of charge for the servicer. Servicers and investors often incur costs associated with delinquency and foreclosure initiation and those costs mount the longer the delinquency remains outstanding. Servicers also use up valuable resources and incur costs to perform loss mitigation. Borrowers who redefault repeatedly drive up these costs making loss mitigation not viable or financially sound.

One way the industry is attempting to reduce the recidivism problem is to engage in "stipulated payment to modification plans." These "stip to mods" require the borrower to make timely payments according to the proposed revised terms of the mortgage for three or four months. . . .

Contractual Requirements: Despite many efforts to relieve some of the legal barriers to executing modifications, servicers are under a contractual duty to follow the requirements of their pooling and servicing agreement and to maximize the recovery to the trust. As we have explored in the past, many PSAs permit workouts that are "consistent with industry practice." This poses a challenge to define common industry practice, especially when new approaches such as streamline modifications are under-taken. Others, albeit a minority, prohibit modifications altogether or limit the length of repayment plans. Yet others have conflicting provisions, for example, permitting servicers to follow standard industry practices for delinquent borrowers, but prohibiting changes to the interest rate in other sections of the document. These legal issues are difficult to manage and servicers are reluctant to err against the investor for fear of liability.

While we are certain these limitations or conflicts would be resolved if investors could get together and agree, many MBS are widely held and getting the necessary number of investors together to change the PSA terms has proven impossible. Servicers are not remaining idle, however. Servicers are advancing new concepts by creating industry standards through coordinated approaches led by industry groups and seeking approval of actions by the American Securitization Forum, the SEC and IRS. The industry is working as a whole to obtain favorable results for homeowners while not violating their contracts. . . .

Security Requirements: In some cases, a modification cannot be executed until the borrower is delinquent. For example, Ginnie Mae does not permit a loan to be modified and remain in the security. To modify a loan, it must be repurchased from the pool. Servicers, however, are prohibited from repurchasing a loan from the pool until the borrower is 90 days delinquent. This policy has merit to curb run-off at the security level. Unfortunately, in today's environment, it also inhibits the servicer's ability to execute modifications when a borrower is current—but default is imminent—or when the borrower is delinquent by a month or two.

Failure to Respond: While the rate of borrower response has improved dramatically since last year, still far too many borrowers are unresponsive or fail to follow through on workout offers. Some borrowers will request loss mitigation assistance, but when asked to provide necessary documentation, such as income verification or letters describing their financial hardship, the borrowers do not respond. Servicers have also seen borrowers get approved for a modification, but then fail to sign and return a modification agreement that executes the deal. Despite follow up efforts, no action is taken and the servicer is forced to consider the request abandoned. We do not know for certain why these situations are happening. We presume several things. In some cases, the borrower cannot demonstrate a financial hardship. We also believe that the borrower may get overwhelmed with notices and collection calls from other creditors and, therefore, stops opening mail and taking calls. We also believe that some borrowers become suspicious of signing an agreement despite communicating with the servicer. We are sure there are many other reasons. Unfortunately, they are all speculation since servicers are unable to reach these borrowers.

Changing Behavior: Servicers are finding in many cases that borrowers' expenses exceed their income. While income may be sufficient to afford the home and reasonable household expenses, other spending habits and debts incurred by the borrower are draining surplus funds. To retain the home, borrowers must change their spending habits and address their other debts. Servicers are willing to provide assistance by modifying terms of the loan to clear the delinquency and provide more affordable terms. However, borrowers may still also have to negotiate with unsecured creditors to reduce credit card balances in order to continue to afford the home. Servicers are not forcing borrowers to bring down these balances before executing a workout. Servicers will give the borrower the benefit of the doubt and will execute a plan, stop the foreclosure if applicable, and trust that the borrower will take action to reduce their expenses and other debts. . . .

Secondary Marketing Risk: Servicers of FHA and VA loans are subject to secondary marketing risk when modifying loans. As stated previously, in order to modify an FHA or VA loan, the servicer must repurchase the loan from the pool. The servicer generally borrows funds from a bank to make the repurchase at the unpaid principal balance. The repurchase obligation creates risk for the servicer. Servicers who repurchase mortgages out of Ginnie Mae securities incur interest rate risk associated with these modifications. Interest rate risk is the risk that the new modified rate offered to the borrower will be below the prevailing market interest rate (par) and the servicer will incur a principal loss for delivering a less valuable asset. Historically the interest rate risk has been far less than the loss from foreclosure. Servicers do not incur redelivery risk with most private label securities because modified loans do not have to be repurchased from pools to be modified.

Conclusion

Servicers want to assist borrowers who are having difficulty paying their mortgages. Not only do servicers want to preserve the client relationship, but servicers and investors have an economic incentive to avoid foreclosure. As a result, servicers are performing a growing number of workouts, including modifications, as evidenced by the HOPE NOW data. Servicers have increased staff, have funded new technology, are sponsoring homeownership workshops and are funding advertising to educate borrowers about foreclosure prevention options. They are paying for housing counseling sessions so that they remain free to homeowners and are working with regulators and others to resolve legal impediments to performing loss mitigation. Servicers are using third parties in innovative ways, even going door-to-door to reach borrowers, and are paying incentives to staff and third parties for successful workouts. All these efforts demonstrate the industry's dedication to avoiding foreclosure and helping delinquent borrowers get back on their feet. The industry is working to keep pace with changes. We are not standing idle, but seeking new and financial responsible ways to increase workouts.

The incentives of the mortgage servicer are generally in line with the borrower who is in trouble. We are doing our part. Thank you for the opportunity to share our thoughts with the Committee.

Notes

1. The Mortgage Bankers Association (MBA) is the national association representing the real estate finance industry, an industry that employs more than 370,000 people in virtually every community in the country. Headquartered in Washington, D.C., the association works to ensure the continued strength of the nation's residential and commercial real estate markets; to expand homeownership and extend access to affordable housing to all Americans. MBA promotes fair and ethical lending practices and fosters professional excellence among real estate finance employees through a wide range of educational programs and a variety of publications. Its membership of over 2,400 companies includes all elements of real estate finance: mortgage companies, mortgage brokers, commercial banks, thrifts, Wall Street conduits, life insurance companies and others in the mortgage lending field. For additional information, visit MBA's Web site. . . .

2. See Darryl E. Getter, "Understanding Mortgage Foreclosure: Recent Events, the Process, and Costs," CRS Report for Congress (November 5, 2007), pp. 9, 11.

3. See Desiree Hatcher, "Foreclosure Alternatives: A Case for Preserving Homeownership," Profitwise News and Views (a publication of the Federal Reserve Bank of Chicago) (February 2006), p. 2 (citing a GMAC-RFC estimate); Craig Focardi, "Servicing Default Management: An Overview of the Process and Underlying Technology," TowerGroup Research Note, No. 033-13C (November 15, 2002). See also Congressional Budget Office (CBO), "Policy Options for the Housing and Financial Markets," (April 2008), p. 17.

4. Karen M. Pence, "Foreclosing on Opportunity: State Laws and Mortgage Credit," Board of Governors of the Federal Reserve System (May 13, 2003), p. 1. See also CBO, p. 17; Community Affairs Department, Office of the Comptroller of the Currency (OCC), "Foreclosure Prevention: Improving Contact with Borrowers," Community Developments (June 2007), p. 3.

5. Amy Crews Cutts and William A. Merrill, "Interventions in Mortgage Default: Policies and Practices to Prevent Home Loss and Lower Costs," Freddie Mac Working Paper #08-01 (March 2008), p. 30 and Table 6.

6. Cutts and Merrill, p. 32.

7. CBO, p. 17; Getter, p. 9; Cutts and Merrill, p. 33.

8. Mortgagee Letter 2008–13 (May 7, 2008).

9. See, for example, Said, Carolyn: "More in Foreclosure Choose to Walk Away," San Francisco *Chronicle*: March 16, 2008. . . .

10. "Mortgage Loss Mitigation Statistics" HOPE NOW issued July 2008. . . .

11. "Streamlined Foreclosure and Loss Avoidance Framework for Securitized Subprime Adjustable Rate Mortgage Loans," American Securitization *Forum*, December 6, 2007 and updated July 8, 2008. . . .

12. Jay Brinkmann, Ph.D., "An Examination of Mortgage Foreclosures, Modifications, Repayment Plans, and Other Loss Mitigation Activities in the Third Quarter of 2007," Mortgage Bankers Association (January 2008).

DAVID G. KITTLE, was appointed in 2008 as the chairman of the Mortgage Bankers Association, a national association representing the real estate finance industry. He is also the executive vice president of Vision Mortgage Capital.

Julia Gordon

NO

A Review of Mortgage Servicing Practices and Foreclosure Mitigation

The U.S. economy faces significant challenges today, as 20,000 foreclosures take place every single week.[1] It is not an overstatement to say that the way we choose to deal with these issues today has implications for nearly every American. The negative spillover effects from these foreclosures are substantial: a single foreclosure causes neighborhood property values to drop, collectively adding up to billions of dollars of losses. Empty homes lead to higher crime rates. Lost property tax revenue hurts cities and counties that are already strapped. Millions of Americans who depend on a robust housing market are losing jobs and income. As foreclosures accelerate during the next two years, these economic effects will be felt even more strongly.

In announcing the Federal Reserve Board's new rules governing mortgage origination, Federal Reserve Board Chairman Ben Bernanke acknowledged that unfair and deceptive practices by lenders have played a major role in the current housing crisis. According to Bernanke, too many loans were "inappropriate or misled the borrower."[2] As a result, the Federal Reserve will now require all lenders to verify a consumer's ability to afford a mortgage before selling it, and will prohibit a variety of abusive and dangerous practices.

While it is too late to stop the housing crisis that has been caused by reckless lending, it is not too late to minimize the massive damage ahead. Skillful loan servicing can convert distressed mortgages into stable loans that generate revenue for investors, build ownership for families, and contribute to stronger and more stable communities. Ineffective or abusive loan servicing, on the other hand, can produce the opposite results. That is why national policies governing loan servicing ultimately will have enormous implications—not only for people facing foreclosure, but for the future prosperity of our country.

In short, abusive and inappropriate loans were mass-marketed for years, and now, to prevent further damage to the economy, these bad loans must be mass-repaired. The most effective way to repair distressed loans is through loan "modifications" that alter the loan's terms in a way that allows homeowners to continue paying their debt and building equity. Unfortunately, as I will discuss in more detail, today even the best-intentioned loan servicers face major obstacles to making loan modifications, and others lack the incentive or motivation to fix mortgages so that people can stay in their homes. To put it bluntly, it is far harder to

obtain an affordable loan modification for an unsustainable loan than it was to take out the loan in the first place. As a result, voluntary efforts aimed at increasing loan modifications have done little to stem the overwhelming tide of foreclosures that are dragging down our economy. . . .

I. We Face a Severe Foreclosure Crisis That Will Grow Even Worse Without Significant Government Action

Just one year ago, some in the mortgage industry claimed that the number of coming foreclosures would be too small to have a significant impact on the overall economy.[3] No one makes that claim today. As foreclosures reach an all-time high and are projected to grow higher,[4] the "worst case is not a recession but a housing depression."[5] Projections by Fitch Ratings indicate that 43 percent of recent subprime loans will be lost to foreclosure,[6] and at least two million American families are expected to lose their homes to foreclosures initiated over the next two years.[7] What's more, industry projections forecast that by 2012, 1 in 8 mortgages—that's all mortgages, not just subprime mortgages—will fail.[8] Robert Schiller recently noted that the meltdown and resulting crisis has erased any gains in the homeownership rate made since 2001, and the rate stands to fall further yet.[9]

The negative effects of foreclosures are not confined to the families who lose their homes. Forty million of their neighbors—those who are paying their mortgages on time—will see their property values decline as a result by over $350 billion.[10] Other ripple effects include a reduced tax base, increased crime, further downward pressure on housing prices, and loss of jobs in the industry. According to the IMF, direct economic losses stemming from this crisis will likely top $500 billion, and consequential costs will total close to a trillion dollars.[11]

Sadly, many of the families losing their homes to foreclosure today might not have found themselves in this position if they had been given the type of loan that they actually qualified for. Last December, the *Wall Street Journal* found that of the subprime loans originated in 2006 that were packaged into securities and sold to investors, 61 percent "went to people with credit scores high enough to often qualify for conventional [i.e., prime] loans with far

Gordon, Julia. Illinois House of Representatives, July 25, 2008, pp. excerpts.

better terms."[12] Even those borrowers who did not qualify for prime loans could have received sustainable, thirty-year, fixed-rate loans for—at most—50 to 80 basis points above the "teaser rate" on the unsustainable exploding ARM loans they were given.[13]

Wall Street's appetite for risky loans incentivized mortgage brokers and lenders to aggressively market these highly risky ARM loans instead of the sustainable loans for which borrowers qualified. As former Federal Reserve Chair Alan Greenspan told Newsweek:

> The big demand was not so much on the part of the borrowers as it was on the part of the suppliers who were giving loans which really most people couldn't afford. We created something which was unsustainable. And it eventually broke. If it weren't for securitization, the subprime loan market would have been very significantly less than it is in size.[14]

Market participants readily admit that they were motivated by the increased profits offered by Wall Street in return for risky loans. After filing for bankruptcy, the CEO of one mortgage lender explained it this way to the New York Times, "The market is paying me to do a no-income-verification loan more than it is paying me to do the full documentation loans," he said. "What would you do?"[15] Even the chief economist of the Mortgage Bankers Association, when asked why lenders made so many loans that they knew were unsustainable, replied, "Because investors continued to buy the loans."[16]

Currently, 30 percent of families holding recent subprime mortgages owe more on their mortgage than their home is worth.[17] These families are at an increased risk of foreclosure because their negative equity (being "underwater") precludes the homeowner from selling, refinancing or getting a home equity loan or using any other mechanism for weathering short-term financial difficulty.[18] Regulators like the Chair of the Federal Reserve Board and other economists are increasingly cautioning that loan balances must be reduced to avoid unnecessary foreclosures that will further damage the economy.[19] Unnecessary foreclosures are those that could be avoided with an economically rational, sustainable loan modification that yields the creditor or investor pool at least as much as would be recovered in foreclosure.

II. Voluntary Loan Modifications Have Proven Insufficient to Prevent the Foreclosure Crisis from Continuing to Escalate

To date, Congress and the regulatory agencies have responded to this crisis largely by encouraging voluntary efforts by servicers to reduce the number of foreclosures. Yet despite the loss mitigation encouragement by HOPE NOW, the federal banking agencies, and state agencies, voluntary efforts by lenders, servicers and investors have failed to stem the tide of foreclosures. Seriously delinquent loans are at a record high for both prime and subprime loans.[20] The number of families in danger of losing their homes continues to be near record highs: in May, an estimated 1,977,000 loans were 60 days or more delinquent or had entered foreclosure, the second highest number since the program began reporting data last July. This is an astonishing 43 percent increase since July of last year.[21]

There is an emerging consensus that half-measures in the private sector are not working. FDIC Chairman Sheila Bair recently said that the current economic situation calls for a stronger government response, since voluntary loan modifications are not sufficient.[22] The necessity of government action also is gaining recognition among Wall Street leaders. In April, a senior economic advisor at UBS Investment Bank stated that, "when markets fail, lenders and borrowers need some sort of regulatory and legislative framework within which to manage problems, rather than be forced to act in the chaos of the moment."[23] Moreover, as former Federal Reserve Board Vice Chairman Alan Blinder recently noted, the fact that most of the mortgages at issue have been securitized and sold to investors across the globe "bolsters the case for government intervention rather than undermining it. After all, how do you renegotiate terms of a mortgage when the borrower and the lender don't even know each other's names?"[24]

While the HOPE NOW initiative claims to be making significant progress, its most recent data report reveals that the current crisis in the housing market dwarfs the servicing industry's response. According to their most recent report, almost four times as many families lost their home or are in the process of losing their home as received loan modifications from servicers.[25] The State Foreclosure Prevention Working Group, made up of state Attorneys General and Banking Commissioners, found that seven out of ten seriously delinquent borrowers are *still* not on track for any loss mitigation outcome that could lead to preventing a foreclosure.[26]

There are a number of reasons for this lack of loss mitigation activity. One reason is that the way servicers are compensated by lenders creates a bias for moving forward with foreclosure rather than engaging in foreclosure prevention. As reported in *Inside B&C Lending*, "Servicers are generally dis-incented to do loan modifications because they don't get paid for them but they do get paid for foreclosures." In fact, "it costs servicers between $750 and $1,000 to complete a loan modification."[27] Even when a loan modification would better serve investors and homeowners, some loan servicers have an economic incentive to proceed as quickly as possible to foreclosure.

But even those servicers who want to engage in effective loss mitigation face significant obstacles. One such obstacle is the fear of investor lawsuits, because modifying loans typically affects various tranches of securities differently. Another obstacle is the existence of junior liens on many homes. When there is a second mortgage, the holder of the first mortgage has no incentive to provide modifications that would free up borrower resources to make payments on the second mortgage. At the same time, the holder of the second mortgage has no incentive to support an effective modification, which would likely cause it to face a 100 percent loss; rather, the holder of the second is better off waiting to see if a homeowner can make a few payments before foreclosure. A third to a half of the homes purchased in 2006 with subprime mortgages have second mortgages as well.[28]

It is also important to note the gap between rhetoric and reality about how easy it is to get a loan modification.[29] Servicers coming before Congress often excuse the paucity of loan modifications by claiming that their efforts to modify loans are stymied by homeowners' refusal to respond to servicers' calls and letters. While this no doubt happens in some cases, the bigger problem by far is the reverse. We repeatedly hear from homeowners and housing counselors that the numerous homeowners who actively reach out to their servicers face the same problem: despite repeated calls to the servicer and many hours of effort, they cannot get anyone on the phone with the authority or ability to help. Many professional housing counselors are demoralized by the servicers' practice of incessantly bouncing the caller around from one "on hold" line to another, such that desperate homeowners never reach a live person or one with decision-making authority.

III. When Modifications and Other Workouts Are Made, They Are Frequently Temporary or Unsustainable, Leading to Re-Default and Placing Homeowners in an Even Worse Economic Position Than When They Started

More than a year ago, leading lenders and servicers publicly and unanimously endorsed a set of principles announced at the Homeownership Preservation Summit hosted by Senate Banking Committee Chairman Christopher Dodd, which called upon servicers to modify loans to "ensure that the loan is sustainable for the life of the loan, rather than, for example, deferring the reset period."[30]

Unfortunately, many of the modifications now being made have not adhered to this pledge. To date, neither HOPE NOW nor the Mortgage Bankers Association has been willing to disclose what proportion of the loan modifications entail reductions of principal or long-term reductions of interest rates, what proportion simply entail the capitalization of arrearages or short-term adjustments, and what proportion require the payment of fines and fees as a precondition to getting any modification at all. However, it is clear that most loan modifications or workouts have not fundamentally changed the unsustainable terms of the mortgage by reducing the principal or lowering the interest rate, but instead just add fees and interest to the loan

balance and amortize them into the loan, add them to the end of the loan term, or provide a temporary forbearance.

Reduction in interest rates is a key way to provide relief for homeowners whose interest rates jumped significantly— far above market rates—as a result of rate resets. Modification of principal is particularly important for the approximately 30 percent of recent subprime loans whose owners now owe more than the house is worth by reducing principal. In calling for more loan modifications that reduce principal, Chairman Bernanke recently noted that such loan modifications involving principle have been "quite rare."[31] The State Foreclosure Prevention Working Group agrees.[32]

Unsurprisingly, given the minimal relief these "modifications" frequently provide, a report just released by Moody's has found a high number of re-defaults among the modified loans. Of the servicing companies surveyed by Moody's (accounting for roughly 50 percent of the total U.S. subprime servicing market), fully 42 percent of the loans modified in the first half of 2007 were at least 90 days delinquent as of March 31, 2008. The vice chair of Washington Mutual, who helps run HOPE NOW, admits that many of the homeowners who have sought their assistance "will not receive long-term relief and could ultimately face higher total costs."[33]

Another obstacle to sustainable modifications is the common servicer practice of charging exorbitant fines and "junk" fees. The reasonableness of most default fees is highly doubtful, with many of the "costs" unjustifiable and vastly exceeding the prevailing market rates in a community. Indeed, the fact that mortgage servicers systematically charge unreasonable fees is well-documented by courts.[34] A recent analysis of over 1,700 foreclosures across the country showed that questionable fees were added to borrowers' bills in almost half the loans.[35] Servicers often require that these fees be paid in full before the homeowner receives a loan modification or workout, thereby depleting whatever limited funds the financially strapped homeowner can scrape together and leaving no cushion for short-term cash-flow needs, which results in a much higher possibility of re-default.

Compounding the problem, servicers frequently misapply monthly mortgage payments first to the fees, rather than to the principal and interest owed. In this way, a homeowner who is timely repaying interest and principal nevertheless falls further behind on the mortgage and accumulates still more fees, continuing a vicious cycle.

IV. In Many Cases, Voluntary Loan Modifications or Workouts Are Further Disadvantaging Homeowners in Trouble Because the Servicer Forces Homeowners to Waive All Their Rights, Even Those Unrelated to the Workout

As a precondition to modifications and workout, lenders have been requiring shockingly broad waivers that strip homeowners of fundamental legal rights. These waivers threaten almost all of the borrowers' legal defenses to a foreclosure if the modification is unsustainable. Thus, if the modification fails, the lender can argue the borrower waived all of his federal (such as Truth in Lending or HOEPA) and state law defenses to foreclosure. The waivers also could be read to prevent claims questioning the reasonableness of fees charged.

Indeed, some releases go so far as to waive future claims that have not arisen, including seeking a free pass for future violations of such important federal laws as the Fair Credit Reporting Act, the Fair Housing Act, and Fair Debt Collection Practices Act, and some even ask homeowners to waive rights that are deemed unwaivable under state law. For example, here is one such waiver required by Countrywide:

> In consideration for Countrywide entering into this Agreement, you agree to release and discharge Countrywide, and all of its investors, employees, and related companies, from any and all claims you have or may have against them concerning the Loan. Although California law (specifically Section 1542 of the California Civil Code) provides that "[a] general release does not extend to claims which the creditor does not know or suspect to exist in his favor at the time of executing the release, which if known by him must have materially affected his settlement with the debtor," you agree to waive that provision, or any similar provision under other state or federal laws, so that this release shall include all and any claim whatsoever of every nature concerning the Loan, regardless of whether you know about or suspect such claims including, but not limited to, claims arising under the Mortgage Disclosure Act, Electronic Fund Transfer Act, Truth in Lending Act, Real Estate Settlement Procedures Act, Fair Credit Reporting Act, Fair Housing Act, and Fair Debt Collection Practices Act. This release shall remain effective even if this Agreement terminates for any reason.[36]

Other institutions include similar clauses in their loan modification agreements.[37] One Option One agreement even forces the homeowner to "admit" that "the Arrearage is the Borrowers' full responsibility and was produced solely by the actions or inactions of the Borrowers."[38]

Given that these waivers are typically signed when a family's only other choice is to lose their home, and given that they are required not just for life-of-the-loan modifications but even for temporary forbearances, we believe they risk compounding the foreclosure crisis. A homeowner should not be coerced into giving up potential defenses if a foreclosure ultimately takes place. As noted below, H.R. 5679 would prohibit these waivers. However, in the absence of legislative action, we strongly recommend that servicers stop requiring such waivers as a condition of modification and that HOPE NOW require its participating servicers to refrain from requiring such waivers. The servicers also should publicly state they will

not seek to enforce the waiver clauses in the modifications they have made to date.

V. H.R. 5679, the Foreclosure Prevention and Sound Mortgage Servicing Act of 2008 Will Help Prevent Foreclosures, Improve Servicing Practices, and Enhance Data Collection

Earlier this year, Representative Maxine Waters introduced H.R. 5679, the Foreclosure Prevention and Sound Mortgage Servicing Act of 2008. This bill requires loan servicers to engage in loss mitigation efforts prior to foreclosure, although it does not mandate any particular outcome or result.

Legislation establishing minimal servicing standards is needed because loan servicing is not an industry subject to typical economic incentives. As Tara Twomey of the National Consumer Law Center notes, homeowners "cannot choose the servicer that handles their loan and cannot change servicers if they are dissatisfied."[39] Instead, servicers are driven by the desire to maximize their own profits and to maximize returns to the investors who now stand in the shoes of the original lender.[40]

By requiring loan servicers to engage in loss mitigation prior to foreclosure, this legislation will assist homeowners, lenders, investors, and communities. The bill prioritizes continued homeownership as the highest goal of servicers. It requires that homeowners be able to reach a live person with decision-making authority, and it prohibits the coercive waivers described in Section IV above.

Perhaps most important, the legislation requires that any agreement reached through loss mitigation be affordable by the homeowner. We think careful consideration of the borrower's income as well as any expenses, including debt and residual income left over for other living expenses, is critical in determining the affordability of any solution intended to keep homeowners in their home. . . .

VI. H.R. 6076, the Home Retention and Economic Stabilization Act, Will Provide a Necessary Timeout for Overburdened Servicers and Homeowners with Unsustainable Loans

Given the extensive nature of the foreclosure crisis and the fact that servicers have been unable to reduce foreclosures sufficiently, more time is needed to develop and implement strategies to keep homeowners in their homes. H.R. 6076, the Home Retention and Economic Stabilization Act, is a temporary deferment plan that provides a much-needed "timeout" that will enable lenders and servicers to increase their capacities to meet current need, for credit markets to stabilize, and for legislative solutions, such as the FHA refinancing program under consideration in Congress, to take effect. . . .

VII. Court-Supervised Loan Modifications Are a Necessary Complement to Any Voluntary Efforts

Even if all of the legislation and other suggestions described above are enacted, a significant proportion of troubled homeowners will ultimately face foreclosure because the loan servicer cannot modify the loan due to a conflict between multiple lienholders or other constraints. In those cases, the failure to modify will be to the clear detriment of investors as a whole. It is critical, as a last alternative to foreclosure, to permit a bankruptcy court to adjust the mortgage if the borrower can afford a market rate loan that will be preferable to foreclosure for the creditor or investor pool and the homeowner alike.

Currently, bankruptcy courts can modify any type of loan, including mortgages on yachts and vacation homes, with the exception of one type: primary residences. Removing this exclusion would help homeowners (not speculators) who are committed to staying in their homes, without bailing out investors and without costing taxpayers a dime. The Emergency Home Ownership and Mortgage Equity Protection Act (H.R. 3609) provides a narrow, time-limited mechanism for enabling court-supervised loan modifications to break the deadlock that is forcing families who can afford a market rate loan into foreclosure.[41] The bill has been marked up in both Chambers, and is an important part of any effective solution to the foreclosure crisis.

We believe that the court-supervised loan modifications bill is a necessary complement to the Foreclosure Prevention and Sound Mortgage Servicing Act because it provides an important backstop for families who cannot get a sustainable loan modification due to junior liens or for whatever other reason. Moreover, as loans get modified through the bankruptcy process, these modifications will effectively create a "template" for modification that will ease the process of loss mitigation for servicers, as all parties involved will have a better idea of how the courts would handle a particular situation.[42] . . .

Conclusion

The foreclosure crisis is far from over. Already we have seen the tremendous costs imposed by this crisis. Yet it is not too late to take action to prevent many more foreclosures and a much higher cost. By moving homeowners from abusive loans into sustainable ones, we can keep families in their homes, ensure a continued stream of income to investors, and prevent the neighborhood and societal costs of mass foreclosures. . . .

Notes

1. *See Moody's Economy.com: Hearing before House Subcommittee on Commercial and Administrative Law* (January 28, 2008), (written testimony of Mark Zandi) . . . *See also* Center for Responsible Lending, *Subprime Spillover*, (Rev. Jan. 18, 2008) . . . [hereinafter Subprime Spillover].

2. Statement of Chairman Ben S. Bernanke, Federal Reserve Board, commenting on new FRB regulatory amendments on mortgage lending (July 14, 2008) at . . .

3. *See, e.g.*, Statement of John M. Robbins, CMB, Chairman, Mortgage Bankers Association at the National Press Club's Newsmakers Lunch—Washington, DC (May 22, 2007) (Speaking of predicted foreclosures, Mr. Robbins stated: "As we can clearly see, this is not a macro-economic event. No seismic financial occurrence is about to overwhelm the U.S. economy."); Julia A. Seymour, *Subprime Reporting, Networks blame lenders, not borrowers for foreclosure 'epidemic,'* Business & Media Institute, Mar. 28, 2007 ("[T] here are experts who say the subprime 'meltdown' is not the catastrophe reporters and legislators are making it out to be. 'We don't believe it will spill over into the prime market or the U.S. economy,' said [Laura] Armstrong [Vice President, Public Affairs] of the Mortgage Bankers Association.").

4. Renae Merle, *Home Foreclosures Hit Record High*, Washington Post, March 6, 2008.

5. David M. Herszenhorn and Vikas Bajaj, *Tricky Task of Offering Aid to Homeowners*, The New York Times, Apr. 6, 2008 (quoting Susan M. Wachter, a real estate finance professor at the Wharton School of the University of Pennsylvania. According to Professor Wachter, "In the market that we have in front of us, prices decline and supply increases, driving prices down further.").

6. Fitch Ratings estimates total losses of 25.8 percent of original balance in Q4 2006 loans placed in MBS they rated, and that loss severity will be at 60 percent, which means that 43 percent of the loans are projected to be lost to foreclosure (25.8/60); lack of home price appreciation said to increase defaults. Glenn Costello, Update on U.S. RMBS: Performance, Expectations, Criteria, Fitch Ratings, at 17-18 (not dated, distributed week of February 25, 2008). According to Michael Bykhovsky, president of Applied Analytics, an estimated 40 percent of outstanding subprime mortgage loans could go into default over the next three years; the dire outlook due to declining home values (press briefing at the Mortgage Bankers Association's National Mortgage Servicing Conference, February 27, 2008).

7. *See Moody's Economy.com Hearing before House Subcommittee on Commercial and Administrative Law* (January 28, 2008) (written testimony of Mark Zandi) . . .

8. Rod Dubitsky et al., *Foreclosure Trends—A Sobering Reality*, Credit Suisse, Fixed Income Research, Apr. 28, 2008.

9. Robert J. Schiller, *The Scars of Losing a Home*, New York Times, May 18, 2008 (noting that the homeownership rate has fallen from 69.1 percent in 2005 to 67.8 percent in the first quarter of 2008, nearly the 67.5 percent rate at the beginning of 2001).

10. See Center for Responsible Lending, *The Impact of Court-Supervised Modifications on Subprime Foreclosures*, (Feb. 25, 2008) . . . for CRL's methodology for computing spillover, *see Subprime Spillover*, *supra* note 1 (Rev. Jan. 18, 2008) . . .

11. Christopher Swann, *IMF Says Financial Losses May Swell to $945 Billion*, April 8, 2008 . . .

12. Rick Brooks and Ruth Simon, Subprime Debacle Traps Even Very Credit-Worthy As Housing Boomed, Industry Pushed Loans to a Broader Market, The Wall Street Journal at A1 (Dec. 3, 2007).

13. Letter from CFAL to Ben S. Bernanke, Sheila C. Bair, John C. Dugan, John M. Reich, JoAnn Johnson, and Neil Milner (January 25, 2007) at 3.

14. Jon Meacham and Daniel Gross, *The Oracle Reveals All*, NEWSWEEK, Sept. 24, 2007, at 32, 33.

15. Vikas Bajaj and Christine Haughney, *Tremors at the Door—More People with Weak Credit Are Defaulting on Mortgages*, The New York Times, Jan. 26, 2007, at C1, C4.

16. Les Christie, *Subprime Loans Defaulting Even Before Resets*, CNNMoney.com, February 20, 2008 . . .

17. Edmund Andrews, *Relief for Homeowners Is Given to a Relative Few*, New York Times, March 4, 2008 (loans originated in 2005 and 2006).

18. Kristopher Gerardi, Adam Hale Shapiro & Paul S. Willen, *Subprime Outcomes: Risky Mortgages, Homeownership Experiences, and Foreclosures*, 3-4 (Federal Reserve Bank of Boston, Working Paper No 07-15, Dec. 3, 2007) (this otherwise good article misses the fact that certain loans themselves can create the cash flow shortfall that causes underwater loans to fail, when they are structured with initial low payments that are scheduled to rise, such as subprime 2/28 hybrid ARMs, and that certain loan terms have been statistically demonstrated to increase foreclosures, such as prepayment penalties).

19. Federal Reserve Chairman Ben Bernanke recently said, "When the mortgage is 'underwater,' a reduction in [loan] principal may increase the expected payoff by reducing the risk of default and foreclosure." "Preventable foreclosures" could be reduced, he said, by enabling loan servicers to "accept a principal writedown by an amount at least sufficient to allow the borrower to refinance into a new loan from another source." This would "remove the downside risk to investors of additional writedowns or a re-default." See Chair Ben S. Bernanke, "Reducing Preventable Mortgage Foreclosures" (March 4, 2008) . . . ; see also, Edmund L. Andrews, Fed Chief Urges Breaks for Some Home Borrowers, The New York Times,

Mar. 4, 2008; John Brinsley, Bernanke Call for Mortgage Forgiveness Puts Pressure on Paulson, Bloomberg.com, Mar. 5, 2008; Phil Izzo, Housing Market Has Further to Fall, The Wall Street Journal, Mar. 13, 2008 ("Last week, Federal Reserve Chairman Ben Bernanke suggested that lenders could aid struggling homeowners by reducing their principal—the sum of money they borrowed—to lessen the likelihood of foreclosure. Some 71 percent of respondents [i.e., economists surveyed by the NYT] agreed with the suggestion.").

20. Press Release, Center for Responsible Lending, Statement on HOPE NOW, (July 2, 2008) . . .

21. *Id.*

22. FDIC Chairwoman Sheila Bair (stating "We've got a real problem. And I do think we need to have more activist approaches. And I think it will be something we need to be honest with the American public about. We do need more intervention. It probably will cost some money."), Real Time Economics, The Wall St. Journal (April 7, 2008) . . .

23. George Magnus, *Large-scale action is needed to tackle the credit crisis*, Financial Times, Apr. 8, 2008.

24. Alan S. Blinder, *From the New Deal, a Way Out of a Mess*, The New York Times, Feb. 24, 2008.

25. Furthermore, the data provided by HOPE NOW understates the number of loans in foreclosure, as it only includes those homes that entered foreclosure and those that completed foreclosure during the month, not the total number currently in the foreclosure process. In fact, 1.1 million families were in foreclosure at the end of March.

26. Conference of State Bank Supervisors, *Analysis of Subprime Servicing Performance, Data Report No. 2*, (April 2008), at 1 . . . [hereinafter *Analysis of Subprime Servicing*].

27. Center for Responsible Lending, *Inside Mortgage Finance Reprints, Subprime Debt Outstanding Falls, Servicers Pushed on Loan Mods* (Nov. 16, 2007) . . . (quoting Karen Weaver, a managing director and global head of securitization research at Deutsche Bank Securities).

28. Credit Suisse Report, *Mortgage Liquidity du Jour: Underestimated No More* (March 12, 2007) at 5.

29. *See generally*, Gretchen Morgenson, *Silence of the Lender: Is Anyone Listening?* New York Times, July 13, 2008.

30. Homeownership Preservation Summit Statement of Principles (May 2, 2007) . . . (The Principles were announced by Senator Dodd, and endorsed by the Mortgage Bankers Association, CitiGroup, Chase, Litton, HSBC, Countrywide, Wells, AFSA, Option One, Freddie Mac, and Fannie Mae).

31. Statement of Federal Reserve Chairman Ben Bernanke on March 4, 2008, reprinted by Bloomberg .com and . . . ("Bernanke statement").

32. *Analysis of Subprime Servicing*, *supra* note 26, at 9 (the majority of servicers are not reporting significant levels of modifications that reduce principal alone, although principal reductions may be

combined with other modifications and therefore may not evidenced in our reporting).

33. David Cho and Renae Merle, *Merits of New Mortgage Aid Are Debate—Critics Say Treasury Plan Won't Bring Long-Term Relief*, The Washington Post, Mar. 4, 2008 (citing remarks of Bill Longbrake, senior policy adviser for the Financial Services Roundtable and vice chair of Washington Mutual).

34. Court have repeatedly found servicers' inspection fees, broker price opinions, forced place insurance, and legal fees either unreasonable or unjustifiable. See e.g., *In re Stewart*, 2008 WL 2676961, No. 07-11113 (Bankr. E.D. La. July 9, 2008) (Wells Fargo charging unnecessary inspection fees, unnecessary broker price opinions, and requiring excessively priced forced-place insurance); *In re Payne*, 387 B.R. 614, 628 (Bankr. D. Kan. 2008) (Everhome charging unjustified inspection fees, late fees, and foreclosure costs); *In re Jones*, 366 B.R. 584, 597-98 (Bankr. E.D. La. 2007) (Wells Fargo charging unreasonable inspection fees, unreasonable attorney's fees).

35. Gretchen Morgenson & Jonathan D. Glater, *Foreclosure Machine Thrives on Woes*, The New York Times, Mar. 30, 2008 (citing Katherine Porter, Misbehavior and Mistake in Bankruptcy Mortgage Claims, University of Iowa College of Law Legal Studies Research Paper Series, *Misbehavior and Mistake in Bankruptcy Mortgage Claims*, (Nov. 7, 2007) . . .

36. Countrywide, Repayment Plan Agreement (February 5, 2007) (on file with Center for Responsible Lending).

37. *Id*; Countrywide, Loan Modification Agreement (June 17, 2008); Homecomings Financial, Foreclosure Repayment Agreement, July 18, 2007; Ocwen Loan Servicing LLC, Forbearance Agreement (May 16, 2008); Ocwen Loan Servicing LLC, Proposed Modification Agreement (June 26, 2008); Option One Mortgage Corporate, Forbearance Agreement (August 24, 2007); NovaStar, Repayment Plan Agreement, (January 2008) (on file with Center for Responsible Lending).

Ocwen: By executing this modification, you forever irrevocably waive and relinquish any claims, action or causes of action, statute of limitation or other defense, counterclaims or setoffs of any kind which exist as of the date of this modification, whether known or unknown, which you may now or hereafter assert in connection with the making, closing, administration, collection or the enforcement by Ocwen of the loan documents, this modification or any other related agreements.

By executing this modification, you irrevocably waive all right to a trial by jury in any action, proceeding or counterclaim arising out of or relating to this modification and any related agreement or documents or transactions contemplated in this modification. Ocwen Loan Servicing LLC, Proposed Modification Agreement, June 26, 2008 (on file with Center for Responsible Lending). Customer expressly relinquishes and waives any rights, claims, and defenses Customer may have under any of the Code of Civil Procedure Sections or under the Loan with regard to any whole or partial payment, whether current, pass or future. Homecomings Financial, Foreclosure Repayment Agreement, July 18, 2007 (on file with Center for Responsible Lending).

38. Option One Mortgage Corporate, Forbearance Agreement (August 24, 2007) (on file with Center for Responsible Lending).

39. *Hearing before the U.S. House of Representatives Subcommittee on Housing and Community Opportunity*, 8 (April 16, 2007) (testimony of Tara Twomey, National Consumer Law Center).

40. *Id*. at 7 (Cutting costs is one reason for heavy reliance on often frustrating voicemail and touch tone menu options, as well as for the lack of adequate staff to handle requests for negotiation or information).

41. CRL Issue Brief, *Solution to Housing Crisis Requires Adjusting Loans to Fair Market Value through Court-Supervised Modifications*, (Apr. 1, 2008). . . .

42. *Straightening Out the Mortgage Mess: How Can WE Protect Homeownership and Provide Relief to Consumers in Financial Distress: Hearing before the House Judiciary Committee, Subcommittee on Commercial and Administrative Law* 5 (Oct. 30, 2007) (Testimony of Richard Levin, Partner, Cravath, Swaine & Moore LLP, on behalf of the National Bankruptcy Conference). . . .

Julia Gordon is associated with the Policy Council at the Center for Responsible Lending, a not-for-profit, nonpartisan research and policy.

EXPLORING THE ISSUE

Is Loan Mitigation the Answer to the Housing Foreclosure Problem?

Critical Thinking and Reflection

1. Is it right that loan servicers shoulder all the costs that fall to them when a loan is delinquent? Why or why not?
2. Why would it be that foreclosure costs vary significantly from state to state?
3. What might constitute a situation in which a short sale would be the most advisable course of action?
4. Should the American consumer trust the voluntary efforts of the mortgage industry? Explain.

Is There Common Ground?

It is one of the most dreaded words a homeowner could possibly hear: foreclosure. Yet, in the land of the American Dream—where owning one's own home is at the core of that dream—foreclosure has become a very real nightmare. To cite Julia Gordon, "20,000 foreclosures take place every single week." She goes on to say that the "most effective way to repair distressed loans is through loan 'modifications' that alter the loan's terms in a way that allows homeowners to continue paying their debt and building equity."

Yet, Gordon does *not* represent the "Yes" side to the question of whether loan mitigation is the answer to the housing foreclosure problem. The common ground, therefore, is established right out of the gate. The mortgage crisis is an indisputable fact. And the value of loan mitigation is not disputed either.

While this might suggest an "argument without an argument," all is not common ground. What it comes down to is this: David Kittle believes that the mortgage industry is vigilantly using foreclosure mitigation to noteworthy effectiveness. Gordon contests that this simply is not so, and that such voluntary modifications must be replaced by enforced regulation.

Create Central

www.mhhe.com/createcentral

Additional Resources

Hartman, Chester and Squires, Gregory D., eds., *From Foreclosure to Fair Lending* (New Village Press, 2013)

Kenney, *Foreclosure Prevention: Loss Mitigation Specialist* (Eiram Publishing, 2011)

Mitchell, Frank P. and Rehman, George A., eds., *Foreclosure Mitigation and Mortgage Irregularities: Housing Issues, Laws and Programs* (Nova Science Publishers, 2011)

Internet References . . .

LawHelpNewMexico: "Easing the Effects of Foreclosure: Alternatives, Loss Mitigation, and Working with the Bank"

www.lawhelpnewmexico.org/?q=content/easing
-effects-foreclosure-alternatives-loss-mitigation-and
-working-bank

Nolo: "Foreclosure Mediation and Loss Mitigation Programs in Bankruptcy"

www.nolo.com/legal-encyclopedia/foreclosure
-mediation-loss-mitigation-programs-bankruptcy.html

U.S. Department of Housing and Urban Development: "FHA NSC Loan Servicing and Loss Mitigation Frequently Asked Questions"

http://portal.hud.gov/hudportal/HUD?src=/program
_offices/housing/sfh/nsc/faqnsctc

Selected, Edited, and with Issue Framing Material by:
Eric Strahorn, *Florida Gulf Coast University*

ISSUE

Are Biofuels Like Ethanol the Answer to U.S. Energy Problems?

YES: Tom Buis, from "Testimony before the House Committee on Energy and Commerce Subcommittee on Energy and Power," U.S. House of Representatives (July 23, 2013)

NO: Charles T. Drevna, from "Testimony before the House Committee on Energy and Commerce Subcommittee on Energy and Power," U.S. House of Representatives (July 23, 2013)

Learning Outcomes

After reading this issue, you will be able to:

- Describe technical specifications of different types of biofuels and fossil fuels such as E15 and biodiesel.
- Identify the types of data necessary to measure policy outcomes like consumer choice and energy independence.
- Apply a cost-benefit analysis to the Renewable Fuel Standard.

ISSUE SUMMARY

YES: Tom Buis argues that the Renewable Fuel Standard has been a success that has created jobs, revitalized rural America, increased competition in the vehicle fuels market, lowered prices at the pump, improved the environment, and increased American energy independence.

NO: Charles Drevna argues that the Renewable Fuels Standard has not worked as intended and should be repealed. It has led to higher food and fuel costs, increased pollution, harmed refiners, and lead to the creation of fuels that can damage engines.

The term "biofuels" usually refers to ethanol and biodiesel. Biofuels are liquid fuels made from biomass, that is, organic nonfossil material of biological origin, and are largely used for transportation. Ethanol can be made from agricultural crops such as corn, barley, and sugarcane. Most biodiesel in the United States is currently produced from soybean oil (and recently also from waste animal fats or recycled grease from restaurants). The commercial viability of cellulosic ethanol, considered an "advanced" biofuel (made from woody biomass such as bark or switchgrass, which is a native prairie grass), has not yet been demonstrated.

The use of ethanol increased after the Energy Policy Act of 2005 set the Renewable Fuels Standard (RFS) mandating that transportation fuels sold in the United States contain a minimum volume of renewable fuels, the level of which will increase each year until 2022. In December 2007, the Energy Independence and Security Act (EISA) of 2007 increased the mandatory level to a total of 36 billion gallons by 2022, including 16 billion gallons of cellulosic biofuels. Corn ethanol is capped at 15 billion gallons from 2015 on, while other categories of renewable fuel continue to rise until 2022. The purpose of the EISA is to reduce U.S. dependence on imported oil produced in politically unstable areas like the Mideast and thereby contribute to American energy independence.

According to the U.S. Energy Information Administration, "most" gasoline sold in the United States has some ethanol in it. The most common blend is E10 which is 10 percent ethanol while E15 which is 15 percent ethanol is available mostly in the Midwest. In 2012 about 134 billion gallons of gasoline, which contained about 13 billion gallons of ethanol, were consumed in the United States. In the U.S. production of fuel, ethanol has been relatively constant with 13.3 billion gallons produced in 2010, 13.9 billion in 2011, and 13.2 in 2012. During the same period the production of biodiesel nearly tripled with 343 million gallons produced in 2010, 967 million in 2011, and 991 million in 2012.[1]

The selections that follow were taken from a hearing on "Overview of the Renewable Fuel Standard: Stakeholder Perspectives" held by the U.S. House of Representatives House Committee on Energy and Commerce Subcommittee on Energy and Power on July 23–24, 2013. Those testifying included representatives from the American Petroleum Institute, American Fuel & Petrochemical Manufacturers, Renewable Fuels Association, Advanced Biofuels Association, Union of Concerned Scientists, Growth Energy, Alliance of Automobile Manufacturers, Briggs & Stratton Corporation, American Automobile Association, Society of Independent Gasoline Marketers, National Association of Convenience Stores, National Biodiesel Board, National Corn Growers Association, National Chicken Council, National Council of Chain Restaurants, and Environmental Working Group. According to the Committee's Background Memo, the purpose of the hearing was to "undertake an assessment of the RFS" since "it has been more than five years since the RFS was last revised, and there is now a wealth of actual implementation experience with its use. In some respects, the RFS has unfolded as expected, but in others it has not. Several implementation challenges have emerged that received little if any consideration prior to passage of EISA."[2]

Notes

1. U.S. Energy Information Administration www .eia.gov/totalenergy/data/monthly/#renewable? src=Renewable-f2.
2. U.S. House of Representatives Subcommittee on Energy and Power, Background Memo http:// energycommerce.house.gov/hearing/overview -renewable-fuel-standard-stakeholder-perspectives

YES ↵

Tom Buis

Testimony before the House Committee on Energy and Commerce Subcommittee on Energy and Power

My name is Tom Buis, and I am the CEO of Growth Energy, the country's leading trade association of ethanol and renewable fuel producers. We represent 79 ethanol plants in 14 different states and 81 associate members involved in the value chain of producing ethanol. In addition, we have over 40,000 supporters in our grassroots group called Growth Force. Our plants produce ethanol from grain and are leaders in innovating second-generation fuels from sources like plant wastes, algae, and woody biomass.

We see the RFS as an overwhelming success that has created American jobs, revitalized rural America, injected much-needed competition into a monopolized vehicle fuels market, lowered the price at the pump, improved the environment, and made our nation more energy independent. That is a great record of accomplishment—one that I would call a resounding success and a modern American success story.

In particular, the RFS:

- Cracks the monopoly stranglehold petroleum-based fuels have on our transportation system, injecting much needed competition and providing drivers a choice at the pump.
- Provides a template to get safe and effective ethanol fuel blends like E-15 into the marketplace. When approving this fuel, the Department of Energy tested 86 different vehicles and drove them a total of 6 million miles, while the oil industry-funded study by the Coordinating Research Council (CRC) tested only 8 vehicles, including 2 that had known engine durability problems.
- Lowered the price at the pump by 83 cents a gallon in 2011 according to a recent LSU study.
- Supports 400,000 American jobs and $42 billion in annual economic activity.

These are real, tangible results that benefit every American today. But if some of the panelists had their way, we would throw all of this progress away so the oil industry can shut out competition and maintain its grip on the wallets of American drivers.

We see a different path forward for the United States. The Renewable Fuel Standard and higher-level blends of ethanol present the first real opportunity to create fuel diversity in the United States. It has been over 100 years since Americans had a choice in what they use in their automobiles. Now, the oil lobby has begun a sustained, multipronged campaign to kill our industry just as it ramps up and decreases oil's market share.

But the premise that America's newfound oil and gas resources mean we no longer need renewable fuels is simply not true. If the past is any indication of the future, more oil drilling has not done anything to reduce gas prices. Despite having record levels of domestic oil production, gas prices are still high and only going higher. This is because we don't control the cost of oil. The price of oil is still set in the global marketplace, and OPEC countries and Middle East politics still control the cost movements of oil. No matter how much we drill, we will still be subject to global events if we maintain the oil monopoly in this country.

With the success of the RFS, the United States is on the brink of energy independence and energy diversity. On behalf of Growth Energy, the biofuel industry, and America's farming communities, I urge you stay true to the Renewable Fuel Standard that is working and already showing results while still in its infancy.

The RFS has created competition in the vehicle fuels market. It has reduced fuel costs for American families, has freed the taxpayer from having to hold up the agricultural economy, and spurred significant investments in rural America. My testimony today covers eight key topics. . . .

E15 Is Safe and Ready for Use

When the RFS was first created, it was apparent that our nation's energy infrastructure and economy needed a wider market for renewable fuels. Even under fuel-use assumptions made in 2007 when the RFS was expanded, lawmakers knew higher-level ethanol blends like E15 would be required in order to meet the volumes originally set when the RFS was enacted. Unfortunately, the oil industry has decided to erect every legal, legislative, public relations, and regulatory hurdle possible to avoid moving to any

Buis, Tom. From U.S. House of Representatives, July 23, 2013.

fuel containing more than 10 percent ethanol. Instead of working to accommodate fuel choice for consumers, the oil industry has chosen to shut out competing fuels from their vertically integrated monopoly. . . .

Over four and a half years ago, Growth Energy led the way by filing a waiver with the U.S. EPA to allow the sale of ethanol blends up to E15 beyond the current 10 percent ethanol in today's current fuel supply. By moving the nation to E15, we would reduce the price at the pump, add 136,000 new American jobs, reduce greenhouse gas emissions, and could reduce the demand of gasoline from foreign oil by 7 billion gallons. In addition, E15 would reduce the use of aromatics in gasoline, which are petroleum-derived fuel components known to harm human health.

When Growth Energy filed the original waiver for E15 with the U.S. EPA, we sought approval for all gasoline-powered engines and provided ample data to demonstrate this fuel's safety and efficacy. The Environmental Protection Agency (EPA) chose to narrow their specific testing by putting E15 on a path for approval for only 2001 and newer vehicles because they concluded that finding vehicles with low enough mileage to run a lifetime of miles for testing was extremely difficult. And, in fact, more testing was done on E15 than any other fuel ever approved by EPA under the Clean Air Act, with the Department of Energy (DOE) testing 86 vehicles for a total of 6 million miles. DOE's testing found absolutely no issues with emissions equipment or with engine durability. With DOE's data in hand, the EPA ultimately approved our waiver in January, 2011 for all 2001 and newer passenger vehicles—over 80 percent of the vehicles on the road today. In fact, Ford, General Motors, and Volkswagen have already started labeling their vehicles as approved for E15—General Motors for model years 2012 and 2013, Ford for model year 2013, and Volkswagen starting with model year 2014. Further, NASCAR has been running on E15 for 3 years for a total of 4 million miles in some of the world's toughest driving conditions and they have seen an increase in horsepower and no mileage loss suggesting that E15 is more than safe for use in everyday automobiles.

The only studies questioning the safety of E15 were conducted with no scientific basis whatsoever and used dubious technical assumptions. Like recent advertisements levied by the oil industry, little regard seems to be given to a factual underlying basis. For example, an oil industry funded-study of E15 by the Coordinating Research Council (CRC) is significantly flawed and DOE itself publicly released a direct critical response entitled "Getting It Right: Accurate Testing and Assessments Critical to Deploying the Next Generation of Auto Fuels" (http://energy.gov/articles/getting-it-right-accurate-testing-and-assessments-critical-deploying-next-generation-auto).

First, the CRC was extremely limited—only testing eight vehicles while the DOE tested 86. Second, CRC failed to test the engines on E10, the standard consumer gasoline found throughout the United States. Third, CRC only tested 3 of the 8 vehicles on ethanol-free gasoline

and even one of those failed. Fourth, and perhaps most disturbing, CRC chose two engines that had existing durability issues—one of which had even been recalled. Finally, the test used was specifically designed to overly stress the engine valve train, so as to be unrealistic with real-world conditions. To sum up their findings, DOE said, "We believe the [CRC] study is significantly flawed."

It has also been argued by the oil lobby that gas mileage takes a major hit if E15 is used. This is not true. Any mileage loss is negligible, and any reduction is substantially offset by price reduction of fuel. Further, it is worth noting that refiners often make sub-octane gasoline, which is cheaper, poorer quality gasoline, because they can utilize the high octane and high performance benefits of ethanol to meet minimum octane standards.

It should be made clear to all on this Committee that E15 is a voluntary choice both for retailers and for consumers. Furthermore, fuel retailers who follow the misfueling mitigation rules should not face any significant incremental risk for offering E15. In addition, the decision to offer E15 is voluntary and based on a retailer's assessment of return on invested capital, customer mix, and retail station configuration.

We expect retailers to begin to adopt E15 because it is good business. At the close of business on Friday, ethanol was trading 65 cents lower than gasoline, and the upcoming corn harvest could push the spread to over a dollar. Because of this steep discount, increasing the ethanol blend in gasoline will save consumers even more and will give retailers offering E15 or higher level ethanol blends an edge in marketing to consumers, who largely base their fuel choice on price and performance. At a time of record gas prices, it only makes sense for refiners to comply with the law and allow sale of E15 and higher ethanol blends in the fuel marketplace as renewable fuels ensure competition in the marketplace.

For small and marine engines, and any other gasoline engine other than 2001 and newer passenger cars and light duty vehicles, the law explicitly prohibits E15. Further, the EPA has issued a specific rule to mitigate consumer misfueling, including a label specific to E15. In fact, ethanol is the only fuel that requires a warning label at the pump. . . .

Therefore, because E15 is a highly-tested, legal, cheaper, and better quality fuel than gasoline, the United States will benefit from its continued rollout across the nation.

The So-Called "Blend Wall"

Recently, the oil industry has falsely blamed the Renewable Fuel Standard as the cause of higher gasoline prices. These stories revolve around a false premise—that prices for a RFS compliance mechanism demanded by the oil industry when the RFS was first passed into law—Renewable Identification Numbers (RINs)—are responsible for the increase in domestic gasoline prices. In reality, these charges are clearly an attack organized by the oil industry to keep their stranglehold on America's fuel supply, eliminate consumer choice at the pump, and eliminate the competition from domestically produced renewable fuels.

It is a charge that is also objectively false. RIN prices are not the cause of higher gas prices. RINs for ethanol are provided free of charge to oil companies when they blend ethanol. Any added value comes from trading RINs in an opaque marketplace between oil companies. Ethanol has consistently been trading and will likely continue trading significantly cheaper than gasoline. At the close of business on Friday, wholesale ethanol was 65 cents less expensive than wholesale gasoline.

Yet, RIN prices are increasing because of refiners' unwillingness to blend ethanol and instead are willing to pay a premium specifically **not** to blend additional ethanol, even though it is cheaper in price. This is a business decision made by refiners, **not** by ethanol producers. Put simply, the blend wall is a self-inflicted wound because the oil industry is afraid of competition. Meanwhile, oil companies are currently making record margins. EPA clearly stated there is not a shortage of RINs for 2013. In fact there are over 2.6 billion carry-over RINs from 2012.

The simple solution to this oil industry created problem is to require the higher level ethanol blends such as E15. As soon as the oil companies adopt the higher blends, plenty of RINs will become available. The oil industry has erected hurdle after hurdle to defeat E15 and mid-level ethanol blends and continue to fight to try to eliminate the RFS. By refusing to sell higher ethanol blends, the oil companies only maintain the status quo: high gas prices for the consume, and record profits for the five largest oil companies. . . .

Many have termed this the "blend wall," and breaking the blend wall is vital to the success of the RFS. Ethanol is consistently trading at a significant discount to wholesale gasoline while yet again oil has climbed over $100 a barrel and gasoline is climbing toward $4 a gallon. It makes little sense to prevent E15 and even higher ethanol blends into entering the market, unless the objective is to benefit the oil industry. With the goal of the RFS to reach 36 billion gallons of renewable fuel by 2022, it was clear at the outset of the authorizing legislation in 2007 (EISA 2007) that higher blends of ethanol would be required regardless of the level of fuel consumption.

In fact, the Volumetric Ethanol Excise Tax Credit (VEETC) was designed to provide a financial incentive to provide ethanol blenders—not ethanol producers—to blend ethanol and make sure the blend wall didn't occur. The primary recipients of this incentive were integrated oil companies. VEETC paid out tens of billions of dollars to help these integrated oil companies upgrade their distribution network to meet the future need for higher inclusion rates of ethanol. Obviously they did not spend the proceeds on infrastructure upgrades to allow for higher blends at retail stations.

Success of Renewable Fuel Standard (RFS)

The RFS is the bedrock federal policy that has spurred billions of dollars of investment in America's cutting-edge biofuels industry. It has been the primary driver behind the only large-scale, commercially-viable alternative to regular gasoline—ethanol. Because of the forward-looking, long-term nature of the policy, the United States leads the world in innovation in biofuels, attracting investment from around the world. Today, because of the RFS, there are more than 200 ethanol biorefineries across the country and dozens of projects that will make advanced or cellulosic biofuels.

The RFS has provided U.S. drivers with a vehicle fuel that is made up of 10 percent biofuel, and that fuel blend is available in all 50 states. If the U.S. ethanol industry were a foreign suppler, only Canada would supply the U.S. with more fuel than the U.S. ethanol industry. This newfound biofuel supply is a key component to reducing our dependence on foreign oil by 25 percent since 2005.

Advanced and cellulosic biofuels research, investment, and development are occurring right now. Growth Energy has several members who are producing these fuels because of the market signal provided by the RFS. . . .

. . . Advanced and cellulose fuels that are now under development would provide benefits and economic opportunity to every state in the country. Any change to the RFS would kill investment in any advanced or cellulosic fuel project. Changing the RFS would put at risk an entire American-made, American-built industry at a time we can least afford to lose jobs. Also, amending the RFS would put at risk future research and development of advanced and cellulosic biofuels, which occupy the largest portion of the RFS. We are just 5 years into a 15-year plan, and we are just three years removed from when the Environmental Protection Agency finalized RFS regulations. Yet there are those in the oil industry who would look at the minor challenges we have faced in the short-term and embellish them in hopes of killing a rising competitor.

How the RFS Has Revitalized Rural Economies

The RFS has a tremendous positive impact on rural communities and the agriculture sector. Net farm income grew by 51 percent from 2005 to 2011 due in part by the RFS. The RFS also supports 400,000 jobs and over $40 billion in economic activity.

In addition, renewable fuels helped create a balance in supply and demand for crop commodities that alleviated the need for most forms of government payments and created a market-based, rather than a government-based, agricultural economy. This in turn drives farmers to utilize technology and soil resources to produce crops. According to USDA, since 2004, planted acres of corn increased from 80.93 million acres to 97.28 million acres for 2013.

Harvested corn acres increased from 73.63 million acres in 2004 to 87.38 million acres in 2012. Similarly, production drives technology and efficiency—since 2000, corn yields went from 137 bushels per acre up to 153 bushels per acre in 2010.

Like any commodity, the market responds to natural forces such as supply and demand. The market for corn is no different. While the RFS created additional demand for corn, more importantly, it drives additional corn production that otherwise would not occur. For decades, farmers were paid far less than the price of production for their corn, and the American taxpayer heavily subsidized the price. Last year, ethanol critics alleged the RFS caused prices to rise more than $8 per bushel, when, in fact, the price increase was a direct result of one of the worst droughts in our nation's history. In fact, those purchasing corn could have locked in prices for under $5 per bushel as late as June 2012. On Friday, the price of corn was $5 per bushel and actually was trading under $5 for part of the day. The RFS has the flexibility built in that allows states to waive the RFS in cases of severe economic harm. Twice, states petitioned the EPA to waive the RFS and both times the petitioners failed to make the case.

A final point that should not be overlooked concerns the taxpayer savings from reduced farm program payments that occurred as the RFS was implemented. According to data from the Congressional Budget Office, the average federal farm program payments to corn producers averaged over $4.4 billion per year for the 2002–2006 crop years. Corn payments averaged about $1.9 billion per year from 2007 to 2011, a reduction in taxpayer costs of almost 57 percent.

How the RFS Has Helped Livestock Producers

Biofuel production only removes the starch from the corn. The protein, fiber, and oil are returned to the animal feed supply in the biofuel feed co-product known as distiller's grains. Distiller's grains amount to one third of the corn used in ethanol production. According to USDA, 80 percent of the calories from the decline of corn-based livestock feed are returned to the livestock industry in this form. Distiller's grains also replace soybean meal in feed rations, meaning there is less demand for soybeans, requiring fewer acres planted to soybeans. . . .

American corn growers demonstrated they have more than enough capacity to satisfy all demand for livestock feed, exports, and ethanol. Because of new technology that allows farmers to grow more crops on fewer acres of land, corn farmers are poised to increase plantings even more to take advantage of the growing market for renewable fuels. On July 11, 2013 USDA pegged this year's corn crop at 14 billion bushels.

One of the biggest myths perpetuated by those who dislike the RFS is that 40 percent of the corn crop goes to biofuels. This is not only wildly false, it is completely misleading. . . .

In the fall of 2012, Growth Energy put together significant comments to the EPA in response to requests to waive the RFS from various state governors. In those comments, we demonstrated that waiving the RFS would jeopardize farmers, rural jobs and economies and would increase consumers' prices at the pump. Specifically, we estimated that waiving the RFS could result in up to $7.8 billion in lost revenue and 8,300 jobs lost in ethanol producing areas. Additionally, waiving the RFS would result in a cost of $7.5 billion a year to consumers in higher fuel costs and between a $5.8 and $27 billion loss to American farmers. Finally, companies already spent billions of dollars building facilities, harvesting cellulosic materials and planning on the certainty of a fifteen-year RFS program as they move to the next generation of biofuels.

In fact, under the most recent corn usage data from USDA, it is estimated that the corn demand lost from 2011 to 2012 due to the drought was far greater for ethanol than for livestock feed. The demand lost from the ethanol industry was over 350 million bushels from 2011 to 2012, while the demand lost from animal feed was less than 100 million bushels. And with a 14 billion bushel crop projected this year (a 31 percent increase compared to last year's 10.7 billion bushel crop), corn demand for animal feed is projected to increase by 16 percent to 5.2 billion bushels, while corn demand for ethanol production is projected to increase by 5 percent to 4.9 billion bushels.

Despite overwhelming data, some leaders in the livestock and poultry industry blamed ethanol for rising feed costs and declining profit opportunities throughout the livestock production sector. The difference between the total value of U.S. livestock and poultry production and the cost of feed is increasing, not declining. In fact, for the 7 years prior to the enactment of the RFS, the margin averaged $83.4 billion per year. In the 7 years since RFS became law, the margin increased by nearly 18 percent to an average of $98.2 billion per year. . . .

When prices are viewed in conjunction with production, one must question the veracity of the statements by those who suggest the RFS is causing the demise of the U.S. livestock industry. Not only has livestock production increased since the enactment of the RFS, but prices for beef, pork, broilers, and turkey also rose compared to the years prior to the RFS. . . .

Biofuel Production's Limited Impact on Food Price

There are many factors that impacted food prices, including crop production shortfalls and increased demand overseas. On June 26, 2013, Dr. Joseph Glauber, Chief Economist at the United States Department of Agriculture testified before the Subcommittee on Energy and Power of the House Committee on Energy and Commerce that the total impact of changes in the corn market on retail food prices was small. This is consistent with prior analysis done by USDA, the World Bank, and many other independent groups.

Countless academic, economic, and government studies disprove the misplaced notion that biofuels production increased the cost of food. These studies instead found that record-high oil prices, Wall Street speculators and the high costs of manufacturing, packaging, and transportation have far more impact than ethanol on everyday grocery prices. There is no substantial link between ethanol production and grocery prices. Despite the proven facts, misinformed critics still actively try to stoke illegitimate fears that demand for ethanol will somehow drive up food prices.

Corn is only a fraction of overall food and grain costs. For every $1 spent at a grocery store, 85.9 cents go to marketing, which includes labor, transportation, energy, and packaging costs. Just 14.1 cents are associated with farm costs, and of that, only 3 cents are associated with the value of corn. The USDA forecasts that the price of food will increase by 3.5 percent in 2013, slightly above historical inflation averages of approximately 3 percent per year. Food prices rise when oil prices rise. The price of food is driven up by transportation and packaging—not by renewable fuels like ethanol. Food processing is energy intensive, and packaging frequently uses petroleum-based raw materials. Transporting food worldwide also requires large amounts of fuel and, subsequently, large amounts of oil. . . .

Since 2005, the CPI for food increased about 18.3 percent, roughly in line with the CPI for all items including food and gasoline which rose by about 16 percent. The index for gasoline increased by nearly 40 percent, and in recent years, the trend has followed a very steep upward path. Interestingly, this is occurring as we increased the amount of ethanol blended into our gasoline supply. Every credible analysis concluded that consumer gas prices would be even higher if it were not for ethanol holding prices down. . . .

The primary cause of increased consumer prices rests not with livestock producers or those who process their products, but with the same food companies who complain about the RFS. According to the World Bank, over 50 percent of the global increase in food prices is due to energy costs, and for the U.S. the increase in the retail price spreads suggest that either energy costs and other non-farm cost factors are passed on to consumers or retained by the food companies as increased profit margins.

The takeaway conclusion from the independently generated World Bank report: certain actors are taking advantage of rising food prices which are, in turn, caused by oil price increases.

Environmental Benefits of Biofuels

The RFS is one of the most successful energy policies of the last forty years. It is reducing greenhouse gas emissions, reducing our dangerous dependence on foreign oil, and creating American jobs. The EPA estimates that by 2022, the RFS will reduce greenhouse gas emissions by 138 million metric tons or the equivalent of taking 27 million passenger vehicles off the road. In particular, studies show that traditional corn ethanol reduces greenhouse gas emissions as much as 59 percent compared to gasoline (*Improvements in Lifecycle Energy Efficiency and Greenhouse Gas Emissions of Corn-Ethanol*, Liska et al., which can be found here: http://onlinelibrary.wiley.com/doi/10.1111/j.1530-9290.2008.00105.x/abstract).

As we move to the next generation of biofuels, greenhouse gas emissions will be even further reduced. Recent studies show that using switchgrass and corn stover to produce cellulosic ethanol will reduce greenhouse gases as much as 94 percent and over 100 percent respectively (*Energy and Greenhouse Gas Emission Effects of Corn and Cellulosic Ethanol with Technology Improvements and Land Use Changes*, Wang et al., which can be found at www.sciencedirect.com/science/article/pii/S0961953411000298).

The long-term certainty of the RFS drove significant investment in the next generation of biofuels and new technologies both in ethanol production and in agriculture. By increasing yields, increasing efficiency, and deploying new technologies, ethanol and agriculture production continues to soften its footprint on the environment—particularly as fossil fuels like crude oil and natural gas become harder and harder to extract. Just in the past four years, we saw significant results—we get more ethanol from each bushel of corn: 2.82 gallons/bushel in 2012 vs. 2.78 gallons/bushel in 2008, using less water: 2.70 gallons of water per gallon of ethanol in 2012 vs. 2.72 gallons of water per gallon of ethanol in 2008, and are using less energy to produce a gallon of ethanol: 23,862 BTU/gallon in 2012 vs. 26,208 BTU/gallon in 2008 (Mueller and Kwik, *2012 Corn Ethanol: Emerging Plant Energy and Emerging Technologies*, www.erc.uic.edu/PDF/mueller/2012_corn_ethanol_draft4_10_2013.pdf). . . .

National Security Benefits of the RFS

The U.S. continues to be extremely vulnerable to shocks in the oil supply and price disruptions—from both foreign supply and the domestic supply chains. During the last decade, the price of oil nearly quadrupled, going from roughly $25 per barrel in 2001 to over $100 per barrel today. That price disruption had a significant impact on American consumers and the American economy, with the price of gasoline rising from $1.09 per gallon in 2001 to $3.67 per gallon today. Despite significant increases in domestic oil production, we still import millions of barrels per day of foreign oil sending more than $400 billion overseas last year alone. These imports are from a number of countries in unstable regions, like the Middle East, that have little interest in the United States' energy security (data from the U.S. Energy Information Administration http://eia.gov).

We also spend billions of dollars each year to protect oil supply routes in the Middle East—these costs could be dramatically reduced if we turned to more home-grown renewable ethanol. As an example, according to RAND, the U.S. spends between $67 billion and $83 billion per year protecting global oil interests ("Imported Oil and U.S. National Security," RAND Corporation, 2009). Critics of renewable fuels point to Canada as our largest source of our imported oil, but even Canada has recently developed assets, such as the Enbridge Northern Gateway Pipeline, aimed at exporting oil to China rather than exporting to the United States (www.northerngateway.ca/).

All of this additional oil is purchased on the global market that is still largely controlled by OPEC. So any time there is a supply disruption or OPEC arbitrarily decides to cut production, it hurts American consumers. We have seen Iran choke off the Strait of Hormuz, workers strike in Venezuela, pipelines burst, massive oil spills off our shores, oil-laden rail cars destroy small towns, and the list goes on—all of these situations both impacted the supply of oil and the cost American consumers pay at the pump. Even in the past few weeks here in the United States, we watched refineries being taken offline for seasonal maintenance in the Midwest, thus causing outrageous price increases in Minneapolis and other places across the region ("Pain at the Pump as Gas Prices Soar above $4," http://kstp .com/article/stories/s3034685.shtml; "Spike in Twin Cities Gas Prices Leaves Drivers Frustrated", www.startribune.com /business/190374421.html). . . .

Conclusion

The RFS is a policy that is working. It is working to the benefit of the American people, and to the detriment of the age-old big oil monopoly. To implement the suggestions of some of the witnesses today and repeal or modify the RFS would effectively cede control of all transportation fuels to the oil industry. This would be a radical and poorly advised decision—one that history would judge as a colossal mistake.

The key to reducing prices at the pump is to inject competition in transportation fuels, and the RFS does that. If you want to reduce greenhouse gas emissions, the only statute that has required GHG reduction is the RFS. If you want to expand American made energy, the RFS does that. If you want to reduce foreign oil, the RFS does that.

The bottom line is that this is a policy that benefits all Americans. With oil prices yet again well over $100 a barrel and gasoline yet again climbing to $4 a gallon, we can no longer afford to be 90 percent dependent on fossil fuels. . . .

TOM BUIS is the chief executive officer of Growth Energy. He joined Growth Energy in March 2009 as the CEO of the organization. Prior to joining Growth Energy, Buis was elected National Farmers Union's 13th president. Buis had been with the organization since March 1998, previously serving as vice president of government relations. Buis served for nearly five years as senior agriculture policy advisor to Senate Majority Leader Tom Daschle, D-S.D. In addition, Buis worked for U.S. Rep. Jim Jontz, D-Ind., for nearly five years as legislative assistant and legislative director. He was also special assistant for agriculture to U.S. Sen. Birch Bayh, D-Ind. Before moving to Washington, DC in 1987, Buis was a full-time grain and livestock farmer in Putnam and Morgan Counties in West Central Indiana, with brothers Mike and Jeff, who continue to operate the family farm.

NO

Testimony before the House Committee on Energy and Commerce Subcommittee on Energy and Power

Charles T. Drevna

. . . Background

The RFS was established with the goals of enhancing both energy security and environmental protection, while providing development opportunities to rural America. Many also believed advanced biofuels would be developed that could work in existing infrastructure and be produced from non-food feed stocks. In practice, however, the RFS has operated contrary to these goals and most of its foundational assumptions turned out to be false. Refiners are now forced to comply with an unworkable law that places consumers at risk of high food and fuel costs, engine damage, and environmental harm.

This hearing takes place against a backdrop of greatly increased domestic oil and gas production that promises to create energy security for the U.S., without mandates or subsidies. Meanwhile, second generation renewable fuels have not materialized as the reality becomes clear that policymakers cannot mandate innovation or favorable economics. Perhaps most critically in 2013, fuel demand, which was projected to steadily increase when RFS2 was established in 2007, has declined and is expected to decline further. The annually increasing amounts of biofuel required to be blended into a declining fuel supply mean the federal biofuel mandate threatens to create fuel supply shortfalls and risk damaging consumer engines. The combination of these factors demonstrates that the RFS is unnecessary, unworkable, and should be repealed.

Changes since RFS2 Was Adopted

Energy supply landscape. In 2007 the energy discussion in the United States was one of scarcity, not abundance. Since that time, the U.S. began to unlock its true energy potential—without the use of mandates or subsidies. Just last week, the Energy Information Administration (EIA) testified before the Senate Energy and Natural Resources Committee that between 2007 and 2012, domestic oil production increased by 1.5 million barrels per day, or 30 percent, with most of the growth occurring over the past three years.[1] Onshore oil production in the lower 48 states rose 64 percent between February 2010 and February 2013 alone.[2] During that time, U.S. petroleum imports declined from 61 percent of consumption to 41 percent in 2012.

The United States' newfound energy abundance is not a short-term phenomenon. Indeed, comparing its 2007 and 2012 estimates for 2022, EIA projects a 23-percent increase in oil production and a 62-percent increase in natural gas production. The International Energy Agency reported in November that the U.S. is on pace to surpass Saudi Arabia as the world's largest oil producer in 2020, and can become a net oil producer by 2025. EIA testified in this Committee on June 26th that ethanol was only a minor factor in the drop in petroleum imports. Ironically, and as detailed below, by placing refining infrastructure at risk, the RFS will also undermine this important economic and security American advantage.

Failure of cellulosic and other advanced biofuels and increased imports. At the same time that the U.S. has been increasing oil and gas production, development of many advanced biofuels hoped for in the RFS has not occurred. Given this reality, the RFS essentially mandates fuels that do not exist. The law requires specific advanced biofuels to be blended into the fuel supply, including biomass-based diesel, cellulosic biofuels, and other advanced biofuels. When the RFS was written into law, policy makers envisioned 1 billion gallons of cellulosic biofuel would be consumed in 2013, increasing to 16 billion gallons by 2022. In reality, zero gallons of cellulosic biofuel were produced in 2010 and 2011, and only 21,093 gallons were produced in 2012 (20,069 of which were exported and unavailable for compliance). The rate of production in 2013 has been slower than 2012, with only 4,900 gallons produced between January and May. EIA now projects that only 0.5 of the 16-billion-gallon-cellulosic mandate will be produced in 2022. In addition, EIA projects that drop-in biofuels[3] will only grow to approximately 341 million gallons by 2022—enough to satisfy .07 percent of gasoline demand.[4]

Ironically, for a law with "energy independence" in its title, EPA projects that approximately 80 percent of the other advanced biofuels mandated will be met by imported sugarcane ethanol (primarily from Brazil). The prevalence of imports and failure of the RFS to develop domestic second and third generation biofuels ensures that RFS will continue to rely heavily on corn-based ethanol production to satisfy its volumes. This situation undermines the argument that the law is enhancing energy independence

Drevna, Charles T. From U.S. House of Representatives, July 23, 2013.

and, as explained later, ensures the required use of biofuels generating more emissions and other environmental issues than arise from using gasoline.

Fuel Demand. While the energy supply picture has been changing, so has fuel demand. Largely due to the recession, a stagnant economy, and recent fuel economy/automobile GHG standards, projections for gasoline[5] use have shifted significantly between 2007 and 2012. The 2007 EIA Annual Energy Outlook projected a 12 percent higher demand for gasoline in 2013 than is actually occurring. The 2013 Annual Energy Outlook (AEO) now projects 2022 gasoline demand will be 27 percent lower than the 2007 AEO projection for 2022. Importantly, and as described below, the combination of decreased gasoline demand and rising biofuels mandates has exacerbated the onset of the E10 blendwall—the point after which blenders are unable to safely add additional ethanol to the fuel mix. We are now at the point where existing delivery infrastructure and the consumer vehicle fleet are not capable of safely handling increased use of fuel containing higher concentrations of ethanol.

Flawed Implementation Concept

The RFS is implemented in a way that makes fuel manufacturers responsible for consumer fuel demand. The mandate establishes how much biofuel volume must be consumed, but quixotically places the obligation for such consumption on upstream fuel manufacturers, who do not have the ability to control downstream ethanol blending or retail operations. Refiners and importers must demonstrate that for every gallon of gasoline and diesel fuel they sell into the U.S. market, a certain amount of renewable fuel was consumed. This requirement holds despite the fact that refiners have no control over either consumer purchasing habits or (in the majority of cases) retail decisions on what fuels to sell to the public or whether to replace dispensers and other refueling infrastructure to accommodate corrosive ethanol blends. Additionally, the structure of the mandate allows compliance credits, called Renewable Identification Numbers (RINs), to be held by non-obligated parties, boosting compliance costs for obligated parties.

Penetration of new fuels requires that consumers see a benefit to buying the fuel and that retailers see adequate incentives to install equipment or make other changes necessary to offer the fuel. A common misconception is that refiners or importers own/control retail operations. Refiners own less than 5 percent of the retail stations in the U.S. In June 2011, GAO reported that the major integrated companies own only 1 percent of the stations and only half of stations are "branded" franchises. . . .

Retailers must see the financial benefit in offering a new fuel, including an affordable cost and consumer acceptance. Penetration was not quick in many areas, even in cases where much of the infrastructure was in place. One alternative fuel currently available on the market is E85, which contains up to 85 percent ethanol and 15 percent gasoline. It can only be used in flex fuel vehicles (FFVs), which consist of less than five percent of the total consumer vehicle fleet. The infrastructure and vehicles are not in place for the widespread adoption of E85, and acceptance of this fuel has moved much more slowly than E10, with sales in key states that promote E85 actually declining last year. These realities place a functional cap on the amount of biofuel that can be blended into the fuel supply at E10. This creates significant barriers to implementing the. . . .

In addition to the market acceptance and penetration issues, a perverse compliance mechanism exacerbates the adverse implications of the RFS. Obligated parties (mainly refiners and importers) must obtain an appropriate number of RINs to turn into EPA to demonstrate compliance. A RIN is generated when a gallon of renewable fuel is produced. It stays with this gallon until it can be separated when an obligated party purchases the gallon of biofuel or when that gallon is blended into the fuel supply. Refiners do not often own the terminals where the biofuel is blended, or do not own enough terminal capacity to satisfy their full obligation in any given year and must therefore rely upon unrelated third parties to blend ethanol and make the separated RINs available to the marketplace. Many refiners and importers simply sell gasoline blendstocks into the wholesale market, where a third party terminal or marketing company purchases them and blends in ethanol to produce finished fuel. Unless an obligated party owns the terminals or other marketing assets that can cover its full obligation, or has a contractual agreement with the owner of those assets, the obligated party must buy RINs from marketers or off the open market. As a result, a company purchasing its RINs on the open market at $1.00 each incurs an implied $0.10 per gallon increase in cost to produce a gallon of gasoline. . . .

After understanding changing market dynamics since the inception of the RFS and the intricacies of its implementation, it is important to focus on the serious short-term problem of the blendwall and highlight the long-term issues of the RFS. However, AFPM would like to reiterate that it is neither anti-biofuels nor anti-ethanol. Two of AFPM's members are among the top five ethanol producers, and at least one makes more ethanol than 97 percent of the Renewable Fuels Association's membership. Biofuels can and do play an important role in the fuel mix, provided they are safely integrated into the fuel supply and consumers demand them. In testimony before this Committee on June 26th, 2013, both EIA and USDA indicated that as long as ethanol is economical to use, refiners and blenders would likely continue to use it—even in the absence of a mandate. However, AFPM opposes mandates and subsidies, including the RFS, because they limit consumer choices and stifle innovation. Moreover, and as this testimony demonstrates, the law is unworkable at its core, threatening to significantly raise consumer costs. For these reasons, Congress should repeal the RFS.

Serious Short-Term Issue: The Blendwall

The U.S. currently faces the onset of the E10 "blendwall," which will fundamentally compromise the fuel industry's ability to simultaneously meet the requirements of the RFS and to meet U.S. transportation fuel demand. The E10 blendwall refers to the point where nearly all the gasoline supplied domestically contains 10 percent ethanol, which is the effective, practical limit on the amount of ethanol that can safely be blended into the fuel supply without risking engine or infrastructure damage.

RFS Volumes Create Blendwall Challenges in 2013 and 2014

As referenced above, gasoline demand is falling in the United States. EIA's current projection of gasoline demand for 2013 is 132.9 billion gallons, and is expected to fall an additional 200 million gallons to 132.7 billion gallons in 2014.[6] At these levels of demand, the 10 percent (E10) saturation point is approximately 13.2 billion gallons. This year, the RFS requires obligated parties to obtain and submit 13.8 billion conventional biofuel renewable identification numbers (RINs) to demonstrate that the requisite gallons of renewable fuel were blended into the fuel supply. The conventional biofuel mandate is primarily filled by corn-based ethanol. In addition to conventional biofuels, the RFS requires volumes of cellulosic biofuel, other advanced biofuel (included sugar-cane-based ethanol), and biomass-based biodiesel. These RFS volumes are "nested" mandates. When you add the requirements for each of these biofuel types together, EPA has proposed a renewable fuel obligation totaling 16.55 billion gallons in 2013 (14.63 billion gallons, or 88 percent, of which is projected to be ethanol from both conventional and advanced fuel mandated categories). Therefore, the proposed EPA RFS obligation for 2013 is already requiring much more ethanol than the E10 system can safely handle. In 2014, as obligated parties run out of banked credits from over-complying in previous years,[7] and as gasoline demand declines further while facing an implicit ethanol mandate of 14.4 billion gallons, the math becomes even more problematic.

Market Already Showing Blendwall Effects Through RIN Prices

The market is currently anticipating that the combination of higher mandates and declining gasoline consumption will force the blendwall in 2013, with the full effects starting to be felt in 2014. This is most apparent in the RIN market, which reflects the expectation of how much ethanol can be blended into gasoline. This RIN supply/demand tightening is not due to ethanol shortages, but to the inability to push more ethanol into the fuel supply and generate more RINs. As the mandates increase, the demand for RINs increases, but the RIN supply is tighter because the mandate is higher, meaning fewer companies have excess RINs to sell. . . .

Finally, the RFS requires companies to buy RINs for biofuel that may need to be blended into products they do not even make. For instance, hypothetically, if the year's renewable fuel obligation is 10 percent, a company that produces 100,000 gallons of gasoline and diesel incurs an obligation to produce 10,000 RINs divided among the nested RFS categories—regardless of their ratio of fuels produced. Thus, a company that produces very little diesel still incurs an obligation to purchase biomass-based diesel RINs at more than $1.00 each.

This leads to the question of what options are available to obligated parties. Obligated parties have limited options to remain in compliance with the requirements of the RFS as the blendwall hits. First, obligated parties will maximize the amount of E10 sold and for a short period of time, some may be able to rely on RINs generated from over compliance in previous years. EIA reported in June that the small amount of RINs that are allowed to be carried over from last year, which exist from companies that may have over-complied with the mandate last year, are expected to fall to zero in 2014.[8] . . .

E85 Will Not Solve the Blendwall

E85[9] will not (and cannot) generate sufficient RINs to alleviate the effects of the blendwall—particularly in the short term. Due to limited infrastructure, the limited number of flex-fuel vehicles (FFVs) in commerce, and lack of interest in the fuel from FFV owners with access to the fuel, E85 will not solve the blendwall problem. In particular, the Department of Energy estimates that approximately 2,347 retail stations (less than 1.5 percent of stations nationwide) carry E85.[10] . . .

According to EIA, based on observations of Brazil's experience, consumers buy fuels based on energy adjusted price. A gallon of gasoline has 50 percent more energy than a gallon of ethanol, meaning that the average E85 blend has 76-percent of the energy content of gasoline and consumers lose 24-percent of the fuel mileage.[11] E85 has not been price competitive with regular gasoline at any point since the inception of the RFS, a major reason for stagnant consumer interest. For example, the AAA Fuel Gauge Report, which displays energy-adjusted prices for E85 and other fuels, regularly shows that E85 is more expense than regular gasoline.[12] In fact, E85's lackluster sales extend to the heart of the corn belt. Sales of E85 in Minnesota, which has the nation's most developed E85 infrastructure, decreased from a peak of 22 million gallons in 2008 to 15 million in 2012 even as the number of FFVs in the Minnesota marketplace increased.[13] . . .

The future is not much brighter for E85. The 2011 CAFE standards began to phase out credits for FFV production, creating a disincentive for automakers to continue producing FFVs. Even assuming significant increases in the installation rate of flex-fuel pumps (which will still not help obligated parties alleviate the blendwall in 2013 and 2014), E85 is also unlikely to break through in the long term. In its 2010 regulatory impact analysis, EPA estimated that to meet the volumes envision by the RFS, 70 percent of the nation would need access to E85 at one in every four pumps they pass, and FFV owners would need to fill up with E85 74 percent of the time in 2022—a far cry from the market realities nationwide and the Minnesota experience.[14] . . .

E15 Will Not Solve or Delay the Blendwall

In 2011, EPA approved a 50-percent increase in the amount of ethanol (from 10 percent to 15 percent, or E15) that may be used in model year 2001 and new automobiles. However, E15 creates significant market and legal concerns among fuel manufacturers, distributors, and retailers as well as small engine manufacturers and automakers. E15 provides a limited and problematic path to RFS compliance, but ultimately does not solve the blendwall even as it creates an entirely new set of problems for consumers.

Engine Compatibility. Critically, despite EPA assertion that E15 is safe to use in model year 2001 and newer cars, no automaker will warranty those cars. Only two automakers—General Motors and Ford—recently announced they'd start to warranty 2012 and 2013 models. The disconnect between EPA's assertion about E15's safety and the automakers concerns stems from the depth and breadth of testing that EPA and DOE undertook. In particular, in evaluating E15 for use in 2001 and newer vehicles, EPA only tested the emissions control devices (e.g. catalytic converters) of the automobiles, but overlooked other critical engine components, such as fuel pumps. Subsequent testing undertaken by the Coordinating Research Council (CRC) demonstrates the inadequacy of EPA's approval process. In two studies conducted on engine durability and fuel pumps, CRC found that a substantial number of the 29 million 2001–2007 light duty vehicles (LDVs) on the road today are susceptible to system failure and other mechanical damage from E15—notwithstanding EPA's approval. It is important to note that EPA and DOE were both participants in the CRC testing. There are no other non-road or off-road engines (motorcycles, lawnmowers, boats, etc) approved to use E15. Historically, nonroad, heavy duty gasoline vehicles, and motorcycles consumed about 8 percent of gasoline in the U.S.[15] However, the hap-hazard way EPA has allowed for the introduction of E15 into the marketplace could lead to significant consumer misfueling of these non- or off-road engines. The fact that E15 is not backward compatible with existing gasoline engines creates a significant potential liability throughout the fuel supply chain and represents one of the most significant hurdles to the provision of E15 in the marketplace.

Infrastructure compatibility. The lack of engine compatibility is exacerbated by the lack of infrastructure compatibility. A 2010 study by the National Renewable Energy Laboratory (NREL) found that using E15 in fuel dispensers already approved for E10 resulted in reduced levels of safety and performance. . . .

All equipment used to store and dispense flammable and combustible liquids must be certified by a nationally recognized laboratory, such as Underwriters Laboratories (UL). Significantly, UL will not retroactively certify existing infrastructure to handle E15 and has not approved significant numbers of pump configurations. Moreover, underground storage tanks (USTs) must likewise be certified for higher ethanol blends. EPA reports that because USTs have a life-span approaching 30 years, many USTs in commerce are not able to handle E15. As a result, and much like E85, large investments must be made by small businesses in order to sell E15.

Misfueling and Consumer Awareness. A new fuel, like E15, introduced into commerce without sufficient misfueling mitigation will likely lead to misfueling and damage consumers' engines. Unfortunately for consumers, EPA's only misfueling mitigation requirement is a small 4×4 label calling "attention" to E15's appropriate uses, but does not include requirements for a physical barrier to misfueling like those that were present during the switchover from leaded to unleaded gasoline. . . .

Other issues. Finally, E15 does not qualify for the one-pound Reid Vapor Pressure (RVP) waiver legislated for E10. EPA regulates RVP, a measure of gasoline's volatility, to control evaporative emissions. According to EIA, E15 would not be an environmentally complaint fuel in summer months using most current gasoline blendstocks. . . .

Biomass-Based Diesel Will Not Solve the Problem

Another pathway for generating additional RINs for RFS compliance is to use more biodiesel, which generates 1.5 RINs for each gallon use and which is not currently facing the biodiesel blendwall (commonly understood to be a maximum of 5 percent biodiesel that can be blended into petroleum diesel). Biodiesel comprises approximately 2 percent of the diesel consumption, but the real challenge facing biodiesel is its feedstock supply. EIA projects that only 1.28 and 1.49 billion gallons of biodiesel will be produced in 2013 and 2014, respectively, far short of the required volumes for the RFS and wholly inadequate to fulfill the RFS obligations triggered from the sale of diesel fuel. A major impediment for biodiesel is cost, as biodiesel typically costs at least $1.00 or more, on average, to produce than petroleum diesel. Coupled with the $1.00 per gallon biodiesel tax credit, consumers are paying $2.00 or more (through higher cost fuel and their tax bills) per gallon of biodiesel consumed than a petroleum diesel alternative. . . .

A related, unanticipated, effect of the RFS is its treatment of diesel. Due to a combination of the RFS structure, a modest biomass-diesel supply, and the practical cap on biodiesel that can be blended into diesel fuel, for each gallon of diesel a refiner produces, it incurs a "diesel deficit" that requires additional ethanol RINs for compliance. Put another way, a refiner's obligation is determined by the total volume of gasoline and diesel produced or imported for domestic consumption. For each gallon of diesel fuel added to the fuel supply, an obligated party must produce RINs for each of the nested mandates. Because biodiesel can only make up a limited portion of the fuel supply (currently less than 3 percent), and petroleum diesel is only able to use biodiesel as an additive, there is a significant shortfall in RINs that must be filled by additional ethanol RINs. . . .

Other Options for Obligated Parties and Resultant Impacts

After understanding how E15, E85 or greater biodiesel use are not viable pathways for addressing the blendwall, it becomes apparent that refiners are left with few options for compliance. If obligated parties are unable to purchase RINs in the open market at an affordable price, the remaining RFS compliance options are reducing gasoline and diesel supplied to the U.S. through a combination of reduced refinery runs, reduced imports, and increased exports. . . . Due to the respective blendwalls of ethanol and biodiesel, coupled with the RIN equivalence values, a refiner has incentive to cut back on diesel production first. . . .

The macro economic implications of this situation are significant. Diesel is the primary fuel used to transport a wide variety of goods through truck and rail, as well as a major input into agricultural production. In 2011, for example, U.S. farms consumed approximately 2.9 billion gallons of diesel. NERA Consulting recently modeled the implications of the blendwall and found that by 2015 the blendwall will cause a $770 billion decline in GDP, a reduction of $2700 in household consumption, a 30 percent increase in the cost of producing gasoline, and a 300 percent increase in the cost of producing diesel. . . .

Long-Term RFS Issues Beyond the Blendwall

Two of the major objectives of the RFS were to move towards energy independence with increased domestic fuel supply and improve the environment through reduced greenhouse gas emissions. The RFS is doing little towards meeting these goals. We are meeting the energy independence through the surprising increase in U.S. and Canadian production of crude oil and natural gas, not anticipated in 2007, the development of technologies for economic production of more environmentally friendly second generation fuels has not occurred, and the promised environmental benefits of conventional biofuels have been called into question. We must rethink the nation's energy policies in light of these new realities.

Environmental Impacts

In light of biofuels' purported environmental benefits as a central rationale for the RFS, it is important to recognize the actual impacts biofuels are having on the environment. It is now clear that, using EPA data and peer-reviewed data from the National Academy of Sciences, the RFS is not only failing to achieve its promised environmental benefits, but that it is undermining progress compared to a gasoline-only baseline. In particular, EPA's own data shows that the overwhelming majority of ethanol produced this year will actually raise greenhouse gas (GHG) emissions compared to gasoline. For the typical natural gas fired dry mill plants,[16] GHG emissions are increasing by 33 percent over gasoline.

Moreover, a comprehensive 2011 study by the NAS found that lifecycle emissions of major air pollutants (CO, NOx, PM2.5, SOx, and NH3) are higher for corn and cellulosic ethanol than for gasoline. NAS states, in part, "overall production and use of ethanol was projected to result in increases in pollutant concentration for ozone and particulate matter than gasoline on a national average, but the local effects could be variable. Those projected air-quality effects from ethanol fuel would be more damaging to human health than gasoline use." . . .

According to EPA's 2010 Regulatory Impact Analysis, RFS2 will raise ozone levels 0.46 ppb over the RFS1 baseline, placing dozens of counties in danger of falling into non-attainment. In addition to the air quality and GHG impacts, ethanol requires an enormous amount of water to produce. NAS estimates that a gallon of gasoline requires between 1.4 and 6.6 gallons of water to produce. By comparison, corn ethanol requires 15–2400 gallons and switchgrass cellulosic ethanol requires 2.9–1307 gallons. . . .

Inadequate Process for Dealing with the Failed Cellulosic Biofuel Mandate

"Do a good job cellulosic producers. If you fail, we'll fine your consumers."

—U.S. Court of Appeals for the DC Circuit, opining on EPA's management of the cellulosic mandate. *API v. EPA*, 706 F.3d 474, 480 (D.C. Cir. 2013).

Cellulosic biofuels—produced from feedstocks such as corn stover, switchgrass and woodchips—are a subcategory of the advanced biofuels mandate. The RFS calls for 16 billion gallons of cellulosic biofuels in addition to the 4 billion gallon of non-cellulosic advanced biofuels in 2022. . . .

Each year, EIA is required to send a letter to EPA detailing its estimates on cellulosic production for the following calendar year. EPA is required to take those estimates and to base its final proposal based on EIA's estimate. In 2010 and 2011, the RFS called for a combined 350 million gallons of cellulosic biofuel. Recognizing that the industry would not produce that much, EIA projected a combined total of 10.28 million gallons. EPA, in an attempt to provide a greater market for the still non-existent fuel, set the final mandates at 12.5 million gallons. . . .

Therefore, in order to stay in compliance with the RFS, obligated parties were forced to purchase "waiver credits" from EPA. A January 2013 court decision rescinded the requirement in 2012, but in 2010 and 2011, credits totaling more than $14.9 million dollars were purchased. Unfortunately, EPA also denied retroactive petitions from the industry asking for a waiver recognizing that the fuel was not produced.

Recognizing the absurdity of the situation, in January 2013 the U.S. Court of Appeals for the D.C. Circuit vacated the 2012 cellulosic mandate and admonished EPA to base the mandates using more realistic projections. Yet less than a week after the Court's decision, EPA doubled down and once again proposed raising the mandate, this time to 14 million gallons. Through the first 5 months of the year, a total of 4,901 gallons of cellulosic biofuels were produced (and only during the month of March). . . .

Unintended Consequence of Increasing Imports and Emissions

As described previously, the mandate for other advanced fuels can only be met with by importing sugar cane based ethanol, mainly from Brazil. At the same time, the U.S. is exporting corn ethanol to Brazil. This "fuel shuffling" between countries increases total GHG emissions due to unnecessary transportation that would not occur absent the RFS. . . .

Another Implementation Consequence: Biodiesel Fraud

In November 2011 and February 2012, EPA issued Notices of Violation (NOVs) to obligated parties that unknowingly purchased and used invalid RINS sold by EPA registered biodiesel producers. The fraud was perpetuated by three companies, which (in total) sold 140 million RINs to unsuspecting obligated parties. For context, 140 million RINs equaled approximately 5–12 percent of the biodiesel market during 2010 and 2011. These companies were registered by EPA, which required registration paperwork such as third-party engineering reports. In addition to fining the victims of the fraud (obligated parties), EPA forced those parties to go into the market and purchase replacement RINs—which cost more than $1.00 each and without obligated parties knowing whether they were valid. AFPM estimates that the fines and replacement RINs cost the industry nearly $200 million in 2012. . . .

Conclusion

Laws, while often passed with the best of intentions, should be consistently re-examined to ensure they are having their intended impacts. The RFS is no different. In 2007, the energy landscape was markedly different than it is today and policy makers did not have the wealth of information now available demonstrating the unintended consequences of biofuel mandates. Just as the European Union recently decided to roll back its biofuel mandates in response to concerns about the environmental and agricultural impacts, the U.S. Congress should look at the facts and take action to stem the consequences of this law before they grow worse. In addition to the technological innovations in oil and gas production leading to an energy renaissance in the U.S., we now know that the RFS is raising food and fuel costs, increasing GHG emissions, reversing advancements in air and water quality, and increasing the likelihood of engine damage. While the law is flawed at its core, its implementation has demonstrated the extent of the mandate's unworkability.

AFPM believes a two-step process is needed to alleviate the problems. First, EPA should waive the 2013 and 2014 mandates using its discretionary waiver authority. This authority is merely a band-aid, however, as EPA's authority extends only a year at a time. This will provide some time to establish the long term certainty that the market requires. Congress needs to take action to repeal this unworkable and anti-consumer mandate—and soon. . . .

Notes

1. Testimony of EIA Administrator Adam Sieminski before the Senate Committee on Energy and Natural Resources (July 16, 2013).
2. *Id.*
3. Drop-in biofuels can move in pipelines, trucks, and barges without equipment modification; are usable in existing fueling stations without modification, and are usable by existing vehicle fleet without modification.
4. EIA, *Drop-In Biofuels in the AEO*, EIA Biofuels Workshop, March 20, 2013.
5. Gasoline includes blends of up to 10 percent ethanol.
6. EIA Short Term Energy Outlook (July 9, 2013).
7. Obligated parties have the ability to carry over 20 percent of RINs for one year. In previous years, blenders used more ethanol than mandated, creating a "RIN bank" that will likely be drawn down by 2014 as obligated parties use RINs for compliance.
8. www.eia.gov/todayinenergy/detail.cfm?id=11551
9. E85 contains 51–83 percent ethanol
10. EIA Biofuels Issues and Trends at 29 (Oct. 2012), citing www.afdc.energy.gov/fuels/ethanol_locations .html
11. EIA, *Biofuels Issues and Trends*, at 29 (Oct. 2012).
12. AAA Fuel Gauge Report available at http:// fuelgaugereport.aaa.com/?redirectto=http:// fuelgaugereport.opisnet.com/index.asp
13. http://mn.gov/commerce/energy/images/E-85-Fuel -Use-Data.pdf
14. EPA RFS 2 Regulatory Impact Analysis at 291.

15. EPA RFS2 Regulatory Impact Analysis at 288.
16. EPA estimates about 80 percent of corn ethanol plants are natural gas fired, and 88 percent are drymill facilities.

CHARLES T. DREVNA is the president of American Fuel & Petrochemical Manufacturers. Since 2007 he has served as president of the American Fuel & Petrochemical Manufacturers, the national trade association that represents 98 percent of refining capacity in the United States. Drevna joined the association in 2002 as director of policy and planning and named executive vice president in 2006. Drevna has over 40 years of extensive experience in legislative, regulatory, public policy, and marketplace issues involving energy and the environment. His previous positions include director of state and federal government relations for Tosco, Inc.; director of government and regulatory affairs for the Oxygenated Fuels Association; vice president at the Washington consulting firm of Jefferson Waterman International; several positions at Sunoco, including vice president for public affairs for Sun Coal Company; director of environmental affairs for the National Coal Association; and supervisor of environmental quality control for the Consolidation Coal Company.

EXPLORING THE ISSUE

Are Biofuels Like Ethanol the Answer to U.S. Energy Problems?

Critical Thinking and Reflection

1. Both authors lead industry trade groups whose members have a direct financial stake in whether or not the Renewable Fuels Standard is retained. In evaluating their arguments how do we separate the facts from the self-interested rhetoric?
2. While ethanol is the best known biofuel, there are many different types of biofuels available. What are the benefits and costs of each type of biofuel? Which types of biofuel appear to be viable alternatives to fossil fuels?
3. Both authors assert that their preferred policy will lead to greater consumer choice. How do they define what they mean by consumer choice? How can the opposite policies both achieve the same goal?

Is There Common Ground?

Both authors agree on the virtues of consumer choice, lower fuel prices, less pollution, and energy independence. They use similar terminology such as blend wall, Renewable Identification Number, greenhouse gas emissions, second generation biofuels, and energy security.

They both draw on data from two federal government agencies: the Environmental Protection Agency and the Energy Information Administration.

Create Central

www.mhhe.com/createcentral

Additional Resources

Gupta, Vijai Kumar and Tuohy, Maria G. (eds.), *Biofuels Technologies: Recent Developments* (Springer, 2013)

James, Tom, *The Global Biofuels Market: Trading and Operations* (Wiley, 2013)

Jansen, Roland A., *Second Generation Biofuels and Biomass: Essential Guide for Investors, Scientists and Decision Makers* (Wiley, 2013)

Pimentel, David (ed.), *Global Economic and Environmental Aspects of Biofuels* (CRC Press, 2013)

Schobert, Harold, *Chemistry of Fossil Fuels and Biofuels* (Cambridge University Press, 2013)

Internet References . . .

American Petroleum Institute, Fuels Policy

www.api.org/policy-and-issues/fuels

Science Daily Alternative Fuel News

www.sciencedaily.com/news/matter_energy
/alternative-fuels

U.S. Department of Energy, Alternative
Fuels Data Center

www.afdc.energy.gov

U.S. Energy Information Administration,
Renewable and Alternative Fuels

www.eia.gov/renewable

U.S. Environmental Protection Agency,
Renewable Fuels Standard

www.epa.gov/otaq/fuels/renewablefuels

Selected, Edited, and with Issue Framing Material by:
Eric Strahorn, *Florida Gulf Coast University*

ISSUE

Is Climate Change a Threat That Requires Urgent Action?

YES: Franklin W. Nutter, from "Testimony before the Senate Committee on Environment and Public Works," statement before U.S. Senate (July 18, 2013)

NO: Diana Furchtgott-Roth, from "Testimony before the Senate Environment and Public Works Committee," statement before U.S. Senate (July 18, 2013)

Learning Outcomes

After reading this issue, you will be able to:

- Describe the evidence used to support or deny the assertion that global temperatures are rising and extreme weather events are becoming more common.
- Apply a cost-benefit analysis to the climate change mitigation proposals identified by both authors.
- Analyze the idea that economic growth and environmental protection are not compatible and that growth should be the higher priority.

ISSUE SUMMARY

YES: Franklin W. Nutter argues that anthropogenic climate change is real, and the effects are already being felt. We need to consider mitigation action to reduce emissions of greenhouse gasses as well as adaptation efforts to avoid the predicted future impacts.

NO: Diana Furchtgott-Roth argues that climate change does not appear to be happening and even if greenhouse gasses are affecting the climate, unilateral action by the United States would not have any tangible effect and would instead harm the U.S. economy.

Scientists began expressing concerns over human-influenced changes in climate nearly a century ago, but research into it intensified in the 1970s. By the 1990s debate over it had spread far beyond academic circles. In the debate over climate change there are numerous allegations of political bias, undeclared economic self-interest, fraudulent data, and pseudoscience. A majority of scientists contend that climate change is currently happening and is anthropogenic, that is, caused by humans. They predict that the effects will be harmful with rising sea levels, more frequent extreme weather events, and changing climatic zones that disrupt agriculture, forests, and ocean fish stocks.

Opponents (often called skeptics) of mainstream climate science advance different arguments, including (1) climate change is not happening at all, (2) climate change is happening but is a natural process unaffected by human activity, and (3) climate change is happening, but

the effects will be minor so little needs to be done to cope with it. Critics of the skeptics often refer to them as climate change "deniers" who seek to obfuscate the issue at the behest of coal and oil companies. The skeptics deny this and say that they are exposing errors in the mainstream science, and some of them allege that mainstream scientists have unstated political agendas of their own. Senator James Inhofe (R-OK) claims that climate change is the "greatest hoax ever perpetrated on the American people" by the United Nations and "the Hollywood elite."[1] However, mainstream scientists argue that there is a substantial consensus among climate scientists in which 97 percent of them "agree that climate-warming trends over the past century are very likely due to human activities."[2]

A significant step in the development of climate science was the creation of the Intergovernmental Panel on Climate Change (IPCC) in 1988 by the United Nations Environment Program and the World Meteorological Organization to "provide the world with a clear scientific view on the current state of knowledge in climate change and its potential environmental and socio-economic impacts."[3] The IPCC does not conduct original research but synthesizes existing research from around the world. In 2007 the IPCC was awarded the Nobel Peace Prize, but controversy erupted over one of its reports. In Chapter 10 of the 2007 Working Group II report ("Impacts, Adaptation and Vulnerability") a paragraph contained the statement that the glaciers of the Himalayas would disappear by 2035. The IPCC conceded that this was a factual error, and this claim was not included in later reports. Climate-change skeptics charged that this error was the tip of the iceberg and that the IPCC lacked any credibility. The IPCC has a variety of critics from different perspectives. Some of its critics charge that it is too conservative and underestimates the dangers of climate change while others charge that it exaggerates those dangers and promotes unnecessary anxiety over climate issues.

Today, climate science is rapidly evolving with the development of better climate models, faster computers, and an increasing volume of historical and contemporary climate data. There are three key issues that are addressed by climate science: evidence of past and present changes in the climate, modeling of future changes, and analysis of the causes of climate change. The evidence for past and present climate change includes such factors as the concentration of greenhouse gasses (including carbon dioxide and methane), the size of mountain glaciers and polar icecaps, and sea level. Predictions of future changes in climate are based on computer models and depend on such factors as available computer power and the sophistication of the algorithms used. The possible causes of climate change include a variety of human and non-human factors. Non-human (non-anthropogenic) causes include changes in solar output and plate tectonics, which over millions of years can alter the global distribution of warm and cold water in the oceans. The primary human (anthropogenic) activity that can affect global temperature is the burning of fossil fuels, although deforestation and certain agricultural practices can contribute to the process. Proposals to reduce the rate of temperature increase are centered on reducing the emission of greenhouse gasses through replacing the burning of fossil fuels with the use of non-fossil sources of energy like wind and solar, the creation of carbon credits that provide a financial incentive to reducing emissions, and the removal of carbon dioxide through carbon sequestration. The mitigation of the effects of warming can include measures like the building of larger sea walls and the relocation of cities from the expanded flood zones.

The key political and policy questions are centered on a cost-benefit analysis that compares the potential environmental and economic damage of climate change with what it may cost to prevent or remediate that damage. There are several variables that need to be taken into account but the most important is to estimate the actual rate of future warming. Many of the estimates predict a 2°C rise in global temperature, although there are higher estimates. The higher the rise in temperature, the more glaciers and icecaps will melt and raise sea level; the greater the acidification of the oceans, the increased number and size of extreme weather events and shifts in rainfall patterns and growing seasons. Cost-benefit analyses of climate change are complicated by the difficulty of quantifying certain factors like human health, ecosystem services, and the migration of plant and animal species to new climate zones.

The selections that follow were taken from a hearing on "Climate Change: It's Happening Now" held by the U.S. Senate Committee on Environment & Public Works on July 18, 2013. According to the committee chairman Barbara Boxer (D-CA), the purpose of the hearing was to "focus on climate change and the serious threat it poses to our nation. The body of evidence is overwhelming, the world's leading scientists agree, and predictions of the impact of climate change are coming true before our eyes."[4] Those testifying included representatives from Climate Central, the Reinsurance Association of America, Climate Solutions, the Manhattan Institute for Policy Research, and the Institute for Energy Research. There were also academics from Rutgers University, Woods Hole Oceanographic Institution, Florida Atlantic University, the University of Colorado, and the University of Alabama, Huntsville.

Notes

1. Jillian Rayfield, "Climate Committee Republicans: 'Ridiculous Pseudo-Science'" (*The Guardian* 29 July 2013), www.theguardian.com/environment/2013/jul/29/climate-committee-republicans.
2. NASA, http://climate.nasa.gov/scientific-consensus.
3. Intergovernmental Panel on Climate Change, www.ipcc.ch/organization/organization.shtml#.UoF3lo11GHl.
4. U.S. Senate Committee on Environment and Public Works; www.epw.senate.gov. No other members of the committee made an opening statement.

YES

Franklin W. Nutter

Testimony before the Senate Committee on Environment and Public Works

My name is Frank Nutter and I am President of the Reinsurance Association of America (RAA). The RAA is a national trade association representing reinsurance companies doing business in the United States. RAA membership includes reinsurance underwriters and intermediaries licensed in the U.S. and those that conduct business on a cross border basis. . . .

Reinsurance is essentially insurance for insurance companies. It is a risk management tool for insurance companies to reduce the volatility in their portfolios and improve their financial performance and security. It is widely recognized that reinsurance performs at least four primary functions—(1) helps insurance companies manage their risks; (2) stabilizes loss experience; (3) provides transfer for insurers of major natural and man-made catastrophe risk; and (4) increases insurance capacity.

Reinsurers have assisted in the recovery from every major natural and man-made catastrophe over the past century. 60% of the insured losses related to the events of September 11, 2001 were absorbed by the global reinsurance industry. In 2005, 45% of the insured losses from Hurricanes Katrina, Rita and Wilma were paid by reinsurers; in 2011, insured losses for the New Zealand earthquakes totalled $17 billion, with reinsurers paying 73% of that total. In 2012, "Superstorm" Sandy caused an estimated $18 billion in insured losses. Reinsurers are expected to pay up to 40% of the insured losses.

Property casualty insurers are more dependent on the vagaries of climate and weather than any other financial services sector. Within the insurance sector, reinsurers have the greatest financial stake in appropriate risk assessment. The industry is at great financial peril if it does not understand global and regional climate impacts, variability and developing scientific assessment of a changing climate. Integrating this information into the insurance system is an essential function.

Insurance is a critical component for economic and social recovery from the effects of extreme weather and climate driven events. Through its pricing structure it is also a mechanism for conveying the consequences of decisions about where and how we build and where people chose to live. In this regard, it must be proactive and forward-looking in a changing climate/weather environment.

Our industry is science based. Blending the actuarial sciences with the natural sciences is critical in order to provide the public with resources to recover from natural events. As the scientific community's knowledge of changes in our climate and the resulting weather continue to develop, it is important for our communities to incorporate that information into the exposure and risk assessment process, and that it be conveyed to stakeholders, policyholders, the public and public officials that can, or should, address adaptation and mitigation alternatives. Developing an understanding about climate and its impact on droughts, heat waves, the frequency and intensity of tropical hurricanes, thunderstorms and convective events, rising sea levels and storm surge, more extreme precipitation events and flooding is critical to our role in translating the interdependencies of weather, climate risk assessment and pricing.

Exposure Assessment

Insurers see climate primarily through the prism of extreme natural events. Research by Munich Re reflects a rising number of natural catastrophes globally and in the U.S. . . .

In the 1980's, the average number of natural catastrophes globally was 400 events per year. In recent years, the average is 1000. Munich Re's analysis suggests the increase is driven almost entirely by weather-related events. North America has seen a fivefold increase in the number of such events since 1980. In comparison, Europe has seen a twofold increase.

In this regard, it is indisputable that the recent rise in damages, insured, economic and uninsured, is heavily influenced by the concentration of people and property in geographically vulnerable areas. Urbanization, increased development and population shifts have placed more people with destructible assets in areas most impacted by extreme weather. NOAA's recent State of the Coast report observes that in a U.S. population of 313 million (based on the 2010 census), coastal shoreline counties comprise 39% or 123 million people; watershed counties comprise 52% of the U.S. population. In coastal shoreline counties, NOAA reports there are 49 million housing units with an expected increase in population of 10 million people before the next census in 2020. The NOAA report notes that an average of 1355 building permits are issued per day in these shoreline counties. . . .

Nutter, Franklin W. U.S. Senate, July 18, 2013.

The Insurance Information Institute and Munich Re report that insured coastal property values on the East and Gulf coasts total nearly $10 trillion. Florida and New York each have nearly $3 trillion of insured coastal values.

Research and consulting firm Core Logic reports there are 4.2 million homes along the Gulf and Atlantic coast exposed to storm surge—the most significant factor in damages associated with Superstorm Sandy. Most of these storm surge affected properties are in 10 metropolitan areas. One million of these are in the category of extreme risk to storm surge and another 839,000 in the high risk category. Core Logic notes that 23 of the 25 most populous U.S. counties are ocean-facing.

Catastrophe modeling firm AIR estimates the insured value of coastal properties (defined as replacement cost not market value) is expected to increase at a rate of 7% per year which means that values would double every decade.

Together with changes in weather patterns, intensity, and number of events, the result, of course, is an inevitable rise in insured and uninsured damages globally and in the U.S.

Hurricane related losses tend to dominate the pattern of large losses.

The pattern is recent. Ten of the 12 most costly hurricanes have occurred in the last nine years.

However, other climate/weather related perils also cause major damage.

Tornado losses in the U.S. exceeded $1 billion only once prior to 1998. Since then, there have been 29 such events.

Severe wind is not the only peril reflecting this pattern. Goldman Sachs Global Economics reports the 2012 U.S. drought alone cut crop yields, reducing 3rd quarter 2012 GDP by .4%—the equivalent of another Superstorm Sandy. Droughts are now the third most costly category of natural catastrophe loss with crop losses dominant.

Recent wildfire major events have destroyed homes and threatened communities.

Future Assessment

But what if the past is not prologue and, in a changing climate, weather, economic and social trends exacerbate the impact. The Insurance Information Institute projected future losses from past events that reflect rising exposures in areas proven to be at high risk to major climate/weather events.

In a study on Climate Change Impacts conducted for FEMA by AECOM, the firm concluded that the typical 100 year floodplain nationally would grow by 45% and by 55% in coastal areas (with significant regional variations and assuming a fixed shoreline). Notably the report attributed 70 percent of the projected growth in 100 year floodplains to climate change and 30 percent to expected population growth (the analysis assumes 4 feet of sea level rise by the year 2100). The study recommends immediate attention to the implications for the Federal government's

National Flood Insurance Program, which is already $26 billion in debt.

Disaster assistance is already a major expense to the Federal government and has set records in recent years.

Dr. David Cummins of Temple University's School of Risk Management estimates the subsidization of disaster-prone areas embedded in Federal disaster assistance practices has encouraged development and increased Federal exposure. He estimates the expected average annual bill for Federal disaster assistance related to natural catastrophes at $20 billion. Current funding for FEMA's Disaster Relief Fund is $1 billion. Dr. Cummins estimates this unfunded liability over the next 75 years at $1.2 to $5.7 trillion, at the high end, essentially the unfunded obligations for Social Security.

Adaptation and Mitigation Strategies

Swiss Re has been a leader in addressing climate change for many years. "Today, global warming is a fact. Since the beginning of industrialization and the rapid growth of world population, man's activities—along with natural variability—have contributed to a change of climate manifesting itself as a considerable increase in global temperature. Climate change has the potential to develop into our planet's greatest environmental challenge of the 21st century.

As an enabler of change, the financial services industry can help guide society towards an effective response. However, the industry can only be effective in this role if the regulatory and legislative framework establishes the right incentives for emissions reduction and adaptation on a global scale."

Munich Re shares this view:

> "Anthropogenic climate change is believed to contribute to this trend (a jump in catastrophe losses) though it influences various perils in different ways.
>
> In order to realize a sustainable model of insurance, it is crucially important for us as risk managers to learn about this risk of change and find improved solutions for adaptation and mitigation." (Peter Roeder)
>
> "Globally, climate change alone will increase worldwide losses by 100% by the end of the 21st century. The overall increase in losses in the United States due to climate change alone will be more than 70% by the end of the century according to a wind-based model."

The Geneva Association (International Association for the Study of Insurance Economics) states the need for action as follows:

> "The economic and social impacts of climate change could be immense; there is therefore a

need for urgent and concerted *mitigation* action to reduce GHG emissions, supported by strong incentives from policy-makers. But regardless of the action taken to mitigate climate change, we can expect many decades of changing climate risks due to inertia within the climate system. We therefore also need concerted *adaptation* to avoid the predicted impacts of climate change and especially to protect the most vulnerable populations."

Congressional Action

As Congress considers the impact of climate change, the RAA suggests the following legislative principles or actions to consider:

- Provide tax credits to individuals for specified mitigation and resiliency actions associated with extreme weather and climate change.
- Incent communities to develop and implement mitigation and resiliency initiatives.
- Reform the National Flood Insurance Program to reflect extreme weather and climate risk in its rates.
- Apply Federal standards to state/local building codes and incorporate climate and extreme weather risk into these standards.
- Purchase or relocate properties near coastal or river areas at repeat risk.
- Use nature to mitigate risk before and after extreme events.
- Transfer development rights from coastal and river properties to areas inland (Strengthen the Coastal Barrier Resources Act)
- Fund adequate remote sensing for NOAA and NASA.
- Require the Army Corps of Engineers to assess climate risk for all projects.
- The Federal government should lead by example: GSA should assess its buildings and critical facilities in light of climate and extreme weather information.
- Fund climate and weather research through the National Science Foundation, NOAA and other Federal agencies at priority levels.
- Use disaster assistance as an incentive for local communities for climate and extreme weather sensitive, forward looking recovery.

Conclusion

The Reinsurance Association and its member companies welcome the attention of Congress to the critical issues of extreme weather and climate. We are committed to work with you to address the exposure of citizens and their property to extreme weather risk and to seek ways to improve the resilience of our communities.

Resources

- Core Logic: Storm Surge Report: Residential Storm Surge Exposure Estimate for the US Coastal Areas (2012)
- Federal Financial Exposure to Natural Catastrophe Risk, David Cummins, Michael Suher and George Zanjani (2010)
- Goldman Sachs, Global Economics, Commodities and Strategy Research
- ClimateWise, Summary of the IPCC Special Report on Managing the Risks of Extreme Events and Disasters
- Applied Insurance Research Coastline at Risk: Update to the Estimated Insured Value of US Coastal Property (2013)
- NOAA State of the Coast National Coastal Population Report (March 2013)
- Geneva Association (International Association for the Study of Insurance Economics): The Insurance Industry and Climate Change (July 2009)
- Munich Reinsurance, Climate Variability and Climate Change
- AECOM: The Impact of Climate Change and Population Growth on the national Flood Insurance Program through 2100 (June 2013)

FRANKLIN W. NUTTER has been the president of the Reinsurance Association of America (RAA) since 1991. He held the same position with the RAA from 1981 to 1984. In the interim, he was president of the Alliance of American Insurers and the Property Loss Research Bureau, which have now merged to be part of the PCI (Property Casualty Insurance Association of America). Nutter currently serves on the Advisory Board of the Center for Health and the Global Environment at the Harvard University School of Public Health, the Advisory Board of the OECD's International Network for the Financial Management of Large Scale Disasters, and the RAND Center on Catastrophic Risk Management and Compensation. He has recently served on the Council of the American Meteorological Society and the Board of the University Center for Atmospheric Research, a consortium of universities managing the National Center for Atmospheric Research sponsored by the National Science Foundation. He has served as a member of the board of directors of the Advocates for Highway and Auto Safety, the Insurance Institute for Highway Safety and the Worker's Compensation Research Institute, the board of overseers of the Institute for Civil Justice, a subsidiary of the RAND Corporation, and on the board of the Bermuda Institute for Ocean Sciences.

Diana Furchtgott-Roth

Testimony before the Senate Environment and Public Works Committee

If Climate Change Is Happening Now, What Do We Do?

. . . I am a senior fellow at the Manhattan Institute. From 2003 until April 2005 I was chief economist at the U.S. Department of Labor. From 2001 until 2002 I served at the Council of Economic Advisers as chief of staff. I have served as Deputy Executive Secretary of the Domestic Policy Council under President George H.W. Bush and as an economist on the staff of President Reagan's Council of Economic Advisers.

Is climate change happening now? Since 2003 global temperatures appear to have reached a plateau.[1] With rising greenhouse gas emissions from Asia and other emerging economies, many predicted that temperatures would continue to rise. Why they have not done so is a puzzle.

With an apparent stall in global warming, the focus has switched to "climate change." For instance, on July 11, 2013, the Department of Energy issued a report entitled *U.S. Energy Sector Vulnerabilities to Climate Change and Extreme Weather*. The report projects increases in storm and flood frequency.

However, a review of the data over the past 100 years does not show a steady increase in major storms such as hurricanes, nor a steady increase in the number of floods, even though greenhouse gas emissions increased. The National Oceanic and Atmospheric Administration shows the number of hurricanes over the past 100 years has been volatile, with no clear trend. There were seven floods reported by the NOAA's Mid-Atlantic River Forecast Center in 2012, the precise number reported in 1912. In between, some years have shown higher numbers, others have shown lower numbers. The data have been sporadic at best.

Despite Congress's decision not to pass cap-and-trade legislation, on June 25, in a speech at Georgetown University, President Obama called for similar regulatory measures to reduce greenhouse gases. He announced that he will use his executive powers to reduce greenhouse emissions from existing power plants, as well as future plants. He also plans to increase efficiency standards for appliances and authorize the placement of wind farms and solar power plants on federal lands. He asked the Department of Defense to install 3 gigawatts of renewable power

on bases. He announced that over the next 7 years, 20 percent of the energy the federal government will consume will come from renewable sources. He mentioned plans for federal tax dollars to fund building infrastructure, such as seawalls for communities.

The 111th Congress failed to pass legislation to regulate emissions in 2009–2010, when Democrats had majorities in the House and Senate. The cost of the legislation is a major reason for the failure of the Waxman-Markey and Kerry-Lieberman "cap-and-trade" bills, which would have capped emissions and encouraged firms to buy and sell rights to pollute.

The bill would have required EPA to shrink greenhouse gas allowances steadily to 2050. When any year's emissions would have exceeded a firm's cap, the firm would have to purchase allowances from the government or other companies. That is a tax under another name, driving up costs that would be passed on to consumers.

The costs of the Kerry-Lieberman and Waxman-Markey bills were too large for a Democratic Congress to support, even with Obama's backing. The revenues from the bills, about $646 billion over 8 years, would have at that time been the largest tax increase in history.

Even if rising greenhouse gas emissions are affecting the climate, actions by the United States will not be helpful in the absence of changes by China and India. The U.S. global share of greenhouse gases is 17 percent.

Other countries are increasing emissions. China, India, and Germany are expanding coal consumption, according to the International Energy Agency. Global coal use will rise by 1.2 billion tons in five years. "By 2017," according to a December 2012 IEA report, "coal will come close to surpassing oil as the world's top energy source."[2] Mr. Obama's reductions in U.S. emissions, with their associated costs, will just be a drop in the global bucket.

Polls show that many believe protecting the environment is less important to Americans than economic growth.[3] With the slowdown in many measures of global warming over the past decade, climate change is playing second fiddle to jobs. Americans know that no reduction in global warming will occur if America reduces greenhouse gases without similar action by China and India, and these countries have not agreed to comparable steps.

Furchtgott-Roth, Diana. U.S. Senate, July 18, 2013.

U.S. greenhouse gas emissions have been declining since 2007, and fell by 1.6 percent between 2010 and 2011, the Environmental Protection Agency announced earlier this year.[4] Required use of alternative energy technology might reduce greenhouse gas emissions further, but the new technologies make fuel and electricity more expensive, reducing economic growth and adversely affecting employment.

The message that government can create more total jobs by requiring more costly technology is seductive but empty. Yes, some Americans might be employed building the technology, but others lose jobs due to more expensive energy.

Although President Obama advocates green jobs, the Labor Department's green jobs survey for 2011, released in March 2013, found only 3.4 million such jobs, despite $500 million in the stimulus bill for green jobs training. By the end of 2011, combined expenditures of the Energy Training Partnership, Pathways out of Poverty, and State Energy Sector Partnership green jobs stimulus programs totaled $257.3 million.

However, only 5,400 new jobs through the programs were retained at least 6 months, yielding a cost of $47,754 per job. The Bureau of Labor Statistics has announced that it will discontinue its green jobs survey due to the sequester.

However, the White House website writes in its 4th report on the stimulus "A central piece of the ARRA is more than $90 billion in government investment and tax incentives to lay the foundation for the clean energy economy of the future" and references "$3 billion for Green Innovation and Job Training to invest in the science, technology, and workforce needed for a clean energy economy."[5] The most recent quarterly report does not mention the Green Innovation and Job Training funding.[6]

The $90 billion includes items like the loan guarantee money (some of which will be recovered), and other items like grants for weatherizing and retrofitting.

The president's climate change measures will reduce economic growth by raising energy prices. As well as reducing jobs in the mining industry—over 100 coal-fired power plants have closed since the beginning of 2010—it will also discourage energy-intensive manufacturing.

Manufacturers are returning to America due to low-cost energy, and the president's proposals will drive them away and discourage others. The new French Vallourec Star pipe mill in eastern Ohio is making tubes for the electric pipe industry. Other companies making similar investments are Luxembourg's Tenaris and China's Tanjin Pipe. Royal Dutch Shell is building a $4 billion ethane cracker plant in Pennsylvania, and is planning on hiring 5,000 construction workers.

Since 2009, the German chemical company BASF has invested more than $5.7 billion into North America, including a formic acid plant under construction in Louisiana. BASF officials say that energy prices in America are lower than in Europe, where fracking is discouraged.

Other European countries planning to invest in America due to low energy prices include Austrian steelmaker Voestalpine (an iron-ore processing plant in Texas), and South Africa-bases Sasol (a natural gas to diesel conversion plant in Louisiana).

If these companies run into difficulties, their investors and shareholders will bear the losses. But when the government picks investments in risky new technology, as the president recommends, taxpayers and the federal budget lose if the projects fail. Of the 33 energy loan guarantees made since 2009 under the Energy Department's programs, 30, or over 90 percent, have shown signs of trouble, ranging from missed production goals to bankruptcy filings.

Companies which received loans or grants from the Energy Department during the Obama administration then filed for bankruptcy include Solyndra, Abound Solar, A123, Ener1, Evergreen Solar, Solar Trust of America, Energy Conversion Devices, and Beacon Power. Grant recipients Ecototality, SunPower, and Smith Electric have reported losses.

The Inspector General of the Energy Department, Gregory Friedman, found that employees of LG Chem, a battery manufacturer in Holland, Michigan, "spent time volunteering at local non-profit organizations, playing games and watching movies during regular working hours." LG Chem, meanwhile, sold batteries made in South Korea to U.S. firms rather than producing the batteries in Michigan.

Raising the cost of energy at any time is poor economic policy, but especially when economic growth is slow. After four years of economic "recovery," U.S. annualized GDP growth was 1.8 percent in the first quarter of 2013. America has 2.1 million fewer nonfarm payroll jobs than in December, 2007, the start of the recession. Now is not the time for Obama to overrule Congress and slow the economy further.

Electricity from natural gas, of which America has a 200-year supply, is less expensive than electricity produced from alternative fuels. The U.S. Energy Information Administration has estimated that the average levelized cost for natural gas-fired plants entering service in 2018 is $67 per megawatt hour, compared to $144 per megawatt hour for solar-powered plants, $87 per megawatt hour for wind power, and $111 per megawatt hour for biomass.[7]

The bottom line: households have far higher electricity bills using alternative energy than natural gas.

This disproportionately affects low-income Americans, who spend a higher share of their income on energy. Data from the Labor Department released September 2012 show those in the lowest fifth of the income distribution spend an average of 24 percent of income on energy, compared to 10 percent of income for those in the middle fifth, and 4 percent of income for those in the top fifth.

A CBO report shows that emissions reduction programs would cause job losses in coal mining, oil and gas extraction, gas utilities, and petroleum refining. In addition, workers' wages adjusted for inflation would be lower than otherwise because of the increase in prices due to a cap and trade program. CBO concludes that some workers, therefore, would leave the labor market, because at the new lower wages they would prefer to stay home.[8]

Any reader of the CBO report would realize that it is not in the interests of American workers to embark on an emissions reduction program with our current high unemployment rate. According to CBO, "While the economy was adjusting to the emission-reduction program, a number of people would lose their jobs, and some of those people would face prolonged hardship." Workers laid off in declining industries would find it hard to get new jobs.

The CBO report points out that "In cases in which a shrinking industry was the primary employer in a community, the entire community could suffer." The tax base would dwindle and real estate would lose its value as unemployed workers moved elsewhere. The community's personal income would diminish and real estate values would fall as the jobless moved away.

That is why a carbon tax would harm the U.S. economy.

A \$15 tax per metric ton of CO_2 would result in an increase in gasoline prices of 15 cents per gallon, 75 cents per thousand cubic feet of natural gas, \$6.45 per barrel of oil, and \$28.50 per ton of coal. A \$50 CO_2 tax rate would raise the price of gasoline by 50 cents per gallon, natural gas by \$2.50 per thousand cubic feet, oil by \$21.50 per barrel, and coal by \$95 per ton.[9]

The carbon tax is a favorite of many academic economists for restructuring the tax system.[10] Proponents suggest that the tax be used to replace other taxes, such as the individual income tax, the corporate income tax, or a Kerry-Lieberman-style cap-and-trade system.

However, as tax practitioners know, a carbon tax is complex to set up. It requires adjustments to make sure that the tax is not unduly regressive and does not encourage consumption of imports relative to domestic production. A carbon tax without such offsets would be another add-on levy, with exemptions for friends and punishments for enemies.

A carbon tax raises the price of energy and so discourages consumption and production, as manufacturers choose to locate elsewhere.

One major problem with the carbon tax is that it is regressive. Since low-income people use more energy as a percent of their income than high-income people, a switch to a carbon tax would have to be accompanied by transfers to low-income groups.

Academics suggest that offsets be returned to taxpayers through lower income taxes, perhaps with the proceeds going chiefly to low-income households (individuals and families), which are disproportionately hurt by what is in essence an energy consumption tax. This could be done by adjustments of the income tax.

However, low-income earners are not required to file returns, and they would have to do so in order to be identified and compensated. That means extra work for them, and for the Internal Revenue Service.[11] And, as recent events have shown, the IRS is not prepared to take on more responsibilities with its current level of funding.

Another problem is that carbon-intensive sectors, such as coal, would be the biggest losers under the new tax. Politicians from coal-producing regions are influential in Congress and they would demand a share of revenues.

Finally, a carbon tax would raise the prices of energy-intensive goods relative to imports from countries without carbon taxes. So Americans would prefer to buy imports, and American firms would lose business. Proponents of the tax suggest putting tariffs on imports in proportion to their carbon content so that American companies will not be at a disadvantage. But the precise quantities are complex to calculate, and such tariffs might be illegal under World Trade Organization regulations.

So for a carbon tax to make our tax system more efficient, its revenues would have to be used to offset other taxes in the economy. Its negative effects on low-income Americans and on energy-intensive regions would have to be ameliorated. Some border adjustment would have to be made so that domestic goods were not disfavored.

But the legislative process makes it difficult to craft a carbon tax with these attributes. It is more likely that any tax on carbon would be an additional tax. It would hurt the poor and raise domestic prices relative to prices of imports.

To reduce global greenhouse gas emissions in a less costly manner, America could assist China and India develop shale gas from hydrofracturing and build natural-gas fired plants to reduce their reliance on coal. Or, America could ship coal to China, because U.S. coal burns cleaner than Chinese coal. The majority of China's coal (54 percent) is bituminous, which has a carbon content ranging from 45 to 86 percent.[12] On the other hand, 47 percent of the U.S.'s coal, a plurality, is subbituminous, which contains a carbon content of only 35 to 45 percent.[13]

Congress could fund research into geoengineering measures. More needs to be done to study solar radiation management, which potentially diminishes the warmth caused by the sun's rays. This could be done by injecting fine sulfur particles or other reflective aerosols into the upper atmosphere to reflect incoming radiation, or spraying clouds with salt water to increase their reflectance.

Clouds seeded with salt water would be thicker, and would reflect more heat back toward the sun, away from Earth. Cooling effects—as well as other, adverse consequences—have been observed after volcanic eruptions.

Another avenue of research is to explore making the surface of the planet more reflective, by brightening structures and painting roofs white, as well as increasing the reflectivity of deserts and oceans.

Such measures would cost a fraction of what cap-and-trade regulations and therefore do less damage to the economy. . . .

Notes

1. National Aeronautics and Space Administration, *Global Land-Ocean Temperature Index*, http://data.giss.nasa.gov/gistemp/graphs_v3/Fig.A2.txt

2. International Energy Agency, *Medium-Term Coal Market Report*, December 2012, http://www.iea.org/publications/medium-termreports/#coal.

3. Gallup Poll, April 2013, http://www.gallup.com/poll/161594/americans-prioritize-economy-environment.aspx.

4. Environmental Protection Agency, *Inventory of U.S. Greenhouse Gas Emissions and Sinks: 1990–2011*, April 12, 2013, http://www.epa.gov/climatechange/Downloads/ghgemissions/US-GHG-Inventory-2013-Main-Text.pdf, p. 26.

5. Council of Economic Advisors, *Recovery Act Fourth Quarterly Report—The Public Investment Provisions of the Recovery Act*, 2010, http://www.whitehouse.gov/administration/eop/cea/factsheets-reports/economic-impact-arra-4th-quarterly-report/section-4#14.

6. Council of Economic Advisors, *The Economic Impact of the American Recovery And Reinvestment Act of 2009: Ninth Quarterly Report*, February 1, 2013, http://www.whitehouse.gov/sites/default/files/docs/cea_9th_arra_report_final_pdf.pdf

7. U.S. Energy Information Administration, *Levelized Cost of New Generation Resources in the Annual Energy Outlook 2013*, January 28, 2013, http://www.eia.gov/forecasts/aeo/electricity_generation.cfm.

8. Congressional Budget Office, *How Policies to Reduce Greenhouse Gas Emissions Could Affect Employment*, May 5, 2010, http://www.cbo.gov/sites/default/files/cbofiles/ftpdocs/105xx/doc10564/05-05-capandtrade_brief.pdf.

9. Ramseur, Jonathan L., Jane A. Leggett, and Molly F. Sherlock, Carbon Tax: Deficit Reduction and Other Considerations, Congressional Research Service, September 17, 2012, p. 11, http://www.fas.org/sgp/crs/misc/R42731.pdf.

10. Carbon Tax Center, "Supporters," March 24, 2012, http://www.carbontax.org/who-supports.

11. Dinan, Terry, *Offsetting a Carbon Tax's Costs on Low-Income Households*, Congressional Budget Office Working Paper Series, November 2012, http://www.cbo.gov/sites/default/files/cbofiles/attachments/11-13LowIncomeOptions.pdf.

12. U.S. Energy Information Administration, *International Energy Outlook 2011*, Table 10, http://www.eia.gov/forecasts/ieo/table10.cfm.

13. U.S. Energy Information Administration, *Subbituminous and bituminous coal dominate U.S. coal production*, 2011, http://www.eia.gov/todayinenergy/detail.cfm?id=2670/.

DIANA FURCHTGOTT-ROTH, the former chief economist of the U.S. Department of Labor, is director of economics and senior fellow at the Manhattan Institute for Policy Research. She is a contributing editor of RealClearMarkets.com and a columnist for the *Washington Examiner,* MarketWatch.com, and *Tax Notes.* From 2003 to 2005, Furchtgott-Roth was chief economist of the U.S. Department of Labor. From 2001 to 2002 she served as chief of staff for President George W. Bush's Council of Economic Advisers. Furchtgott-Roth served as deputy executive director of the Domestic Policy Council and associate director of the Office of Policy Planning in the White House under President George H.W. Bush from 1991 to 1993, and she was an economist on the staff of President Reagan's Council of Economic Advisers from 1986 to 1987. Furchtgott-Roth is a frequent guest on *FOX Business News,* and she has appeared on numerous other TV and radio shows, including CNBC's *Larry Kudlow Show,* C-SPAN's *Washington Journal,* and PBS's *The NewsHour* with Jim Lehrer.

EXPLORING THE ISSUE

Is Climate Change a Threat That Requires Urgent Action?

Critical Thinking and Reflection

1. Furchtgott-Roth claims that the evidence does not indicate that climate change is actually happening, so why does she propose several methods to combat it?
2. Nutter proposes several steps to reduce the emission of greenhouse gasses and adapt the country to the effects of climate change. Will these proposals have a tangible effect in mitigating climate change or will they only reduce the insurance industry's financial liability from natural disasters?
3. The two authors utilize almost completely different sources and disagree on the basic facts. Among those sources used, which are the most persuasive? What important and useful sources could they have used to find agreement on the facts?

Is There Common Ground?

Both authors use some of the same terminology, including the terms "greenhouse gasses" and "global warming." There is little overlap in the datasets used, but there is one source used by both authors: the National Oceanic and Atmospheric Administration. Both do propose ways to reduce emissions of greenhouse gasses and mitigate effects of warming.

Create Central

www.mhhe.com/createcentral

Additional Resources

Charles Fletcher, *Climate Change: What the Science Tells Us* (Wiley, 2013)

Susanne C. Moser and Maxwell T. Boykoff, eds., *Successful Adaption to Climate Change: Linking Science and Policy in a Rapidly Changing World* (Routledge, 2013)

J. D. Neelin, *Climate Change and Climate Modeling* (Cambridge University Press, 2011)

William D. Nordhaus, *The Climate Casino: Risk, Uncertainty, and Economics for a Warming World* (Yale University Press, 2013)

Roy W. Spencer, *The Great Global Warming Blunder: How Mother Nature Fooled the World's Top Climate Scientists* (Encounter Books, 2012)

Internet References . . .

American Enterprise Institute

www.aei.org/policy/energy-and-the-environment/climate-change/

Brookings Institution

www.brookings.edu/research/topics/climate-change

Intergovernmental Panel on Climate Change

www.ipcc.ch

NASA Global Climate Change

climate.nasa.gov

Nature Climate Change

www.nature.com/nclimate/index.html

ISSUE

EXPLORING THE ISSUE

Can U.S. Deficit and Debt Problems Be Solved Without Increases in Taxes?

YES: Chris Edwards, from "Statement before the National Commission on Fiscal Responsibility and Reform" (June 30, 2010)

NO: Robert Greenstein and Jim Horney, from "Statement before the National Commission on Fiscal Responsibility and Reform" (June 30, 2010)

Learning Outcomes

After reading this issue, you will be able to:

- Enumerate the four types of budget-cutting reforms set forth by Edwards.
- Identify the "big three entitlements."
- Explain the embodiment of federalism in the Tenth Amendment.
- Give a profile of the purpose and practices of the Center on Budget and Policy Priorities.
- Discuss the merits and detriments of imposing tax hikes to address the deficit.

ISSUE SUMMARY

YES: Chris Edwards, the director of tax policy at the Cato Institute, believes that "unless massive deficit spending is reduced, the nation is headed for fiscal calamity." He proposes four types of reform that will make significant cuts in government spending. These include the restructuring of entitlements and the elimination of unneeded programs.

NO: Robert Greenstein, the executive director of the Center on Budget and Policy Priorities, and Jim Horney, the director of federal fiscal policy at the Center on Budget and Policy Priorities, believe that deficits need to be reduced and this requires tax increases as well as spending cuts. They support increases in corporate taxes and taxes on high-income taxpayers. They suggest that tax increases on taxpayers with incomes less than $250,000 per year will also be necessary.

The Full Employment and Balanced Growth Act of 1978 lists a number of economic goals for the U.S. federal government. Besides the familiar objectives of full employment, price stability, and increased real income, the act specifically mentions the goal of a balanced federal budget. This means that the government is to collect in taxes an amount equal to its expenditures. Despite this legislative call to action, the government has, with few exceptions, failed to balance its budget.

What is of concern today is not so much the fact of a U.S. federal government budget deficit but its size. Between fiscal years 2007 and 2010 the deficit increased from $161 billion to an estimated $1,556 billion, from 1.2 percent of Gross Domestic Product (GDP) to 10.6 percent (see Tables B-78 to B-89 in the *2010 Economic Report of the President*). No matter how they are measured, the current deficits are the largest since World War II. Of course,

every dollar of deficit means a dollar increase in debt. For fiscal year 2010, the gross federal debt stood at an estimated $13,787 billion or about 99 percent of GDP. The dollar size of the current debt is, of course, the largest ever while the relative size of the debt is the largest since the end of World War II.

Why did the deficit increase so dramatically between 2007 and 2010? The Great Recession as well as the federal government's efforts to improve economic conditions explain most of this change. Consider first the decline in economic activity. This will decrease government revenues (when incomes fall, income tax collections decrease) and increase government expenditures (persons who become unemployed and are eligible will now receive unemployment compensation). But as the financial crisis and the recession unfolded, the U.S. federal government took action. One action taken late in 2008 by the Bush administration was the Emergency Economic Stabilization Act that included the Troubled Assets Relief Program, which authorized outlays of $700 billion (much of the assistance provided to financial institutions was to be recovered over time). Another action taken in early 2009 by the Obama administration was the American Recovery and Reinvestment Act; this action involved a combination of tax cuts and spending changes that approximated $800 billion (see Issue 9 in this volume).

Why the deficits and the debt problems for the U.S. economy? With respect to the deficits, the standard argument is that government borrowing increases the demand for loanable funds and raises interest rates. This, in turn, makes private borrowing more expensive and reduces growth-enhancing investment. A second argument is that to the extent the Federal Reserve monetizes government borrowing and the money supply increases, it is inflationary. As for the problems caused by the debt, there is great concern regarding the income redistribution: taxes must be collected and then paid as interest to the holders of the debt. This is particularly notable when foreign companies, foreign individuals, and foreign governments (mainly foreign central banks) own significant amounts of the debt. In June 2010, the total public debt was estimated at $13,202 billion with foreign and international holdings

estimated at $4,005 billion; that is, approximately one third of the U.S. federal government's debt is held abroad (see *U.S. Treasury Bulletin* available at http://www.fms.treas.gov/bulletin/index.html). Thus, income is taken from Americans, reducing their ability to purchase goods and services, and transferred abroad. Another drawback of extensive foreign holdings of U.S. federal government debt is a loss of political and economic independence. For example, many are worried that China may be able to influence U.S. policy by threatening to sell its substantial holdings of U.S. securities.

Almost everyone agrees that the United States would be better off if it were able to reduce its deficit and eventually its debt, especially after the economy returns to more prosperous conditions. The disagreement is over how deficit reduction should be achieved. For this reason, President Obama established the National Commission on Fiscal Responsibility and Reform. The conservative position favors deficit reduction through spending cuts. Chris Edwards outlines just such an approach. The liberal approach generally favors deficit reduction through tax increases, especially increased taxes on persons with high incomes. Greenstein and Horney include such actions, along with tax increases on persons with lower incomes, in their plan.

YES

Chris Edwards

Statement before the National Commission on Fiscal Responsibility and Reform

Unless today's massive deficit spending is reduced, the nation is headed for a fiscal calamity. The freedom and prosperity of young people will be crushed by debt piling up at over $1 trillion a year.

Both parties are responsible for the deep fiscal hole we are in. The last president presided over the fastest annual average real growth in federal spending since Lyndon Johnson.[1] The current president has embraced shortsighted and dangerous Keynesian economic theories, which favor large deficit spending.

Policymakers need to reverse course and begin cutting the budget to stop the massive flow of red ink. Cato is building the website www.downsizinggovernment.org to describe ways to cut spending in every federal department.

There are four types of reform we should pursue in cutting the budget: restructuring the big three entitlements, terminating unneeded programs, reviving federalism, and privatization. This testimony provides examples of each type of reform.

Restructuring the Big Three Entitlements

There are straightforward ways to slow the growth of Social Security, Medicare, and Medicaid. For Social Security, initial benefits could be indexed to the growth in general prices, not wages, as under current law. If we were to make that change, it would reduce Social Security spending by roughly $60 billion annually by 2020 and rising amounts after that. That reform would encourage younger Americans to increase their personal savings, which would be beneficial for the nation's economic growth. Congress could support such a policy change with pro-savings reforms to the tax code.

For Medicaid, a simple and dramatic reform would be to convert the program into a block grant for the states. Block granting was the successful approach taken with federal welfare reform in 1996. A block grant would encourage the states to trim their Medicaid programs, combat fraud and abuse, and pursue cost-effective health care solutions. Turning Medicaid into a block grant and freezing spending at the 2011 level would save federal taxpayers about $190 billion annually by 2020.

For Medicare, I like the approach developed by Rep. Paul Ryan (R-WI) to fund elderly health care by way of vouchers.[2] The Ryan plan would provide retirees with a voucher averaging $11,000, which would be adjusted based on age, health status, and income level. The voucher would grow in value over time based on the blended growth rate of general inflation and medical inflation. That would restrain Medicare's growth compared to the baseline and generate large savings over time. The reform would help reduce waste and fraud in Medicare, while creating a range of incentives to improve efficiency and quality in the overall health care system.

Terminating Unneeded Programs

The Cato website www.downsizinggovernment.org lists dozens of major programs that should be terminated, including business subsidies, housing subsidies, energy subsidies, and other inefficient hand-outs. One high-priority area for cuts is agricultural subsidies.

The extensive federal welfare system for farm businesses is costly to taxpayers and it distorts the economy.[3] Subsidies induce farmers to overproduce, which pushes down prices and creates political demands for further subsidies. Subsidies inflate land prices in rural America, and they can damage the environment and harm our international trade relations. The flow of federal subsidies also hinders farmers from innovating, cutting costs, diversifying their land use, and taking other actions needed to prosper in the global economy.

Farm subsidy programs effectively tax average families to fund a small group of well-off farm businesses. The largest 10 percent of recipients receive about 72 percent of all subsidy payments.[4] Furthermore, federal data for 2007 show that the average income of farm households was $86,223, or 28 percent higher than the $67,609 average of all U.S. households.[5] We should end this welfare program for the well-to-do and save about $30 billion annually.

Reviving Federalism

Under the Constitution, the federal government was assigned specific limited powers and most government functions were left to the states. The Tenth Amendment to the Constitution embodies federalism, the idea that federal and state governments have separate areas of activity and that federal responsibilities were "few and defined," as James Madison noted.

Edwards, Chris. U.S. Senate, June 30, 2010.

Unfortunately, policymakers and the courts have mainly discarded federalism in recent decades.[6] Congress has undertaken many activities that should be reserved to the states and the private sector. Grants-in-aid are a primary mechanism that the federal government has used to extend its power into state and local affairs. Grants are subsidy programs that are combined with federal regulatory controls to micromanage state and local activities.

The number of different federal grant-in-aid programs for the states soared from 463 in 1990 to more than 800 today.[7] The federal government spends more than $500 billion annually on aid to the states. State aid programs are notoriously bureaucratic and inefficient, and they stifle local innovation. Furthermore, by involving all levels of government in just about every area of policy, the federal aid system creates a lack of government accountability.

The federal government should start shedding properly state and local activities. A good place to start would be the Department of Education.[8] The department funds about 150 different subsidy programs, which come with an array of regulations that extend federal control over local schools, as under the No Child Left Behind law.[9]

Despite an enormous increase in federal K-12 spending in recent decades, national academic performance has generally not improved. Math and reading scores have been largely flat, graduation rates have stagnated, and researchers have found serious shortcomings with many federal education programs.

Having quality K-12 education is a concern of most Americans, but that does not justify having a federal Department of Education. Canada provides an interesting comparison. It is a high-income nation with an advanced economy, yet it has no federal department of education. Public education in Canada is the sole concern of provincial and local governments. That decentralized approach has resulted in experimentation and innovation, including school vouchers and charter schools. International achievement data suggest that Canadian students generally outperform U.S. students in reading, math, and science.[10]

The states need to recognize that federal aid is ultimately funded by the taxpayers who live in the 50 states, and thus it provides no free lunch. There is no important policy reason for the federal government to be involved in K-12 education and other local activities. Ending federal K-12 education spending would save about $60 billion annually.

Privatization

Governments on every continent have sold off state-owned assets to private investors in recent decades.[11] Airports, railroads, and many other assets have been privatized. The U.S. government privatized some activities during the 1980s and 1990s, but we lag behind other nations in realizing the potential of this type of reform.

Germany and the Netherlands, for example, have privatized their postal services, while Chile, Australia, and other nations have privatized their Social Security systems.

The Department of Transportation is a good target for privatization reforms.[12] Rising federal control over transportation has resulted in the political misallocation of funds, bureaucratic mismanagement, and costly one-size-fits-all regulations on the states. The solution is to devolve DOT activities back to state governments and the private sector.

The federal government should end highway aid, and the states should seek private funding for their highways. Virginia is adding toll lanes on the Capital Beltway, which are partly privately financed, and that state is also home to the Dulles Greenway, a 14-mile private highway in operation since 1995. Ending federal highway aid would accelerate the trend toward such innovative projects.

The federal government should end subsidies to Amtrak and high-speed rail. Amtrak has a poor on-time record, its infrastructure is in bad shape, and it carries only a tiny fraction of intercity passengers. Politicians prevent Amtrak from making cost-effective decisions regarding its routes, workforce polices, and capital investments. Amtrak should be privatized to save money and give the firm flexibility to operate efficiently. As for high-speed rail, even in countries such as Japan and France virtually all high-speed rail lines are money losers, and they carry only a small fraction of intercity passengers.

The federal government should end aid to airports, which are owned by state and local governments. State and local governments should be encouraged to privatize their airports and have them operate without subsidies. In recent decades, many airports have been partly or fully privatized in major cities such as Amsterdam, Auckland, Frankfurt, London, Melbourne, Sydney, and Vienna.

Finally, the air traffic control system should be privatized. The Federal Aviation Administration has a poor record in implementing new technologies in a timely and cost-effective manner. Many nations have moved toward a commercialized ATC structure, and the results have been very positive. Canada privatized its ATC system in 1996 in the form of a nonprofit corporation, NavCanada, which has a very good record on safety and innovation.

Conclusions

To some policymakers, the sorts of cuts discussed here will seem drastic. But rising debt will eventually force policymakers to make radical budget changes whether they like it or not. However, it would be better to make needed reforms now before the federal government's debt grows even larger.

Policymakers may hesitate to make budget reforms because of concerns regarding possible negative effects. But experience shows that we usually underestimate the ability of individuals and communities to adjust after the withdrawal of government subsidies. Before the 1996 welfare reform, for example, opponents in Congress made apocalyptical warnings about the supposed harm that would come to low-income families. Yet the 1996 welfare reform turned out to be a huge success, as most policy-makers now concede.

Other nations have made dramatic fiscal reforms, and they emerged stronger for it. New Zealand, for example, ended virtually all its farm subsidies in 1984, which was a bold stroke because the country is far more dependent on farming than the United States.[13] The changes were initially met with resistance, but New Zealand farm productivity, profitability, and output have soared since the reforms.[14] New Zealand's farmers have cut costs, diversified their land use, and developed new markets.

Another example is Canada, which allowed government spending to soar to 53 percent of gross domestic product in the early 1990s. The high spending in turn caused government debt to jump to more than 70 percent of GDP. But policymakers changed course and undertook dramatic reforms, which caused government spending and debt to fall rapidly.[15] The Canadian government cut programs, privatized assets, consistently balanced its budget, and began to pre-fund its retirement system.

There is no reason why America can't undertake similar reforms. Budget cuts would strengthen the U.S. economy and expand personal freedom to everyone's benefit. America became so prosperous because of our system of limited and decentralized government—not because of federal subsidy programs.

References

1. www.cato-at-liberty.org/2009/12/19/george-w-bush -biggest-spender-since-lbj.
2. Rep. Paul Ryan (R-WI), House Committee on the Budget, "A Roadmap for America's Future, Version 2.0," January 2010.
3. www.downsizinggovernment.org/agriculture/subsidies.
4. Environmental Working Group, Farm Subsidy Database, www.ewg.org/farm. This is a nine-year average, 1995 to 2003.
5. www.ers.usda.gov/briefing/wellbeing/farmhouse income.htm.
6. www.downsizinggovernment.org/fiscal-federalism.
7. Chris Edwards, "Federal Aid to the States: Historical Cause of Government Growth and Bureaucracy," Cato Institute Policy Analysis no. 593, May 22, 2007.
8. www.downsizinggovernment.org/education /k-12-subsidies.
9. Chris Edwards, "Number of Federal Subsidy Programs Tops 1,800," Cato Institute Tax and Budget Bulletin no. 56, April 2009.
10. The 2006 Progress in International Reading Literacy Study included five Canadian provinces, and four outperformed the United States. The 2006 Program for International Student Assessment tested Canadians as a whole, and the nation finished ahead of the United States in science, reading, and mathematics.
11. www.downsizinggovernment.org/privatization.
12. www.downsizinggovernment.org/transportation.
13. Chris Edwards and Tad DeHaven, "Save the Farms—End the Subsidies," op-ed, *Washington Post*, March 3, 2002.
14. Vaudine England, "Shorn of Subsidies, New Zealand Farmers Thrive," *International Herald Tribune*, July 2, 2005.
15. Chris Edwards, Jason Clemens, and Niels Veldhuis, "Great Right North," *Washington Post*, May 17, 2009.

CHRIS EDWARDS is the director of tax policy at the Cato Institute. Before joining the Cato Institute, he served as a senior economist on the congressional Joint Economic Committee and as an economist with the Tax Foundation. He holds both BS and MA degrees in economics.

**Robert Greenstein
and Jim Horney**

➜ **NO**

Statement before the National Commission on Fiscal Responsibility and Reform

The Center on Budget and Policy Priorities is a nonpartisan research and policy institute that focuses both on fiscal policy and on programs and policies of particular importance to low- and moderate-income Americans. We have long argued that the federal budget is on an unsustainable path under current policies—we are among the few policy institutes that regularly develop and issue long-term budget projections—and have for some time urged lawmakers to begin taking the steps necessary to deal with the problem.

So we salute the President for establishing this commission to develop a plan to improve the medium- and longer-term budget outlook. We would like to make a few suggestions about important matters for you to keep in mind as you move forward in this process.

First, we think that the President's emphasis on the goal of stabilizing the ratio of debt held by the public to Gross Domestic Product around the middle of this decade is the right goal. Achieving that goal—which under current projections could be achieved if deficits are reduced to about three percent of GDP—would be a major accomplishment. It would send an important message to the American public and world financial markets that policymakers are serious about getting our fiscal house in order. However, putting in place policies that would achieve that goal by 2015 may prove extremely difficult for several reasons.

In addition, we would urge the Commission to keep in mind the President's recent admonition against too much fiscal restraint while the recovery is still fragile and unemployment remains so high. It would not be wise to have significant fiscal retrenchment take effect in the next couple of years. To the contrary, the economy now badly needs the federal government to extend measures such as extended unemployment benefits and state fiscal relief; failure to do so will further weaken the economy and *delay* the point at which serious fiscal consideration measures can safely be instituted. This reality, combined with the usual desirability (for both policy and political reasons) of phasing in program cuts and tax increases, may make it difficult to achieve sufficient deficit reduction to hit the target by as early as 2015. Doing so may require a few additional years.

Furthermore, even aside from the problem of what year to start phasing in savings—which will depend upon the nature and pace of the recovery—it is likely to be very hard to get substantial savings by 2015 in the three biggest federal programs. In the long run, it will prove impossible to put the budget on a sustainable path if we do not significantly reduce the rate of growth of Medicare and Medicaid. (Let me note that we think the only way to do that in a sensible fashion is to slow the rate of growth of per-person health care costs systemwide—that is, to slow cost growth in privately funded care as well as publicly funded care.) But the recently enacted health reform legislation included almost every measure for Medicare savings that health experts have agreed makes sense at this time; for instance, most of the proposals that MedPac—the Medicare Payment Advisory Commission—had been proposing for years were adopted as part of health reform. That legislation also included many significant provisions—research projects, pilot programs, and experiments in alternative methods or organizing and paying for health care—that should help inform policymakers about further changes in the health care system that could slow the rate of growth of health care costs in coming decades. As the results of these studies become available, further changes must be made in the health care system to slow the rate of cost growth. But we won't have these results in time to secure significant savings by 2015, and as a result, it is hard to see how significant savings in Medicare can be achieved in time to help hit a 2015 deficit target.

Similarly, it is hard to see how savings in Social Security could make a significant contribution to deficit reduction by 2015. Unlike some others, we believe there are good reasons why the commission could consider policy changes that would strengthen the finances of Social Security, and in so doing, also improve the long-term outlook for the budget as a whole. But under any sensible approach, such changes would likely be phased in slowly (there is wide agreement that it would be inappropriate to make changes that would significantly affect people who are either currently collecting benefits or are about to become eligible for the program). That means changes in Social Security will not provide significant savings by 2015.

Certainly, it should be possible to find some savings by 2015 in some other mandatory programs and in discretionary programs. But without significant savings from Medicare and Social Security, there is a limit on how big program savings will be.

Greenstein, Robert and Horney, Jim. U.S. Senate, June 30, 2010.

This means that to hit a 3-percent-of-GDP target by 2015, increases in revenues almost certainly will have to account for a considerably larger share of the total deficit reduction in 2015 than in the longer run, when the savings from health care, and to a lesser degree Social Security, will grow. That would not represent unreasonable policy. But you are constrained by the need to reach agreement within the commission and the desire to submit a proposal that has a chance to be enacted by the current Congress. It likely will be hard to get agreement if increases in revenues account for a significant majority of the proposed savings in 2015. If that turns out to be the case, we believe that—rather than trying to make deeper cuts by 2015 in Medicare, Social Security, or other programs (which probably also would make it impossible for the Commission to agree to a plan that could be enacted) or giving up on reaching agreement among commissioners—you should be willing to move the 3 percent of GDP target back if you need to. It would be far preferable to propose a balanced and politically feasible plan to stabilize the debt starting in 2017 or 2018 than to reach a deadlock in your deliberations or adopt a plan with big program cuts that would be very harmful if enacted and likely would be unacceptable on Capitol Hill in any case. Stabilizing the debt within a few years after 2015 would still represent a tremendous accomplishment that signals seriousness about getting deficits and debt under control. Once policies have been put in place to accomplish that goal, policymakers could begin to consider further efforts to ensure that deficits do not start growing again in subsequent years and, perhaps, achieve reductions in the size of the debt relative to the economy.

As I noted earlier, such efforts will have to include steps to slow the rate of growth of health care costs. Given that the only way to achieve significant savings in Medicare and Medicaid without undercutting the important role that those programs play in ensuring quality health care for the elderly and poor in this country is to slow the rate of growth of costs systemwide, we strongly supported the excise tax on high-cost employer-provided health insurance plan. We believe that the federal government in the future should take further steps in this direction and should also put in place strong incentives for private health care plans and medical professionals to provide, and consumers to demand, more cost-effective delivery of health care.

In Social Security, we think the plan developed by current OMB Director Peter Orszag (before he became head of CBO and then OMB) and noted MIT economist Peter Diamond provides a good starting point for reform. One element not included in their plan that we would endorse is to change the measure of inflation used in the annual adjustment to Social Security and other program benefits and in the adjustment of various parameters of the tax code to a chained CPI. Many analysts believe the chained CPI is a more accurate indicator of inflation than the regular CPI. We believe strongly that the savings from

this step should be devoted to deficit reduction, not to offset the costs of tax cuts or program increases (except that a small amount of the savings should be devoted to providing some relief for lower-income Social Security and SSI beneficiaries who live to age 80 or thereabouts, as they already face a struggle to get by on currently promised benefits and would be impacted by the chained CPI).

We also would note that Social Security benefits are much more modest than many people realize. The average Social Security retirement benefit is now only $1,170 a month, or about $14,000 a year. Social Security checks now replace about *39 percent* of an average worker's pre-retirement wages—significantly less than similar programs in most other Western countries. And because of the currently scheduled increase in the normal retirement age and the projected rise in Medicare premiums (which are deducted from Social Security checks), that figure will gradually fall from 39 percent to about 32 percent over the next two decades, under current law.

Over 90 percent of the aged receive Social Security, and on average it accounts for nearly two-thirds of their income. It provides over 90 percent of income for nearly one-third of its beneficiaries. In considering changes in Social Security, policymakers should keep these realities in mind.

We believe that an increase in revenues also is an essential part of any package to put the budget on a sustainable path. As I already mentioned, we believe increased revenues will have to represent the major share of savings needed to get the deficit down to three percent of GDP in this decade, and they will need to make a substantial contribution to the required long-term deficit reduction as well.

Revenues can be increased to levels significantly above the historical average without harming the economy if the revenue-raising procedures are well designed. The average level of total taxes raised in other developed countries relative to the size of the economy is significantly higher than in the United States (taking taxes at all levels of government into account) without discernible negative effects on their economies. If we are careful about the way we raise revenues—for instance, by curbing tax expenditures (which Alan Greenspan once termed "tax entitlements") that encourage the inefficient allocation of resources—we can raise revenues without sacrificing economic growth. In the case of corporate income taxes in particular, claims that the tax burden on American firms in general is too high and makes those firms less competitive are misguided. It is true that the top *statutory* tax rate on corporate income in this country is higher than in most other developed countries. But because a host of special tax preferences reduce the size of our corporate tax base more than in other large developed economies, the total amount of revenues raised from corporate taxes relative to GDP or corporate income (i.e., the average effective tax rate on corporate income) is not out of line with the rates in other countries. With sensible base broadening, we can reduce the inequities and inefficiencies in the corporate income tax code, lower the top corporate rate, boost competitiveness, and raise somewhat more revenues. We certainly should *not* take steps that would reduce the amount of corporate taxes collected.

We believe that high-income taxpayers in this country should pay higher taxes than they are paying now. The first step is certainly to allow the 2001 and 2003 tax cuts for high-income taxpayers to expire as scheduled. While further steps should be taken to raise revenues from the most well-off Americans (particularly by curbing inefficient tax expenditures), we do not believe it will be possible to raise the revenues needed to fund the benefits and services that Americans will expect and demand in coming decades if we protect all taxpayers with income below $250,000 a year from any tax increase.

Finally, in developing a proposal to reduce the deficit, the Commission should take special care to protect the most vulnerable people in this country. The Commission should strive to ensure that the policies it proposes taken together, would not push more Americans into poverty or make those already in poverty worse off. The big deficit reduction packages enacted in 1990 and 1993 succeeded on this front—they avoided harming those at the bottom of the income spectrum. In fact, those packages contained provisions that improved the situation of some of the most

vulnerable people in the country and thereby reduced deficits and poverty at the same time. We would encourage you to do as the negotiators of the 1990 budget agreement did and request from the Congressional Budget Office a distributional analysis that would show the overall impact on Americans, by income category, of the major elements of any package of proposals you are seriously considering. Such analyses will help you to develop proposals that can achieve the necessary fiscal retrenchment without making struggling low-income families and individuals worse off.

ROBERT GREENSTEIN is the founder and executive director of the Center on Budget and Policy Priorities. He has also served as the administrator of the Food and Nutrition Services at the U.S. Department of Agriculture. He received a MacArthur Fellowship in 1996 and the Heinz Award in Public Service in 2008. He is a graduate of Harvard College.

JIM HORNEY is the director of federal fiscal policy at the Center on Budget and Policy Priorities. He has also served as the deputy democratic staff director at the Senate Budget Committee and as the chief of the projections unit in the budget analysis division of the Congressional Budget Office. He holds a PhD in government and politics from the University of Maryland.

EXPLORING THE ISSUE

Can U.S. Deficit and Debt Problems Be Solved Without Increases in Taxes?

Critical Thinking and Reflection

1. Of the four reforms suggested by Edwards, which would spawn the least objection? Explain.
2. How reasonable is it to project that younger Americans would be encouraged to increase their personal savings if Social Security spending were reduced? Why?
3. Describe in practical terms how Republican Paul Ryan's voucher approach would affect Medicare recipients.
4. Give a brief analysis of the ramifications of immediate debt stabilization tactics versus a plan to start stabilizing in 2017 or 2018.

Is There Common Ground?

The one bridge that seems to traverse the common territory of this debate is the simple fact that the current U.S. deficit is significantly large and thus unhealthy. Also, it is not the intention of either side to say that this is the doing of any one party or president. The history on that speaks for itself, so the contest of views really begins and ends with the policies and practices involved with deficit spending—in other words, how should taxation be factored into the debt-resolution equation?

That is the hot-button question that divides parties, principles, and perspectives. With Edwards coming in with strong reasons not to increase taxes, in an immediate application, and Greenstein and Horney coming in with equally strong reasons in favor of a longer-term process that would rely on an increase in certain taxes (such as corporate), the bridge becomes quite tenuous indeed.

Create Central

www.mhhe.com/createcentral

Additional Resources

Edwards, Chris, *Downsizing the Federal Government* (Cato Institute, 2005)

Ippolito, Dennis, S., *Deficits, Debt, and the New Politics of Tax Policy* (Cambridge University Press, 2013)

Newton, David B., ed., *Crisis of Confidence: How Federal Taxes, Deficits, Debt, and Entitlements Threaten the American Private Sector* (Free Market Press, 2012)

Internet References . . .

Cato Institute: "Spending Freezes in History"

www.cato.org/publications/commentary/spending -freezes-history

Center on Budget and Policy Priorities: "Size and Reach of Federal Government Are Not Exploding"

www.cbpp.org/cms/index.cfm?fa=view&id=3696

Christian Science Monitor: "US Budget Deficit: Finding Solutions"

www.csmonitor.com/USA/2010/0224/US-budget -deficit-Finding-solutions

ISSUE

Is China's Currency Undervalued, and Should the United States Take Action to Correct This Undervaluation?

YES: Jack W. Shilling, from "Testimony before the U.S. Senate Banking, Housing, and Urban Affairs Committee, Subcommittee on Economic Policy" (April 22, 2010)

NO: Daniel J. Ikenson, from "Testimony before the U.S. Senate Banking, Housing, and Urban Affairs Committee, Subcommittee on Economic Policy" (April 22, 2010)

Learning Outcomes

After reading this issue, you will be able to:

- Enumerate the seven factors that come into play when a supplier and a customer enter a purchasing agreement.
- Assess the applicability of the formula "import value = price × quantity."
- Describe GOES (grain-oriented electrical steel) and discuss it as a trade commodity.

ISSUE SUMMARY

YES: Jack W. Shilling, the executive vice president and chief technical officer, Alleghany Technologies, and the chairman, Specialty Steel Industry of North America, argues that China has intervened in foreign exchange markets to keep its currency undervalued. Since this is "undermining U.S. competitiveness," he believes the United States should impose countervailing or antidumping duties on imports from China.

NO: Daniel J. Ikenson, the associate director of Cato Institute's Center for Trade Policy Studies, claims that there is only a weak relationship between China's undervalued currency and the U.S. trade deficit with China, on the one hand, and between the trade deficit and U.S. job losses, on the other. Rather than threatening China with sanctions, the United States should "allow China to appreciate its currency at its own pace."

A country that chooses to fix (peg) the value of its currency to another currency or a basket of currencies—China pegs its currency to the U.S. dollar—has to defend its official exchange rate by buying or selling its currency as needed. For example, a country with a trade surplus vis-à-vis another country faces an excess supply of the foreign currency that threatens an appreciation of its own currency unless it buys the excess foreign currency with an equivalent amount of its own currency. Other things being equal, a country that persistently acts to prevent its currency from appreciating accumulates foreign currency reserves. A country with a chronic imbalance of its balance of payments can rectify this by a change in its official exchange rate, that is, by a currency revaluation to correct a surplus, or by a devaluation to counteract a payments deficit.

An undervalued currency helps the country's export sector and makes imports to the country more expensive.

Economic theory shows that free trade based on comparative advantage leads to an increase in national welfare as productivity and levels of output, income, and consumption rise. Comparative advantage, however, may diverge from competitive advantage when money wages, money prices, and exchange rates are not priced correctly and so do not reflect economic values. Arguments for protection are familiar: job protection, protection from cheap foreign labor, "fairness" or a leveling of the playing field, national security, and so forth.

The U.S. Treasury reports twice a year to Congress on International Economic and Exchange Rate Policies as required by the Omnibus Trade and Competitiveness Act of 1988. Under Section 3004 of the Act, the Treasury must consider "whether countries manipulate the rate of exchange between their currency and the U.S. dollar for purposes of preventing effective balance of payments adjustments or gaining unfair competitive advantage in international trade." The Treasury's first report for 2010 was due on April 15, 2010. On March 24, the House Ways and Means Committee held a hearing to consider the impact of China's exchange rate policy on the United States and global economic recoveries (specifically on U.S. job creation), and the steps that could be taken to address the issue. In his opening statement, Chairman Sander M. Levin (D-MI) noted that the administration had "to decide whether to label China a currency manipulator in [Treasury's] report." To him, "What seems undisputed on this much disputed issue is that China has a persistent economic strategy, a policy, key to which is the pegging of its currency to the dollar at an undervalued rate." On April 3, 2010, Treasury Secretary Geithner announced a delay in the publication of the report in view of the meetings of G-20 finance ministers and central bank governors later that month, the Strategic and Economic Dialogue with China in May, and the G-20 finance ministers and leaders meetings in June—which

he believed "are the best avenue for advancing U.S. interests at this time."

The debate continues, although the Treasury's report released on July 8, 2010, concluded that "no major trading partner of the United States met the standards identified in Section 3004" for manipulating its exchange rate, noting China's announcement on June 9, 2010, that it was ending its peg to the dollar in favor of an exchange rate that was "more market-based." On September 15, 2010, the House Ways and Means Committee held another full committee hearing to determine whether China had made material progress in allowing its currency to appreciate since June and what action might need to be taken by Congress. Treasury Secretary Geithner advised the Committee that in the three months since China's announcement, China allowed the RMB to appreciate by only 1 percent against the dollar and the RMB had *depreciated* against the weighted average of the currencies of its trading partners.

YES

Jack W. Shilling

Testimony before the U.S. Senate Banking, Housing, and Urban Affairs Committee, Subcommittee on Economic Policy

I. To What Extent Is China's Currency Misaligned?

For the past 16 years, China has engaged in the protectionist policy of currency depreciation by effectively pegging the renminbi ("RMB") to the U.S. dollar, and other countries have compounded this problem by undervaluing their currencies in an attempt to remain competitive with China.

There is a broad consensus that the RMB is substantially undervalued. The Peterson Institute estimates that the renminbi remains misaligned by about 25 percent on an overall, real-effective-exchange-rate basis and by about 40 percent relative to the U.S. dollar on a bilateral, real-exchange-rate basis. This 40-percent undervaluation vis-à-vis the U.S. dollar is as large today as it was 6 years ago before a modest revaluation and nominal appreciation of the RMB by China between July 2005 and July 2008. China's intervention in the exchange markets is now approximately \$30–\$40 billion per month, and China's foreign reserves are estimated to be at least \$2.4 trillion and possibly as much as \$3 trillion.[1] These numbers are staggering and contribute to a huge, artificial and competitive advantage for China in various ways.

II. What Effect Does the RMB's Undervalued Misalignment Have on the Trade Deficit and U.S. Employment?

A. Background

The U.S. manufacturing base has been eroding for a long time, while manufacturing capability in China has been increasing dramatically over the same time period. This shift has been well documented by others. The large and growing trade imbalance with China is one confirmation of this situation.

Loss of our domestic manufacturing base presents serious economic and national security problems as documented recently in the President's Framework for Revitalizing American Manufacturing. These problems

include a significant loss of more highly compensated employment opportunities for our citizens. There are many factors affecting the competitiveness of U.S. manufacturers that are far more important than labor rates, which are often cited incorrectly as the reason for this loss of competitiveness.

One of the most important and most easily understood factors undermining U.S. competitiveness is the impact of exchange rates, and particularly the actions of the Chinese government to prevent the RMB from appreciating relative to the U.S. dollar. In order to understand the importance of exchange rates to competitiveness and, therefore, to the U.S. trade imbalance with China and loss of American jobs, it is helpful to understand how products are generally sold and then to apply that knowledge to both imports and exports in various market segments. Some examples are provided below.

B. How Products Are Sold

The following factors come into play when a decision is made by a supplier and a customer to enter into a purchasing agreement: (1) price and its impact on profit margin; (2) availability; (3) supply-chain management issues; (4) quality; (5) product capability; (6) short-and long-term customer–supplier relationships; and (7) strategic considerations. All other things being equal, price becomes the dominant issue where exchange rates have a direct and obvious impact. However, in order to understand a specific purchasing decision, it is often necessary to consider some or all of the other factors just mentioned.

C. Imports from China into the United States

A 40% undervalued RMB has a dramatic impact on imports. When a product made in China is sold in the United States, the invoice is paid in dollars and then converted to RMB in China to pay the Chinese producer. If the Chinese product is sold for \$100 in the United States, approximately 683 RMB are provided to the supplier in China under the current exchange rate between the RMB and the U.S. dollar. If the costs of manufacturing are 500 RMB in China, the Chinese producer's operating profit is 183 RMB.

Shilling, Jack W. U.S. Senate, April 22, 2010.

If, on the other hand, the RMB were allowed to appreciate to market rates, 40% higher in value, only 409 RMB would be generated in China, resulting in an operating loss of 91 RMB. The net result would be an unwillingness by the Chinese producer to export that product to the United States at the original price of $100, and the Chinese producer's export price would rise, making U.S.-origin products more competitive.

Note that the Chinese producer's export price to the United States would not necessarily rise by 40%. The specific price increase would depend upon the degree to which costs could be lowered in China and the minimum profit margin that would be acceptable to the Chinese producer. The Chinese producer's price increase would also depend on some of the other factors mentioned above, such as product availability from U.S. domestic suppliers and strategic considerations, including the ability of the Chinese supplier to decrease prices over time through cost reductions, the Chinese producer's ability to supply other products of interest to the U.S. purchaser, and the perceived long-term importance of the business to the Chinese supplier and U.S. customer.

Importantly, a 40% revaluation of the RMB could have a significant favorable impact on a Chinese producer's costs. A central consideration is the benefit the Chinese producer would realize when purchasing raw materials or energy in U.S. dollars with a more valuable RMB. For instance, over 50% of the value of stainless steel is in inputs such as nickel, chromium, molybdenum, and natural gas that are priced globally based on U.S. dollars. With reference to the previous illustration, if 50% or 250 RMB of the Chinese producer's total costs of 500 RMB were in U.S. dollar commodities, with a 40% revaluation of the RMB the Chinese producer's costs would decrease by 100 RMB to 400 RMB, and the loss of 91 RMB after revaluation of the RMB that was postulated above would become a small operating profit of 9 RMB. Nevertheless, such a large revaluation would still have a substantial, unfavorable effect on profitability even after taking such purchasing benefits into consideration.

To summarize, above all else a long-term, chronic undervaluation of the RMB has led and will always lead to the gradual loss of American manufacturing competitiveness, particularly when the undervaluation is so large. The larger the exchange-rate misalignment, and the longer in time that this misalignment is allowed to persist, the more price will become the determining factor and allow the Chinese producer time to resolve all other issues at least to parity with the U.S. domestic producer. In addition, the longer this misalignment is allowed to persist, the higher the probability is that U.S. competitors will cease to exist when the misalignment is corrected.

D. Exports to China from the United States

The same logic that applies to imports into the United States from China, as discussed above, also applies to exports by the United States to China. In this case, the important issue is how many U.S. dollars a U.S. producer will receive when the U.S. product is sold in China in RMB and the RMB are then converted back into U.S. dollars. If the price in RMB doesn't change and the RMB–U.S.$ exchange rate is allowed to appreciate by 40%, a U.S. producer in the abstract should receive an effective price increase of over 60% in U.S. dollars.[2]

Such a huge revenue increase would be expected to significantly improve U.S. competitiveness and result in U.S. producers quoting on business in China that otherwise would produce inadequate margins. However, it is unlikely that such success would be completely realized. One reason relates to cost reductions that would occur for Chinese producers associated with dollar-denominated purchases of input materials and energy, as discussed above. In addition, it is critically important to the Chinese government that China be able to maintain a large GDP growth rate. If it is assumed that current prices produce acceptable profit margins to Chinese producers, many of whom have significant ownership by the Chinese government, it seems very likely the Chinese government would intervene in the future in some manner other than an undervalued RMB to prevent a significant disruption to the ability of Chinese producers to supply their own market. In other words, price has not been, nor will it be, the only factor considered in purchasing decisions made in China. We can all speculate on how China would accomplish this, but it seems highly likely that following a significant currency realignment, e.g., by 40%, action can and would be taken by the Chinese government to protect China's ability to continue to grow its own GDP and keep its citizens employed.

Because of its impact on jobs and national security, it is my opinion that the impact of Chinese currency manipulation on imports into the United States from China and the resulting inability of U.S. domestic manufacturers to supply their own U.S. market is a much larger problem than a lost opportunity to export products from the United States to China, although both are important.

E. Example 1: Specialty Metals

1. Titanium Condenser Tubing

This is a high-tech product used for seawater cooling in conventional and nuclear power plants. The important issues to understand here are (a) this product is critical to the functioning of these systems and (b) China has not had the capability to supply their own market with acceptable quality product. In situations like this, China has been unable to export product and depends on imports. Pricing relative to Chinese competition has not been a factor, and therefore the exchange rate has not been an issue. Orders are frequently quoted in U.S. dollars, and the currency risk (although there is none if the exchange rate is pegged) is assumed by the purchaser.

However, as China builds this ability over time (as it is attempting to do today), most likely using foreign technology, pricing will become a factor for both imports and exports of this product as discussed above, and exchange rates will become very important. So, as we look to the future, it is very important that we act now to help preserve the technology advantage that currently exists with high-tech products like titanium condenser tubing produced by U.S. manufacturers.

2. Grain-Oriented Electrical Steel ("GOES")

This steel also is a high-tech specialty metal product critical to the efficient distribution of electricity in any advanced or emerging economy. Electrical power is generated in power plants. In order to use this electricity, it must be distributed widely to all sectors of the economy. These distribution systems employ many large transformers, and GOES is critical to their efficient operation.

Ten years ago, the story of GOES in China was much the same as the titanium condenser tubing story. But over the intervening time period, China has added sufficient capacity using foreign technology for the most part so that Chinese producers can now supply their own market. The Chinese government recently implemented antidumping and countervailing duties claiming trade agreement violations by U.S. producers of GOES. The U.S. industry feels these decisions are unjustified and is considering its options.

During the last 5 years or so, imports of this product into the United States from China have not been significant, because China did not have an adequate domestic supply. Exports from U.S. producers to China, however, have occurred because of inadequate supply in China. As China increased capacity over this time period, exchange rate issues became more of a factor. With large import duties now imposed due to China's trade cases against the U.S. producers, exchange rate issues are of significant importance. If and when these duties are removed, exchange rates will remain important to future U.S. exports of GOES to China and will be *critically* important to the ability of U.S. producers of GOES to supply their own domestic market assuming increasing imports into the United States of Chinese product. . . .

F. Example 2: Consumer Products

Gas grilles are an instructive example of how the RMB's enforced undervaluation affects trade between China and the United States in consumer products. Most gas grilles sold in big box stores were developed originally in the United States. But now, virtually all of these products are made in China and imported into the U.S. market.

These gas grilles are sold strictly on the basis of price. Were the exchange rate allowed to appreciate by 40%, it is highly likely that imports from China would be reduced over time as U.S. manufacturers restored capacity allowing significant production to return to the United States. Not only would such a transition benefit the U.S. producers of gas grilles, but a significant benefit would accrue as well to the U.S. domestic manufacturers of gas grilles' component parts and raw materials, such as commodity stainless steel. At the same time, it is unlikely that U.S. exports to China would increase to nearly the same extent for the

reasons discussed above along with the fact that significant Chinese capacity now being used for the U.S. market would need to be diverted to the Chinese market. . . .

III. What Happened When China Allowed the RMB to Appreciate from 2005–2008? Why Did the U.S. Trade Deficit Not Narrow During This Time?

Between July 2005 and July 2008, the Chinese government allowed the RMB to appreciate *nominally* relative to the U.S. dollar by 17.6 percent, from 8.28 RMB/U.S.$1 to the current rate of 6.82 RMB/U.S.$1. During those three years, China's foreign reserves rose from $711 billion to $1.8 trillion, and the U.S. trade deficit and number of jobs lost likewise increased substantially. There are two basic reasons why China gained ground and the United States lost ground despite this appreciation of the RMB during those three years.

First, the time between July 2005 and July 2008 was one in which China's economy was growing rapidly, and China's ability to supply the U.S. market was increasing dramatically, both in terms of manufacturing costs and product capability. Moreover, as seen in the examples above, as Chinese producers have become more self-sufficient there has been less reason for China to import from the United States. Each of these influences contributed to a more pronounced trade deficit by the United States with China. . . .

Second, the RMB's appreciation between July 2005 and July 2008 was in *nominal* terms, but then as now the RMB's undervaluation relative to the U.S. dollar was around 40% on *a bilateral, real-exchange-rate basis*. What was needed then, in other words, was a meaningful revaluation of the RMB in that amount in accordance with *inflation-adjusted, trade-weighted exchange rates*. The same is true today.[3]

IV. If China Were to Allow for a Currency Revaluation, What Is an Appropriate Appreciation? What Tools Should Congress Consider to Remedy This Imbalance? What Are the Multilateral Policy Options?

What is needed is for China to revalue the RMB relative to the U.S. dollar by 40% on *a bilateral, real-exchange-rate basis*. But what should we do if this does not happen in a timely manner? Unfortunately, while the International Monetary Fund for the last five or six years especially has been sounding the alarm about China's undervaluation of the renminbi, the IMF's authority is so limited under its Articles of Agreement that China has been able to block publication of the IMF's 2007, 2008, and 2009 reports on China's currency policy. It is apparent that a strengthening of the multilateral rules on protracted currency depreciation is imperative.

In the absence of unilateral action by China to appropriately revalue its currency, a first step that can be taken by Congress and the Executive Branch against this protectionist practice is to authorize the imposition of countervailing or antidumping duties against imports from any country with a fundamentally undervalued currency. This approach would be a reasonable implementation in U.S. domestic law of the World Trade Organization's provisions, would assist materially injured U.S. industries and workers, would act as a deterrent, and would underscore that protracted currency depreciation will not be tolerated.

V. Conclusions

Currency manipulation by the Chinese government has significantly affected the bilateral trade deficit of the United States with China, primarily through its effect on the levels of imports into the United States from China. From 2002 to 2009, the United States ran a cumulative trade deficit of nearly $5.4 trillion for All Merchandise, including a deficit of almost $1.6 trillion with China. China's share of the U.S. trade deficit in All Merchandise rose from 22 percent in 2002 to 45.3 percent in 2009.[4]

... As the Economic Policy Institute reported in a study last month, the RMB's substantial undervaluation has been a major reason for the United States' imbalanced trade with China, the loss of 1.6 million manufacturing jobs in the United States between 2001 and 2008, and depressed and lower wages for many more millions of U.S. workers.[5]

As devastating to the United States as these trends are, the longer-term prognosis if China persists in its behavior is even more troubling. In addition to further trade deficits and lost jobs, the renminbi's undervalued misalignment is an important factor in making investment in China more attractive and feasible than investment in the United States. It is not necessary or even desirable to stop investment overseas by multinational companies, but it is critical that the protectionist policy of China's enforced undervaluation of the RMB should not be tolerated. If not countered, that policy will increasingly drain the United States of knowledge and expertise, continue to contribute to the demise of its basic manufacturing capability, as well as jobs and revenue, by weakening companies in areas such as the U.S. specialty metals industry, which are constantly developing new technology that has essential applications to the U.S. economy and national defense.

The major benefit associated with China allowing the RMB to appreciate by 40% to market levels, or otherwise mitigating this problem, will be to allow U.S. manufacturers to recapture the U.S. market that has been lost or will be lost to Chinese imports. Less benefit to exports of U.S. products into China is anticipated, because the Chinese government's emphasis on large increases in GDP each year will almost certainly be reflected in other measures that favor Chinese domestic production and sales, thereby compensating in part for any meaningful revaluation of the RMB.

Virtually all segments of the U.S. economy should benefit, but major sectors representing high levels of imports into the United States from China would be advantaged the most. . . .

The importance of this issue, and its potential impact, is directly proportional, or perhaps even geometrically proportional, to the magnitude of the currency misalignment and its remediation. Current estimates of 40% misalignment are enormous in this context. Likewise, token efforts to reduce this misalignment will be generally ineffective.

It is critically important that we act now. Pushing the problem ahead will only produce a bigger problem in the future as U.S. GDP weakens and U.S. manufacturing and technology capability is lost. In the absence of unilateral action by China to appropriately revalue its currency, a first step that can be taken by Congress and the Executive Branch is to authorize the imposition of countervailing or antidumping duties against imports from any country with a fundamentally undervalued currency.

Notes

1. *See* Fair Currency Coalition, "Fact of the Week—China's Record Reserves" (Jan. 26, 2010), *available at*, www.faircurrency.org.
2. If the unit price in China remained at 100 RMB for a U.S. producer's product, for instance, the U.S. producer would receive only U.S.$14.64 at the current exchange rate of 6.83 RMB/U.S.$1, but would receive U.S.$24.45 at the revalued exchange rate of 4.09RMB/U.S.$1, an increase of 67%.
3. Morgan Stanley has said that it expects China will permit the renminbi to appreciate to 6.54 RMB/U.S.$1 by the end of 2010 and to 6.17 RMB/U.S.$1 by the end of 2011. Morgan Stanley, "China Economics—Renminbi Exit from USD Peg: Whether, Why, When, How," at 1 (Apr. 5, 2010). Yet that nominal appreciation from the current rate of 6.83 RMB/U.S.$1 would be only 9.7 percent, about the same pace over the next 21 months as the pace China set between July 2005 and July 2008. That pace of nominal appreciation will be no more effectual than the RMB's nominal appreciation was between July 2005 and July 2008.
4. *See* Fair Currency Coalition, "Fact of the Week—RMB Peg Fuels China Trade Surpluses, Undercuts U.S. Recovery" (Feb. 23, 2010), *available at*, www.faircurrency.org.
5. Robert E. Scott, "Unfair China Trade Costs Local Jobs" (Economic Policy Institute, Mar. 23, 2010).

Jack W. Shilling is the executive vice president, corporate development, and the chief technical officer of Allegheny Technologies, Inc. He is also the vice chairman of a trade association, Specialty Steel Industry of North America. He holds a PhD degree in metallurgical engineering from the University of Pittsburgh.

Daniel J. Ikenson

Testimony before the U.S. Senate Banking, Housing, and Urban Affairs Committee, Subcommittee on Economic Policy

Introduction

Many economists believe that the Renminbi is undervalued, but there is disagreement about the magnitude. Disagreement is to be expected. After all, nobody can know the true value of the RMB unless, and until, it is allowed to float freely and restrictions on China's capital account are removed.[1] Short of that, economists produce estimates of undervaluation—and those estimates vary widely. So that begs a practical question: How will we know when we are there?

That question is important because Congress is once again considering legislation to compel the Chinese government to allow RMB appreciation under the threat of sanction. Regardless of whether sanctions take the form of an across-the-board surcharge or are the product of a countervailing duty investigation or are manifest in exchange rate conversions in antidumping calculations, a precise estimate of the market value of the Renminbi would have to serve as the benchmark. But respected economists from reputable institutions have produced a range of undervaluation of approximately 10 to 40 percent. So what should be the benchmark?

Of course the sanctions approach is fraught with dangers. Not only would it amount to a tax on U.S. producers and consumers—felt particularly acutely by lower- and middle-income families—but it could spark retaliation from China and run afoul of U.S. World Trade Organization obligations at a time when the Obama administration is planning to hold our trade partners more accountable to their own WTO commitments, as part of its National Export Initiative.

Many in Washington blame the undervalued Renminbi for the trade deficit with China, and blame the deficit for U.S. job losses. But those relationships are weak. Before doing something unnecessary or counterproductive, Congress should consider whether, and to what extent, RMB appreciation would even lead to more balanced bilateral trade. Recent evidence casts plenty of doubt.

Laser-Like Focus on the Trade Deficit

For many in Washington, it seems the issue is not that the Chinese currency is undervalued per se, but that the United States has a large bilateral trade deficit with China,

which is popularly attributed to the undervalued RMB.[2] Currency revaluation for many policymakers is just a proxy for reducing the trade deficit to zero—or better still, turning it into a surplus. . . .

What matters for the trade account is *how much* Americans reduce their purchases of Chinese goods and *how much* the Chinese increase their purchases of U.S. goods. Import value equals price times quantity, so if the percent increase in price (appreciation of the RMB) exceeds the percent reduction in quantity of imports consumed (in absolute value), then import value will *increase*. For example, if the RMB appreciates by 25 percent and U.S. consumers reduce consumption of Chinese imports by only 10 percent, then the value of U.S. imports from China will be greater than before (*adding* to the trade deficit). The same 25 percent increase in RMB value, however, should lead to an unequivocal increase in U.S. exports to China because the dollar price charged (the price used to measure U.S. exports) remains the same, while the quantity sold to China increases because Chinese consumers, by virtue of RMB appreciation, face lower relative prices, and demand more goods. Thus, RMB appreciation should unambiguously increase U.S. export value, reducing the trade deficit. But its effect on U.S. import value *is* ambiguous.

Whether the aggregate change in U.S. import and export value results in a lower trade deficit depends on the relative responsiveness (price elasticity) of American and Chinese consumers to the price changes they face. . . . If U.S. consumers are not responsive (they reduce the quantity of their purchases by a smaller percentage than the price increase), then import value will rise and Chinese consumers would have to increase their purchases of American goods by a large enough percentage to offset the increased U.S. import value, if the U.S. trade deficit is to be reduced.[3]

Weak Link Between Currency Values and Trade Flows

Recent evidence suggests that RMB appreciation will not reduce the U.S. trade deficit and undermines the common political argument for compelling China to revalue. Between July 2005 and July 2008, the RMB appreciated by

21 percent against the dollar—from a value of $.1208 to $.1464.[4] During that same period (between the full year 2005 and the full year 2008), the U.S. trade deficit with China increased from $202 to $268 billion. . . .

In 2005—the first year in which there was a slight RMB appreciation—the value of exports increased by $6.8 billion. Exports jumped another $12.5 billion in 2006, a year in which the RMB appreciated by 2.8 percent. But in 2007, despite an even stronger 4.7 percent RMB appreciation, the increase in exports was only $9.3 billion. And in 2008, the RMB appreciated by a substantial 9.5 percent, but the increase in exports fell to $6.8 billion. If currency value were a strong determinant, then export growth should have been much more robust than it was in 2007 and, especially, in 2008. Other factors, such as Chinese incomes and Chinese savings propensities, must have mitigated the lower relative price effects.

On the import side, recent experience is even more troubling for those who seek deficit reduction through currency revaluation. The evidence that an appreciating RMB deters the U.S. consumption of Chinese goods is not very compelling. During the period of a strengthening RMB from 2005 to 2008, U.S. imports from China increased by $94.3 billion, or 38.7 percent. Not only did Americans demonstrate strong price inelasticity, but they actually *increased* their purchases of Chinese imports. One reason for continued U.S. consumption of Chinese goods despite the relative price increase is that there may be a shortage of substitutes in the U.S. market for Chinese-made goods. In some cases, there are no domestically produced alternatives.[5] . . .

It is doubtful that members of Congress, who support action to compel Chinese currency appreciation, would proudly announce to their constituents that they intentionally reduced their real incomes. But that is the effect of relative dollar depreciation.

Globalization Mutes the Effect of Currency Changes

Something else is evident about the relationship from those 2005 to 2008 data. The fact that a 21 percent increase in the value of the RMB was met with a 38.7 percent increase in import value means that the quantity of Chinese imports demanded after the price change increased by nearly 15 percent.[6] Higher prices being met with greater demand would seem to defy the law of demand.

Chinese exporters must have lowered their RMB-denominated prices to keep their export prices steady. That would have been a completely rational response, enabled by the fact that RMB appreciation reduces the cost of production for Chinese exporters—particularly those who rely on imported raw materials and components. According to a growing body of research, somewhere between one-third and one-half of the value of U.S. imports from China is actually Chinese value-added.[7] . . .

RMB appreciation not only bolsters the buying power of Chinese consumers, but it makes China-based producers and assemblers even more competitive because the relative prices of their imported inputs fall, reducing their costs of production. That reduction in cost can be passed on to foreign consumers in the form of lower export prices, which could mitigate entirely the effect desired by Congress, which is to reduce U.S. imports from China. That process might very well explain what happened between 2005 and 2008, and is probably a reasonable indication of what to expect going forward.

A 2006 Cato paper on the topic of exchange rates and trade flows found that despite considerable dollar depreciation between 2002 and 2005 against the Canadian dollar, the [e]uro, the Japanese yen, the Korean won, and the Brazilian real, the U.S. trade deficit expanded during that period with Canada, Europe, Japan, Korea, and Brazil.[8] Factors other than currency movements, such as income and the availability of substitutes, influence trade flows, particularly when exporters are willing to absorb the costs of those currency changes.

In a recently published paper from the U.S. International Trade Commission, economist Cathy L. Jabara observes a weak relationship between exchange rates and U.S. import prices, particularly with respect to imports from Asia. Exchange rate pass-through is quite low because exporters often "price to market" to absorb costs and maintain market share. She notes that the economic literature supports her findings of low exchange rate pass-through, particularly for consumer goods. Ironically, she also notes that economist Paul Krugman, who is among the most outspoken advocates of U.S. intervention on the currency issue, was one of the first to explore and describe the potential for exchange-rate pass-through to mitigate the impacts on trade flows.[9]

Economic Benefits

Although it may be fashionable to think of China as the country to which the U.S. manufacturing sector was offshored in exchange for tainted products and a mountain of mortgage debt, the fact is that the bilateral relationship has produced enormous benefits for people in both countries, including most Americans. China is America's third-largest export market, and has been our fastest-growing market for a decade, providing 20.2 percent annual sales growth for U.S. businesses between 2000 and 2008, when overall annual export growth to all countries stood at just 6.8 percent.[10]

American businesses, portfolio investors, and 401(k) participants also have benefited handsomely from China's high rate of sustained economic growth. Likewise, American consumers have benefited from their access to Chinese goods. Imports from China have helped keep prices in check, raising real incomes and easing the strain on family budgets.

What is perhaps less well known—because they are often portrayed as victims—is that large numbers of American producers and workers benefit from the bilateral relationship, as well. This is the case because the U.S.

economy and the Chinese economy are highly comple-mentary. U.S. factories and workers are more likely to be collaborating with Chinese factories and workers in production of the same goods than they are to be com-peting directly. . . .

Though the focus is typically on American workers who are displaced by competition from China, legions of American workers and their factories, offices, and labora-tories would be idled without access to complementary Chinese workers in Chinese factories. Without access to lower-cost labor in places like Shenzhen, countless ideas hatched in U.S. laboratories—which became viable com-mercial products that support hundreds of thousands of jobs in engineering, design, marketing, logistics, retail-ing, finance, accounting, and manufacturing—might never have made it beyond conception because the costs of production would have been deemed prohibitive for mass consumption. Just imagine if all of the compo-nents in the Apple iPod had to be manufactured and assembled in the United States. Instead of $150 per unit, the cost of production might be multiple times that amount.[11] . . .

The *Atlantic*'s James Fallows characterizes the com-plementarity of U.S. and Chinese production sharing as following the shape of a "Smiley Curve" plotted on a chart where the production process from start to fin-ish is measured along the horizontal axis and the value of each stage of production is measured on the verti-cal axis. U.S. value-added comes at the early stages—in branding, product conception, engineering, and design. Chinese value-added operations occupy the middle stages—some engineering, some manufacturing and assembly, primarily. And more U.S. value-added occurs at the end stages in logistics, retailing, and after-market servicing.[12] Under this typical production arrangement, collaboration, not competition, is what links U.S. and Chinese workers.

Economic Frictions

Despite the enormous benefits of the bilateral relation-ship, Americans are more likely to be familiar with the sources of friction. Americans have heard that under-handed Chinese policies have had a deleterious impact on U.S. manufacturing. They have been told that China manipulates its currency to secure an unfair trade advan-tage; "illegally" dumps and sells government-subsidized products in U.S. markets; maintains policies that discrimi-nate against imports and favor domestic industries; steals American intellectual property; treats its workers poorly; degrades the environment; sells us tainted products; and even caused the U.S. financial crisis by lending America too much money.[13] There is some truth in some of those claims. But there is also a good deal of exaggeration, mis-information, and hypocrisy in them. Some ring hollow because the U.S. government—usually at the behest of the same interests clamoring for action against China—commits the same sins.

Manufacturing the Myth of Decline[14]

Nefarious Chinese trade practices are often blamed for the decline of U.S. manufacturing. But the first problem with that presumption of causation is that U.S. manufactur-ing is simply not in decline. Until the onset of the recent recession (when virtually every sector in the economy con-tracted), U.S. manufacturing was setting new performance records year after year in all relevant statistical categories: profits, revenues, investment returns, output, value-added, exports, imports, and others. In absolute terms, the value of U.S. manufacturing has been growing continuously, with brief hiccups experienced during recessions over the past several decades. As a percentage of our total economy, the value of manufacturing peaked in 1953 and has been declining since, but that is the product of rapid growth in the services sectors and not—as evidenced by its absolute growth—an indication of manufacturing decline.

. . . American factories are, in fact, the world's most prolific, accounting for 21.4 percent of global manufac-turing value-added in 2008, while China accounted for 13.4 percent.[15] The main reason for continued American industrial preeminence is that the U.S. manufacturing sec-tor has continued its transition away from labor-intensive industries toward higher value-added production.

Regardless of manufacturing's operating perfor-mance, the metric that matters most politically is the number of jobs in the sector. That figure reached a zenith of 19.4 million jobs in 1979 and has been trending downward along roughly the same trajectory ever since. China's entry into the WTO and the subsequent increase in bilateral trade did nothing to accelerate the decline. Manufacturing job loss has very little to do with trade and a lot to do with changes in technology that lead to productivity gains and changes in consumer tastes. China has also experienced a decline in manufacturing jobs. In fact, many more jobs have been lost in Chinese manu-facturing and for the same reasons—productivity gains. According to a 2004 study published by the Conference Board, China lost 15 million manufacturing jobs between 1995 and 2002, a period during which 2 million U.S. manufacturing jobs were lost.[16]

Policymakers in Washington have been citing a figure from the Economic Policy Institute that attrib-utes 2.4 million manufacturing job losses between 2001 and 2008 to the bilateral trade deficit with China. But that figure approximates job gains from export value and job losses from import value, as though there were a straight line correlation between the figures. And it assumes that imports do not create or support U.S. jobs. But U.S. producers—purchasing raw materials, compo-nents and capital equipment—account for more than half of the value of U.S. imports annually, according to the U.S. Bureau of Economic Analysis. Those imports support U.S. jobs in a wide range of industries. . . .

In a 2006 paper, Stanford University economist Law-rence Lau found that Chinese value-added accounted for about 37% of the total value of U.S. imports from China.[17]

In 2008, using a different methodology, U.S. International Trade Commission economist Robert Koopman, along with economists Zhi Wang and Shang-jin Wei, found the figure to be closer to 50%.[18] In other words, despite all the hand-wringing about the value of imports from China, one-half to nearly two thirds of that value is not even Chinese. Instead, it reflects the efforts of workers and capital in other countries, including the U.S. In overstating Chinese value by 100% to 200%, the official U.S. import statistics are a poor proxy for job loss.

The fact that China surpassed Germany to become the world's largest exporter last year—a milestone that prompted a string of "end-of-Western-civilization" newspaper commentaries—says less about Chinese economic might than it does about the extent of global economic integration. The global division of labor enabled by intricate transnational production and supply chains still assigns to China primarily lower-value production and assembly operations.[19] . . .

Less Provocative Alternatives

Another reason the Chinese government worries about RMB appreciation is that Chinese investors own about $800 billion of U.S. debt. A 25 percent appreciation in the RMB would reduce the value of those holdings to approximately $640 billion. That's a high price for China to pay, especially in light of the fact that U.S. inflation is expected to rise in the coming years, which will further deflate the value of those holdings (and ease the burden of repayment on U.S. taxpayers). Likewise, mass dumping of U.S. government debt by Chinese investors—the much ballyhooed "leverage" that China allegedly holds over U.S. policy—would precipitate a decline in the dollar as well, which also would depress the value of Chinese holdings. The assertion that China holds U.S. debt as a favor to America, and would withdraw that favor on a whim, is a bit far-fetched.

China, it seems, is guilty of a failure to heed the first law of investment: it failed to diversify its portfolio adequately. The overwhelming investment focus on U.S. public debt has left China exposed to heavy losses from dollar inflation and RMB appreciation. The fact that the inflation rate is in the hands of U.S. policymakers makes China even more reluctant to allow large-scale or, at least, precipitous, RMB appreciation.

As of the close of 2008, Chinese direct investment in the United States stood at just $1.2 billion—a mere rounding error at about 0.05 percent of the $2.3 trillion in total foreign direct investment in the United States. That figure comes nowhere close to the amount of U.S. direct investment held by foreigners in other big economies. U.S. direct investment in 2008 held in the United Kingdom was $454 billion; $260 billion in Japan; $259 billion in the Netherlands; $221 billion in Canada; $211 billion in Germany; $64 billion in Australia; $16 billion in South Korea; and even $1.7 billion in Russia.[20] . . .

A large inflow of investment from China would have a similar impact as a large increase in U.S. exports to China on the value of both countries' currencies, and on the level of China's foreign reserves. In light of China's large reserves and its need and desire to diversify, America's need for investment in the real economy, and the objective of creating jobs and achieving sustained economic growth, U.S. policy should be clarified so that the benchmarks and hurdles facing Chinese investors are better understood. Lowering those hurdles would encourage greater Chinese investment in the U.S. economy and a deepening of our mutual economic interests.

To reduce bilateral tensions and foster greater cooperation from China with respect to market access, intellectual property theft, and other legitimate U.S. concerns, the United States should offer to reform its punitive trade remedies practices toward China. Ending the practice of treating China as a non-market economy in antidumping cases would probably do more to improve bilateral economic relations than just about any other possible reform. . . .

Short of graduating China to market economy status, U.S. policymakers could reduce bilateral tensions by addressing another systemic, methodological problem that results in Chinese exporters being penalized twice for the same alleged infraction. Since the Commerce Department resumed applying the countervailing duty law to non-market economies in 2007 (after a 22-year moratorium), it has failed to account for the problem of "double-counting" in cases where imports are subject to both the antidumping and countervailing duty laws. . . .

Some Hypocrisy in U.S. Allegations

Claims are numerous that China maintains discriminatory policies that impede imports and foreign companies. Indeed, some of those claims have been substantiated and remedied. Others have only been substantiated. And still many more have been merely alleged.

. . . On eight occasions, the United States decided that bilateral process alone was insufficient, and lodged official complaints with the WTO Dispute Settlement Body about various Chinese practices. Outcomes in two of the cases are still pending, but six of the eight cases produced satisfactory outcomes from the perspective of the U.S. government: either China agreed during consultations to change its rules or practices, or a dispute panel affirmed most of the U.S. complaints and issued opinions requesting that China bring its practices into conformity with the relevant WTO agreements.

It is difficult to find merit in the suggestion that U.S. trade policy toward China should change tack and become more unilateralist or provocative, when the WTO dispute settlement system has worked well as a venue for resolving U.S. complaints. The United States has brought 19 cases against Europe in the WTO, but there is not much talk about adopting a more strident trade policy toward the EU. . . .

One of the costs of bringing cases against Chinese market barriers or policies that favor domestic firms would be the exposure of U.S. hypocrisy. The U.S. government subsidizes chosen companies and industries, too. The past 18 months is littered with examples, such as General Motors and Chrysler. Though the U.S. business community is concerned about the emergence of technical market barriers in China favoring local companies, the U.S. government maintains opaque technical barriers in a variety of industries, which [hamper] and [preclude] access to the U.S. market for foreign food products, in particular. Mexican trucks cannot even operate on U.S. highways. There is an element of the pot calling the kettle black in U.S. allegations.

By and large, though, the Office of the U.S. Trade Representative, in its December 2009 report to Congress about the implementation of China's WTO commitments, strikes the right tone and reassures that the economics can and should be shielded from the vicissitudes of politics:

> China has taken many impressive steps over the last eight years to reform its economy, while implementing a set of sweeping WTO accession commitments that required it to reduce tariff rates, to eliminate non-tariff barriers, to provide national treatment and improved market access for goods and services imported from the United States and other WTO members, to protect intellectual property rights, and to improve transparency. Although it still does not appear to be complete in every respect, China's implementation of its WTO commitments has led to increases in U.S. exports to China, while deepening China's integrations into the international trading system and facilitating and strengthening the rule of law and the economic reforms that China began 30 years ago.[21]

Conclusion

The world would be better off if the value of China's currency were truly market-determined, as it would lead to more optimal resource allocations. The impact on the bilateral trade account—meaningless as that statistic is in a globalized economy—would be impossible to predict. But compelling China to revalue under threat of sanction could produce adverse consequences—including reductions in Americans' real incomes and damaged relations with China—leaving us all worse off without even achieving the underlying policy objectives.

For now, it would be better to let the storm pass and allow China to appreciate its currency at its own pace.

Notes

1. To float its currency and let markets determine the value, China would have to remove restrictions on its capital account, so that investment can flow in and out of the country freely. If China did this, it is not entirely clear that the value of the RMB would appreciate. It is possible that there would be more capital flight than inflow, as domestic savings are able to pursue investment options outside of China. This capital flight would have a depreciating effect on the value of the RMB.

2. Of course, there are many other important determinants of the trade account besides relative currency values.

3. There is also an "income effect" from the change in currency values. When the dollar declines in value, U.S. consumers experience a decline in real income, which affects their consumption choices. Even though Chinese imports might be relatively more expensive than they were before the currency rise, they may still be less expensive than the alternatives. Accordingly, U.S. consumers with lower real incomes might be inclined to purchase more Chinese imports.

4. Federal Reserve Board, *Federal Reserve Statistical Release G5.A, Foreign Exchange Rates (Annual)*, release dates January 4, 2010, and January 2, 2009. Since July 2008, the value of the Yuan against the dollar has not changed measurably.

5. The dearth of substitutes is probably a function of retailers not wanting to incur the costs of having to reconfigure their supply chains. If the cost of reconfiguring and sourcing products from other countries is similar to the cost of maintaining Chinese suppliers with their exchange-induced higher prices, then retailers may be more likely to stick with the status quo and pass on their higher costs to consumers.

6. Assume that the price of imports is $1 and the quantity demanded is one unit. The import value is then $1. If a 15.2 percent increase in price leads to a 38.7 percent increase in value, then quantity must increase by 20.4 percent because: $(1.152 \times \text{price}) * (1.204 \times \text{quantity}) = 138.7$.

7. Robert Koopman, Zhi Wang, and Shang-jin Wei, "How Much of Chinese Exports Is Really Made in China? Assessing Foreign and Domestic Value-Added in Gross Exports," U.S. International Trade Commission, Office of Economics, Working Paper no. 2008-03-B, March 2008.

8. Daniel J. Ikenson, "Currency Controversy: Surplus of Controversy, Deficit of Leadership," Cato Free Trade Bulletin no. 21, May 31, 2006.

9. Cathy L. Jabara, "How Do Exchange Rates Affect Import Prices? Recent Economic Literature and Data Analysis," U.S. International Trade Commission, Office of Industries Working Paper no. ID-21 (revised), October 2009.

10. U.S. Department of Commerce, Bureau of the Census, Foreign Trade Statistics, http://www.census.gov/foreign-trade/balance/c5700.html#2009. China was the fastest-growing market among America's top 25 largest export markets between 2000 and 2008. In 2009, overall U.S. exports declined 12.9 percent, but exports to China held steady, declining by just 0.23 percent.

11. Production of Apple iPods is the quintessential example of the benefits of transnational production and supply chains. The degree of international collaboration embedded in the value of an iPod has been described in a few other Cato publications, including: Daniel Ikenson, "Made on Earth: How Global Economic Integration Renders Trade Policy Obsolete," Cato Trade Policy Analysis no. 42, December 2, 2009.

12. James Fallows, "China Makes, the World Takes," *Atlantic*, July/August 2007, http://www.theatlantic.com/doc/200707/shenzhen.

13. It is particularly ironic to hear this last accusation from spendthrift members of Congress who overlook the fact that their own profligacy is what brought China to the U.S. debt markets in the first place.

14. For more comprehensive treatments refuting the myth of manufacturing decline in the United States, see: Daniel Ikenson, "Thriving in a Global Economy: The Truth about Manufacturing and Trade," Cato Trade Policy Analysis no. 35, August 28, 2007; Daniel Ikenson and Scott Lincicome, "Audaciously Hopeful: How President Obama Can Help Restore the Pro-Trade Consensus," Cato Trade Policy Analysis no. 39, April 28, 2009, pp. 12–16; and Daniel Griswold, "Trading Up: How Expanding Trade Has Delivered Better Jobs and Higher Living Standards for American Workers," Cato Trade Policy Analysis no. 36, October 25, 2007.

15. United Nations Industrial Development Organization, "National Accounts Main Aggregates Database, Value Added by Economic Activity," (2008 data are the most recent available), http://unstats.un.org/unsd/snaama/resQuery.asp.

16. Yuan Jiang, Yaodong Liu, Robert H. McGuckin, III, Matthew Spiegelman, and Jianyi Xu, "China's Experience with Productivity and Jobs," Conference Board Report Number R-1352-04-RR, June 2004, http://www.conference-board.org/publications/describe.cfm?id=809.

17. Lawrence J. Lau et al., *Estimates of U.S.-China Trade Balances in Terms of Domestic Value-Added*, working paper no. 295 (Palo Alto, CA: Stanford University, October 2006; updated November 2006).

18. Robert Koopman, Zhi Wang, and Shang-jin Wei, "How Much of Chinese Exports Is Really Made in China? Assessing Foreign and Domestic Value-Added in Gross Exports," U.S. International Trade Commission, Office of Economics, working paper no. 2008-03-B, March 2008.

19. For a more comprehensive treatment of this topic, see Daniel Ikenson, "Made on Earth: How Global Economic Integration Renders Trade Policy Obsolete," Cato Trade Policy Analysis no. 42, December 12, 2009.

20. Bureau of Economic Analysis, "Foreign Direct Investment in the United States: Selected Items by Detailed Industry of U.S. Affiliate," 2004–2008, http://www.bea.gov/international/xls/LongIndustry.xls.

21. United States Trade Representative, *2009 Report to Congress on China's WTO Compliance*, December 2009, p. 4.

Daniel J. Ikenson is the associate director of the Center for Trade Policy Studies at the Cato Institute. Before joining the Cato Institute, he was the director of international trade planning for an international accounting and business advisory firm. He holds an MA degree in economics from George Washington University.

EXPLORING THE ISSUE

Is China's Currency Undervalued, and Should the United States Take Action to Correct This Undervaluation?

Critical Thinking and Reflection

1. In a U.S. attempt to correct the RMB's devaluation, how might a sanctions approach *not* be "fraught with danger"?
2. How exactly does the impact of exchange rates undermine U.S. competitiveness?
3. Why would it be that, on the import side, the currency-value/trade-flow situation is particularly troubling for those who seek deficit reduction through currency revaluation?

Is There Common Ground?

Since the issue examined here is presented as a two-question challenge—"Is China's currency undervalued? Should the United States take action to correct this undervaluation?"— indications of common ground must be considered in two parts as well. In doing so, it is apparent that only the first question lends itself to an agreeable discourse, as the prevailing opinion is, yes, China's currency is undervalued.

Even though this accepted fact does qualify as common ground, it must be regarded as conditional at best. Shilling points out that there is a "broad consensus that RMB is substantially undervalued," and the strength of his argument is largely derived from the statistical evidence that supports this consensus. Ikenson, however, asserts that the magnitude of the RMB's devaluation is widely disputed among economists. For Ikenson, such discrepancy is what veers him away from sharing Shilling's resolve.

Create Central

www.mhhe.com/createcentral

Additional Resources

Bhalla, Surjit S., *Devaluing to Prosperity: Misaligned Currencies and Their Growth Consequences* (Peterson Institute, 2012)

Farlow, Andrew, *Crash and Beyond: Causes and Consequences of the Global Financial Crisis* (Oxford University Press, 2013)

Hartquist, David, Beckington, Jeffrey, and Collis, Ariel, *China's Policy of Substantially Undervaluing the Renminbi* (CreateSpace Independent Publishing Platform, 2008)

Internet References . . .

Bloomberg: "China, Germany Criticized by U.S. for Account Imbalances"

www.bloomberg.com/news/2013-10-30/china-germany
-criticized-by-u-s-for-current-account-imbalances.html

CNN Business 360: "Undervalued Currencies: China's Not Alone"

http://business.blogs.cnn.com/2010/10/04/undervalued
-currencies-chinas-not-alone/

The Free Library: "Is the Chinese Currency, the Renminbi, Dangerously Undervalued and a Threat to the Global Economy?"

www.thefreelibrary.com/Is+the+Chinese
+currency%2c+the+renminbi%2c+dangerously
+undervalued+and+a...-a0100545302

ISSUE

Do the Testing and Accountability Elements of the No Child Left Behind Act Prevent a Proper Cost-Benefit Evaluation?

YES: George Miller, from "Should Congress Make Fundamental Changes in the No Child Left Behind Act?" *Congressional Digest* (May 2008)

NO: Raymond Simon, from "Should Congress Make Fundamental Changes in the No Child Left Behind Act?" *Congressional Digest* (May 2008)

Learning Outcomes

After reading this issue, you will be able to:

- Discuss the Improving America's Schools Act of 1994.
- Identify Miller's six key components for a renewed American education policy.
- Explain what Simon means by "the '2014 is today' schools."
- Describe how a slide-rule/calculator analogy applies to our system of education.

ISSUE SUMMARY

YES: Chairman of the Education and Labor Committee of the United States House of Representatives, California Democrat George Miller states that schools and students are not making enough progress and significant changes must be made to the law so that its goals may be achieved. "America needs and must have an educational law that insists on accountability with high expectations and high-quality assessments; that closes the achievement gap; and helps all children to learn."

NO: Deputy Secretary, U.S. Department of Education, Raymond Simon states that NCLB is working for students. Simon believes that there is consensus for a limited number of changes. He claims that NCLB's insistence on scientifically based research and the gathering and usage of reliable data has been one of its major successes.

The passage of the Elementary and Secondary Education Act (ESEA) in 1965 imparted an important federal component to spending on education that is mostly financed by state and local taxes. Americans are concerned about public education for a variety of reasons. One reason is that public spending absorbs a significant amount of tax dollars. But Americans are also concerned because the results of all the spending are less than impressive. This dissatisfaction goes back to at least 1983, when the National Commission on Excellence in Education released its report, entitled *A Nation at Risk*. This report identified a variety of problems in public education. In spite of a number of "reforms" that have been put in place since then, the dissatisfaction with public education continued into the twenty-first century. For example, the U.S. Department of Education reported that in 2003, "Even after four

years of public schooling, most students perform below proficiency in both reading and mathematics." And for the year 2000, the Department reported: "Upon graduation from high school, few students have acquired the math and science skills necessary to compete in the knowledge-based economy."

In his presidential campaign in 2000, candidate George W. Bush emphasized educational reform. He signed the No Child Left Behind Act (NCLBA) into law on January 8, 2002. NCLBA was a bipartisan effort; it passed the House by a 381–41 margin and the Senate with an 87–10 vote. A leading Democrat, Senator Ted Kennedy (D-MA), was a chief sponsor of the legislation in the Senate.

As to its broad objectives, former Secretary Rod Paige states that NCLBA "ensures accountability and flexibility as well as increased federal support for education," and that it "continues the legacy of the *Brown v. Board* decision by creating an education system that is more inclusive, responsive, and fair." Turning to more specific provisions, NCLBA mandates that every state set standards for grade-level achievement and develop a system to see if students are reaching those standards. NCLBA rededicates the country to the goal of having a "highly qualified teacher" in every classroom, where "highly qualified" means the teacher holds a bachelor's degree, holds a certification or licensure to teach in the state of his or her employment, and has proven knowledge of the subjects he or she teaches.

The NCLBA has generated a good deal of controversy beginning just a few years after its passage. Six years later as the law came up for reauthorization, there are those like Deputy Secretary, U.S. Department of Education, Raymond Simon who believe the legislation is generating positive results and that only a few changes might be in order. At the same time, there is a significant vocal opposition, represented by George Miller, chairman of the Education and Labor Committee of the U.S. House of Representatives, one of the original coauthors of the NCLBA,

who believes that the law brought some positive changes but "We didn't get it all right when we enacted the law," and "there are no votes in the U.S. House of Representatives for continuing the No Child Left Behind Act without making serious changes to it." He identifies six key elements, of which assessment and accountability are a major component: "The heart of No Child Left Behind is accountability."

An epilogue is in order about budgetary provisions and the fate of the reauthorization of NCLBA. As to the first, the 2009 budget provides only $125 million above 2008 for NCLB, "a cumulative shortfall of $85.6 billion."

As to the reauthorization: the Educator Roundtable November Bulletin reported that it failed, since a compromise that would satisfy all the critics of NCLB could not be reached. The law continues until it is repealed.

In April 2008, the Department of Education proposed new regulations for Title I of the ESEA covering state assessment and accountability systems. George Miller denounced these as "a series of piecemeal changes to a law that really needs a comprehensive overhaul."

YES

George Miller

Should Congress Make Fundamental Changes in the No Child Left Behind Act?

Over 40 years ago, President John F. Kennedy had a vision of sending a man to the moon and bringing him home again. That vision fueled a massive investment by this Nation in all levels of education—an investment that drove nearly four decades of discovery, innovation, and economic growth, allowing America to have the world's strongest economy and lead the community of nations for generations.

Sadly, this investment fell off over the years. With the report *A Nation at Risk,* America woke up and saw an education system that no longer served all its children and was failing our future.

America had an education system that was operating under a policy of acceptable losses. Where only about half of all minority children could read proficiently. Where black and Hispanic 17-year-olds were being taught math to the same level as white 13-year-olds. Where 40,000 teachers in California were without the credentials necessary to teach in the schools.

Nearly four decades after President Kennedy's decision, America realized that its education system was threatening the country's world leadership. Six years ago we decided to do something bold about it.

We made a decision as a Nation to raise our expectations of what America's schools and schoolchildren could achieve. We made a decision to insist upon high standards. We said that it was not good enough for a majority of the children in a school district to be learning and performing at grade level if their success was allowed to mask the fact that many other children were falling behind.

We asked the States to set higher standards for their schools and students, because we believed that every single child—if given access to a highly qualified teacher and a good curriculum in a decent school—could achieve educational success.

We made performance at our schools transparent, and we made schools accountable for their performance.

Today, five and a half years after its enactment, the No Child Left Behind Act has brought some positive changes.

A recent Center on Education Policy study of all 50 States found gains in students' reading and math proficiency and the narrowing of the achievement gap among groups of students since the implementation of No Child Left Behind.

There are more qualified teachers in the classroom today, because we made it a priority. The law is shining a bright light on the achievement gaps among different groups of students in the United States and among the States. Now—for the first time—we know exactly which students, and which groups of students, are not learning and performing at grade level. This information makes it impossible for us to ignore those students who are not succeeding.

And finally, the law has provoked an energetic national debate about our Nation's system of public education and the need for the next generation of investment in our schools, students, principals, and teachers. That is a good thing.

Let me be clear, though: Schools and students are not making enough progress. Not for a country as great as ours. We didn't get it all right when we enacted the law.

Throughout our schools and communities, the American people have a very strong sense that the No Child Left Behind Act is not fair. That it is not flexible. And that it is not funded. And they are not wrong.

The question is what we are going to do next. America needs and must have an education law that insists on accountability with high expectations, high standards, and high-quality assessments; that closes the achievement gap; and that helps all children to learn. And America needs and must have an education law that treats schools and children fairly, that provides educators and administrators with the flexibility they need to meet high standards, and that delivers to schools the resources they need to improve and succeed. We can and we must meet these objectives in this next stage of education reform in the United States.

We would be wrong to waver when it comes to the existing goals and standards of the No Child Left Behind law. We would also be wrong if we failed to respond to the serious concerns with the law raised by people who sincerely care about America's educational future.

I can tell you that there are no votes in the U.S. House of Representatives for continuing the No Child Left Behind Act without making serious changes to it. It is my intention as chairman of the Education and Labor Committee to pass a bill in September, both in committee and on the floor of the House.

We want a bill that is fair and flexible—that maintains the integrity of the law through accountability while responding to the legitimate concerns that have been raised.

I have always said that I am proud to be one of the original coauthors of the No Child Left Behind Act. But what I really want is to be the proud coauthor of a law that works.

To that end, for the last five years I have traveled this country listening to teachers, administrators, students, parents, governors, and many others about how the law can be improved. I have listened carefully, as have my colleagues. We have heard an emerging consensus about needed changes.

The process by which this bill is being developed is open, transparent, and bipartisan. It reflects the input of Members of Congress from both parties and across the ideological spectrum, many of whom testified before and submitted suggestions to our committee.

It reflects testimony delivered in nearly two dozen congressional hearings begun last year by then-Chairman [Rep. Buck] McKeon [R-CA]. Congressman McKeon and I have been working together on this reauthorization for many months. He has been very helpful to this process.

And it reflects our review of recommendations from more than 100 education, civil rights, and business organizations. Congressman Dale Kildee [D-MI], the subcommittee [on Early Childhood, Elementary and Secondary Education] chair, and I have met with many of these organizations.

My vision for this next bill is to take America's education policy in a new direction by doing six key things:

- Provide much-needed fairness and flexibility.
- Encourage a rich and challenging learning environment and promote best practices and innovation taking place in schools throughout the country.
- Support teachers and principals.
- Continue to hold schools accountable for students' progress.
- Join the effort to improve America's high schools.
- Invest in our schools.

First, the legislation will provide much-needed fairness and flexibility. We hear concerns that schools don't get credit they deserve when their students make real progress over time. The legislation I will introduce will contain a growth model that gives credit to States and schools for the progress that their students make over time. This builds on a pilot effort started by [U.S. Education] Secretary [Margaret] Spellings. The Secretary deserves great credit for her leadership on this important issue.

These growth models will give us fairer, better, and more accurate information. The information will be timely and helpful to teachers and principals in developing strategies for improvement and in targeting resources. In addition, many Americans do not believe that the success of our students or our schools can be measured by one test administered on one day. I agree with them. This is not fair.

We hear concerns that the law has forced schools to focus on math and reading instruction at the expense of history, art, social studies, music, and physical education. This is not required under the Act—nor should it be—but we must help ensure that all students in all schools have access to a broad, rich curriculum.

Our legislation will continue to place strong emphasis on reading and math skills. But it will allow States to use more than their reading and math test results to determine how well schools and students are doing. We will allow the use of additional valid and reliable measures to assess student learning and school performance more fairly, comprehensively, and accurately. One such measure for high schools must be graduation rates.

The legislation will also drive improvements in the quality and appropriateness of the tests used for accountability. This is especially important for English language learners and students with disabilities who should be given tests that are fair and appropriate, just as they should continue to be included in our accountability system.

In exchange for increased resources, States will be allowed to develop better tests that more accurately measure what all students have learned. These tests will be more useful to teachers and will drive richer classroom instruction.

Second, the legislation will encourage a rich and challenging learning environment, and it will promote best practices and innovation taking place in schools throughout the country. In so many meetings I have had in my district and elsewhere, employers say that our high school graduates are not ready for the workplace. Colleges say that our high school graduates are not ready for the college classroom. This is unacceptable.

In my bill, we will ask employers and colleges to come together as stakeholders with the States to jointly develop more rigorous standards that meet the demands of both.

Many States have already started this process. We seek to build on and complement the leadership of our Nation's governors and provide them with incentives to continue. This requires that assessments be fully aligned with these new State standards and include multiple measures of success.

These measures can no longer reflect just basic skills and memorization. Rather, they must reflect critical thinking skills and the ability to apply knowledge to new and challenging contexts. These are the skills that today's students will need to meet the complex demands of the American economy and society in a globalized world.

Schools must no longer prepare our students to be autonomous problem solvers. The workplace they enter tomorrow will increasingly require them to work in teams, collaborating across companies, communities, and continents. These skills cannot be developed solely by simple multiple choice exams.

For too long we have settled for standards and assessments that do not measure up to the high goals we have for our kids or the skills they must achieve. But let none of us for a moment believe that our students will be able to participate in this interactive and participatory culture and workplace if they cannot read, write, and understand math.

Therefore, the bill will say that if States take this step and commit to the students of their States that they will prepare them for the universities and jobs of the future, then we will provide them with incentives and assistance to do so.

Third, the legislation will support teachers and principals. Even with all of these changes, we will not meet our national goal of closing the achievement gap until and unless we close the teacher quality gap. No factor matters more to children's educational success than the quality of their teachers and principals. All children deserve their fair share of teacher talent and expertise. We must do more to ensure that poor and minority students are taught by teachers with expertise in the subjects they are teaching.

I have heard from so many teachers who feel they are no longer viewed as critical partners in an educational system but merely an instrument to satisfy a minimum attainment goal. As a Nation, we are not offering teachers the respect and support they deserve today, and as a result we are facing a very real teacher shortage crisis. Particularly in urban and rural communities, in subjects like math, science, foreign language, and for children with disabilities and children learning English, we must hire, train, and retain excellent teachers.

For these reasons, the legislation I will introduce will provide for performance pay for principals and teachers based on fair and proven models, teacher mentoring, teacher career ladders, and improved working conditions. It will also provide incentives consistent with the Teach Act that I introduced two years ago that will help bring top teacher talent into the classrooms that need this the most.

Fourth, the legislation will continue to hold schools accountable for students' progress. The heart of No Child Left Behind is accountability. Our bill will continue to hold schools accountable for all students, including minority and low-income students, students learning English, and those with disabilities. All of these students deserve an improved accountability system. Under current law, schools whose students have not made adequate achievement gains are all treated the same—with the same interventions and sanctions taking place over the same period of time. We need to distinguish among different schools and the challenges facing them, as well as their needs for addressing those challenges.

Schools with specific problems in specific areas should be allowed to use instructional interventions that are appropriate to their needs. High-priority schools, meanwhile, must receive more intensive support and assistance.

I am pleased that the House Appropriations Committee has already committed significant new funding for this purpose next year.

Fifth, the legislation will join the effort to improve America's high schools.

I believe this is part of the solution to addressing our unacceptably high dropout rate. Over 30 percent of all high school students do not receive a diploma. America is better than that. We can no longer give up on these students by allowing them to give up on school.

The bill will include comprehensive steps to turn around low-performing middle and high schools. It will include uniform standards for measuring graduation rates that are fair, accurate, and reliable, and will do more to keep students in school. I tip my hat to the governors for their leadership in this area, and look forward to working with them as we benefit from and build on their reforms.

We must also remember that there are remarkable examples of schools in difficult environments where students are soaring and the achievement gap is closing. We must celebrate and reward these successes. Our bill will help sustain them, build on them, and bring them to scale.

Sixth, and finally, this legislation will invest in our schools. This new direction for education in America is premised on the growing consensus that there is a need for greater and sustained investments in American education.

In the new Congress, the Democratic Leadership has begun this new era of investment—first with the continuing resolution funding, then the appropriations bill, the Innovation and Competitiveness Agenda, and the College Cost Reduction Act.

I expect this legislation to follow suit.

Much has been made of the unusual political coalition that developed the No Child Left Behind Act and the important role that President [George W.] Bush played. Now the discussion has shifted to No Child Left Behind as the most important domestic legacy for this President.

I would only say this: President Bush's legacy will not be established if he vetoes the education funding in the Labor-Health and Human Services-Education Appropriations bill. The legacy of a great American education system for our children and our country cannot be built on the cheap. America deserves better.

I want to close today by talking about why it's so important that we get this right.

Our public education system plays many critical roles in our society. So much of who we are and where we are going is a product of this system combined with our families and our communities.

Social and economic opportunity begins in the classroom. Discovery and innovation begin in the classroom. Economic growth and economic disparity begin in the classroom.

That is why it is essential to have a high-quality and engaged education system to carry out the continuous quest of redeeming America's promise of equality for all people to fully participate in a thriving democratic system.

With this new direction for education in America, I believe we will have a new opportunity to succeed. So many leaders from the education community, the business community, and the civil rights community have already contributed so much understanding and rigor to this reauthorization process.

I am as excited and hopeful today as I have been at any time in the more than 30 years that I have served in Congress about the prospects for finally realizing the vision of excellent educational opportunities for all children in America.

GEORGE MILLER is a democratic congressman representing the seventh district of California. He was first elected to the House in 1974, and he currently chairs the House Committee on Education and Labor.

Raymond Simon   ➡ **NO**

Should Congress Make Fundamental Changes in the No Child Left Behind Act?

A reading of the U.S. Constitution finds no mention of the Federal Government's role in the education of its citizens, thereby relegating that responsibility primarily to individual States. Although constitutionally absent, events in our country's history have nonetheless established a clear national interest in an educated citizenry, with Federal law so reflecting that.

Most pertinent to today's topic are events dating back to 1965 with the passage of the Federal Elementary and Secondary Education Act (ESEA), beginning for the Nation a new era of responsibility for our country's poorest school children. ESEA was designed to level the playing field between the rich and poor by focusing Federal money on high-poverty areas. The law has been in existence continually since that time, undergoing periodic renewal (what we call reauthorization) roughly every seven years. No Child Left Behind represents its latest reauthorization.

I began my teaching internship just a few weeks after the signing of that historic law. At that time, learning standards were almost exclusively teacher-based. My standards were not necessarily those of the teacher in the adjacent room teaching the same subject. As long as I covered the textbook or major portion thereof, and did it in a way that kids were learning, no one really cared.

Federal financial support, although limited, was welcomed and offered opportunity for new programs beyond what State and local funding provided. Schools met the accountability requirements of the law primarily by documenting that the money was spent on allowable products and services, such as equipment or professional development. State education departments and local school districts were the principal drivers of school reform.

By the late 1980s, even longtime supporters of the law were becoming concerned about the lack of evidence that the Federal funds were making a substantial difference in the education of poor and minority children. It was then that the Federal interest began to shift to standards and accountability for academic achievement.

The 1994 reauthorization, known as the Improving America's Schools Act, required States to develop more rigorous standards, establish tests to measure against those standards, and disaggregate the testing data to identify which population subgroups were being underserved. Because the 1994 version lacked accountability

mechanisms for rigorous enforcement, by the time of NCLB in 2001, only 11 of our 50 States were in compliance.

NCLB, signed by President George W. Bush with overwhelming bipartisan support in the Congress, expanded the law's requirements even further, establishing meaningful achievement and compliance provisions. Both the President and Congress made it very clear that this time they really did mean it—children must be able to read and do math at or above grade level. No more excuses.

Today, learning standards are State-based, with annual State-developed and -administered tests in reading and math required in each of the grades three through eight and once in high school. The goal is that every child performs at or above grade level in those subjects by 2014.

Accountability is measured at the school level, with each State setting the improvement trajectory for its schools, taking them from their current level of performance to 100 percent by 2014. In order to accomplish this, every child is expected to have a highly qualified teacher every year.

Schools report annually to parents and the public on how well they are doing. Those that fail to meet their annual improvement goals have additional sums of money targeted to interventions that will help their students get better, including tutoring and, in some cases, allowing children to transfer to another school that is meeting its targets. Schools that chronically under-perform are subject to more extreme interventions, including replacing staff, being taken over by other public or private entities, or eventual closure.

Federal aid has been substantially increased under NCLB and now stands at an all-time high, but still accounts for only about 9 percent of the average school district's financial support. In exchange for this money, a State voluntarily agrees to be held accountable for the law's provisions, submitting a plan that sets out the manner in which it will fulfill these requirements. This includes proof that its standards are indeed aligned with its testing and that highly qualified teachers are being distributed equally among the classrooms of poor children and their more affluent counterparts.

Each year, each State is told how much it will receive in Federal funds, and each year the State is free to decline those funds and thus avoid any obligation to implement its plan. No State has yet refused the money. The Federal

From *Congressional Digest*, May 2008. Published by Pro & Con ® Publishers, a division of Congressional Digest Corporation.

Government, although a minority funding partner in a voluntary endeavor, is now driving much of the country's school reform efforts.

Some question whether the mission of NCLB, getting every child to grade level or above in reading and math by 2014, is doable. The fact is, it is already being done in a growing number of schools around the country, schools where today all or most of students are meeting that standard. These are what I call the "2014 is today" schools.

What distinguishes these successful schools from those similarly situated in terms of demographics and other measures, but that are not making progress or are among the chronic underperforming schools?

First and foremost, successful schools know what to do—and what to do centers around a really good teacher. Specifically, these schools believe that their students can achieve to high standards. These standards, and the expected behavior to reach them, are clearly communicated to the students and their parents. Highly qualified, effective teachers use data to guide instruction daily and they work with an outstanding school-level administrator who has knowledge and authority to effect change, reward innovation, and enforce high expectations.

One of the immediate challenges for educators and policymakers is to provide information to all schools about what really works and what doesn't. Then, we must have the wisdom and courage to stop what doesn't work and concentrate exclusively on what does.

Does anybody know what this is? It's a slide rule, a calculating device that has its origins dating back to the seventeenth century. I don't mind telling you I had a time getting this through airport security; some of the younger screeners were convinced it was some sort of weapon, but just couldn't prove it.

Slide rules came in various sizes and were made of various materials, including fiberglass, wood, plastic, and metal. The one I am most proud of, and which was given to me in 1963 by my brother as a high school graduation present, is made of fiberglass and has numerous advanced features that are not on the plastic version I hold in my hand. Unsure of whether or not this would be allowed on the plane, I just couldn't risk bringing the better one.

The accuracy of the instrument varied, depending on the material of construction, giving different answers depending on the temperature, relative humidity, and nervousness of the operator. A slight twitch at any point in the process could skew the final answer significantly. The operator had to be good at estimating the answer; for instance, multiplying 572 times 1,320 required the same settings as multiplying 5.72 by 13,200.

No mathematician, scientist, or engineer dared do his or her work without the slide rule. You especially looked cool when you could wear one on your belt in a leather carrying case. The slide rule remained the machine of choice for computation even into the computer age. The first calculators were called "electronic slide rules," just like the first cars were called "horseless carriages." In 1951, IBM bragged that it took 150 slide rules to match the power of one of its new computers.

American engineering achievements that owe their existence to this device include the Empire State Building, Hoover Dam, Golden Gate Bridge, Boeing 707 airliner, and the Saturn 5 rocket used by the Apollo and Skylab programs.

This instrument, that carried the world from the Renaissance to the moon, was rendered obsolete overnight. It was replaced with the microprocessor, represented here by an electronic calculator. These devices are millions of times faster and infinitely more accurate. They are the machine of choice for computation for today's generation.

It took a wizard to use the slide rule, and only after weeks of training and persistent use. Anyone can use a calculator with only a few minutes of training—but you can't look cool carrying it on your belt.

I use this analogy between the slide rule and calculator to illustrate where I believe the United States as a nation finds itself in discussing our system of education and the reforms necessary to make it work better for students.

One of the major successes of NCLB has been in its insistence on scientifically based research and the gathering and use of reliable data—data that can tell the truth, whether or not we want to hear it. There exists in too many of our schools what President Bush has called the "soft bigotry of low expectations" for certain subgroups of students, including those in special education, those whose first language is not English, and our poor and minority children.

Only half of African-American and Hispanic students graduate from high school on time. Ninety percent of the fastest-growing jobs require postsecondary education or training, yet 60 percent of Americans have no postsecondary credentials at all. Only 10 percent of Latinos earn bachelor's degrees by age 29.

Among countries participating in the Organization for Economic Co-operation and Development, the United States ranks first in the percent of the population 55 to 64 years old who have completed both high school and college. When you look at those same statistics among 25 to 34 year olds, we rank tenth in each category. These and other similar statistics illustrate that a large number of our students lack the skills to succeed in the global knowledge economy. If we choose to ignore this reality, too many of our citizens run the risk, as history has documented for the slide rule, of being rendered obsolete overnight.

These young people are being released with slide rule skills to compete in job markets that demand the ability to work not only with multifunctional calculators, but also with advanced computer systems.

Our very best schools are extraordinary, but there is a diversity of quality in far too many, where expectations for students haven't been set high enough. In other words, contentment with the status quo equates to losing ground. When business as usual fails our students, informed innovators need to step forward and give the status quo the heave ho.

On a positive note, it is apparent that No Child Left Behind, in partnership with State and local school reform efforts, is working for students. In addition to annual State testing, the law requires that all States participate every two years in reading and math portions of the National Assessment of Educational Progress (NAEP) at grades four and eight. NAEP, known as our Nation's report card, is the only true national exam given.

Results from the 2007 administration show that at fourth grade, reading and math scores are higher than ever, with math gains between 2003 and 2007 equivalent to adding an extra half-year of instruction. Math scores at eighth grade are higher than ever. The biggest gains in both grades and both subjects came from our Hispanic and African-American students, among those traditionally left behind by our education system.

Similar results have been shown on the State-administered tests. Highly qualified teachers are now found in over 90 percent of our classrooms, which is an all-time high.

To ensure that the goals of NCLB continue to be met for all students, the President has proposed a series of modifications for the Act's current reauthorization. These refinements are meant to foster and honor further innovation, where such new thinking will increase the opportunities for teachers to teach and students to learn. He wants to make sure that the law works better for States, schools, and the children they serve, while not sacrificing its core principles of accountability, high standards, enhanced choices for parents, and sound, proven methods of instruction.

We have learned a lot over the past six years—what works well and what needs to be changed. We have heard from students, teachers, parents, administrators, and policymakers from all levels of school governance, the business community, and advocacy groups. Consensus has generally formed around a limited number of changes, some of which Secretary of Education Margaret Spellings has already addressed through her limited authority provided in the law to waive certain aspects of its provisions.

The Secretary has already made allowances for a limited group of special education students and for those children whose first language is not English. We have worked with States and local districts to make it easier for them to offer more tutoring options for children who fall behind.

We believe the law needs to be changed to accommodate the use of what is known as a growth model, where schools can get credit for improving the performance of the same students over time as they move from grade to grade. When NCLB began, few States had the data capacity to calculate such individual academic progress. The Secretary has already permitted nine States to use this method and recently announced its future availability to all others eligible.

We need to increase the flexibility and capacity for States and school districts to help them turn around struggling schools by going from the current pass–fail system to a more nuanced approach that makes distinctions between those chronic underperformers and those schools that are missing their targets in just one or two areas. This involves both intervening early when signs of trouble develop and being more innovative and aggressive at the other extreme when chronic underperforming schools just don't seem to be able to get it right.

We need to make sure our children graduate prepared for the jobs of the twenty-first century by increasing accountability and access to a more rigorous curriculum in our high schools. States should be required to develop course-level academic standards for English and mathematics that prepare those students to succeed in college and the global workplace, administer assessments aligned to these standards, and publicly report how well the students are doing. Consistent graduation rate calculations should be used, so that we know for sure how many of our students actually finish twelfth grade.

We need to reward our best and most effective teachers by paying them more for helping students achieve to high standards and for working in our most challenging schools. Talented and qualified professionals from math, science, and technology fields outside of education should be encouraged to teach middle and high school courses, especially in low-income areas.

I believe the days are numbered for the traditional system of starting work in an organization or company and then moving up through the ranks to eventually assume leadership or ownership at middle-age or older. We must get these young people ready to lead immediately. They will not all have the luxury of learning on the job or learning, for the first time, what we should have taught them before graduation. In many instances, they will be creating the jobs in which they work.

Let's look ahead to the day that whatever ground some students have lost in the arena of global competitiveness is fully recovered. That day should be viewed not as the end of our efforts, but the beginning. If we become overly satisfied with achieving the goals I just mentioned, if we become content with the fact that we indeed are producing microprocessors rather than slide rules, then we run the risk of becoming complacent. Complacency very likely could lead to the following scene unfolding.

It is the year 2040. One of my grandchildren, Alex now six or Ana now three, is giving an RSA lecture on the relevance of education. At some point he or she will hold this instrument up for view—"Does anybody know what this is? It is a microprocessor-based electronic calculator. It was the machine of choice for computation in the late twentieth and early twenty-first centuries when my granddad was still working. It became obsolete overnight."

RAYMOND SIMON was appointed to the position of deputy secretary in the U.S. Department of Education in 2005. He previously served as chief state school officer for Arkansas and as superintendent of the Conway Arkansas School District.

EXPLORING THE ISSUE

Do the Testing and Accountability Elements of the No Child Left Behind Act Prevent a Proper Cost-Benefit Evaluation?

Critical Thinking and Reflection

1. Why has the academic emphasis of NCLB always been on math and reading, and is this appreciably detrimental to the teaching and learning of other subjects?
2. Why would it be that, by 2001, only 11 of 50 states were in compliance with the Improving America's Schools Act of 1994?
3. Are teachers justified when they lament being seen as instruments to satisfy minimum standards, as opposed to being critical partners in an educational system? Explain.

Is There Common Ground?

Simon's testimony to Congress gives an approving nod to the No Child Left Behind (NCLB) Act. In his overview of education reform since 1965, he assesses the legislative provisions that ultimately led to NCLB, and he is pleased to report that the "meaningful achievement" established by the act is working. Miller's testimony gives an approving nod to NCLB as well, even though he is far less satisfied than Miller with its current measures of success.

The principles and objectives of NCLB are not at the heart of this dispute, as both sides seem to share a genuine appreciation for NCLB. The pivotal argument begins with Miller's assertion that the benefits of this legislation cannot be optimized without much greater government investment geared toward better testing and accountability. Simon, who himself is not against the idea of NCLB

revisions, does however insist that if changes are needed (specifically in measuring benefits), they are minimal.

Create Central

www.mhhe.com/createcentral

Additional Resources

Olivas, Michael A., *No Undocumented Child Left Behind* (NYU Press, 2012)

Reese, William J., *America's Public Schools: From the Common School to "No Child Left Behind"* (Johns Hopkins University Press, 2011)

Vinovskis, Maris, *From a Nation at Risk to No Child Left Behind* (Teachers College Press, 2008)

Internet References . . .

Education and the Workforce:
"Kline Releases Draft Accountability,
Teacher Effectiveness Legislation"

http://edworkforce.house.gov/news/documentsingle
.aspx?DocumentID=273999

Education and the Workforce
(Democrats): "Miller Statement on
10th Anniversary of No Child Left
Behind Act"

http://democrats.edworkforce.house.gov/press
-release/miller-statement-10th-anniversary-no-child
-left-behind-act

Policy Insider: "House Passes CEC-Opposed
ESEA Rewrite; Contains Major Accountability
Loopholes for Students with Disabilities"

www.policyinsider.org/2013/07/house-passes-cec
-opposed-esea-rewrite-contains-major-accountability
-loopholes-for-students-with-disabilities.html?cid=6a
00d83452098b69e2019b00a4ebca970b

WebWire: "Deputy Secretary of Education
Raymond Simon Highlights No Child Left
Behind in Denver, Colorado"

www.webwire.com/ViewPressRel.asp?aId=61163#
.Unp4k9wo5kg

Selected, Edited, and with Issue Framing Material by:
M. Reza Ramazani, *Saint Michael's College*

ISSUE

Is the Inequality in U.S. Income Distribution Surging?

YES: Steven J. Markovich, from "The Income Inequality Debate," *Council on Foreign Relations Backgrounder* (September 17, 2012)

NO: Thomas A. Garrett, from "U.S. Income Inequality: It's Not So Bad," *Inside the Vault* (Spring 2010)

Learning Outcomes

After reading this issue, you will be able to:

- Identify how income inequality is defined, what causes it, and what the consequences of income inequality are.
- Identify how income inequality in the United States has changed over time.
- Understand why there are political differences and debates over the size of the income inequality as well as ways to reduce it.
- Understand how government intervenes to soften the blow to market adjustments when there is a major economic crisis, such as the Great Recession of 2007.
- Understand that society should have a reduction in income and wealth inequality as a goal, in addition to achieving economic efficiency, although this may come at the expense of lower economic growth.

ISSUE SUMMARY

YES: Steven J. Markovich, contributing editor for the Council on Foreign Relations, believes that the level of income and wealth inequality has increased in the United States as well as in every European country during the past few decades. However, the disparity in income inequality is much higher in the United States than in most other developed countries of Europe and North America. His analysis shows that the average real family income of the top 1 percent rose to 275 percent from 1979 to 2007.

NO: Thomas A. Garrett, assistant vice president and economist at the Federal Reserve Bank of St. Louis, does not deny the fact that income and wealth inequality has been rising in the United States since 1970. However, he rejects the notion that the United States is experiencing a surge in inequality. He cautions that the data used by economists to measure income inequality overstate the true degree of inequality for several reasons.

It is well known that the level of income inequality has increased in the United States as well as in every European country during the past few decades. However, the level of income inequality stretches much higher in the United States than in most of the other developed countries of Europe and North America.

Growing inequality is one of the biggest social, economic, and political challenges that the United States is experiencing today. Despite the fact that the U.S. economy has grown considerably during the past three decades, there is a strong and prevailing public perception that the middle class and the poor have been left behind. Many economists believe that the woes of the middle class and the poor are in large part a consequence of globalization and technological change as well as a significant drop in union membership. In addition, culture may also play a role. The consensus of mainstream economists has long been that under the capitalist system, both the input and product markets are competitive; wages are determined by worker productivity and the market value of output produced. More educated and productive workers should receive higher wages than less educated and unproductive workers. In other words, any market economy has some workers whose skill levels and education are so low that income-earning possibilities are bleak. Therefore, it is important to understand that the income and wealth inequality is a by-product of a well-functioning capitalist system. However, if markets do such a good job in directing an economy's scarce resources and improving our economic condition, then why have we experienced so much skepticism about the virtues of capitalism in the past few years?

Economic analysis can provide some insight into why income inequality exists in a market economy. Income distribution can be skewed by any of the following factors:

- Discrimination based on race, age, and gender.
- Unequal opportunities to skills training, education, and other productivity-enhancing options.
- Labor market discrimination.

In addition, there are other sources of income and wealth inequality in the United States such as:

- Changing attitudes toward family formation: the rise in single-family female-headed households and high divorce rates.
- Old age and the decline of income and wealth.
- Unfortunate events, such as illness, accidents, and mental health problems.
- Culture and society, including lack of effective role models and development of behavioral traits that lead to failure, such as teenage pregnancies, school dropouts, weak work ethics, and low aspirations.

This issue looks at income inequality in the United States, providing a brief historical analysis of income inequality, its trends, its causes, as well as instruments for measuring it, and tools available to policymakers for reducing it. Two important tools used by economists and policymakers to measure income inequality are referenced by both Markovich and Garrett in this issue—quintile distribution of income and the Gini coefficient.

To analyze family and personal income distribution, the Census Bureau sorts households from the lowest incomes to the highest. It then divides these households into quintiles, or fifths, from the lowest 20 percent of households to the highest 20 percent. After totaling and averaging household incomes for each quintile, the Census Bureau calculates the percentage of income that goes to each quintile. If a society wishes to achieve absolute income equality, then all quintiles should receive 20 percent of aggregate income.

U.S. Income Distribution in 2010

Income group	Income range	Average income	Percent of total income
Bottom quintile	Less than $20,000	$11,034	3.3
Second quintile	$20,000 to 38,043	$28,636	8.5
Third quintile	$38,043 to $61,735	$49,309	14.6
Fourth quintile	$61,735 to $100,065	$79,040	23.4
Top quintile	More than $100,065	$169,633	50.2
Top 5 percent	More than $180,810	$287,686	21.3
Mean income = $67,530		Median income = $49,445	

Source: U.S. Census Bureau

Based on this measurement, over the past three decades, income distribution in the United States has been growing more unequal. As the table below shows, in 2010 the average income of the poorest fifth of households was less than a quarter of the average income of households in the middle, and the richest fifth had an average income of more than three times that of households in the model. Furthermore, the incomes of the richest fifth of the households were, on average, about 15 times as high as those of the poorest fifth. However, it is important to know that these numbers are only based on money income before taxes and ignore the value of employment-based fringe benefits and government-provided noncash benefits such as food stamps, Medicaid, and public or subsidized housing.

The second tool that is used by economists and policymakers to evaluate income distribution is the Gini coefficient. It is named after the Italian statistician Corrado Gini, who designed it in 1912. The coefficient values vary between 0 and 1—with 0 meaning that everyone has exactly the same income (absolute income equality) and 1 meaning that one person has all of the income and everyone else has none (absolute income inequality). During the 1970s, the Gini coefficient was 0.316 in the United States; however, it had increased to 0.378 by the late 2000s.

Income inequality, as measured either by the quintile distribution of income or the Gini coefficient, is only a snapshot of outcomes. Unfortunately, they do not explain why these income gaps have appeared or what the trend is over time. Like any snapshot, they can be misleading. Income inequality can increase for good reason, such as workers being more productive and rewarded with higher wages or poor children not having the same opportunities as wealthy ones. In addition, it is important to distinguish between equality of opportunity vs. equality of outcome. Some countries like the United States, China, and India put more emphasis on the equality of opportunity to help their population achieve upward mobility. On the other hand, the European countries seem to be more egalitarian, believing that there should not be a big income gap between rich and poor.

In the following selections, two authors explore a question that will be of primary focus for American economists as well as policymakers for many years to come. Is the inequality in U.S. income distribution surging? Markovich identifies several causes of income inequality and explains the possible economic, social, and political costs of surging inequality in the United States. In addition, he introduces several policy recommendations that might help reduce income inequality. Garrett's analysis is very similar. He does not deny the fact that income is distributed unequally in the United States. However, he rejects the notion that the United States is experiencing a surge of inequality. He cautions that the data used by economists to measure income inequality overstate the true degree of inequality for several reasons. For example, he argues that the data represent a snapshot for a single year, whereas the income of any individual household changes over time.

YES

Steven J. Markovich

The Income Inequality Debate

Introduction

In September of 2011, the Occupy Wall Street protests began in New York and quickly spread across the globe. Its "We are the 99 percent" slogan encapsulated popular angst over income inequality that had been rising steadily over the years. Today, inequality in the United States, measured by the standard Gini coefficient, is substantially higher than almost any other developed nation, and even some developing countries such as Russia and India.

While income inequality can be summarized in a few words, its multiple potential causes are more complex. Globalization and technological change have simultaneously led to greater competition for lower-skilled workers—many of whom have also lost union membership—while giving well-educated, higher-skilled workers increased leverage. Changes to tax rates, including favorable treatment for capital gains, may also play a role.

Rising U.S. Income Inequality

Income inequality in the United States has been rising for decades, with the top echelon of earners rapidly outpacing the rest of the population. According to the Congressional Budget Office, the average real after-tax household income of the top 1 percent rose 275 percent from 1979 to 2007. Meanwhile, income for the remainder of the top quintile (81st to 99th percentile) grew 65 percent. Income for the majority of the population in the middle of the scale (21st through 80th percentiles) grew just 37 percent for the same period. And the bottom quintile experienced the least growth income at just 18 percent.

Furthermore, in 1965, a typical corporate CEO earned more than twenty times a typical worker; by 2011, the ratio was 383:1, according to the Economic Policy Institute.

While many of the suspected drivers of rising income inequality—globalization, technological change and the rising value of education—affect other nations as well, few have seen as stark a rise in inequality. From 1968 to 2010, the share of national income earned by the top 20 percent rose from 42.6 to 50.2 percent, with gains concentrated at the very top. Meanwhile, the "middle class," the middle 60 percent, saw its share decline from 53.2 to 46.5 percent. This increasing income inequality is captured by the steady rise in the U.S. Gini coefficient, from 0.316 in the mid-1970s to 0.378 in the late 2000s. Today,

the U.S. income distribution is one of the most uneven among major developed nations.

Globalization and De-Unionization

Economic forces underlie the growth of income inequality. Highly skilled workers have greatly benefited from worldwide opportunities, from the star actor whose movies reach a global audience to the entrepreneur who can quickly and cheaply bring a new product to market through Chinese contract manufacturing (*Forbes*).

Meanwhile, globalization has brought tough competition to other American workers who have seen jobs move overseas, wages stagnate, and unions decline. The median union member earns roughly a quarter more than a non-union counterpart. Forty years ago, a quarter of private sector workers were represented by unions, but today it is only 6.9 percent. Despite a workforce one-fifth of the size, the public sector has more union members.

Immigration likely pays a role in stagnant wages, especially among workers without a high school degree, of which immigrants make up about half. One study found that a 10 percent increase in the local immigrant population correlated with a 1.3 percent decline in the price of labor-intensive services, but it is difficult to disentangle this competitive effect from others on the labor market.

A noted free trade advocate, Alan Blinder, said that while beneficial for the United States as a whole, the increased labor competition from globalization will be painful for many Americans. He advocated for helping displaced workers through a stronger safety net, reforming education, and encouraging innovation and entrepreneurship (*WashPost*). Fellow Princeton economist Paul Krugman believes that "we need to restore the bargaining power that labor has lost over the last thirty years, so that ordinary workers as well as superstars have the power to bargain for good wages" (*NYT*).

Education and Technological Change

Most high wages come from high-skill jobs that require a commensurate level of education. After decades of gradually narrowing, the college wage premium has grown dramatically since 1980, as the annual growth in the college educated workforce (2 percent) failed to keep pace with rising demand (3.27 to 3.66 percent) driven by technological change. In 2011, the median earnings of a worker with a bachelor's degree were 65 percent higher than a high school graduate's; holders of professional degrees (MD, JD, MBA) enjoyed a 161 percent premium. Higher educational attainment correlates both with higher earnings and lower unemployment.

However, college degrees do not guarantee good jobs. Falling communication and computer costs are leading to the offshoring and automation of some jobs that were once the purview of well-paid professionals, from scientists in pharmaceutical labs to finance and accounting jobs (*Businessweek*). There is a widening wage premium between those with advanced degrees and those with a bachelor's degree only. Since the 2000s, the wage premium for those with only a four-year degree has remained flat, while for those with advanced degrees it has continued to grow.

Gary S. Becker and Kevin M. Murphy of the University of Chicago see education as the major driver of rising income inequality. "In the United States, the rise in inequality accompanied a rise in the payoff to education and other skills. We believe that the rise in returns on investments in human capital is beneficial and desirable, and policies designed to deal with inequality must take account of its cause" (*TheAmerican*). To address income inequality, they argue for policies that would increase the percentages of American youth who complete high school and college, and against making the tax code more progressive.

In a recent survey, 80 percent of economic experts agreed that a leading reason for rising U.S. income inequality was that technological change has affected workers with some skill sets differently than others, but not all prominent economists agree. James K. Galbraith believes that "the skills bias argument—the notion that inequality is being driven by technological change and education and the supply of skills—is comprehensively rebutted by the evidence." He argues instead that the credit cycle has concentrated income in specific sectors, such as finance, tech and real estate (*WashPost*).

Income Tax Rates

One tool for addressing income inequality is a more progressive tax code. While some argue that shifting some money from the rich to the poor means that money can be used to create more social utility—the economic concept of declining marginal utility—other see this shift as unfair and unwise because it reduces the ability of more productive citizens to re-invest in the skills and businesses responsible for their higher relative income, thus retarding overall growth. While economic models and theories can attempt to quantify the relationship between inequality and growth, the optimum balance cannot be empirically determined.

The United States has generally cut top income tax rates over the past half century. When John F. Kennedy entered the White House in 1961, the top ordinary income tax bracket—applied to wages and savings interest—was more than 90 percent. Ronald Reagan slashed the top rate from 70 percent in 1981 to 28 percent after 1986. Tax increases under the first President Bush and President Clinton brought the top rate to 39.6 percent, but tax cuts signed by President George W. Bush and reauthorized by President Obama set it to 35 percent.

Tax rates on investment income in the form of capital gains taxes and dividends have also declined, with the current rate of 15 percent the lowest since 1933. Investment income ultimately is derived from the after-tax profits of corporations, whose tax rate has also declined since the Eisenhower-era, from more than 50 percent to today's marginal rate of 35 percent. Corporate income tax has declined steadily as a share both of corporate profits and as a percentage of GDP over the past half century.

The Social Security payroll tax, which funds both old age pensions and Medicare, is regressive because it is a flat rate that only applies to the first $110,100 of wages, in 2012. On the other hand, roughly half of U.S. taxpayers pay no additional federal income tax.

A Tax Policy Center analysis of all federal taxes found overall progressive taxation, with each quartile paying a successively higher rate and the top 0.1 percent paying an effective rate of 30.4 percent. While higher than the 14.1 percent borne by the middle quartile, 30.4 percent is lower than the historical rates paid by this small group, which is earning its largest share of national income since the Great Depression.

Social Program Support

The poverty rate tends to generally follow the economic cycle. As the economy reached new heights in 2000, the poverty rate fell to 11.1 percent—a rate not seen since 1973—but in 2010 the poverty rate had jumped back up to 15.1 percent.

Under President Lyndon Johnson's Great Society, most assistance was in the form of cash benefits to needy families. Through the 1970s and 1980s, non-cash benefit programs were created or accelerated, including college grants, food stamps, and housing assistance. The 1990s ushered in welfare reform, replacing federal cash assistance with TANF block grant to states, with work requirements and time limits. The refundable earned income tax credit, (created in 1975) was greatly expanded at this time, providing extra cash to workers in an effort to "make work pay."

Today, record numbers receive food stamps, though one in five Americans struggle to afford food (Stateline). The number of Social Security Disability Insurance recipients has surged by more than 22 percent since the recession began, as that program effectively acts as a long-term unemployment benefit for some (Bloomberg).

From Medicaid to unemployment benefits, many social support programs are driven by decisions at the state level. States have less flexibility to run deficits and many have cut programs to needy citizens. Pennsylvania recently joined other states in eliminating its general assistance program (Stateline). One caseworker observed: "My clients have lost an important source of funds for life's necessities, while they face longer waitlists for job training programs."

Bred for Success?

A longer-term source of income disparity is strengthening: It is increasingly difficult to reach a higher economic status than your parents. Many Americans take pride in the belief that everyone has a chance to "make it big" and rags-to-riches stories are almost legends. But today, more than 40 percent of those born into the lowest income quintile will stay there, and less than 30 percent will make an above-average income.

Among developed countries, only the United Kingdom has less class mobility; in 2006, the Brookings Institution found that 47 percent of U.S. parents' income advantages are passed to their children, greater than in France (41 percent), Germany (32 percent) or Sweden (27 percent). The countries with the highest mobility were Canada, Norway, Finland and Denmark, where less than 20 percent of economic advantages are passed to children.

Political Impact

The growing gap between the rich and poor may exacerbate political disunity. Economist Joseph E. Stiglitz of Columbia University examined this in his recent book, *The Price of Inequality,* and argued that no one has an interest in stark inequality. "The rich do not exist in a vacuum. They need a functioning society around them to sustain their position. Widely unequal societies do not function efficiently and their economies are neither stable nor sustainable" (*Vanity Fair*).

The Pew Research Center found increasing anxiety among America's middle class, with 85 percent expressing greater difficulty in maintaining their standard of living. While a majority of Americans see income inequality as a big problem (*TheHill*), polls also show more desire for economic growth and greater equality of opportunity (Gallup).

During the debate in late 2010 over whether to extend the Bush-era tax rates, influential behavioral economist Richard H. Thaler asked "whether we want a society in which the rich take an ever-increasing share of the pie, or prefer to return to conditions that allow all classes to anticipate an increasing standard of living" (*NYT*). The former chairman of Bush's Council of Economic Advisers, N. Gregory Mankiw, argued that raising his marginal tax rate would lead him—and many others—to work less (*NYT*). This tension between equality and growth is likely to remain unresolved for the foreseeable future.

Finally, an August 2012 paper by the Hoover Institution of Stanford argued that income inequality is not rising. Their analysis considered after tax income and added in non-cash benefits from employers and government programs, and calculated a decline in the U.S. Gini coefficient from 1993 to 2009. The authors argued that reducing income inequality would not improve economic well-being, and policymakers should instead target opportunity inequality.

STEVEN J. MARKOVICH is contributing editor for Council on Foreign Relations and market manager at Valspar. He holds an MBA from University of Chicago Booth School of Business as well as bachelor's and master's degrees in chemical engineering from Case Western Reserve University.

Thomas A. Garrett

➡ **NO**

U.S. Income Inequality: It's Not So Bad

Each year, the U.S. Census Bureau releases data on the income levels of America's households. A comparison of the annual data over time reveals that the income of wealthier households has been growing faster than the income of poorer households—the real income of the wealthiest 5 percent of households rose by 14 percent between 1996 and 2006, while the income of the poorest 20 percent of households rose by just 6 percent.

As a result of these differences in income growth, the income of the wealthiest 5 percent of households grew from 8.1 times that of the income of the poorest 20 percent of households in 1996 to 8.7 times as great by 2006. Such figures commonly lead to the conclusion that income inequality in the United States has increased. This apparent increase in income inequality has not escaped the attention of policy makers and social activists who support public policies aimed at reducing income inequality. However, the common measures of income inequality that are derived from the census statistics exaggerate the degree of income inequality in the United States in several ways. Furthermore, although many people consider income inequality a social ill, it is important to understand that income inequality has many economic benefits and is the result of—and not a detriment to—a well-functioning economy.

An Inaccurate Picture

The Census Bureau essentially ranks all households by household income and then divides this distribution of households into quintiles. The highest-ranked household in each quintile provides the upper income limit for each quintile. Comparing changes in these upper income limits over time for different quintiles reveals that the income of wealthier households has been growing faster than the income of poorer households, thus giving the impression of an increasing "income gap" or "shrinking middle class."

One big problem with inferring income inequality from the census income statistics is that the census statistics provide only a snapshot of income distribution in the U.S., at a single point in time. The statistics do not reflect the reality that income for many households changes over time—i.e., incomes are mobile. For most people, income increases over time as they move from their first, low-paying job in high school to a better-paying job later in their lives. Also, some people lose income over time because of business-cycle contractions, demotions, career changes,

retirement, etc. The implication of changing individual incomes is that individual households do not remain in the same income quintiles over time. Thus, comparing different income quintiles over time is like comparing apples to oranges, because it means comparing incomes of different people at different stages in their earnings profile.

The U.S. Treasury released a study in November 2007 that examined income mobility in the U.S. from 1996 to 2005. Using data from individual tax returns, the study documented the movement of households along the distribution of real income over the 10-year period. The study found that nearly 58 percent of the households that were in the lowest income quintile (the lowest 20 percent) in 1996 moved to a higher income quintile by 2005. Similarly, nearly 50 percent of the households in the second-lowest quintile in 1996 moved to a higher income quintile by 2005. Even a significant number of households in the third- and fourth-lowest income quintiles in 1996 moved to a higher quintile in 2005.

The Treasury study also documented falls in household income between 1996 and 2005. This is most interesting when considering the richest households. More than 57 percent of the richest 1 percent of households in 1996 fell out of that category by 2005. Similarly, more than 45 percent of the households that ranked in the top 5 percent of income in 1996 fell out of that category by 2005.

Thus it is clear that over time, a significant number of households move to higher positions along the income distribution, and a significant number move to lower positions along the income distribution. Common reference to "classes" of people (e.g., the lowest 20 percent or the richest 10 percent) is quite misleading because income classes do not contain the same households and people over time.

Another problem with drawing inferences from the census statistics is that the statistics do not include the noncash resources received by lower-income households—resources transferred to the households—and the tax payments made by wealthier households to fund these transfers. Lower-income households annually receive tens of billions of dollars in subsidies for housing, food and medical care. None of these are considered income by the Census Bureau. Thus the resources available to lower-income households are actually greater than is suggested by the income of those households as reported in the census data.

At the same time, these noncash payments to lower-income households are funded with taxpayer dollars—mostly from wealthier households, since they pay a majority of overall taxes. One research report estimates that the share of total income earned by the lowest income quintile increases roughly 50 percent—whereas the share of total income earned by the highest income quintile drops roughly 7 percent—when transfer payments and taxes are considered.

The census statistics also do not account for the fact that the households in each quintile contain different numbers of people; it is differences in income across people, rather than differences in income by household, that provide a clearer measure of inequality. Lower-income households tend to consist of single people with low earnings, whereas higher-income households tend to include married couples with multiple earners. The fact that lower-income households have fewer people than higher-income households skews the income distribution by person. When considering household size along with transfers received and taxes paid, the income share of the lowest quintile nearly triples and the income share of the highest quintile falls by 25 percent.

Is Policy Needed?

Income inequality will still exist even if the income inequality statistics are adjusted to account for the aforementioned factors. Given the negative attention income inequality receives in the media, it is important to ask whether reducing income inequality is a worthy goal of public policy. It is important to understand that income inequality is a byproduct of a well-functioning capitalist economy. Individuals' earnings are directly related to their productivity. Wealthy people are not wealthy because they have more money; it is because they have greater productivity. Different incomes reflect different productivity levels.

The unconstrained opportunity for individuals to create value for society—and the fact that their income reflects the value they create—encourages innovation and entrepreneurship. Economic research has documented a positive correlation between entrepreneurship/innovation and overall economic growth. A wary eye should be cast on policies that aim to shrink the income distribution by redistributing income from the more productive to the less productive simply for the sake of "fairness." Redistribution of wealth increases the costs of entrepreneurship and innovation, with the result being lower overall economic growth for everyone.

Poverty and income inequality are related, but only the former deserves a policy-based response. Sound economic policy to reduce poverty would lift people out of poverty (increase their productivity) while not reducing the well-being of wealthier individuals. Tools to implement such a policy include investments in education and job training.

Income inequality should not be vilified, and public policy should encourage people to move up the income distribution and not penalize them for having already done so.

GLOSSARY

Adjusted gross income Total income less statutory adjustments.

Business cycle The periodic but irregular up-and-down movements in economic activity, measured by fluctuations in real GDP and other macroeconomic variables.

Capitalism Economic system characterized by the following: ownership of private property; individuals and companies that are allowed to compete for their own economic gain; and free-market forces that determine the prices of goods and services.

Income Earnings received as wages, rent, profit or interest; payments received for providing natural, human capital and entrepreneurial resources in the market.

Inflation A sustained increase in the average price level.

Poverty A condition that occurs when people do not enjoy a certain minimum level of living standards, as determined by a government.

Productivity A ratio of output to input during a specified period of time. For example, output per worker is a measure of the productivity of labor during an hour, week, month or year. The productivity of workers can be increased through division of labor, investment in human capital and investment in capital resources.

Purchasing power A measurement of the relative value of money in terms of the quality and quantity of goods and services it can buy.

Quintile One of five equal parts of a range of data, each being 1/5th (20 percent) of the range.

Real income Income expressed in terms of the goods and services it can purchase.

Standard of living A measure of the goods and services available to a person in a country; the dollar value is calculated as per capita GDP.

Subsidies Financial assistance given by the government to individuals or groups.

Taxes Mandatory government fees on business and individual income, activities or products.

Taxable income Adjusted gross income less standardized or itemized deductions.

Transfer payments Payments by governments—such as social security, veterans' benefits and welfare—to people who do not supply goods, services or labor in exchange for the payments.

Wealth Accumulated assets such as money and/or possessions, often accumulated as a result of saving and investment.

THOMAS A. GARRETT is assistant vice president of the Federal Reserve Bank of St. Louis. He holds a PhD in economics from West Virginia University.

EXPLORING THE ISSUE

Is the Inequality in U.S. Income Distribution Surging?

Critical Thinking and Reflection

1. Outline the range of major policy options available to the U.S. government to reduce the income and wealth inequality. Which policy or policies do you believe are absolutely essential, and which are important but not crucial?
2. Are higher economic growth and more equitable distribution of income necessarily conflicting objectives? Outline the arguments both for and against the presumed conflict of objectives.
3. What are the major causes of income and wealth inequality in the United States today?
4. Name and explain the two measures used to determine the extent of income inequality.
5. How would you design a program aimed at reducing income and wealth inequality in the United States?

Is There Common Ground?

Income inequality and poverty are among the most contentious issues facing economists and politicians today. No one denies that income is distributed unequally in America. In fact, many believe that income inequality is a natural consequence of a well-functioning market economy. However, what should be the acceptable level of inequality in order to allow the market economy to achieve the desirable level of economic efficiency and growth? Should the market economy be concerned about issues, such as economic equity, social justice, and fairness?

How serious an issue is income inequality in the United States today? As we have already seen, income inequality has increased substantially since the 1970s. Today a large percentage of the American population does not share in the country's overall prosperity, even though it contributes a great deal to its success. Increasing income inequality is one of the most important reasons for why the poverty rate has not improved in the United States over the past 40 years despite the fact that the United States as a whole has become much wealthier. In addition to economic cost, there might be also a political cost associated with the high level of income inequality. For example, the extreme inequality in many developing countries, such as in Latin America, is usually associated with political instability because of tension between a very rich minority and the rest of the population that lives in poverty for the most part.

Many economists including Steven J. Markovich and Thomas A. Garrett are concerned about this widening income disparity. They believe that it might have long-lasting and damaging side effects. In theory, there is an ambiguous relationship between inequality and economic growth and prosperity. The existence of income inequality might help the country achieve a higher rate of economic growth because rich people save and invest by far more than poor people. In addition, people generally work harder, save, and invest more in response to incentives. However, a large income gap can be very inefficient for a country. It can prevent a large segment of the populations that is smart, hardworking, but poor from access to education and can cause resentment and anger, which might negatively affect the country's economic growth policies.

Traditionally, education has been one of the most important tools for low- and middle-income Americans to achieve new opportunities and upward economic mobility. However, today in America 40 percent of those born into the lowest income quintile will stay there, and less than 30 percent will make an above-average income. Unfortunately, if we do not provide poor young Americans with the same educational opportunities that we provide to rich young Americans to realize their potential, not only will we harm students, but we might also harm the nation as a whole.

Fundamentally, both Steven J. Markovich and Thomas A. Garrett agree with polices that would increase the percentage of American youth who complete high school and college in order to reduce income and wealth inequality in the United States. In addition, Markovich believes that changes to tax rates, including less favorable treatment for capital gains, may also help. However, unlike Markovich, Garrett is against making the tax code more progressive as a policy solution to reduce income inequality. Garrett concludes that "Income inequality should not be vilified, and public policy should encourage people to move up the income distribution and not penalize them for having already done so."

Create Central

www.mhhe.com/createcentral

Additional Resources

Bonica, Adam, McCarty, Nolan, Poole, Keith T., and Rosenthal, Howard, "Why Hasn't Democracy Slowed Rising Inequality? (pp. 103–124)," *Journal of Economic Perspectives* (vol. 27, no. 3, Summer 2013)

Corak, Miles "Income Inequality, Equality of Opportunity, and Intergenerational Mobility (pp. 79–102)," *Journal of Economic Perspectives*: (vol. 27, no. 3, Summer 2013)

Deaton, Angus *The Great Escape: Health, Wealth, and the Origins of Inequality* (Princeton University Press, 2013)

Mankiw, N. Gregory "Defending the One Percent (pp. 21–34)," *Journal of Economic Perspectives* (vol. 27, no. 3, Summer 2013)

Stiglitz, Joseph E. *The Price of Inequality: How Today's Divided Society Endangers Our Future* (W.W. Norton & Company, 2012)

Internet References . . .

Forbes

www.forbes.com/fdc/welcome_mjx.shtml

Inequality.org

http://inequality.org/

National Bureau of Economic Research

www.nber.org/digest/dec08/w13982.html

NYTimes.com

www.nytimes.com/2013/07/28/us/politics/obama-says-income-gap-is-fraying-us-social-fabric.html

U.S. Census Bureau

www.census.gov/hhes/www/income/